ŚRĪ BHAJANA-RAHASYA

śrī śrī guru-gaurāṅgau jayataḥ

ŚRĪ BHAJANA-RAHASYA

WITH AN ABBREVIATED MANUAL ON DEITY WORSHIP

Compiled by

the best amongst the eighth generation of descendants in the *bhāgavata-paramparā* from Śrī Kṛṣṇa Caitanya Mahāprabhu, and the best of the followers of Śrī Rūpa Gosvāmī

oṁ viṣṇupāda

ŚRĪLA BHAKTIVINODA ṬHĀKURA

with commentary by

ŚRĪ ŚRĪMAD BHAKTIVEDĀNTA NĀRĀYAṆA MAHĀRĀJA

GAUDIYA VEDANTA PUBLICATIONS
GVP

Vṛndāvana, Uttar Pradesh, India

Other titles by Śrīla Nārāyaṇa Mahārāja

The Nectar of Govinda-līlā
Going Beyond Vaikuṇṭha
Bhakti-rasāyana
Śrī Śikṣāṣṭaka
Veṇu-gīta
Śrī Prabandhāvalī
Śrī Bhakti-rasāmṛta-sindhu-bindu
Śrī Manaḥ-śikṣā
Bhakti-tattva-viveka
Pinnacle of Devotion
Śrī Upadeśāmṛta
Arcana-dīpikā
The Essence of All Advice
Śrī Gauḍīya Gīti-guccha
Dāmodara-līlā-mādhurī
Śrīmad Bhagavad-gītā
Śrīmad Bhakti Prajñāna Keśava Gosvāmī – His Life and Teachings
Five Essential Essays
Śrī Harināma Mahā-mantra
Secret Truths of the Bhāgavata
Jaiva-dharma
Śrī Vraja-maṇḍala Parikramā
The Origin of Ratha-yātrā
Śrī Brahma-saṁhitā
Rays of the Harmonist (periodical)

For further information, please visit www.igvp.com or www.gaudiya.net

ISBN 81-86737-11-1
First printing: 5000 copies, June 2003

dedicated to my śrī guru-pāda-padma

ŚRĪ GAUḌĪYA-VEDĀNTA-ĀCĀRYA-KESARĪ NITYA-LĪLĀ-PRAVIṢṬA
OṀ VIṢṆUPĀDA AṢṬOTTARA-ŚATA ŚRĪ ŚRĪMAD

BHAKTI PRAJÑĀNA KEŚAVA GOSVĀMĪ MAHĀRĀJA

The best amongst the tenth generation of descendants in the *bhāgavata-paramparā* from Śrī Kṛṣṇa Caitanya Mahāprabhu, and the founder of the Śrī Gauḍīya Vedānta Samiti and its branches throughout the world.

CONTENTS

Introduction to the Rahasya i
Preface v
Preface to the English Edition ix
Śrī Brahma-Madhva-Gauḍīya Guru-paramparā xiii

CHAPTER ONE:	Prathama-yāma-sādhana *Niśānta-bhajana*	1
CHAPTER TWO:	Dvitīya-yāma-sādhana *Prātaḥ-kālīya-bhajana*	61
CHAPTER THREE:	Tṛtīya-yāma-sādhana *Pūrvāhna-kālīya-bhajana*	125
CHAPTER FOUR:	Caturtha-yāma-sādhana *Madhyāhna-kālīya-bhajana*	151
CHAPTER FIVE:	Pañcama-yāma-sādhana *Aparāhna-kālīya-bhajana*	185
CHAPTER SIX:	Ṣaṣṭha-yāma-sādhana *Sāyaṁ-kālīya-bhajana*	237
CHAPTER SEVEN:	Saptama-yāma-sādhana *Pradoṣa-kālīya-bhajana*	303
CHAPTER EIGHT:	Aṣṭama-yāma-sādhana *Rātri-līlā*	363
APPENDIX:	Saṅkṣepa-arcana-paddhati *(abbreviated manual on deity worship)*	411

Glossary 427
Verse Index (main verses) 455
Verse Index (quoted verses) 461

Introduction to the Rahasya

[translated from the Bengali edition]

Śrī Bhajana-rahasya is compiled by Śrīmad Bhaktivinoda Ṭhākura Mahāśaya. He has collected into the form of a book several confidential hints from his own method of *bhajana* to guide sincere *sādhakas* who are performing *bhajana* under his direction. Some years ago, this destitute person observed him performing *bhajana*. He was constantly reciting and relishing verses such as the ones in this book, thus becoming overwhelmed with *bhagavat-prema*.

For *sādhakas* whose faith is on the neophyte platform, the system of *arcana* is provided. Many people are unable to understand the distinction between *arcana* and *bhajana* and therefore use the word *bhajana* to refer to *arcana*. One can practise *bhajana* by performing the nine kinds of devotion, *navadhā-bhakti*. Because *arcana* is included within *navadhā-bhakti*, it is also considered a part of *bhajana*. There is a difference beween complete *bhajana* and partial *bhajana*. *Arcana* means to worship the deity with awe and reverence; that is, with knowledge of the Lord's opulence and by observing etiquette. It is also *arcana* to serve Bhagavān with various paraphernalia according to rules and regulations and with the mundane conception of identifying oneself with the material body. In *viśrambha-sevā*, service rendered with intimacy and a sense of possessiveness, the hot rays of awe and reverence are still apparent to a small degree, but no one can refuse the excellent sweetness of its cool, pleasant moonbeams. A brief *arcana-paddhati* has been added as an appendix to this book.

Within the framework of this book, the secret meaning of *bhajana* is given in a way that captivates the heart. In the process of *arcana*, one remains more or less entangled in one's relationship with the gross and subtle body. In the realm of *bhajana*, however, the *sādhaka* passes beyond both the gross and subtle bodies to directly serve Bhagavān. The transcendental sentiments that others perceive in great personalities (*mahāpuruṣas*), who perform *bhajana* and who are completely free from all kinds of material designations, are not worldly or illusory. Due to being directly within the proximity of the non-dual Supreme Absolute Truth (*advaya-jñāna-para-tattva*), who is beyond perception, they experience the transcendental sentiments of devotional service that are beyond the range of material senses and material time.

Rahasya means "a profound subject that is instructed by the *guru* and that is required to be known by those with great faith". As a result of first receiving spiritual instructions and then performing *viśrambha-sevā*, which is the third among the sixty-four limbs of *sādhana-bhakti* mentioned in *Bhakti-rasāmṛta-sindhu*, a devotee begins to follow the path of *sādhus*. To do so is to cultivate *bhajana-rahasya*. *Niskiñcana-bhaktas* (renounced devotees) who are absorbed in *bhagavad-bhajana* become freed from material bondage. They therefore also become completely freed from the association of those bound by worldly desires. At that time, the inclination to engage in service throughout the twenty-four hours of the day (*aṣṭa-kāla*) awakens in their hearts. Pure devotees who are intent on rendering *sevā* consider the association of non-devotees, who are attached to either enjoyment or renunciation, to be an obstacle in the attainment of their desired goal. *Anyābhilāṣīs* (those with desires other than to serve Kṛṣṇa), *karmīs* and *jñānīs* do not have a taste for *bhajana-rahasya*. Therefore, due to being unqualified to enter the realm of *bhajana*, which is transcendentally illuminated by the eight divisions of the day, they do not revere this book.

When the day and night are divided into eight parts, each part is known as a *yāma*. There are three *yāmas* during the night, three during the day, one at dawn and one at dusk. Only pure Vaiṣṇavas are able to perform *kṛṣṇa-bhajana* with one-pointed determination in all respects and at all times. Such continuous *bhajana* is not possible as long as one's gross and subtle material conceptions of "I" and "mine" remain. The living entities will not be liberated from this conditioning if they attribute mundane conceptions to matters related to Hari. Vaiṣṇavas devoted to *bhajana* who have achieved their pure identity (*śuddha-svarūpa*) are forever prepared to serve Kṛṣṇa.

The eight verses of *Śikṣāṣṭaka*, composed by Śrī Gaurasundara, contain transcendental sentiments favourable to *bhajana* throughout the eight periods of the day. The eleven verses of Śrī Rūpa Gosvāmī's *Śrī Rādhā-kṛṣṇayor aṣṭa-kālīya-līlā-smaraṇa-maṅgala-stotram** and the poetry that expresses longing for *aṣṭa-kāla-bhajana* composed by all the exalted

* Eight of these verses, which are also found in Śrīla Kṛṣṇadāsa Kavirāja Gosvāmī's *Govinda-līlāmṛta*, are present in this book as the final Text of each chapter.

personalities who follow him, prescribe continuous *bhajana*. Upon becoming completely free from mundane conceptions of time, place and recipient, the servant of the spiritual master should constantly study *Śrī Bhajana-rahasya*.

The servant of the devotees of Śrī Hari,

Dāsa Śrī Siddhānta Sarasvatī

13th November, 1927
Kanpur, Uttar Pradesh

Preface

[translated from the Hindi edition]

Just as the sage Bhagīratha brought the River Bhāgīrathī (Gaṅgā) to this Earth, *oṁ viṣṇupāda* Śrī Śrīmad Saccidānanda Bhaktivinoda Ṭhākura Mahāśaya brought the present flow of the Bhāgīrathī of pure *bhakti* to this world. In his book *Śrī Harināma-cintāmaṇi*, Śrīla Bhaktivinoda Ṭhākura has presented an extensive deliberation on the glories of the holy name, on the distinctions between *nāma*, *nāma-ābhāsa* and *nāma-aparādha*, and on the method of chanting the holy name. He has compiled *Śrī Bhajana-rahasya* as a supplement to *Śrī Harināma-cintāmaṇi*. There are eight pairs of names in the *mahā-mantra*. In this book, Ṭhākura Mahāśaya describes the mercy of these eight pairs of names, and provides a remarkably beautiful glimpse of how to cultivate one's contemplation of *aṣṭa-kālīya-līlā* through the chanting of the *mahā-mantra*.

Several years ago, at the request of the sincere devotees of Mathurā and Vṛndāvana, I continuously spoke on this book for some time. The listeners gave rapt attention and I also felt boundless joy. When I had completed my classes, the faithful listeners repeatedly requested me to publish a Hindi edition of this book. At that time, however, I was busy publishing some books by Śrī Viśvanātha Cakravartī Ṭhākura – in particular his commentary on *Bhagavad-gītā* – and I was also engaged in preaching pure *bhakti*, as practised and propagated by Śrīman Mahāprabhu, around the world. Therefore I was unable to give this project my attention.

Some time later, I returned from preaching in the West to Śrī Keśavajī Gauḍīya Maṭha in Mathurā. During the month of Kārttika, daughter Kumārī Savitā gave me a manuscript of *Śrī Bhajana-rahasya* in Hindi with my commentary, *Bhajana-rahasya-vṛtti*. I was so pleased and asked her how she had prepared it. She humbly replied that she had compiled it from notes she had carefully taken during my lectures and from my *brahmacārīs'* cassette recordings of those lectures. I kept the manuscript with me and after Kārttika-vrata, took it with me when I again went abroad to preach.

We arrived at the very beautiful island of Cebu, which, being part of the Philippines, is situated in the Pacific Ocean. When, in that favourable atmosphere, I looked at the manuscript of *Bhajana-rahasya* to edit it, I became astonished and could not believe that I had actually spoken it. I felt sure that Śrīla Bhaktivinoda Ṭhākura Mahāśaya himself had inspired me to speak this commentary. To compile the manuscript, daughter Savitā had also meticulously searched through many authoritative books on *rāgānuga-bhakti*, thus further enriching the *Bhajana-rahasya-vṛtti* commentary.

The guardian of the Śrī Gauḍīya *sampradāya* and the founder of Śrī Gauḍīya Vedānta Samiti, my most worshipful *gurudeva*, *ācārya-kesarī aṣṭottara-śata* Śrī Śrīmad Bhakti Prajñāna Keśava Gosvāmī Mahārāja, used to mercifully encourage and inspire me, his servant, to publish Hindi editions of the books of Śrīla Bhaktivinoda Ṭhākura Mahāśaya. Today, offering this book into his lotus hands, I feel unbounded joy. All glories unto him! All glories unto him!

The services and great endeavours of daughter Kumārī Savitā in preparing the manuscript of this book, daughter Śrīmatī Jānakī-devī in helping her, Śrī Oṁ Prakāśa Brijabāsī "Sahitya-ratna", Śrīmatī Vṛndā-devī, Śrīmatī Śānti-devī, Śrīman Purandara dāsa Brahmacārī, Śrīman Śubhānanda Brahmacārī "Bhāgavata-bhūṣaṇa", Śrīman Navīna-kṛṣṇa Brahmacārī "Vidyālaṅkāra", Śrīman Parameśvarī dāsa Brahmacārī and others who were involved in composing it on the computer, proofreading and performing other services, are all greatly praiseworthy and notable. My heartfelt prayer at the lotus feet of Śrī Guru-Gaurāṅga-Gāndharvikā-Giridhārī is that They bestow an abundance of merciful blessings upon them.

I am confident that persons eager for *bhakti*, and in particular *sādhakas* of *rāgānuga-bhakti* who are eagerly desirous of *vraja-rasa*, will greatly honour this book, and that by studying it, faithful persons will attain the eligibility to enter the *prema-dharma* of Śrī Caitanya Mahāprabhu.

Finally, may the condensed personification of Bhagavān's compassion, my most worshipful *śrī guru-pāda-padma*, shower me with profuse mercy so that I may attain the eligibility to fulfil his inner-most desire. This is my submissive prayer at his crimson lotus feet.

An aspirant for a particle of mercy
from Śrī Hari, Guru and Vaiṣṇavas,
humble and insignificant,

ŚRĪ BHAKTIVEDĀNTA NĀRĀYAṆA

Śrī Gaura-pūrṇimā
20th March, 2000
Mathurā, Uttar Pradesh

ŚRĪ ŚRĪMAD BHAKTIVEDĀNTA NĀRĀYAṆA MAHĀRĀJA

ŚRĪ ŚRĪMAD A.C. BHAKTIVEDĀNTA SWAMI PRABHUPĀDA

ŚRĪ ŚRĪMAD BHAKTI PRAJÑĀNA KEŚAVA GOSVĀMĪ

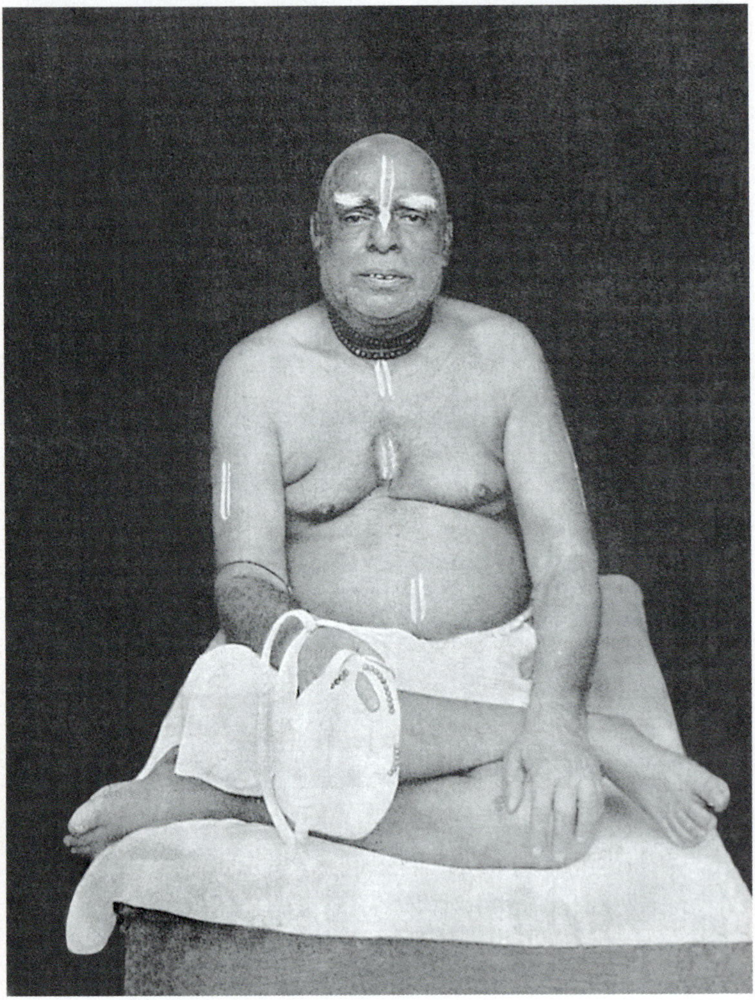

ŚRĪLA BHAKTIVINODA ṬHĀKURA

Preface to the English Edition

In compiling *Śrī Bhajana-rahasya*, Śrīla Bhaktivinoda Ṭhākura has selected specific verses from the Vedic literature that serve to guide the *sādhaka* in awakening his eternal identity as a servant of Kṛṣṇa. He reveals the purpose of each verse with an introductory sentence. These verses are presented in chapters that correspond to the *sādhaka's* level of spiritual practice, from the early stages of faith up to the appearance of *prema*, when one's heart is blossoming with his eternal relationship with Rādhā and Kṛṣṇa.

The book's chapters are also divided according to the eight parts of the day, called *yāmas*. In each *yāma* Śrī Rādhā-Kṛṣṇa enjoy particular pastimes, a general synopsis of which is given in the final verse of each chapter. Following the introductory sentence, the main verse (individually referred to throughout as a "Text") and its translation, are Bengali verses composed by Bhaktivinoda Ṭhākura himself. These verses paraphrase the main Text and also include his commentary.

Just as Śrīla Bhaktivinoda Ṭhākura took the essence of each Text and elaborated upon it in his paraphrases, our beloved *gurudeva*, Śrī Śrīmad Bhaktivedānta Nārāyaṇa Mahārāja, has expanded on the meaning of each verse with a wonderful *vṛtti*, or commentary, named *Bhajana-rahasya-vṛtti*. In most cases direct translations of Bhaktivinoda Ṭhākura's paraphrases have not been provided, as they are generally included within Śrīla Gurudeva's commentary. This commentary reveals his genuine concern for the souls in this world who, under the guidance of *śrī guru* and Vaiṣṇavas, are endeavouring to develop their relationship with Śrī Rādhā-Kṛṣṇa. For this we remain bound to him with affection.

A chart that serves as an overview of *Śrī Bhajana-rahasya* is located at the inside of the back cover. This chart, based on information from Śrīla Gurudeva's commentary on Text 6 of Chapter 1, can be understood as follows.

The *mahā-mantra* is chanted by two types of *sādhaka*: that person in whose heart *bhāva* has not arisen (the *ajāta-rati-sādhaka*) and that person in whose heart *bhāva* has arisen (the *jāta-rati-sādhaka*). How each *sādhaka* chants each pair of names is described in the section outside the chart's concentric circles.

Each pair of names corresponds to a *yāma*, one of the eight periods of the day into which Śrī Rādhā-Kṛṣṇa's eternal pastimes are divided. These pastimes are briefly described under the heading "*jāta-rati-sādhaka*". In other words, this is the constant meditation of such a *sādhaka*.

Each pair of names also corresponds with the *ajāta-rati-sādhaka's* devotional growth, as he progresses through the stages from *śraddhā* to *āsakti*. This development is outlined in the first verse of *Śrī Śikṣāṣṭaka*, which describes the seven progressive results of *śrī-kṛṣṇa-saṅkīrtana*. And each result corresponds with one of the eight successive verses of *Śikṣāṣṭaka*. Once the *sādhaka* attains the stage of *bhāva*, he is no longer an *ajāta-rati-sādhaka*, as described above; hence that title is omitted from that part of the chart onwards.

Although Bhaktivinoda Ṭhākura's analysis of the *mahā-mantra* is outlined in this diagram, one should be careful not to limit this analysis to its two dimensions. Rather, the chart is meant to serve as a springboard to a more developed understanding of the *mahā-mantra* and a deeper approach to chanting.

In the course of doing this translation, quite a number of questions arose. The book contains many technical and subtle points that needed clarification to remove any ambiguity. Śrīpada Bhaktivedānta Mādhava Mahārāja kindly gave his time to clearing confusion and answering questions, although he repeatedly reminded us that many of these concepts are never usually expressed in words and that it is only by the mercy of Śrīla Bhaktivinoda Ṭhākura and Śrīla Gurudeva that they are presented at all. He also pointed out that it is not possible for the material mind to grasp them and we must patiently wait until we attain higher levels of *bhakti* to realise their meaning.

We are also indebted to Umā Dīdī, Mādhava-prīya Brahmacārī, Savitā dāsī and Pūrṇimā dāsī, who were constantly available to answer all varieties of questions. The book would not have come to completion without them

Vraja-sundarī dāsī (England) originally translated most of the book from Hindi into English. Mañjarī dāsī edited the English and Ananta-kṛṣṇa dāsa did a fidelity check of the entire translation. Śyāmarāṇī dāsī reviewed this draft, making English suggestions and clarifying the *siddhānta*. We thank Śrīpada Bhaktivedānta Bhāgavata Mahārāja and Atula-kṛṣṇa dāsa for checking the Sanskrit. Kāntā dāsī compiled the glossary and assisted by doing other computer work.

Sundara-gopāla dāsa (England) made numerous valuable suggestions throughout the manuscript's development, and Giridhārī Brahmacārī proofread the book. Kṛṣṇa-kāruṇya Brahmacārī and Jaya-gopāla dāsa did the graphic design for the enclosed diagram. Kṛṣṇa-prema dāsa designed the cover and provided the layout for the entire book. We are ever grateful to Prema-vilāsa dāsa and Lavaṅga-latā dāsī for providing the final edit and for preparing the book for production.

This English version of *Śrī Bhajana-rahasya* was published by the kind donation of Sundara-gopāla dāsa (Fiji). We also thank Gopīnātha dāsa for his committed support of Śrīla Gurudeva's book production.

It is by the transcendental compassion of Śrīla A.C. Bhaktivedānta Swami Prabhupāda, who introduced the science of *kṛṣṇa-bhakti* to the Western world, that we are now receiving the mercy of Bhaktivinoda Ṭhākura and our *guru-paramparā*. He endured great difficulties for the sole purpose of giving us the most essential teachings, as found in this *Śrī Bhajana-rahasya*. Our feelings of indebtedness to him cannot be expressed in words and we humbly pray that he forever bestow his mercy upon us.

Finally, we would like to thank those devotees dedicated to the service of our *gurudeva* who gave their constant encouragement to this project, and to all those Gauḍīya Vaiṣṇavas who embody the various aspects of the teachings given herein and who are a constant source of inspiration for devotees worldwide.

Vaijayantī-mālā dāsī / Śāntī dāsī

Kāmadā Ekādaśī
13th April, 2003
Gopīnātha-bhavana, Śrī Vṛndāvana

Śrī Brahma-Madhva-Gauḍīya Guru-paramparā

śrī-kṛṣṇa-brahma-devarṣi-
bādarāyaṇa-saṁjñakān
śrī-madhva-śrī-padmanābha-
śrīman-nṛhari-mādhavān

akṣobhya-jayatīrtha-śrī-
jñānasindhu-dayānidhīn
śrī-vidyānidhi-rājendra-
jayadharmān kramādvayam

puruṣottama-brahmaṇya-
vyāsatīrthāś ca saṁstumaḥ
tato lakṣmīpatiṁ śrīman-
mādhavendraṁ ca bhaktitaḥ

tac-chiṣyān śrīśvarādvaita-
nityānandān jagad-gurūn
devam īśvara-śiṣyaṁ śrī-
caitanyaṁ ca bhajāmahe
śrī-kṛṣṇa-prema-dānena
yena nistāritaṁ jagat

mahāprabhu-svarūpa-śrī-
dāmodaraḥ priyaṁ karaḥ
rūpa-sanātanau dvau ca
gosvāmi-pravarau prabhū

śrī-jīvo raghunāthaś ca
rūpa-priyo mahāmatiḥ
tat-priyaḥ kavirāja-śrī-
kṛṣṇa-dāsa-prabhur mataḥ

tasya priyottamaḥ śrīlaḥ
sevāparo narottamaḥ
tad-anugata-bhaktaḥ śrī-
viśvanāthaḥ sad-uttamaḥ

tad-āsaktaś ca gauḍīya-
vedāntācārya-bhūṣaṇam
vidyābhūṣaṇa-pāda-śrī-
baladeva-sadāśrayaḥ

vaiṣṇava-sārvabhaumaḥ śrī-
jagannātha-prabhus tathā
śrī-māyāpura-dhāmnas tu
nirdeṣṭā sajjana-priyaḥ

śuddha-bhakti-pracārasya
mūlībhūta ihottamaḥ
śrī-bhaktivinodo devas
tat priyatvena viśrutaḥ

tad-abhinna-suhṛd-varyo
mahā-bhāgavatottamaḥ
śrī-gaurakiśoraḥ sākṣād
vairāgyaṁ vigrahāśritam

māyāvādi-kusiddhānta-
dhvānta-rāśi-nirāsakaḥ
viśuddha-bhakti-siddhāntaiḥ
svāntaḥ padma-vikāśakaḥ

devo 'sau paramo haṁso
mattaḥ śrī-gaura-kīrtane
pracārācāra-kāryeṣu
nirantaraṁ mahotsukaḥ

hari-priya-janair gamya
oṁ viṣṇupāda-pūrvakaḥ
śrīpādo bhaktisiddhānta
sarasvatī mahodayaḥ

sarve te gaura-vaṁśyaś ca
paramahaṁsa-vigrahāḥ
vayaṁ ca praṇatā dāsās
tad-ucchiṣṭa-grahāgrahāḥ

Guru-paramparā

by Śrīla Bhaktisiddhānta Sarasvatī Ṭhākura

kṛṣṇa haite caturmukha, haya kṛṣṇa sevonmukha,
brahmā haite nāradera mati
nārada haite vyāsa, madhva kahe vyāsadāsa,
pūrṇaprajña padmanābha gati

In the beginning of creation Śrī Kṛṣṇa spoke the science of devotional service to four-headed Lord Brahmā, who in turn passed these teachings on to Nārada Muni, who accepted Kṛṣṇa-dvaipāyana Vyāsadeva as his disciple. Vyāsa transmitted this knowledge to Madhvācārya, who is also known as Pūrṇaprajña Tīrtha and who was the sole refuge for his disciple Padmanābha Tīrtha.

nṛhari mādhava vaṁśe, akṣobhya-paramahaṁse,
śiṣya bali' aṅgīkāra kare
akṣobhyera śiṣya jayatīrtha nāme paricaya,
tāṅra dāsye jñānasindhu tare

Following in the line of Madhvācārya were Nṛhari Tīrtha and Mādhava Tīrtha, whose principal disciple was the great *paramahaṁsa* Akṣobhya Tīrtha. He in turn accepted as his disciple Jayatīrtha, who passed his service down to Jñānasindhu.

tāhā haite dayānidhi, tāṅra dāsa vidyānidhi,
rājendra haila tāṅhā haite
tāṅhāra kiṅkara jayadharma nāme paricaya,
paramparā jāna bhāla mate

From him the line came down to Dayānidhi, then to his disciple Vidyānidhi, then in turn it was introduced to Rājendra Tīrtha, whose servant was the renowned Jayadharma, also known as Vijayadhvaja Tīrtha. In this way the *guru-paramparā* is properly understood.

jayadharma-dāsye khyāti, śrī-puruṣottama yati,
tā' ha'te brahmaṇyatīrtha sūri
vyāsatīrtha tāṅra dāsa, lakṣmīpati vyāsadāsa,
tāhā ha'te madhavendra purī

The great *sannyāsī* Śrī Puruṣottama Tīrtha was a renowned disciple in the service of Jayadharma; from Śrī Puruṣottama the line descended to the powerful Brahmaṇyatīrtha, then to Vyāsatīrtha. He was succeeded by Śrī Lakṣmīpati, who passed the line down to Śrī Mādhavendra Purī.

mādhavendra purīvara, śiṣya-vara śrī-īśvara,
nityānanda śrī-advaita vibhu
īśvara-purīke dhanya, karilena śrī-caitanya,
jagad-guru gaura-mahāprabhu

Śrī Īśvara Purī was the most prominent *sannyāsa* disciple of the great Śrī Mādhavendra Purī, whose disciples also included the *avatāras* Śrī Nityānanda Prabhu and Śrī Advaita Ācārya. Śrī Caitanya Mahāprabhu, the Golden Lord and spiritual preceptor of all the worlds, made Īśvara Purī greatly fortunate by accepting him as *dīkṣā-guru.*

mahāprabhu śrī-caitanya, rādhā kṛṣṇa nahe anya,
rūpānuga janera jīvana
viśvambhara priyaṅkara, śrī svarūpa dāmodara,
śrī-gosvāmī rūpa-sanātana

Śrī Caitanya Mahāprabhu, who is Rādhā and Kṛṣṇa combined, is the very life of the *rūpānuga* Vaiṣṇavas who follow Śrī Rūpa Gosvāmī. Śrī Svarūpa Dāmodara, Śrī Rūpa and Śrī Sanātana Gosvāmīs were the dearmost servants of Viśvambhara (Śrī Caitanya).

rūpa priya mahājana, jīva raghunātha hana,
tāṅra priya kavi kṛṣṇadāsa
kṛṣṇadāsa priya-vara, narottama sevāpara,
jāṅra pada viśvanātha āśa

Dear to Śrī Rūpa Gosvāmī were the great saintly personalities, Śrī Jīva Gosvāmī and Śrī Raghunātha dāsa Gosvāmī, whose intimate disciple was the great poet Śrī Kṛṣṇadāsa Kavirāja. The dearmost of Kṛṣṇadāsa was Śrīla Narottama dāsa Ṭhākura, who was always engaged in *guru-sevā*. His lotus feet were the only hope and aspiration of Śrī Viśvanātha Cakravartī Ṭhākura.

viśvanātha bhakta-sātha, baladeva jagannātha,
tāṅra priya śrī-bhaktivinoda
mahā-bhāgavata-vara, śrī-gaurakiśora-vara,
hari bhajanete jāṅra moda

Prominent among the associates of Śrī Viśvanātha Cakravartī Ṭhākura was Śrī Baladeva Vidyābhūṣaṇa. After him the line descended to Śrīla Jagannātha dāsa Bābājī Mahārāja, who was the beloved *śikṣā-guru* of Śrī Bhaktivinoda Ṭhākura. Bhaktivinoda was the intimate friend of the great *mahā-bhāgavata* Śrīla Gaura-kiśora dāsa Bābājī Mahārāja, whose sole delight was *hari-bhajana*.

śri-vārṣabhanavī-vara, sadā sevya-sevā-para,
tāṅhāra dayita-dāsa nāma
prabhupāda-antaraṅga, śrī-svarūpa-rūpānuga,
śrī-keśava bhakti prajñāna
gauḍīya-vedānta-vettā, māyāvāda-tamohantā,
gaura-vāṇī pracārācāra-dhāma

The most distinguished Śrīla Bhaktisiddhānta Sarasvatī Ṭhākura, whose initiated name was Śrī Vārṣabhānavī Dayita dāsa, was always engaged in divine service to Hari, Guru and Vaiṣṇavas. An internal and intimate disciple of Prabhupāda following in the line of Svarūpa Dāmodara and Rūpa Gosvāmī was Śrī Bhakti Prajñāna Keśava Gosvāmī. Having full knowledge of Vedānta philosophy according to the Gauḍīya *sampradāya*, Śrīla Keśava Mahārāja annihilated the darkness of all *māyāvāda* arguments. He abundantly served Navadvīpa-dhāma, and his life is an example of both the practice and preaching of Mahāprabhu's message.

ei saba harijana, gaurāṅgera nija-jana,
tāṅdera ucchiṣṭe mora kāma

It is my desire to honour the remnants (*ucchiṣṭa*) – their *mahā-prasāda* and their instructions – from the lotus mouths of all these personal associates of Śrī Kṛṣṇa and Śrī Caitanya Mahāprabhu.

śrī śrī kṛṣṇa-caitanya-candrāya namaḥ

ŚRĪ BHAJANA-RAHASYA

(a sequel to *Śrī Harināma-cintāmaṇi*)

1

Prathama-yāma-sādhana

Niśānta-bhajana – śraddhā

(the last six *daṇḍas* of the night:
approximately 3.30 A.M. – 6.00 A.M.)

Text 1

kṛṣṇa-varṇaṁ tviṣākṛṣṇaṁ
sāṅgopāṅgāstra-pārṣadam
yajñaiḥ saṅkīrtana-prāyair
bhajāmi kali-pāvanam

I worship Śrī Gaurāṅgadeva, who delivers the living entities of Kali-yuga (*kali-pāvana*) through the congregational chanting of the Lord's holy names (*śrī-nāma-saṅkīrtana-yajña*). He describes the name, form, qualities and pastimes of Śrī Kṛṣṇa; He performs *kīrtana* of the two syllables *kṛ* and *ṣṇa*; His complexion is fair; He is surrounded by His *aṅgas* (associates, meaning Śrī Nityānanda Prabhu and Śrī Advaita Prabhu), *upāṅgas* (servitors, meaning Śrīvāsa Paṇḍita and other pure devotees) and *pārṣadas* (confidential companions like Śrī Svarūpa Dāmodara, Śrī Rāya Rāmānanda, Śrī Gadādhara Paṇḍita and the Six Gosvāmīs); and He is endowed with His weapon (*astra*) of *harināma*, which destroys ignorance.

A verse similar in meaning to Text 1 is found in *Śrīmad-Bhāgavatam* (11.5.32):

kṛṣṇa-varṇaṁ tviṣākṛṣṇaṁ
sāṅgopāṅgāstra-pārṣadam
yajñaiḥ saṅkīrtana-prāyair
yajanti hi su-medhasaḥ

In the age of Kali, Kṛṣṇa appears with a golden complexion (*akṛṣṇa*). He is constantly singing the two syllables *kṛ* and *ṣṇa*, and He is accompanied by His associates, servitors, weapons and confidential companions. Intelligent people worship Him by performing *saṅkīrtana-yajña.*

kali-jīva uddhārite para-tattva hari
navadvīpe āilā gaura-rūpa āviṣkari

yuga-dharma kṛṣṇa-nāma-smaraṇa kīrtana
sāṅgopāṅge vitarila diyā prema dhana

jīvera sunitya dharma nāma-saṅkīrtana
anya saba dharma nāma-siddhira kāraṇa

"Śrī Hari, who is the Absolute Truth Himself, descended in Navadvīpa as Gaurasundara to deliver the living entities (*jīvas*) of Kali-yuga. Together with His associates, He distributed the treasure of *kṛṣṇa-prema* through *śrī-kṛṣṇa-nāma-saṅkīrtana*, the religion of the current age (*yuga-dharma*). *Nāma-saṅkīrtana* is the living entities' only eternal religion; all other *dharmas* are simply secondary means to attain perfection in chanting."

Bhajana-rahasya-vṛtti

Śrīla Bhaktivinoda Ṭhākura begins this book by praying to Śrīman Mahāprabhu. The *jīva's* only duty is to worship Śrī Gaurasundara, who is resplendent with the lustre and sentiment of Śrī Rādhā. Śrī Kṛṣṇa Caitanya, the central figure (*mūla-tattva*) in *navadvīpa-līlā*, comprises five features (*pañca-tattva-*

ātmaka). He and His four other forms – Śrī Nityānanda Prabhu, Śrī Advaita Ācārya, Śrī Gadādhara and the associates headed by Śrīvāsa – are all supremely worshipful.

The worship and service of Śrī Gaurasundara are performed only through *nāma-saṅkīrtana*. By this process, which is the most powerful of the nine kinds of *bhakti*, all the limbs of *bhakti* are practised. Even if the other types of *sādhana* are not performed during *kīrtana*, *kīrtana* is sufficient in itself; *arcana*, *smaraṇa* and so forth are nourished solely through *kīrtana*. Actual service to Śrī Kṛṣṇa is carried out through *saṅkīrtana*, a process prescribed by *pañca-tattva-ātmaka* Śrī Gaurasundara. Śrīman Mahāprabhu and His associates assembled and showed through *śrī-kṛṣṇa-nāma-saṅkīrtana* how to perform service to and worship of the Lord.

In this first Text the author establishes that Śrī Gaurasundara is Kṛṣṇa Himself. In the word *kṛṣṇa-varṇam* we find the two syllables *kṛ* and *ṣṇa*. Hence the quality of being Kṛṣṇa (*kṛṣṇatva*), which is itself the quality of being Bhagavān (*bhagavattā*), is displayed in the name Śrī Kṛṣṇa Caitanya. *Kṛṣṇa-varṇam* also refers to that person who, by remembering His previous supremely blissful pastimes of *keli-vilāsa*, becomes absorbed in transcendental sentiments due to intense jubilation and always describes (*varṇam*) – here meaning "performs *kīrtana* of" – the name of Kṛṣṇa. He has assumed a fair complexion, and out of supreme compassion has instructed all living entities to chant Kṛṣṇa's name, which will naturally manifest in their hearts simply by receiving Śrī Gaurasundara's *darśana*. Śrī Kṛṣṇa, who possesses the potency to make the impossible possible (*aghaṭana-ghaṭana-paṭīyasī-śaktimān*), accepted the form of a devotee and appeared as Gaurasundara. In other words Śrī Kṛṣṇa Himself directly manifested as Gaurasundara.

This incarnation (*avatāra*) of Śrī Caitanyadeva is extremely difficult for ordinary *sādhakas* to understand. In *Śrīmad-Bhāgavatam* (7.9.38) Prahlāda Mahārāja says: "*channaḥ kalau yad abhavas triyugo 'tha sa tvam* – O Puruṣottama, in Kali-yuga You are concealed. Your name, therefore, is Tri-yuga, the Lord who appears only in three *yugas*, because this covered incarnation is not clearly evident in any scripture."

When the great scholar Sārvabhauma Bhaṭṭācārya saw the brightly shining ecstatic transformations (*sūddīpta-aṣṭa-sāttvika-bhāvas*) in Śrīman Mahāprabhu, he was amazed; he knew that these extremely rare transcendental sentiments are not seen in any human being. Nevertheless, he doubted that Śrīman Mahāprabhu was Kṛṣṇa Himself and expressed this to Śrī Gopīnātha Ācārya:

ataeva 'triyuga' kari' kahi viṣṇunāma
kaliyuge avatāra nāhi – śāstra-jñāna

Śrī Caitanya-caritāmṛta (*Madhya-līlā* 6.95)

[Sārvabhauma Bhaṭṭācārya said:] The verdict of the scriptures is that there is no incarnation of Śrī Viṣṇu in Kali-yuga; hence, one name of Śrī Viṣṇu is Tri-yuga.

Hearing this, Gopīnātha Ācārya said:

kali-yuge līlāvatāra nā kare bhagavān
ataeva 'triyuga' kari' kahi tāra nāma
pratiyuge karena kṛṣṇa yuga-avatāra
tarka-niṣṭha hṛdaya tomāra nāhika vicāra

Śrī Caitanya-caritāmṛta (*Madhya-līlā* 6.99–100)

In Kali-yuga there is no *līlā-avatāra* of Śrī Bhagavān; therefore His name is Tri-yuga. But certainly there is an incarnation in each *yuga*, and such an incarnation is called a *yuga-avatāra*. Your heart has become hardened by logic and arguments and thus you cannot consider these facts.

On the other hand, when Śrī Rāya Rāmānanda, who is Viśākhā Sakhī in *vraja-līlā*, received *darśana* of Mahāprabhu, he clearly realised His identity. He said:

pahile dekhiluṅ tomāra sannyāsī-svarūpa
ebe tomā dekhi muñi śyāma-gopa-rūpa

tomāra sammukhe dekhi kāñcana-pañcālikā
tāṅra gaura-kāntye tomāra sarva aṅga ḍhākā

Śrī Caitanya-caritāmṛta (*Madhya-līlā* 8.268–9)

At first I saw You in the form of a *sannyāsī*, but then I saw You as a dark-complexioned cowherd boy. Now I see a shining figure in front of You, whose golden lustre appears to cover Your entire body.

Statements in various Purāṇas prove that Caitanya Mahāprabhu is Śrī Kṛṣṇa, the source of all incarnations. At the time of Śrī Kṛṣṇa's name-giving ceremony, Śrī Gargācārya said:

āsan varṇās trayo hy asya
gṛhṇato 'nuyugaṁ tanuḥ
śuklo raktas tathā pīta
idānīṁ kṛṣṇatāṁ gataḥ

Śrīmad-Bhāgavatam (10.8.13)

Your son Kṛṣṇa appears in every *yuga* as an *avatāra*. Previously He assumed three different colours – white, red and yellow – and now He has appeared in a blackish colour.

The *Mahābhārata* (*Dāna-dharma* 149.92, 75) states:

suvarṇa-varṇo hemāṅgo
varāṅgaś candanāṅgadī

sannyāsa-kṛc chamaḥ śānto
niṣṭhā-śānti-parāyaṇaḥ

[Bhīṣma said to Yudhiṣṭhira Mahārāja:] Kṛṣṇa first appears as a *gṛhastha* with a golden complexion. His limbs are the colour of molten gold, His body is extremely beautiful, He is decorated with sandalwood pulp and He continuously chants "Kṛṣṇa". Then He accepts *sannyāsa* and is always equipoised. He is firmly fixed in His mission of propagating *harināma-saṅkīrtana* and He defeats the impersonalist philosophers, who are opposed to *bhakti*. He is thus the highest abode of peace and devotion.

Furthermore it is said in *Bhagavad-gītā* (4.8): "*dharma-saṁsthāpanārthāya sambhavāmi yuge yuge* – to re-establish the principles of religion, I appear in every *yuga*." The *āgama-śāstras* state: "*māyāpure bhaviṣyāmi śacī-sutaḥ* – in the future, the son of Śacī will appear in Māyāpura." Śrī Jīva Gosvāmī writes in *Tattva-sandarbha* (*Anuccheda* 2):

antaḥ kṛṣṇaṁ bahir-gauraṁ
darśitāṅgādi-vaibhavam
kalau saṅkīrtanādyaiḥ smaḥ
kṛṣṇa-caitanyam āśritāḥ

I take shelter of Śrī Kṛṣṇa Caitanya, who is outwardly *gaura*, of fair complexion, but is inwardly Kṛṣṇa Himself. In Kali-yuga He displays His associates, servitors and confidential companions while performing *saṅkīrtana*.

And in *Śrī Caitanya-caritāmṛta* (*Madhya-līlā* 8.279) it is said:

rādhikāra bhāva-kānti kari' aṅgīkāra
nija-rasa āsvādite kariyācha avatāra

To taste Your own transcendental mellow You appeared as Śrī Caitanya Mahāprabhu, accepting the sentiment and lustre of Śrīmatī Rādhikā.

The rays of Śrī Kṛṣṇa Caitanya's yellow lustre, which resemble molten gold, destroy the darkness of ignorance. To destroy the darkness of the activities that are opposed to *bhakti* performed by the living entities in Kali-yuga, Śrī Mahāprabhu wanders the Earth together with His *aṅgas* (associates), *upāṅgas* (servitors) and *pārṣadas* (confidential companions), and with the weapon of the *saṅkīrtana* of Hare Kṛṣṇa and other names of Bhagavān. Other incarnations destroyed demons with armies and weapons, but Śrī Kṛṣṇa Caitanya Mahāprabhu's *aṅgas* and *upāṅgas* are His army. According to the scriptures, the word *aṅga* means *aṁśa*, or part, and the *aṅga* of an *aṅga* (part of a part) is called an *upāṅga*. Śrī Nityānanda and Śrī Advaita Ācārya are both Śrī Caitanya's *aṅgas*, and their parts, the *upāṅgas*, are Śrīvāsa and the other devotees who always accompany Mahāprabhu. They preach Bhagavān's name, Hare Kṛṣṇa, which is itself the "sharp weapon" capable of destroying atheism.

In this Text the adjective *saṅkīrtana-prāyaiḥ*, which means "consisting chiefly of congregational chanting", defines *harināma-saṅkīrtana-yajña* as *abhidheya-tattva*, the means to attain the goal. In the incarnation of Śrīman Mahāprabhu the main weapon is *harināma-saṅkīrtana*, by which He destroys the atheism of the atheists and the sins of the sinful. He who worships Śrī Caitanyadeva through *nāma-saṅkīrtana-yajña* is intelligent and attains all perfection; he who does not worship Him is unfortunate, unintelligent and devoid of pious merit (*sukṛti*).

To conclude, in this age of Kali the only objects worthy of meditation are Śrī Caitanya Mahāprabhu's lotus feet, which fulfil all treasured desires. Apart from Śrī Caitanyadeva's mercy, nothing is eternal or permanent; rather, everything is perishable and incapable of fulfilling these desires.

Text 2

Stavāvalī (*Śrī Śacīsūnv-aṣṭaka* (5)) says:

nijatve gauḍīyān jagati parigṛhya prabhur imān
hare kṛṣṇety evaṁ gaṇana-vidhinā kīrtayata bhoḥ
iti prāyāṁ śikṣāṁ caraṇa-madhupebhyaḥ paridiśan
śacī-sūnuḥ kiṁ me nayana-saraṇīṁ yāsyati padam

When will Śacīnandana Gaurahari appear on the path of my eyes? He accepted the Gauḍīya Vaiṣṇavas in this world, who are like bees at His lotus feet, as His own, and He instructed them to chant the Hare Kṛṣṇa *mahā-mantra* by counting a fixed number of rounds.

Bhajana-rahasya-vṛtti

Here Śrīla Raghunātha dāsa Gosvāmī expresses the natural, affectionate mercy of Śrīman Mahāprabhu for the inhabitants of Gauḍa (Bengal). Their relationship with each other is likened to the affectionate relationship of near and dear ones in this mundane world (*laukika-sad-bandhuvat*). This means they have a natural feeling of possessiveness (*madīya-bhāva*, or *mamatā*) towards Śrīman Mahāprabhu, by which they think, "Gaurasundara is ours". In *Śrī Bṛhad-bhāgavatāmṛta*, in the section describing *rāgānuga-bhajana*, Śrīla Sanātana Gosvāmī explains that a mood of *laukika-sad-bandhuvat*, which is characterised by intense possessiveness (*mamatā*) in relation to Bhagavān, is indeed the symptom of deep *prema* for Him.

Although Rasarāja Śrī Kṛṣṇa appeared as Gaurasundara and gave the process of chanting the Hare Kṛṣṇa *mahā-mantra* to the entire world, He displayed special compassion towards the inhabitants of Gauḍa. There, in Śrī Navadvīpa-dhāma, is the place renowned as the *aparādha-bhañjana*, where every kind of offence is vanquished.

Being entirely overwhelmed by *bhāva*, Śrī Gaurasundara, the originator of *saṅkīrtana*, would perform *kīrtana* and dance in the company of the Gauḍīya *bhaktas* in an unprecedented way. As the sentiments in Śrī Gaurasundara's heart swelled more and more upon seeing His affectionate devotees, like bees they would become intoxicated by drinking the honey-like bliss of *prema* at His lotus feet.

At the time of *saṅkīrtana*, Śrī Gaurasundara would dance and sing and become absorbed in ecstatic bliss as He tasted the sweetness of Kṛṣṇa's *rāsa* dance with Śrī Rādhā and the other *vraja-gopīs*. The wonderful expressions of the spiritual sentiments of this sweet and enchanting dance, which is possessed of transcendental *śṛṅgāra-rasa*, thus embellished Him with *prema*, and He became decorated with the ornaments of extraordinary ecstatic symptoms (*aṣṭa-sāttvika-bhāvas*) such as the shedding of tears and the standing of bodily hairs on end.

During the Ratha-yātrā Festival in Jagannātha Purī, Mahāprabhu's ecstatic dancing and *kīrtana* reached their topmost limit. To support Mahāprabhu's sentiments Śrī Svarūpa Dāmodara and Rāya Rāmānanda sang poetry endowed with *samṛddhimān sambhoga-rasa*, the mellows experienced by Śri Rādhā and Kṛṣṇa when They meet after having been far away from each other. Svarūpa Dāmodara sang, *"sei ta parāṇa-nātha pāinu, yāhā lāgī' madana-dahane jhuri' genu* – now I have attained the master of My life. In His absence I was being burned by Cupid and was withering away." Hearing this, Mahāprabhu would gaze upon Jagannātha's lotus face. When Their eyes met, Mahāprabhu's heart would be agitated by waves of ecstatic mellows of *prema*, and He would proceed to dance according to the mood of the song. At such times Śrī Gaurasundara would exhibit extraordinary expressions. He would bite His lips, which were pinkish like the *bandhūka* flower, artistically place His left hand on His hip, and move His right hand to demonstrate wonderful dance postures that were extremely attractive. This sight would overwhelm Śrī Jagannātha Himself with astonishment and supreme bliss. Tasting the sweetness of the unprecedented beauty of Mahāprabhu's dance, Śrī Jagannātha would slowly and gently proceed towards Sundarācala (which represents Vṛndāvana).

The brightly shining golden lustre of Śrīman Mahāprabhu's large body defeated the splendour of a golden mountain. Absorbed in ecstatic bliss, Śrī Gaurasundara loudly chanted His own names, *hare kṛṣṇety uccaiḥ sphurita-rasanaḥ.*[1] Surrounded by His devotees, Mahāprabhu performed *kīrtana*, and His restless lotus feet danced. Tears flowed from His eyes like streams of Gaṅgā and Yamunā water, and His bodily hairs stood erect in a way that was astonishing, thus resembling the filaments of a *kadamba* flower.

Remembering the unprecedented sweetness of Mahāprabhu's *prema*, Raghunātha dāsa Gosvāmī said, "When will Śacīnandana Śrī Gaurahari appear on the path of my eyes?" As Śrī Dāsa Gosvāmī remembered the great compassion of Mahāprabhu, he became overwhelmed by feelings of separation from Him. He offered this prayer, while continuously shedding tears, waiting for the *darśana* of his beloved Lord with the utmost longing and hope. Then Śrī Gaurasundara's own compassion, abundant steadfastness, unsurpassed renunciation and fully transcendental *prema-bhakti* arose in the heart of Dāsa Gosvāmī, who became overwhelmed with ecstatic emotions. He had lived close to Śrī Caitanya Mahāprabhu for a long time and had received unlimited

[1] This verse is from Rūpa Gosvāmī's *Stava-mālā* (*Prathama-caitanyāṣṭaka* (5)). It can have two meanings: "His tongue is always dancing by loudly calling out 'Hare Kṛṣṇa!' " or "the *mahā-mantra* ecstatically dances of its own accord on the theatrical stage of His tongue".

affection, mercy and blessings from Him. The compassion of Śrī Gaurasundara is just like that of a mother. For this reason Dāsa Gosvāmī addresses Him as Śacīnandana, the son of Mother Śacī. Śacīnandana Śrī Gaurahari bestowed His mercy even upon all kinds of unqualified *jīvas*, thus making them fortunate.

Text 3

The *Viṣṇu-rahasya* states:

yad abhyarcya hariṁ bhaktyā
kṛte kratu-śatair api
phalaṁ prāpnoty avikalaṁ
kalau govinda-kīrtanāt

Whatever fruit can be obtained in Satya-yuga by devoutly performing austerities and so on for hundreds of years, can be obtained in the age of Kali simply by chanting the names of Śrī Govinda.

satya-yuge śata śata yajñe haryarcana
kalite govinda-nāme se phala-arjana

"The result received in Satya-yuga by meditation on Bhagavān, in Tretā-yuga by worshipping Bhagavān through great sacrifices, and in Dvāpara-yuga by performing *arcana* of Bhagavān according to proper rules, is obtained in Kali-yuga simply by chanting *nāma-ābhāsa*, a semblance of Śrī Kṛṣṇa's names."

Bhajana-rahasya-vṛtti

In Kali-yuga, Śrīman Mahāprabhu Himself, the saviour of the fallen, accepted the mood and conduct of a devotee and taught the path of devotion to the entire world. The *Bṛhan-nāradīya Purāṇa* states:

harer nāma harer nāma
harer nāmaiva kevalam
kalau nāsty eva nāsty eva
nāsty eva gatir anyathā

In Kali-yuga there is no other way for the *jīva* than chanting *harināma.* There is no other way, there is no other way.

The mention of pure *harināma* three times in this verse demonstrates the need for fixed determination in performing *bhakti* and the need for one to understand the futility of other practices like *karma*, *jñāna* and *yoga.*

Text 4

The *Bṛhad-viṣṇu Purāṇa* states that other kinds of atonement (*prāyaścitta*) are not necessary for one who chants the holy name:

nāmno 'sya yāvatī śaktiḥ
pāpa-nirharaṇe hareḥ
tāvat kartuṁ na śaknoti
pātakaṁ pātakī janaḥ

Śrī Hari's name possesses such potency to destroy sins that it can counteract more sins than even the most sinful person is able to commit.

kona prāyaścitta nahe nāmera samāna
ataeva karma-tyāga kare buddhimān

Bhajana-rahasya-vṛtti

The scriptures describe methods of atonement for many kinds of sins. By chanting *śrī harināma*, however, all kinds of sins are destroyed. Therefore no other kind of atonement is required for one who is chanting the holy name. Nāma Prabhu has the capacity to destroy more sins than a sinful man is able to commit: *eka hari-nāme jata pāpa hare, pāpī haya tata pāpa karibāre nare.*

Text 5

The superiority of *kīrtana* is described in *Vaiṣṇava-cintāmaṇi* (*Hari-bhakti-vilāsa* (11.236)):

aghacchit-smaraṇaṁ viṣṇor
bahvāyāsena sādhyate
oṣṭha-spandana-mātreṇa
kīrtanaṁ tu tato varam

Sins are destroyed with great effort by remembering Viṣṇu, but by chanting His name, they are very easily destroyed. *Kīrtana* is performed simply by using the lips to vibrate the names of Bhagavān and is far superior to *smaraṇa* (remembrance).

tapasyāya dhyāna yoga kaṣṭa sādhya haya
oṣṭhera spandana-mātre kīrtana āśraya

oṣṭhera spandanābhāve nāmera smaraṇa
smaraṇa kīrtane sarva siddhi-saṅghaṭana

arcana apekṣā nāmera smaraṇa-kīrtana
ati śreṣṭha bali śāstre karila sthāpana

"Austerities, meditation, *yoga* and other practices are very difficult to perform in Kali-yuga, but *kīrtana* is easy; one need only vibrate one's lips. *Nāma* chanted without moving the lips is called *nāma-smaraṇa*. The *jīva* can attain all perfection by *nāma-kīrtana* and *nāma-smaraṇa*. The scriptures have therefore concluded that *kīrtana* and *smaraṇa* of the holy name are superior to *arcana*."

Bhajana-rahasya-vṛtti

The practices of *karma*, *jñāna* and *yoga* are difficult and troublesome, but the path of *bhakti* is easy and simple. In *Bhagavad-gītā* (2.40) Śrī Kṛṣṇa says:

nehābhikrama-nāśo 'sti
pratyavāyo na vidyate
svalpam apy asya dharmasya
trāyate mahato bhayāt

> Endeavours on the path of *bhakti-yoga* are neither fruitless nor subject to faults. Even a little performance of *bhakti-yoga* frees one from the great fear of material existence.

Even though mistakes made in the practices of meditation, *yoga* and so forth may be insignificant, as a consequence of those mistakes the desired result is unattainable. Actually, only *bhakti-yoga* is completely *nirguṇa*, free from the influence of the material qualities of goodness, passion and ignorance. Even if a person begins to practise *bhakti-yoga* but for some reason his practice remains incomplete, there is no defect or fault in his endeavour. Neither destruction nor misfortune in this world or the next awaits a person who has fallen from the path of *bhakti-yoga*.

The main limb of *bhakti-yoga* is *nāma-kīrtana*, which is performed merely by vibrating the lips. The holy name is not of this material world. Nāma Prabhu dances on the tongue of the *sādhaka* and, destroying his *prārabdha-karma* and other impediments, bestows everything up to *prema*. In previous *yugas*, a practitioner who was unable to fix his mind in the practice of *yoga* was unable to attain the goal. Yet in Kali-yuga perfection can be attained simply by uttering the holy name. In *Bṛhad-bhāgavatāmṛta*, Sanātana Gosvāmipāda states that *kīrtana* is more powerful than *smaraṇa.* By the process of *kīrtana* both the mind and the tongue attain a special pleasure.

Text 6

Hari-bhakti-vilāsa (11.237) states:

yena janma-śataiḥ pūrvaṁ
vāsudevaḥ samarcitaḥ
tan-mukhe hari-nāmāni
sadā tiṣṭhanti bhārataḥ

O best of the dynasty of Bharata, the holy name of Śrī Hari is eternally present only in the mouth of one who has perfectly worshipped Vāsudeva for hundreds of births.

hare kṛṣṇa ṣolanāma aṣṭayuga haya
aṣṭayuga arthe aṣṭaśloka prabhu kaya

ādi hare kṛṣṇa arthe avidyā-damana
śraddhāra sahita kṛṣṇa-nāma-saṅkīrtana

āra hare kṛṣṇa nāma kṛṣṇa sarva-śakti
sādhu-saṅge nāmāśraye bhajanānurakti

sei ta bhajana-krame sarvānartha-nāśa
anarthāpagame nāme niṣṭhāra vikāśa

tṛtīye viśuddha-bhakta caritrera saha
kṛṣṇa kṛṣṇa nāme niṣṭhā kare aharaha

caturthe ahaitukī bhakti uddīpana
ruci saha hare hare nāma-saṅkīrtana

pañcamete śuddha dāsya rucira sahita
hare rāma saṅkīrtana smaraṇa vihita

ṣaṣṭhe bhāvāṅkure hare rāmeti kīrtana
saṁsāre aruci kṛṣṇe ruci samarpaṇa

saptame madhurāsakti rādhā-padāśraya
vipralambhe rāma rāma nāmera udaya

aṣṭame vrajete aṣṭa-kāla gopī-bhāva
rādhā-kṛṣṇa-prema-sevā prayojana lābha

Bhajana-rahasya-vṛtti

The word *samarcita* in this Text means "properly worshipped". Here Svayam Bhagavān says to Arjuna, "O Arjuna, when one has worshipped Bhagavān Vāsudeva for several births according to rules and regulations, his heart becomes indifferent to lust and so on. Indeed, Mukunda appears in the heart of such a person." The scriptures present the system of *arcana* to enable the neophyte devotee (*kaniṣṭha-adhikārī*) to develop pure, good behaviour and to bring him to the practice of *bhagavad-bhakti*. By performance of *arcana* his heart will gradually become pure and freed from sorrow, anger, fear and so forth. In *Bhakti-rasāmṛta-sindhu* (1.2.115) Rūpa Gosvāmipāda says:

śokāmarṣādibhir-bhāvair
ākrāntaṁ yasya mānasam
kathaṁ tatra mukundasya
sphūrti-sambhāvanā bhavet

How can Mukunda manifest in the heart of a person who is filled with emotions like grief and anger?

In the scriptures, *smaraṇa* is considered to be a part of *arcana*; one remembers the object of worship at the time of *arcana*. For a neophyte devotee *arcana* is superior to *smaraṇa*, but the compilers of the scriptures conclude that one attains the actual fruit of *arcana* only when it is performed with *kīrtana*. This is the rule for performing *arcana* in Kali-yuga.

The *mahā-mantra* is that *harināma* which is composed of sixteen names, or eight pairs of names, and consists of thirty-two syllables. Śrīman Mahāprabhu revealed to the world the meanings of these eight pairs of names in the eight verses of His *Śikṣāṣṭaka*.

The steps from *śraddhā* to *prema* begin from the first verse and continue up to the eighth.

The hidden meaning of the first pair of names – Hare Kṛṣṇa – is that performing *kṛṣṇa-nāma-saṅkīrtana* with *śraddhā* nullifies ignorance and cleanses the mirror-like heart. The second pair of names – Hare Kṛṣṇa – indicates that all potencies, such as mercy, are invested in the holy name. These potencies destroy the ignorance in the heart of the *sādhaka* who performs *nāma-kīrtana*, and they create attachment for *bhajana*, which takes the form of performing *harināma-saṅkīrtana* in the association of devotees. Performance of such *bhajana* gradually destroys all kinds of impediments (*anarthas*) and produces unwavering faith (*niṣṭhā*) in *bhajana*.

When a *sādhaka* on the platform of *bhāva* (a *jāta-rati-sādhaka*) chants the first and second pairs of names – Hare Kṛṣṇa, Hare Kṛṣṇa – he remembers the pastimes in which Rādhā and Kṛṣṇa meet. Under the guidance of Śrī Rūpa Mañjarī and other *vraja-devīs*, he performs *mānasī-sevā* to Śrī Rādhā-Govinda in his internally contemplated form of a *gopī*.

When the *sādhaka* remembers Śrī Rādhā-Kṛṣṇa's eternal forms, pastimes, qualities and so forth, Their *līlā-vilāsa* manifests, as does direct service to Them within these pastimes. This service is the wish-fulfilling tree (*keli-kalpa-taru*) of all treasured yearnings. The *sādhaka* constantly remembers Lalitā and the other *sakhīs*; in other words, he serves in his eternally perfect body (*siddha-deha*) under their guidance.

By continuously chanting Hare Kṛṣṇa, a *sādhaka* who has not attained the stage of *bhāva* (an *ajāta-rati-sādhaka*) has his *anarthas* gradually removed and develops steadfastness in chanting. Consequently his intelligence becomes fixed and he develops resolute attachment (*niṣṭhā*) for *kṛṣṇa-nāma*. Such a *sādhaka* pursues as his ideal the character, service and goal of

Śrīla Rūpa Gosvāmī, Śrīla Raghunātha dāsa Gosvāmī and other pure devotees.

While chanting the third pair of names – Kṛṣṇa Kṛṣṇa – this *sādhaka* follows the ideal character of the pure devotees, their way of chanting a fixed number of rounds, their offering of a fixed number of obeisances, their renunciation of material enjoyment and their utterance of prayers and glorifications. With firm faith he chants the holy name day and night. The *jāta-rati-sādhaka*, on the other hand, remembers the pastimes of Śrī Rādhā and the other *gopīs* when Śrī Kṛṣṇa leaves for cowherding, as well as the moods of separation they experience at that time.

With the fourth pair of names – Hare Hare – unalloyed *bhakti* is stimulated within the heart of the *ajāta-rati-sādhaka* when he performs *nāma-saṅkīrtana* with taste (*ruci*). The *jāta-rati-sādhaka* chants this fourth pair of holy names with great affection, and Śrī Rādhā-Kṛṣṇa's pastimes of meeting awaken within his heart.

While chanting the fifth pair of names – Hare Rāma – the *ajāta-rati-sādhaka* prays for the mood of servitude (*dāsya-bhāva*) to appear in his heart. Attachment (*āsakti*) for *nāma-bhajana* arises at this time and remembrance of pastimes begins. With attachment, that *sādhaka* cultivates the conception that he is a servant of Kṛṣṇa. The *jāta-rati-sādhaka* remembers the pastime of Rādhā and Kṛṣṇa's meeting after Kṛṣṇa returns from cowherding. The *gopīs* see to Kṛṣṇa's bath, dressing and so forth in the house of Nanda, and they help Rohiṇī-devī cook various preparations for Him.

In this way, as the *ajāta-rati-sādhaka* continuously chants the holy name, he attains the inherent mercy of Nāma Prabhu, and his heart begins to soften and melt. *Śuddha-sattva* (unalloyed goodness) then arises in his heart, and his taste for chanting the holy name thickens. In the heart of this *sādhaka*, the mood of *āsakti* sprouts and the nine symptoms of *bhāva* – *kṣāntir avyartha-kālatvam*[2] – begin to manifest.

At this stage the *sādhaka* tastes the chanting of the sixth pair of names – Hare Rāma – and a natural aversion for that which is unrelated to Kṛṣṇa manifests. By the *sādhaka's* chanting of the holy name with complete dedication to Śrī Kṛṣṇa, his heart melts and becomes extremely soft. Tears (*aśru*), horripilation (*pulaka*) and other *aṣṭa-sāttvika-bhāvas* manifest to the degree of *dhūmāyita* (smouldering)[3]. With this pair of names, the *jāta-rati-sādhaka* remembers how Rādhikā becomes completely delighted upon obtaining Kṛṣṇa's remnants through Dhaniṣṭhā. Simultaneously She receives information regarding where Their rendezvous will take place later that evening.

Chanting the seventh pair of names – Rāma Rāma – the *nāma-sādhaka*, who has taken shelter of *mādhurya-rasa* with an exclusive service mood to Śrī Rādhā-Kṛṣṇa Yugala, attains the exclusive shelter of Śrī Rādhā's lotus feet. In other words, he attains the transcendental sentiments of one of Śrīmatī Rādhikā's maidservants (*pālyadāsīs*), whose hearts are one with Hers. He also attains the *ekādaśa-bhāvas* and the five *daśās.*[4] Overwhelmed by the mood of separation (*vipralambha-rasa*), however, the *sādhaka* performs *nāma-saṅkīrtana* considering himself devoid of *bhakti*. At this time an internal transcendental vision (*sphūrti*) manifests in his heart: Śrī Rādhā is intensely eager to meet Kṛṣṇa and, following Vṛndā-devī's instruction, goes to meet Him in a *kuñja* on the bank of the Yamunā. Śrī Rādhā and Kṛṣṇa, fully absorbed in thinking of each other, search for one another.

[2] This refers to verses 1.3.25–6 of *Bhakti-rasāmṛta-sindhu*, which describe the nine symptoms of *bhāva*. A full translation of these verses can be found on p. 241.

[3] An explanation of *dhūmāyita* and the other stages of intensity of the *sāttvika-bhāvas* can be found on p. 247.

[4] These terms are explained on pp. 255–6.

Performing *kīrtana* of the eighth pair of names – Hare Hare – the *sādhaka* engages in the sweet *prema-sevā* of Rādhā-Kṛṣṇa in the manifested Vraja-dhāma throughout the eight divisions of the day and night (*aṣṭa-kāla*). In other words, the *sādhaka* attains service imbued with the mood of the *gopīs* in his eternal form (*svarūpa*). As he performs *nāma-bhajana* of this pair of names, he remembers the pastimes of Śrī Rādhā-Kṛṣṇa's meeting, in which the completely dedicated *mañjarīs* of Śrī Rādhā are serving Śrī Yugala by offering betel, massaging Their feet and so on.

Śrī Bhajana-rahasya is truly a treasure chest of *rahasyas*, intimate secrets. The secret of the qualification to enter *bhajana* is hidden in the first *yāma* of *Bhajana-rahasya*, *niśānta-bhajana*. This secret is *śraddhā*, faith. After the stage of *sādhu-saṅga*, when *sādhana* is executed through the performance of *nāma-saṅkīrtana* under the shelter of the spiritual master and with *sambandha-jñāna*, *anarthas* are eliminated. The first verse of *Śrī Śikṣāṣṭaka*, *ceto-darpaṇa-mārjanam*, indicates the most favourable process of *bhajana* for this stage.

The second *yāma*, *prātaḥ-kālīya-bhajana*, holds the secret of the removal of *anarthas* (*anartha-nivṛtti*) in the association of devotees. *Nāma* (the holy name) and *nāmī* (the possessor of the name) are non-different in *tattva*. Mercy and all other potencies of the personification of *nāma* are placed within the name of Bhagavān, and cleansing the heart (*ceto-darpaṇa-mārjanam*) becomes possible by performing such *bhajana*. The second *yāma* explains the secrets of *nāma-bhajana* in accordance with the mood of the second verse of *Śikṣāṣṭaka*, which begins with the words *nāmnām akāri*.

Bhajana with firm faith (*bhajana-niṣṭhā*) is the subject of the third *yāma*, *pūrvāhna-kālīya-bhajana*. Performing *nāma-bhajana* with *niṣṭhā* extinguishes the blazing forest fire of material existence (*bhava-mahā-dāvāgni*). *Bhajana* that is performed without pride (*amānī*) and with respect for others in relation to their respective positions (*mānada*) is the secret hidden within this *yāma*. This is stated in the words of the third verse of *Śikṣāṣṭaka*, *tṛṇād api sunīcena taror api sahiṣṇunā.*

The secrets of *ruci* are found to be concealed within the fourth *yāma*, *madhyāhna-kālīya-bhajana*. In the stage of *ruci*, the *sādhaka* has no other prominent desire but to serve Śrī Kṛṣṇa. The transcendental sentiments of prayers such as *śreyaḥ kairava-candrikā-vitaraṇam* (*Śikṣāṣṭaka* (1)) and *na dhanaṁ na janam* (*Śikṣāṣṭaka* (4)) explain *bhajana* in this stage.

In the fifth *yāma*, *aparāhna-kālīya-bhajana*, the *nāma-sādhaka* is praying to attain his true identity as an eternal servant of Kṛṣṇa. Here an attachment for both *bhajana* and the object of *bhajana* (*bhajanīya*) is especially awakened. By performing such *bhajana*, one realises that the holy name is without doubt the very life of all transcendental knowledge, *vidyā-vadhū-jīvanam*. At this stage, the mood of the prayer *ayi nanda tanuja kiṅkaram* (*Śikṣāṣṭaka* (5)) appears in the heart of the *sādhaka*.

The secret of performing *nāma-bhajana* with *bhāva* lies hidden within the sixth *yāma*, *sāyaṁ-kālīya-bhajana*. At this stage, the external symptoms of perfection become visible. By performing *nāma-saṅkīrtana* with *bhāva*, the ocean of transcendental bliss begins to expand (*ānandāmbudhi-vardhanam*), and prayers like *nayanaṁ galad-aśru-dhārayā* (*Śikṣāṣṭaka* (6)) arise in the devotee's heart. This is all discussed in this *yāma*.

The seventh *yāma*, *pradoṣa-kālīya-bhajana*, presents a discussion on the internal symptoms of perfection. At this stage, when *nāma-bhajana* is performed with realisation of the mood of separation (*viraha*, or *vipralambha*), it is possible to taste complete nectar at every step, *prati-padaṁ pūrṇāmṛtāsvādanam*. Prayers to obtain *vipralambha-prema*, as described in the seventh verse of *Śikṣāṣṭaka*, *yugāyitaṁ nimeṣeṇa*, begin in this *yāma*.

The secret of *prema-bhajana* is hidden in the eighth *yāma*, *rātri-līlā-bhajana*, which describes perfection together with *aikāntika-niṣṭhā*, one-pointed dependence on Kṛṣṇa. Such a stage bestows *sarvātma-snapanam*, the complete purification of the *jīvātmā*, both inside and out. The desire to obtain *bhāva* (here referring to the stage just prior to *mahābhāva*), which is described in the eighth verse of *Śikṣāṣṭaka*, *āśliṣya vā pāda-ratām*, is contained within this eighth *yāma*.

Text 7

Bhakti-rasāmṛta-sindhu (1.4.15–16) states:

ādau śraddhā tataḥ sādhu-
saṅgo 'tha bhajana-kriyā
tato 'nartha-nivṛttiḥ syāt
tato niṣṭhā rucis tataḥ

athāsaktis tato bhāvas
tataḥ premābhyudañcati
sādhakānām ayaṁ premṇaḥ
prādurbhāve bhavet kramaḥ

[This verse describes the gradual development of the *sādhaka's* devotion.] *Sukṛti* that gives rise to *bhakti* generates transcendental faith (*paramārthika-śraddhā*). Faith in the words of the scriptures and a desire to hear *hari-kathā* are the symptoms of this *śraddhā*. Upon its appearance, one gets the opportunity for *sādhu-saṅga*, and then *bhajana-kriyā* (devotional activity) begins. *Anartha-nivṛtti* is also initiated at this time, and thereafter *niṣṭhā* arises in *bhajana*. This is followed by *ruci*, and then *āsakti* arises for both *bhajana* and the object of *bhajana*. When this stage ripens it is transformed into the state of *bhāva*, and thereafter *prema* arises. This is how *prema* gradually manifests in the heart of the *sādhaka*.

bhakti-mūlā sukṛti haite śraddhodaya
śraddhā haile sādhu-saṅga anāyāse haya

sādhu-saṅga phale haya bhajanera śikṣā
bhajana-śikṣāra saṅge nāma mantra dīkṣā

bhajite-bhajite haya anarthera kṣaya
anartha kharvita haile niṣṭhāra udaya

niṣṭhā-nāme yata haya anartha-vināśa
nāme tata ruci-krame haibe prakāśa

ruci-yukta nāmete anartha yata yāya
tatai āsakti nāme bhakta-jana pāya

nāmāsakti krame sarvānartha dūra haya
tabe bhāvodaya haya ei ta niścaya

iti madhye asat-saṅge pratiṣṭhā janmiyā
kuṭīnāṭī dvāre deya nimne phelāiyā

ati sāvadhāne bhāī asat-saṅga tyaja
nirantara parānande harināma bhaja

Text 8

The *Kātyāyana-saṁhitā* (quoted in *Bhakti-rasāmṛta-sindhu* (1.2.51)) states:

varaṁ huta-vaha-jvālā
pañjarāntar-vyavasthitiḥ
na śauri-cintā-vimukha-
jana-saṁvāsa-vaiśasam

Whether I am burned by fire or remain encaged forever, I will never, ever desire the association of those who are averse to Kṛṣṇa.

Text 9

The *Viṣṇu-rahasya* (*Bhakti-rasāmṛta-sindhu* (1.2.112)) states:

āliṅganaṁ varaṁ manye
vyāla-vyāghra-jalaukasām
na saṅgaḥ śalya-yuktānāṁ
nānā-devaikasevinām

It is better to live with or embrace a snake, a tiger or an alligator than to associate with those whose hearts are filled with varieties of material desires and who worship various demigods.

agnite puḍi vā pañjarete baddha hai
tabu kṛṣṇa-bahirmukha saṅga nāhi lai

varaṁ sarpa-vyāghra-kumbhīrera āliṅgana
anyasevi saṅga nāhi kari kadācana

Bhajana-rahasya-vṛtti (for Texts 8–9)

These two Texts instruct the *sādhaka* to seek the association of devotees of Kṛṣṇa who are like-minded and favourable to oneself. The *ācāryas* instruct the *sādhaka* to accept what is favourable for *bhakti* and to reject what is unfavourable. One should completely give up bad association. This means one should renounce association with the opposite sex and with those desiring liberation. The *sādhaka* should exclusively hear and chant the narrations of Śrī Rādhā-Kṛṣṇa Yugala's pastimes. The association of like-minded devotees is beneficial for the performance of this *sādhana*.

A *sādhaka* should also stay far away from the association of demigod worshippers; a good example of this are the followers of the Śrī *sampradāya*, who never enter a temple of Śiva nor worship him. The *sādhaka* should also carefully avoid the company of materialists and persons averse to Kṛṣṇa, for they will pollute his heart. In this regard the example of Śrīla Gaura-kiśora dāsa Bābājī is quite suitable. Occasionally, to avoid the approach of materialists, Śrīla Bābājī Mahārāja would lock himself in a public lavatory and perform his *bhajana* there. He maintained that the stench of excrement was superior to the "odour" of materialistic people. Various kinds of material desires arise in the heart of a *jīva* who has bad association, and he thus becomes degraded. Therefore *sādhakas* of pure *kṛṣṇa-bhakti* should avoid detrimental association.

Text 10

Bhakti-rasāmṛta-sindhu (2.1.103) states that *nāma-ābhāsa* destroys all sins and liberates one from material existence:

taṁ nirvyājaṁ bhaja guṇa-nidhiṁ pāvanaṁ pāvanānāṁ
śraddhā rajyan matir atitarām uttama-śloka-maulim
prodyann antaḥ-karaṇa-kuhare hanta yan-nāma-bhānor
ābhāso 'pi kṣapayati mahā-pātaka-dhvānta-rāśim

O reservoir of good qualities, just faithfully perform *bhajana* of Śrī Kṛṣṇa without duplicity. He is the supreme saviour among all saviours, and the most exalted of those worshipped with poetic hymns. When even a slight appearance of His name, which is like the sun, arises in one's cave-like heart, it destroys the darkness of great sins that are present there.

parama pāvana kṛṣṇa tāṅhāra-caraṇa
niṣkapaṭa śraddhā-saha karaha bhajana

yāṅra nāma sūryābhāsa antare praveśi
dhvaṁsa kare kahāpāpa andhakāra rāśi

ei śikṣāṣṭake kahe kṛṣṇa-līlā-krama
ihāte bhajana-krame līlāra udgama

prathame prathama śloka bhaja kichu dina
dvitīya ślokete tabe haota pravīṇa

cāri śloke kramaśaḥ bhajana pakva kara
pañcama ślokete nija-siddha-deha bara

ai śloke siddha-dehe rādhā-padāśraya
ārambha kariyā krame unnati udaya

chaya śloka bhajite anartha dūre gela
tabe jāna siddha-dehe adhikāra haila

adhikāra nā labhiyā siddha-deha bhāve
viparyaya buddhi janme śaktira abhāve

sāvadhāne krama dhara yadi siddhi cāo
sādhura carita dekhi' śuddha-buddhi pāo

siddha-deha peye krame bhajana karile
aṣṭa-kāla sevā-sukha anāyāse mile

śikṣāṣṭaka cinta, kara smaraṇa kīrtana
krame aṣṭa-kāla-sevā habe uddīpana

sakala anartha yābe pābe prema-dhana
catur-varga phalgu-prāya habe adarśana

Bhajana-rahasya-vṛtti

When the holy name is chanted without any desire other than that for *bhakti*, when it is not covered by *jñāna*, *karma* and so forth, and when it is chanted in a favourable mood with a sense of one's relationship (*sambandha*) with Kṛṣṇa, it is called *śuddha-nāma*, the pure name. If it is not *śuddha-nāma*, it is called *nāma-ābhāsa*, a semblance of the holy name. When one's chanting of the holy name is *aśuddha*, covered with ignorance, or in other words when it has the defects of *bhrama* (the tendency to commit mistakes) and *pramāda* (the tendency to be illusioned), it is called *nāma-ābhāsa*. *Nāma-ābhāsa* also refers to the chanting of the name when one is absorbed in matters unrelated to Kṛṣṇa. And when *aśuddha-nāma* is chanted with desires for liberation and enjoyment, due to the influence of *māyāvāda* (impersonalism) and so on, it is called *nāma-aparādha*.

The semblance of Śrī Kṛṣṇa's name is so powerful that it is capable of putting an end to the darkness of the greatest of sins. *Nāma-ābhāsa* enters the ears of the *jīva*, rises in his cave-like heart and liberates him. Moreover, if one who chants *nāma-ābhāsa* gives up bad association and constantly remains in the association of pure devotees, he will very quickly attain *śuddha-bhakti* and the topmost goal of life – *kṛṣṇa-prema.*

Nanda-nandana Śrī Kṛṣṇa is the ultimate limit of *bhagavattā* (the quality of being Bhagavān). He is all-powerful (*sarva-śaktimān*) and supremely merciful. Even a semblance of His name burns the most terrible sins to ashes and makes the heart pure and pleasant. It is therefore necessary to perform one's *bhajana* sincerely and faithfully.

The process of gradually developing *kṛṣṇa-bhajana* is described in *Śrī Śikṣāṣṭaka.* Kṛṣṇa's pastimes will progressively manifest in the heart of the *sādhaka* who is following this process. First, one should practise according to the rules of *bhajana* mentioned in the first verse. Thereafter, by faithfully following the second, third and fourth verses, one's *bhajana* will gradually become mature. When that is achieved, one should perform *bhajana* according to the sentiments contained in the fifth verse, and one should contemplate one's perfect spiritual body (*siddha-deha*), which develops gradually by taking exclusive shelter of Śrīmatī Rādhikā's lotus feet. By continuously performing *bhajana* in this way, all *anarthas* will be removed and one will receive the eligibility to attain one's *siddha-deha.* As long as *anarthas* are present, one can never attain one's *siddha-deha.* The intelligence of those who try to contemplate their *siddha-deha* without sufficient qualification becomes spoilt due to their lack of strength, and their entire *bhajana* is ruined. This is called *sahajiyā-bhāva*, and it is thoroughly opposed to pure *bhajana.* If there is an honest desire to attain perfection, one should carefully adopt the gradual process of *bhajana* as mentioned previously and follow the path of Śrī Rūpa, Śrī Raghunātha and other *mahājanas* who are expert in *bhajana*.

By performing *bhajana* in this way and having obtained one's *siddha-deha*, one easily attains the happiness of *aṣṭa-kālīya-sevā*, service in Rādhā-Kṛṣṇa's eternal pastimes during the eight periods of the day. Therefore, contemplating the sentiments of *Śikṣāṣṭaka* through *smaraṇa* and *kīrtana* will gradually stimulate *aṣṭa-kālīya-sevā*. All *anarthas* will be removed by this process and one will easily be able to attain *prema-dharma*. At that time the four ultimate goals of human life (*puruṣārthas*) – religiosity (*dharma*), economic development (*artha*), sense gratification (*kāma*) and liberation (*mokṣa*) – will appear very insignificant.

Text 11

The first verse of *Śikṣāṣṭaka* describes the sequence of *bhajana*. First the mirror-like heart is cleansed by the chanting of the holy name:

ceto-darpaṇa-mārjanaṁ bhava-mahā-dāvāgni-nirvāpaṇaṁ
śreyaḥ-kairava-candrikā-vitaraṇaṁ vidyā-vadhū-jīvanam
ānandāmbudhi-vardhanaṁ prati-padaṁ pūrṇāmṛtāsvādanaṁ
sarvātma-snapanaṁ paraṁ vijayate śrī-kṛṣṇa-saṅkīrtanam

Let there be supreme victory for the chanting of the holy name of Śrī Kṛṣṇa, which cleanses the mirror of the heart and completely extinguishes the blazing forest fire of material existence. *Śrī-kṛṣṇa-saṅkīrtana* diffuses the moon rays of *bhāva*, which cause the white lotus of good fortune for the *jīvas* to bloom. The holy name is the life and soul of transcendental knowledge, which is herein compared to a wife. It continuously expands the ocean of transcendental bliss, enabling one to taste complete nectar at every step, and thoroughly cleanses and cools everything, both internally and externally, including one's body, heart, self (*ātmā*) and nature.

saṅkīrtana haite pāpa-saṁsāra nāśana
citta śuddhi sarva-bhakti-sādhana udgama
kṛṣṇa premodgama premāmṛta-āsvādana
kṛṣṇa prāpti-sevāmṛta-samudre majjana

Bhajana-rahasya-vṛtti

The glory of *śrī-kṛṣṇa-saṅkīrtana* is mentioned first in the teachings of Śrī Caitanya Mahāprabhu. Because *śrī-kṛṣṇa-kīrtana* is all-auspicious, the word *param* (supreme) is used in the fourth line of this verse. This word indicates pure *saṅkīrtana*, which is obtained in progressive stages beginning with *śraddhā* and followed by *sādhu-saṅga* and *bhajana-kriyā*. Caitanya Mahāprabhu, the ocean of mercy and compassion, Himself appeared as a *sādhaka-bhakta*. He sang the glories of *śrī-kṛṣṇa-saṅkīrtana*, which is Śrī Kṛṣṇa Himself, in order to enlighten the living entities with the fundamental truths of *sambandha* (relationship), *abhidheya* (the process) and *prayojana* (the goal). For the benefit of the *jīvas*, Śrī Bhagavān Himself appears in the material world in the form of His name, which is the transcendental, inconceivable, non-dual truth (*aprākṛta-acintya-advaya-tattva*).

Our *tattva-ācārya*, Śrī Jīva Gosvāmī, says that the one Absolute Truth (*parama-tattva*) eternally exists in four features by the influence of His inherent inconceivable potency (*svabhāvikī acintya-śakti*). These four features are: (1) *svarūpa* (His original form), (2) *tad-rūpa-vaibhava* (His personal splendour), (3) *jīva* (the living entity) and (4) *pradhāna* (the unmanifest state of material nature). They can be compared to the four aspects of the sun: (1) the effulgence situated in the interior of the sun planet; (2) the sun globe; (3) the atomic particles of light emanating from the sun globe; and (4) the reflected rays of the sun. Although the sun has four aspects, it is one.

Bhagavān's *parā-śakti* (superior potency, also known as *svarūpa-śakti*) is manifest in three forms: (1) *antaraṅga-śakti* (internal potency), (2) *taṭastha-śakti* (marginal potency) and (3) *bahiraṅga-śakti* (external potency). By the *antaraṅga-śakti*, the Absolute Truth in His complete and original feature eternally exists as Bhagavān, devoid of all faults, supremely auspicious and the basis of all transcendental qualities. Moreover, for the accomplishment of His transcendental pastimes, *tad-rūpa-vaibhava* (the Lord's personal splendour, specifically Vaikuṇṭha and other *dhāmas*, His associates, and His forms such as Nārāyaṇa) is eternally established by this same *svarūpa-śakti*.

This same Absolute Truth, when endowed only with the marginal potency (*taṭastha-śakti*), exists as His separate expansion (*vibhinnāṁśa-svarūpa*), which consists of the innumerable infinitesimal conscious *jīvas*. Although the infinitesimal conscious living entities have no separate existence from Bhagavān, they cannot be said to be Bhagavān, nor do they ever become Bhagavān.

Further, *parama-tattva* Bhagavān, by His external potency (*bahiraṅga-śakti*), manifests this entire material world, which is His external splendour. This material world is a transformation of *māyā-śakti*, here meaning *pradhāna*, the unmanifest material elements. In this way it is proved that the living entities (*jīvas*), the material world (*jaḍa-jagat*) and Bhagavān's personal splendour that is manifest as His Vaikuṇṭha existence (*tad-rūpa-vaibhava*), are inconceivably one with and different from (*acintya-bhedābheda*) Bhagavān's original form.

The living entity's eternal identity is understood by the words *ceto-darpaṇa-mārjanam*. In this regard Jīva Gosvāmī has concluded that the individual *jīva* is one minute part of the

Supreme Absolute Truth, who is endowed with the marginal potency represented by the sum total of all *jīvas*. The Supreme Lord is all-pervading consciousness (*vibhu-caitanya*) and the living entity is infinitesimal consciousness (*aṇu-caitanya*). The *jīvas* are innumerable and are either conditioned (*baddha*) or liberated (*mukta*). When the *jīvas* are *vimukha*, indifferent to the Lord, they become conditioned. They become liberated when they are *unmukha*, turned towards Him, and the covering of *māyā* over the pure identity and qualities of the *jīva* is removed.

Just as one's face cannot be seen in a mirror that is covered with dust, the *jīva* cannot perceive his actual *svarūpa* in a heart that is covered by the dirt of ignorance. When the practice of pure *bhakti*, which is the essential function of the *hlādinī-śakti*, begins, one engages in the process of *śravaṇam*, hearing. Thereafter, *śrī-kṛṣṇa-saṅkīrtana* manifests automatically and thoroughly cleanses the dirt of ignorance. When the mirror of the heart is cleansed, it is possible to truly have vision of one's own *svarūpa*. The *jīva's* constitutional occupation (*svadharma*) is to serve Bhagavān.

Bhava-mahā-dāvāgni-nirvāpaṇam – The purport of the word *bhava*, mundane existence, is that the living entity has to repeatedly take birth in this material world. This *bhava-mahā-dāvāgni*, blazing forest fire of material existence, cannot be extinguished by any means other than *śrī-kṛṣṇa-saṅkīrtana*. Here a question may be raised. Upon attaining knowledge of one's *svadharma*, does one cease to perform *śrī-kṛṣṇa-saṅkīrtana*? No, this never happens. *Hari-saṅkīrtana* is the eternal occupation of the living entity, and it is both the process (*sādhana*) and the goal (*sādhya*).

Śreyaḥ-kairava-candrikā-vitaraṇam – For the living entities ensnared by *māyā*, material enjoyment alone is desirable and because of this they inevitably suffer the threefold miseries. In complete opposition to this, it is auspicious (*śreyaḥ*) to always be engaged in serving Śrī Kṛṣṇa. This *śreyaḥ* is compared to the white water lotus, which opens at night by the influence of the moon. *Śrī-kṛṣṇa-saṅkīrtana* diffuses its moon rays of *bhāva* and causes the white water lotus of auspiciousness for the living entities to bloom.

Vidyā-vadhū-jīvanam – The power of *śrī-kṛṣṇa-saṅkīrtana* removes the ignorance of the *jīva*, and then knowledge of one's relationship with Śrī Kṛṣṇa arises. *Śrī-kṛṣṇa-saṅkīrtana* is therefore the life of all transcendental knowledge, which has here been compared to a wife (*vadhū*). Through *saṅkīrtana* the inherent identity of the *jīva* manifests, and if by qualification one is fit to taste *mādhurya-rasa*, he receives the pure spiritual form of a *gopī*. Thus Śrī Kṛṣṇa's *svarūpa-śakti*, which is the embodiment of that transcendental knowledge, is compared to a wife or consort.[5]

Ānandāmbudhi-vardhanam – Here another doubt may arise. Since the inherent nature of the *jīva* is infinitesimal, it may be assumed that his constitutional happiness is also infinitesimal; but factually it is not. *Śrī-kṛṣṇa-saṅkīrtana* unlimitedly expands the inherent transcendental pleasure of the living entity by virtue of the *hlādinī-śakti*. In other words, when the living entity attains his purely spiritual form (*śuddha-svarūpa*), he will gain boundless, transcendental happiness.

Prati-padaṁ pūrṇāmṛtāsvādanam – Upon attaining his *śuddha-svarūpa* and being eternally situated in one of the transcendental *rasas* (*dāsya*, *sakhya*, *vātsalya* or *mādhurya*), the

[5] *Bhakti*, as the essential function of Bhagavān's *svarūpa-śakti*, is always present within the hearts of the *vraja-gopīs*. In particular, Śrīmatī Rādhikā is the personification of *svarūpa-śakti* and, consequently, the personification of *bhakti*. That is why the *svarūpa-śakti* has here been compared to the beloved consort of Śrī Kṛṣṇa.

jīva relishes the sweetness of Bhagavān's form and pastimes in an ever-new way at every moment. In other words, he relishes the nectar of service to Nanda-nandana Śrī Kṛṣṇa in His two-armed form, holding a flute and dressed as a cowherd boy.

Sarvātma-snapanam – At this stage, when the *jīva's* heart is completely pure and devoid of any selfish motive for personal enjoyment, he naturally enjoys the transcendental bliss of the loving pastimes of the Divine Couple. In his internally contemplated spiritual form he serves Them as a maidservant of Śrīmatī Rādhikā, who is the embodiment of *mahābhāva*, the very essence of *hlādinī*. The two words *sarvātma-snapanam* have been used here to indicate supreme purity, completely devoid of the faults of the desire to merge into Brahman and the desire for selfish sense enjoyment.

Text 12

The seventh verse of Śrī Rūpa Gosvāmī's *Nāmāṣṭaka* describes the holy name as the embodiment of concentrated transcendental bliss and knowledge:

sūditāśrita-janārtir-āśaye ramya-
cid-ghana sukha-svarūpiṇe
nāma gokula-mahotsavāya te kṛṣṇa
pūrṇa-vapuṣe namo namaḥ

O destroyer of the numerous sufferings of those who have taken shelter of You! O embodiment of delightful transcendental bliss! O great festival for the residents of Gokula! O all-pervading one! O Kṛṣṇa-nāma, time and again I offer respects to You, who are replete with these qualities.

āśrita janera saba ārtināśa kari
atiramya cidghana svarūpe vihari

gokulera mahotsava kṛṣṇa pūrna-rūpa
hena nāme nami prema pāī aparūpa

nāma kīrtane haya sarvānartha nāśa
sarva śubhodaya kṛṣṇe premera ullāsa

Bhajana-rahasya-vṛtti

Śrī Caitanya Mahāprabhu says, "The name of Kṛṣṇa removes all kinds of distress and sorrow for those who have taken shelter of Him. He especially removes the Vrajavāsīs' extreme pain of separation. *Kṛṣṇa-nāma* sports as Nanda-nandana Śrī Kṛṣṇa, the personification of supremely delightful, condensed, transcendental happiness. The holy name is the great festival of Nanda-Gokula and the very embodiment of Kṛṣṇa Himself. Please let Me attain undivided love for *śrī-kṛṣṇa-nāma*. *Aho*! All *anarthas* will be completely destroyed through *nāma-saṅkīrtana*, and all varieties of auspiciousness, as well as joyful love for Kṛṣṇa, will arise."

A question may arise here. The holy name is able to destroy the thirty-two kinds of *seva-aparādha*, but how can criticism of devotees and saintly persons (*sādhu-nindā*) and the other nine kinds of *nāma-aparādha* be destroyed? The answer is that they can also be destroyed by chanting *harināma*. Mahāprabhu is speaking with this mood.

Text 13

The path of *aṣṭāṅga-yoga* is always full of fear. *Śrīmad-Bhāgavatam* (1.6.35) states:

yamādibhir yoga-pathaiḥ
kāma-lobha-hato muhuḥ
mukunda-sevayā yadvat
tathātmāddhā na śāmyati

The mind that is disturbed by the enemies of lust, anger, greed and so forth does not become subdued or peaceful by practising *yama* and *niyama* on the path of *aṣṭāṅga-yoga*, as it does by performing service to Śrī Mukunda, which completely controls it.

yoge śuddha kari' citte ekāgraha kare
bahusthale e kathāra vyatikrama kare

Bhajana-rahasya-vṛtti

In *Śrī Caitanya-caritāmṛta* (*Madhya-līlā* 22.29) it is stated:

jñānī jīvan-mukta-daśā pāinu kari' māne
vastutaḥ buddhi 'śuddha' nahe kṛṣṇa-bhakti bine

This verse describes how *yogīs* observe the practices of *aṣṭāṅga-yoga*[6], such as *yama* and *niyama*, in order to restrain the senses. They use processes like *prāṇāyāma* to pacify the restless mind, and they use *pratyāhāra* to keep the objects of sense enjoyment far away. By remembering their object of meditation, by repeated *dhāraṇā*, and finally by *samādhi*, they become absorbed in Brahman, which is devoid of transcendental pastimes. Although they go through many difficulties and they practise so much self-control, even if they become successful they only attain a degraded state. The heart of the *jīva* cannot become completely pure by doing *yoga* and so forth, for upon seeing the forms and tasting the objects that attract his senses, he again becomes agitated to attain them. It is because of that desire that he falls down. Examples of this are Maharṣi Viśvāmitra and Saubhari Muni.

The purity desired by the practitioner of *aṣṭāṅga-yoga* is automatically manifest in the devotee who performs *bhakti-yoga*; it naturally comes to the devotee on the strength of *bhakti*. In *bhakti-yoga* the devotees, who are fearless, free from care and sorrow, and without worldly desires, are engaged in the service

[6] Please refer to the *aṣṭāṅga-yoga* Glossary entry for an explanation of the related terms that appear here.

of Mukunda. Śrī Mukunda, being pleased by their unalloyed devotion, protects and maintains them under all circumstances.

Text 14

In *Śrīmad-Bhāgavatam* (1.5.12) *jñāna* and *karma* are condemned:

naiṣkarmyam apy acyuta-bhāva-varjitaṁ
na śobhate jñānam alaṁ nirañjanam
kutaḥ punaḥ śaśvad abhadram īśvare
na cārpitaṁ karma yad apy akāraṇam

Even pure knowledge (*jñāna*), which is the direct *sādhana* to obtain liberation, has no beauty if it is devoid of *bhakti* to Bhagavān. How then can selfless action (*niṣkāma-karma*), which is not offered to Bhagavān, and fruitive action (*kāmya-karma*), which is always inauspicious in both its practice and perfection, be beautiful?

nirañjana karmātīta, kabhu jñāna suśobhita,
śuddha bhakti vinā nāhi haya
svabhāva abhadra karma, haleo niṣkāma dharma,
kṛṣṇārpita naile śubha naya

Bhajana-rahasya-vṛtti

The word *naiṣkarmya* in this Text refers to *niṣkāma-karma*, selfless action. Although such selfless action does not have the variegated nature of *karma-kāṇḍa*, devotees do not accept it because it is devoid of worship of Bhagavān. Devotees also have no connection with *nirañjana-jñāna* (knowledge freed from nescience) if it is not dedicated to Bhagavān. *Vairāgya* (renunciation) that does not lead to attachment for the lotus feet of Bhagavān is also useless. The *ācāryas* have ascertained that the *jīva* who leaves the eternal service of Hari and runs towards inauspicious *karma* or contemptuous *mokṣa* becomes bereft of his own supreme auspiciousness forever.

Text 15

Śrīmad-Bhāgavatam (10.14.4) condemns the path of non-devotion:

śreyaḥ-sṛtiṁ bhaktim udasya te vibho
kliśyanti ye kevala-bodha-labdhaye
teṣām asau kleśala eva śiṣyate
nānyad yathā sthūla-tuṣāvaghātinām

O Lord, devotional service unto You is the main source of all kinds of auspiciousness. Those who give up this path only to cultivate *jñāna* will simply undergo hard work, suffer pain and achieve difficulty, just as the only gain of a person who beats empty husks is hard work, not rice.

bhakti-patha chāḍi' kare jñānera prayāsa
miche kaṣṭa pāya tāra haya sarva-nāśa

ati kaṣṭe tuṣa kuṭi' taṇḍūla nā pāya
bhakti-śūnya jñāne tathā vṛthā dina yāya

Bhajana-rahasya-vṛtti

Brahmājī says, "O Lord, the hard work of those who disrespect the path of all-auspicious *bhakti* and strive to attain *nirviśeṣa-brahma-jñāna* (knowledge aimed at impersonal liberation) will only result in trouble. The path of *bhakti* is extremely straightforward, simple and easily attained without any effort. Bhagavān is pleased merely with a leaf or flower if it is offered with a heart full of love. But someone who leaves the service of Bhagavān and endeavours to merge into Brahman will only obtain misery."

Text 16

The blazing fire of material existence is extinguished by *nāma-saṅkīrtana. Śrīmad-Bhāgavatam* (6.2.46) says:

nātaḥ paraṁ karma-nibandha-kṛntanaṁ
mumukṣatāṁ tīrtha-padānukīrtanāt
na yat punaḥ karmasu sajjate mano
rajas-tamobhyāṁ kalilaṁ tato 'nyathā

For those who desire liberation from the bondage of this material existence, there is no other means than chanting the name of Bhagavān, who sanctifies even the holy places by the touch of His lotus feet. This *nāma-saṅkīrtana* is able to destroy the root cause of all sinful activities, because when the mind has taken shelter of Bhagavān it will never again be caught by fruitive activities. By taking shelter of any atonement other than the name of Bhagavān, the heart will remain affected by the modes of passion and ignorance, and sins will not be destroyed at the root.

karma-bandha sukhaṇḍana, mokṣa prāpti saṅghaṭana,
kṛṣṇa-nāma-kīrtane sādhaya
karma-cakra rajas-tamaḥ, pūrṇa-rūpe vinirgama,
nāma vinā nāhi anyopāya

Text 17

Further, the *Padma Purāṇa* states:

sakṛd uccāritaṁ yena harir ity akṣara-dvayam
baddhaḥ parikaras tena mokṣāya gamanaṁ prati

A person who even once chants the two syllables *ha* and *ri* easily attains liberation.

yāṅra mukhe ekabāra nāma nṛtya kare
mokṣa-sukha anāyāse pāya sei nare

Text 18

The holy name is like the moonlight that causes the white water lotus of all-auspiciousness to blossom. The *Skanda Purāṇa* says:

madhura-madhuram etan maṅgalaṁ maṅgalānāṁ
sakala-nigama-vallī sat-phalaṁ cit-svarūpam
sakṛd api parigītaṁ śraddhayā helayā vā
bhṛguvara nara-mātraṁ tārayet kṛṣṇa-nāma

The holy name is the most auspicious of all that is auspicious, and the sweetest of all that is sweet. It is the fully ripened transcendental fruit of all the creepers of the Śrutis. O best of the Bhṛgu dynasty, if a person even once chants the name of Kṛṣṇa without offence – be it with faith or indifferently – that chanting will deliver him from the bondage of material existence.

sakala maṅgala haite parama maṅgala
cit-svārūpa sanātana vedavallī-phala
kṛṣṇa-nāma ekabāra śraddhāya helāya
yāṅhāra vedane sei mukta suniścaya

Text 19

The holy name is the life of all transcendental knowledge, which is compared to a wife (*vadhū*). This is supported by the following verse from the *Garuḍa Purāṇa*:

yad icchasi paraṁ jñānaṁ
jñānād yat paramaṁ padam
tad ādareṇa rājendra
kuru govinda-kīrtanam

O best of kings, if you desire to obtain the topmost knowledge and the supreme goal of that knowledge, *prema-bhakti*, then chant the holy name of Śrī Govinda with great respect and devotion.

parama jñāna haite ye parama pada pāya
govinda-kīrtana sei karaha śraddhāya

Text 20

In *Śrīmad-Bhāgavatam* (3.5.40) the demigods speak the following:

dhātar yad asmin bhava īśa jīvās
tāpa-trayeṇābhihatā na śarma
ātman labhante bhagavaṁs tavāṅghri-
cchāyāṁ sa-vidyām ata āśrayema

O Vidhātā! O Lord! O Paramātmā! In this material world the living entities, overwhelmed by the threefold miseries, cannot find any peace. Therefore, O Bhagavān, we take shelter of the shade of Your lotus feet, which are full of knowledge.

e saṁsāre tāpa-traya, abhihata jīvacaya,
ohe kṛṣṇa nā labhe maṅgala
tava pada-chāyā vidyā, śubha dātā anavadyā,
tad-āśraye sarva-śubha phala

Bhajana-rahasya-vṛtti

The demigods are praying at the lotus feet of Bhagavān: "O Lord, the *jīva* is experiencing the auspicious and inauspicious fruits of lifetimes of *karma*. By the management of *māyā* he is wandering around in the forest of material existence, overwhelmed by suffering. The *jīva* is endeavouring to find relief from these threefold miseries, sometimes through knowledge and renunciation and sometimes through knowledge of Brahman, but he is unable to find peace. By obtaining liberation he wants to become as if inert, unable to feel anything, just as stones immersed in water cannot feel the pleasure of being in water. Transcendental peace, *para-śānti*, is attained at Śrī Hari's lotus feet. By following the path of *bhakti*, the living entity becomes immersed in an ocean of transcendental peace and bliss. Thus, to take shelter of Your lotus feet is the only means to attain this *para-śānti*."

Text 21

In *Śrīmad-Bhāgavatam* (4.29.49) it is stated:

sā vidyā tan-matir yayā

Knowledge is that by which one's attention is concentrated upon Bhagavān.

ye śaktite kṛṣṇe kare udbhāvana
vidyā-nāme sei kare avidyā khaṇḍana

kṛṣṇa-nāma sei vidyā-vadhūra jīvana
kṛṣṇa-pāda-padme ye karaye sthira mana

Bhajana-rahasya-vṛtti

Bhagavān has only one potency (*śakti*), which has two functions: knowledge (*vidyā*) and ignorance (*avidyā*). Yogamāyā is knowledge and Mahāmāyā is ignorance. Mahāmāyā is responsible for the creation of the material world, and she covers the living entity's eternal identity and inherent qualities.

The word *vidyā* is derived from the verbal root *vid*, "to know" or "to understand". In other words *vidyā* is that through which one can know service to Śrī Kṛṣṇa. When *śuddha-bhakti* arises in the heart of the *sādhaka* by his continuous performance of hearing and chanting, at that time Bhakti-devī removes his ignorance and dispels all desires other than to attain the service of Bhagavān. By *vidyā-vṛtti*, the function of knowledge, she destroys the *jīva's* coverings in the form of his gross and subtle bodies and simultaneously manifests his pure spiritual body according to his inherent nature (*svarūpa*). The life of this transcendental knowledge (*vidyā*), which is compared to a wife, is the holy name of Kṛṣṇa. This *vidyā* fixes a person's mind at the lotus feet of Śrī Kṛṣṇa. Śrī Caitanya Mahāprabhu asked Rāya Rāmānanda:

prabhu kahe – "kaun vidyā vidyā madhye sāra?"
rāya kahe – "kṛṣṇa bhakti vinā vidyā nāhi āra"

Śrī Caitanya-caritāmṛta (*Madhya-līlā* 8.245)

"Which is the most important of all fields of knowledge?" Rāya Rāmānanda replied, "Except for *kṛṣṇa-bhakti*, no other education is important."

Text 22

The chanting of the holy name expands the ocean of transcendental bliss. It is stated in *Śrīmad-Bhāgavatam* (8.3.20):

ekāntino yasya na kañcanārthaṁ
vāñchanti ye vai bhagavat-prapannāḥ
aty-adbhutaṁ tac-caritaṁ sumaṅgalaṁ
gāyanta ānanda-samudra-magnāḥ

The devotees who are exclusively surrendered unto Bhagavān, and who have no other desire than to attain Him, become immersed in an ocean of bliss by performing *saṅkīrtana* of His wonderful and supremely auspicious pastimes.

akiñcana haye kare ekānta kīrtana
ānanda samudre magna haya sei jana

Bhajana-rahasya-vṛtti

This Text comes from Gajendra's prayers to Bhagavān, when Gajendra was being attacked by the crocodile. The *sādhaka* will also realise Bhagavān in his heart by constantly chanting the holy name. *Śrī-kṛṣṇa-saṅkīrtana* unlimitedly expands the *jīva's* inherent transcendental pleasure by virtue of the essential function of the *hlādinī-śakti.* When the *jīva* attains his pure spiritual form, he experiences unlimited bliss. In this condition he is eternally situated in one of the transcendental *rasas* – *dāsya, sakhya, vātsalya* or *mādhurya* – and he relishes complete nectar at every step by virtue of the ever-increasing freshness of his attachment to Śrī Kṛṣṇa (*nava-navāyamāna-anurāga*).

Text 23

Nāma-saṅkīrtana enables one to taste complete nectar at every step; therefore the *Padma Purāṇa* states:

tebhyo namo 'stu bhava-vāridhi-jīrṇa-paṅka-
sammagna-mokṣaṇa-vicakṣaṇa-pādukebhyaḥ
kṛṣṇeti varṇa-yugalaṁ śravaṇena yeṣām
ānandathur bhavati nartita-roma-vṛndaḥ

The devotees whose bodily hairs stand on end and whose hearts tremble with bliss upon hearing the two syllables *kṛ* and *ṣṇa*, deliver the living entities engrossed in material existence. Clear-sighted, intelligent persons who desire eternal auspiciousness surrender to the lotus feet of these *rasika-bhaktas.*

kṛṣṇa-nāma suni' roma-vṛnda nṛtya kare
ānanda kampana haya yāṅhāra śarīre

bhava-sindhu-paṅka magna jīvera uddhāra
vicakṣaṇa tiṅho nami caraṇe tāṅhāra

Bhajana-rahasya-vṛtti

I offer my repeated obeisances unto the lotus feet of those persons whose bodily hairs stand on end, whose hearts tremble with bliss, and from whose eyes tears flow upon hearing the name of Kṛṣṇa. Such devotees, who are most fortunate and magnanimous, are expert in delivering the *jīvas* sunk in the horrible mud of material existence.

Text 24

Chanting the holy name completely cleanses the self. *Śrīmad-Bhāgavatam* (12.12.48) states:

saṅkīrtyamāno bhagavān anantaḥ
śrutānubhāvo vyasanaṁ hi puṁsām
praviśya cittaṁ vidhunoty aśeṣaṁ
yathā tamo 'rko 'bhram ivāti-vātaḥ

Bhagavān Śrī Hari Himself enters the heart of a devotee who describes His name, form, qualities, pastimes and so on, or hears His glories; and He destroys all the darkness of the sins present there. Upon entering the heart of the *jīva*, Bhagavān destroys his offences, impediments, duplicity and material desires, just as the sun drives away darkness or a powerful wind scatters the clouds. This cleanses the mirror-like hearts of those who take shelter of Kṛṣṇa's name, and very quickly they attain their pure transcendental forms.

śruta anubhūta yata anartha saṁyoga
śrī kṛṣṇa kīrtane saba haya ta viyoga

ye rūpa vāyute megha sūrya tamaḥ nāśe
citte praveśiyā doṣa aśeṣa vināśe

kṛṣṇa nāmāśraye citta darpaṇa mārjana
ati śīghra labhe jīva kṛṣṇa prema-dhana

Bhajana-rahasya-vṛtti

The glories of *nāma-saṅkīrtana* are described in this Text. Nāma Prabhu enters the heart of the living entity who is performing *nāma-saṅkīrtana*, destroys all his *anarthas* and makes his heart soft and smooth. Not only that, *nāma-saṅkīrtana* will also destroy all kinds of *anarthas* in a person who merely sees or hears *saṅkīrtana*, just as the sun drives away darkness or the wind drives away the clouds. The scriptures state that the *jīvas'* tendency to enjoy will be completely destroyed on the strength of performing *nāma-kīrtana* in the association of devotees. At the end of *Śrīmad-Bhāgavatam* (12.13.23) Śrī Vedavyāsa glorifies *nāma-saṅkīrtana*:

nāma-saṅkīrtanaṁ yasya
sarva-pāpa-praṇāśanam
praṇāmo duḥkha-śamanas
taṁ namāmi hariṁ param

All sins are completely destroyed by the chanting of Bhagavān's names, and all kinds of miseries are relieved by complete surrender to His lotus feet and by always bowing down to Him. I offer my respectful obeisances unto that Absolute Truth, Śrī Hari.

Text 25

The holy name is Kṛṣṇa Himself and the sweet embodiment of transcendental mellows (*caitanya-rasa-vigraha*). In *Nāmāṣṭaka* (8) it is stated:

nārada-vīṇojjīvana! sudhormi-
niryāsa-mādhurī-pūra!
tvaṁ kṛṣṇa-nāma! kāmaṁ
sphura me rasane rasena sadā

O life of Nārada's *vīṇā*! O crest of the waves upon the transcendental ocean of nectar! O condensed form of all sweetness! O Kṛṣṇa-nāma! By Your own sweet will, may You always appear on my tongue along with all transcendental *rasa*.

muni-vīṇā-ujjīvana-sudhormi-niryāsa
mādhurīte paripūrṇa kṛṣṇa-nāmocchvāsa

sei nāma anargala āmāra rasane
nācuna rasera saha ei vāñchā mane

Bhajana-rahasya-vṛtti

Here Rūpa Gosvāmī prays: "O life of Nārada Muni's *vīṇā*! O crest of the waves on the transcendental ocean of nectar! O condensed form of all sweetness! O Kṛṣṇa-nāma! May You always, by Your own will, dance on my tongue with all transcendental *rasa*. This is my prayer at Your lotus feet."

Text 26

The second verse of *Nāmāṣṭaka* states:

jaya nāmadheya! muni-vṛnda-geya!
jana-rañjanāya param akṣarākṛte!
tvam anādarād api manāg-udīritaṁ
nikhilogra-tāpa-paṭalīṁ vilumpasi

O Harināma, the great sages constantly chant Your glories. To delight the devotees You have appeared in the form of transcendental syllables. All victory unto You! May Your excellence forever be splendidly manifest, and may You display it to all. Prabhu, Your excellence is such that even if Your name is chanted only once and without respect – that is, to indicate something else, jokingly and so forth – it completely destroys the most fearsome of sins, and even sinful thoughts. Thus, make me surrender to You without fail, and by my remembrance of Your power, purify me because I proclaim Your glories.

jīva śiva lāgi' paramākṣara ākāra
muni-vṛnda gāya śraddhā kari' anivāra

jaya jaya harināma akhilogratāpa
nāśa kara helā gāne e baḍa pratāpa

Bhajana-rahasya-vṛtti

O Lord, You have manifested as transcendental syllables (*śabda-brahma*) for the benefit of the living entities. The great *munis* and *maharṣis* always faithfully chant these glories of Yours. All victory, all victory to the holy name, which destroys all fearsome sufferings, even if chanted indifferently.

Text 27

The Vedas (*Ṛg Veda* 1.156.3) describe the truth of the holy name (*nāma-tattva*):

oṁ ity etad brahmaṇo nediṣṭaṁ
nāma yasmād uccāryamāna
eva saṁsāra-bhayāt tārayati
tasmād ucyate tāra iti

One who chants *oṁ*, which is very close to Brahman (here meaning Bhagavān) and which indicates Brahman, is liberated from the fear of the material world by this name. Therefore *oṁ* is famous by the name *tāraka-brahma* (the deliverer).

Text 28

oṁ āsya jānanto nāma-cid-vivaktan mahas te viṣṇo
sumatiṁ bhajāmahe oṁ tat sat

O Viṣṇu, all the Vedas appear from Your name, which is fully conscious and all-illuminating. Your name is the personification of transcendence and supreme bliss, and it is the embodiment of easily obtainable transcendental knowledge. I worship You by thoughtfully performing continuous chanting of Your name.

Text 29

tato 'bhūt trivṛd oṁkāro
yo 'vyakta prabhavaḥ svarāṭ
yat tal liṅgaṁ bhagavato
brahmaṇaḥ paramātmanaḥ

Śrī Bhagavān is imperceptible; He is both undivided and divided. The syllables found in the word *oṁ* are His manifestation, and He is manifest in the three forms of Brahman, Paramātmā and Bhagavān. The three syllables in the *oṁkāra* represent the names Hari, Kṛṣṇa and Rāma. The name of Hari is non-different from Hari Himself.

avyakta haite kṛṣṇa svarāṭa svatantra
brahma, ātmā, bhagavān liṅgatraya tantra

a-kāra u-kāra āra ma-kāra nirdeśa
oṁ hari kṛṣṇa rāma nāmera viśeṣa

hari haite abhinna sakala harināma
vācya-vācaka bhede pūrṇa kare kāma

Bhajana-rahasya-vṛtti

The manifest Brahman, Śrī Kṛṣṇa, is much greater than the unmanifest Brahman and completely independent from it. Parabrahma Śrī Kṛṣṇa is always manifest in the three forms of Brahman, Paramātmā and Bhagavān. The three syllables in the *oṁkāra* – *a*, *u* and *m* – represent Hari, Kṛṣṇa and Rāma, respectively. Śrī Hari is non-different from all the names of Hari. His personal form is known as *vācya* (that which is nameable) and His transcendental name is known as *vācaka* (that which denotes). These two forms fulfil the desires of each and every *sādhaka*. (The syllables in the *oṁkāra* also have the following meaning: *a* – Kṛṣṇa, *u* – Śrī Rādhā, *m* – *gopīs*, and the *candra-bindu* (the dot over the m) – the *jīva*.)

Text 30

Śrī Caitanya-bhāgavata (*Madhya-khaṇḍa* 23.76–8) states:

hare kṛṣṇa hare kṛṣṇa kṛṣṇa kṛṣṇa hare hare
hare rāma hare rāma rāma rāma hare hare

prabhu kahe kahilāma ei mahā-mantra
ihā japa giyā sabe kariyā nirbandha

ihā haite sarva-siddhi haibe sabāra
sarva-kṣaṇa bala ithe vidhi nāhi āra

The Lord said, "Regularly chant *japa* of this *mahā-mantra*. In this way you will attain all perfection. Chant at any time and in any circumstance; there are no other rules for chanting."

Bhajana-rahasya-vṛtti

Śrīman Mahāprabhu says that by chanting the *mahā-mantra* all bondage will vanish and the *jīva* will achieve perfection. In other words, he will attain *kṛṣṇa-prema*. Therefore one should chant the *mahā-mantra* at all times. One is not required to follow any special rules or regulations to chant it.

Text 31

Bhakti-rasāmṛta-sindhu (1.2.103) states:

acirād eva sarvārthaḥ
siddhaty eṣām abhīpsitaḥ
sad-dharmasyāvabodhāya
yeṣāṁ nirbandhinī matiḥ

The holy name is the bestower of all perfection, and those who continuously chant *harināma* with such firm faith and conviction quickly obtain the fruit of *prema*.

nirbandhinī-mati-saha kṛṣṇa-nāma kare
atiśīghra prema-phala sei nāme dhare

Bhajana-rahasya-vṛtti

One who has a firm desire in his heart to know true *dharma* will very quickly have his inner desire fulfilled. The perfection and inner desire of devotees is to attain the service of Govinda's lotus feet. This service is realised by affectionately completing one's fixed amount of *nāma*. By firmly chanting a fixed amount of *harināma*, *prema* will be incited in the heart of the *sādhaka* by the mercy of Nāma Prabhu. Day and night, *nāma-ācārya* Śrīla Haridāsa Ṭhākura was chanting three *lakhas* of *harināma* with determination. His vow was:

khaṇḍa-khaṇḍa hai deha yāya yadi prāṇa
tabu āmi vadane nā chāḍi harināma

Śrī Caitanya-bhāgavata (*Ādi-khaṇḍa* 16.94)

Even if my body is cut to pieces and my life air exits, I will never abandon the chanting of *harināma*.

Text 32

Hari-bhakti-vilāsa gives the following injunctions for chanting:

tulasī-kāṣṭha-ghaṭitair
maṇibhir japa-mālikā
sarva-karmāṇi sarveṣām
īpsitārtha-phala-pradā

go-puccha-sadṛśī kāryā
yad vā sarpākṛtiḥ śubhā
tarjanyā na spṛśet sūtraṁ
kampayen na vidhūnayet

aṅguṣṭha-parva-madhyasthaṁ
parivartaṁ samācaret
na spṛśet vāma-hastena
kara-bhraṣṭāṁ na kārayet
bhuktau muktau tathā kṛṣṭau
madhya-māyāṁ japet sudhīḥ

A *japa-mālā* made of *tulasī* or precious stones fulfils all kinds of inner desires. A *japa-mālā* shaped like a cow's tail or a snake is auspicious. One should not touch the *japa-mālā* with the fore-finger. One should not swing or shake the *mālā* again and again while chanting. Chant and change the direction of the *mālā* using the thumb and the middle finger. Do not touch the *mālā* with the left hand, and do not let it fall from the hand. Those who desire material enjoyment (*bhukti*) and those who desire liberation (*mukti*) chant with the middle finger.

Bhajana-rahasya-vṛtti

Although it is mentioned that one can use a *japa-mālā* of precious stones, such a *mālā* is not used in our *sampradāya.* Also, it is mentioned that chanting with the middle finger is for those desiring sense enjoyment and liberation. Nonetheless, we chant in this way because we should follow the method adopted by our *guru-paramparā.*

Text 33

Hari-bhakti-vilāsa states:

manaḥ saṁharaṇaṁ śaucaṁ
maunaṁ mantrārtha-cintanam
avyagratvam anirvedo
japa-sampatti-hetavaḥ

While chanting, one should be one-pointed and give up talking about mundane topics. With a pure heart, one should think about the meaning of the holy name, and be steadfast and patient in his chanting and remembrance of the holy name.

japa kāle manake ekāgrabhāve laha
citte śuddha thāka, vṛthā kathā nāhi kaha
nāmārtha cintaha sadā dhairyāśraya kara
nāmete ādara kari' kṛṣṇa-nāma smara

Bhajana-rahasya-vṛtti

The method for one to perfect the chanting of his *mantras*, both *harināma* and *gāyatrī*, is described in this Text.

Manaḥ saṁharaṇam – While chanting the holy name, one should fix the mind on the desired name of the Lord and remember pastimes connected with that name. The mind of the conditioned living entity wanders to different subject matters, and therefore one should stay in the association of *sādhus* and control the mind through renunciation and practice.

Śauca – It is necessary for the *sādhaka* to maintain a standard of external cleanliness through bathing and so forth, and to keep his mind pure through internal cleanliness. He can do this by bringing the six enemies headed by lust under control. In this way his mind will not be attracted to anything other than Kṛṣṇa.

Mauna – To speak only *bhagavat-kathā* and reject talk unrelated to Kṛṣṇa is known as *mauna* (silence). One should not talk about anything mundane while chanting.

Avyagratā – The restless nature of the unsteady mind is called *vyagratā*. One should chant with *avyagratā*, a peaceful and undisturbed mind.

Anirveda – One should not become discouraged by moving slowly in his endeavour to attain the desired goal; rather, one should chant with patience.

Nāmārtha-cintana – While chanting the holy name, the *sādhaka* should remember Rādhā-Kṛṣṇa's pastimes of meeting (*milana*) and separation (*vipralambha*). When he chants his *mantras*, he should practise in the following five ways:

(1) The *sādhaka* should know the meaning of the *mantra*, and remember the predominating deity of the *mantra* (the *mantra-devatā*) and his own specific relationship with that deity.

(2) *Nyāsa* – "The deity of the *mantra* is my protector" – this conviction is called *nyāsa*. It is true that success can be attained by uttering the *mantra* one time only; nonetheless, the *mantra* is uttered 10 or 108 times for the pleasure of the *mantra-devatā*. This is also called *nyāsa*.

(3) *Prapatti* – "I take shelter of the lotus feet of the *mantra-devatā*" – this is called *prapatti*.

(4) *Śaraṇāgati* – "I am a *jīva* who is suffering extremely, and therefore I surrender to the deity" – this resolve is *śaraṇāgati*.

(5) *Ātma-nivedana* – "Whatever I have belongs to Him; it is not mine. I am not mine either; I am His for Him to enjoy." This is *ātma-nivedana*.

If one follows the process comprised of these five limbs, he will quickly attain perfection in chanting his *mantras*.

Text 34

Śrī Gopāla-guru explains the meaning of the holy name as follows:

vijñāpya bhagavat-tattvaṁ
cid-ghanānanda-vigraham
haraty avidyāṁ tat kāryam
ato harir iti smṛtaḥ

harati śrī-kṛṣṇa-manaḥ
kṛṣṇāhlāda-svarūpiṇī
ato harety anenaiva
śrī-rādhā parikīrtitā

ānandaika-sukha-svāmī
śyāmaḥ kamala-locanaḥ
gokulānandano nanda-
nandanaḥ kṛṣṇa īryate

vaidagdhī sāra-sarvasvaṁ
mūrti-līlādhidaivatam
rādhikāṁ ramyan nityaṁ
rāma ity abhidhīyate

The Supreme Person Śrī Bhagavān has descended in the form of the holy name, which is the embodiment of condensed knowledge and bliss. While remembering the name of Bhagavān, one should remember that *nāma* and *nāmī* are non-different. In the first stage of a *sādhaka's* progress, the holy name removes ignorance. Therefore He is Hari, "He who removes". The *rasika-ācāryas*, however, taste *harināma* by thinking that, in the *kuñjas* Vṛṣabhānu-nandinī Śrī Rādhā is stealing away the mind of Śrī Hari by Her service. He who chants Hare Kṛṣṇa with this meditation attains *prema-bhakti.* Śrī Rādhā is *kṛṣṇa-hlādinī-rūpiṇī*, the embodiment of Kṛṣṇa's own pleasure potency. She steals away Kṛṣṇa's mind, and therefore Her name is Harā. The vocative form of Harā is Hare. Thus, Hare Kṛṣṇa means Rādhā-Kṛṣṇa Yugala.

The names Rādhā-Kṛṣṇa are *sac-cid-ānanda*, full of eternity, knowledge and bliss. Rādhā and Kṛṣṇa are personally present in Hare Kṛṣṇa. The eternal master of Śrī Rādhā, who is bliss personified, is Śyāma, who has eyes like lotus petals and who desires that Śrī Rādhikā always be happy. Nanda-nandana Śrī Kṛṣṇa, the giver of bliss to the residents of Gokula, is always yearning to taste happiness with Śrī Rādhā. Kṛṣṇa is Līleśvara, a clever *dhīra-lalita-nāyaka*[7]; therefore His name is Rādhā-ramaṇa. The Hare Kṛṣṇa *mahā-mantra* is comprised of names of the Divine Couple. While chanting this *mantra* one should remember Their pastimes.

cid-ghana ānanda-rūpa śrī bhagavān
nāma-rūpe avatāra ei ta pramāṇa

avidyā-haraṇa kārya haite nāma hari
ataeva hare kṛṣṇa nāme yāya tari

kṛṣṇāhlāda-svarūpiṇī śrī rādhā āmāra
kṛṣṇa mana hare tāi harā nāma tāṅra

rādhā-kṛṣṇa śabde śrī sac-cid-ānanda rūpa
hare kṛṣṇa śabde rādhā-kṛṣṇera svarūpa

ānanda-svarūpa-rādhā tāṅra nitya svāmī
kamala-locana śyāma rādhānanda-kāmī

gokula-ānanda nanda-nandana śrī kṛṣṇa
rādhā-saṅge sukhāsvāde sarvadā satṛṣṇa

vaidagdhya-sāra-sarvasva mūrta līleśvara
śrī rādhā-ramaṇa rāma nāma ataḥpara

hare kṛṣṇa mahā-mantra śrī yugala nāma
yugala līlāra cintā kara avirāma

Bhajana-rahasya-vṛtti

Śrī Kṛṣṇa is the personification of condensed eternity, knowledge and bliss (*sac-cid-ānanda*). He is an ocean of compassion. The clear proof of this is that He has appeared on this Earth in the form of His name for the benefit of the living entities. This form of Hari is performing the task of removing ignorance. Therefore those who affectionately chant *harināma* are saved from this illusory world created by ignorance.

[7] A hero who is expert in the sixty-four arts and in amorous sports, always situated in fresh youth, expert at joking, devoid of anxiety and controlled by the *prema* of his beloveds is known as a *dhīra-lalita-nāyaka*.

Śrī Rādhā is the essence of the *hlādinī-śakti*, and She is always giving supreme pleasure to Svayam Bhagavān Śrī Kṛṣṇa. She even steals away the mind of *parama-puruṣa* Śrī Kṛṣṇa with Her sweet form and qualities and by Her service, which is filled with *prema*. Therefore, one of Her names is Harā. "Hare" in the *mahā-mantra* is the vocative form of Harā, which refers to Śrī Rādhā. Thus, the devotee who is exclusively intent on the Divine Couple (the *aikāntika-bhakta*) accepts Rādhā-Kṛṣṇa as the only meaning of Hare Kṛṣṇa. Śrī Rādhā is the personification of bliss (*ānanda-svarūpiṇī*). Kamala-locana Śyāmasundara is Her eternal beloved, *prāṇa-vallabha*. He is always intent on pleasing Śrī Rādhā, but He nonetheless remains indebted to Her. The source of the great festival of bliss of Gokula, Nanda-nandana, is the supremely attractive attractor. Therefore He is named Kṛṣṇa. Even though He always tastes happiness in Śrī Rādhā's association, He always remains eager for it. He is famous as Rādhā-ramaṇa because He, Līleśvara, the personification and essence of all *vaidagdhya* (cleverness in amorous pastimes), is always with Śrī Rādhā, playing (*ramaṇa*) inside and outside Her heart. This Rādhā-ramaṇa Śrī Kṛṣṇa is called Rāma in the *mahā-mantra*. It should be understood that Hare Kṛṣṇa in the *mahā-mantra* means Rādhā-Kṛṣṇa Yugala. Therefore, while performing *japa* or *kīrtana* of the *mahā-mantra*, one should continuously remember the pastimes of Śrī Rādhā-Kṛṣṇa Yugala.

Text 35

The *Bṛhan-nāradīya Purāṇa* states:

harer nāma harer nāma
harer nāmaiva kevalam
kalau nāsty eva nāsty eva
nāsty eva gatir anyathā

In Kali-yuga there is no other way for the *jīva* than chanting the holy name. There is no other way, there is no other way.

anya dharma karma chāḍi harināma sāra
kali-yuge tāhā vinā gati nāhi āra

Bhajana-rahasya-vṛtti

In Kali-yuga, Svayam Bhagavān Śrī Kṛṣṇa has appeared in the form of His name. Through *harināma* the whole world can be delivered. The words *harer nāma* in this Text are used three times to make people with mundane intelligence become fixed in chanting *harināma*. The word *kevala* (meaning "only") is used to make it abundantly clear that *jñāna*, *yoga*, *tapasya* and other activities are to be renounced. Salvation is never possible for one who disregards this instruction of the scriptures. To emphasise this, the words *nāsty eva* (meaning "no other way") are repeated three times at the end of the *śloka*.

Text 36

The *Bhāgavata-nāma-kaumudī* states:

naktaṁ divā ca gatabhir jita-nidra eko
nirviṇṇa īkṣita-patho mita-bhuk praśāntaḥ
yady acyute bhagavati sva-mano na sajjen
nāmāni tad-rati-karāṇi paṭhed vilajjaḥ

If your mind is not absorbed in the name of Śrī Bhagavān Acyuta, then day and night without shyness chant those principal names that are endowed with *rati* (such as Rādhā-ramaṇa, Vraja-vallabha and Gopījana-vallabha). Minimise sleep, eat moderately, and proceed on the path of spiritual truth with a peaceful mind and a disregard for worldly things.

rātra dina unnidra nirvighna nirbhaya
mitabhuk praśānta nirjane cintāmaya

lajjā tyaji kṛṣṇa-rati uddīpaka nāma
uccāraṇa kare bhakta kṛṣṇāsakti kāma

Text 37

Śrīmad-Bhāgavatam (6.3.22) states:

etāvān eva loke 'smin
puṁsāṁ dharmaḥ paraḥ smṛtaḥ
bhakti-yogo bhagavati
tan-nāma-grahaṇādibhiḥ

Only the worship of Bhagavān Śrī Vāsudeva, performed through *nāma-saṅkīrtana*, is called *bhakti-yoga*. This alone is the supreme *dharma* for the living entities.

bhakti-yoga kṛṣṇa-nāma grahaṇādi rūpa
para dharma nāme tāra nirṇīta svarūpa

Bhajana-rahasya-vṛtti

Only *nāma-saṅkīrtana* is directly *bhakti-yoga*, and in Kali-yuga it is the only means by which Śrī Vrajarāja-nandana can be controlled. A question may arise here: if sense enjoyment and so forth are easily attained through *nāma-kīrtana*, why are learned persons teaching *karma-yoga*? The answer is that the intelligence of Yājñavalkya, Jaiminī and the other compilers of *dharma-śāstras* was often bewildered by Māyā-devī. Their minds remained attracted to the beautiful explanations given at that time of the *Ṛg*, *Yajur* and *Sāma Vedas*, and they were engrossed in the various kinds of activities by which, with great difficulty, one obtains the insignificant and temporary result of attaining Svarga, the heavenly planets. The topmost *dharma* is *nāma-kīrtana*, which is easily performed; however, they were unable to understand this.

Text 38

While chanting *harināma*, one should remember Kṛṣṇa's pastimes. "*Niśānte kīrtane kuñja-bhaṅga kare dhyāna, krame krame citta lagne rasera vidhāna* – by remembering and performing *kīrtana* of *niśānta-līlā*, or *kuñja-bhaṅga-līlā*, the mind will gradually relish *rasa*." *Govinda-līlāmṛta* (1.10) states:

rātryante trasta-vṛnderita bahu-viravair bodhitau kīraśārī-
padyair-hṛdyair api sukha-śayanād utthitau tau sakhībhiḥ
dṛṣṭau hṛṣṭau tadā tvoditarati-lalitau kakkhaṭī-gīḥ saśaṅkau
rādhā-kṛṣṇau satṛṣṇāv api nija-nija-dhāmny āpta-talpau smarāmi

At the end of the night, Vṛndā-devī, fearing the approach of day, indicates to the *śuka* (parrot), *śārī* (female parrot) and other birds to make sweet sounds to awaken Śrī Rādhā-Kṛṣṇa. A cool, gentle, fragrant breeze is slowly blowing. With charming calls, the peacocks, peahens, *śuka*, *sārī* and *papīhā* (cuckoos) glorify Śrī Rādhā-Kṛṣṇa's pastimes. They say, "O Vrajarāja-nandana! O Nikuñjeśvarī! When will we receive Your *darśana*?" Although the Divine Couple have been aroused by the sweet chirping of the birds, They embrace each other in fear of being separated and again fall asleep, weary from amorous play. The more Vṛndā-devī tries to wake Them, the more They drowsily pretend to sleep deeply, for They do not desire to leave one another. At that time, the she-monkey Kakkhaṭī loudly cries "Jaṭilā! Jaṭilā!" and They awaken, filled with fear. (The meaning of "Jaṭilā" is "Morning has come and the sun-rays, which look like matted hair (*jaṭā*), are about to appear." But it can also mean "Jaṭilā is coming", Jaṭilā being Śrī Rādhā's mother-in-law.) The *nitya-sakhīs* and *prāṇa-sakhīs* enter the *kuñja*. These *mañjarī-sakhīs* redecorate Rādhā and Kṛṣṇa with clothes and ornaments, concealing the signs of Their amorous pastimes, and then they call the *priya-sakhīs* and *priya-narma-sakhīs*. Kiśora and Kiśorī joke with each other, and Śrī Lalitā performs Their *ārati.* Thereafter They proceed to Their respective residences.

dekhiyā aruṇodaya, vṛndā-devī vyasta haya,
kuñje nānā rava karāila
śuka-sārī-padya suni, uṭhe rādhā nīlamaṇi,
sakhī-gaṇa dekhi hṛṣṭa hailā

kālocita sulalita, kakkhaṭīra rave bhīta,
rādhā-kṛṣṇa satṛṣṇa haiyā
nija-nija gṛhe gelā, nibhṛte śayana kailā,
dūṅhe bhaji se līlā smariyā

ei līlā smara āra gāo kṛṣṇa-nāma,
kṛṣṇa-līlā prema-dhana pābe kṛṣṇa-dhāma

Bhajana-rahasya-vṛtti

Niśānta-līlā, the pastime at night's end, is also called *kuñja-bhaṅga-līlā* because Rādhā and Kṛṣṇa have to separate after Their night-long pastimes in the *kuñja.* The eager *sādhaka* who remembers and performs *kīrtana* of this pastime will very quickly become eligible for the treasure of *kṛṣṇa-prema.*

Thus ends the *Prathama-yāma-sādhana,*
Niśānta-bhajana, of *Śrī Bhajana-rahasya.*

2

Dvitīya-yāma-sādhana

Prātaḥ-kālīya-bhajana – anartha-nivṛtti in sādhu-saṅga

(the first six *daṇḍas* of the morning:
approximately 6.00 A.M. – 8.30 A.M.)

Text 1

There is no consideration of proper or improper time in regard to chanting the Lord's holy names, which are fully endowed with all potencies. This is described in the second verse of *Śikṣāṣṭaka*:

nāmnām akāri bahudhā nija-sarva-śaktis
tatrārpitā niyamitaḥ smaraṇe na kālaḥ
etādṛśī tava kṛpā bhagavan mamāpi
durdaivam īdṛśam ihājani nānurāgaḥ

O Bhagavān, Your names bestow all auspiciousness upon the *jīvas*. Therefore, for their benefit, You are eternally manifest as Your innumerable names, such as Rāma, Nārāyaṇa, Kṛṣṇa, Mukunda, Mādhava, Govinda and Dāmodara. You have invested those names with all the potencies of Their respective forms. Out of Your causeless mercy, You have not even imposed any restrictions on the remembrance of these names, as is the case with certain prayers and *mantras* that must be chanted at specific times (*sandhyā-vandana*). In other words, the holy name of

Bhagavān can be chanted and remembered at any time of the day or night. This is the arrangement You have made. O Prabhu, You have such causeless mercy upon the *jīvas*; nevertheless, due to my *nāma-aparādha*, I am so unfortunate that no attachment for Your holy name, which is so easily accessible and which bestows all good fortune, has awakened within me.

aneka lokera vāñchā aneka prakāra
kṛpāte karila aneka nāmera pracāra

khāite suite yathā tathā nāma laya
deśa-kāla-niyama nāhi sarva-siddhi haya

sarva-śakti nāme dila kariyā vibhāga
āmāra durdaiva nāme nāhi anurāga

Bhajana-rahasya-vṛtti

The innumerable people in this material world have many different kinds of desires. Even so, Bhagavān is supremely merciful and appears in this world as His different names to fulfil these various desires. All perfection is attained by *harināma*, even if it is chanted while eating, drinking, sleeping or moving about; nor are place, time, rules and so forth considerations while chanting. All of Bhagavān's potencies are invested in His names.

The holy names are of two kinds: primary (*mukhya*) and secondary (*gauṇa*). Names related to the material world, like Brahman, Paramātmā and Jagadīśa, are secondary names. Primary names are also of two kinds: those that are full of opulence (*aiśvarya-para*) and those that are full of sweetness (*mādhurya-para*). Names like Hari, Nārāyaṇa and Vāsudeva are full of opulence, and names like Kṛṣṇa, Madana-mohana, Govinda, Gopīnātha and Rādhā-ramaṇa are full of sweetness. From the names of Bhagavān that are related to this world (that is, the secondary names), one attains sense enjoyment (*bhoga*) and liberation (*mokṣa*), from *aiśvarya-para* names one attains the *aiśvarya-prema* of Vaikuṇṭha, and from *mādhurya-para* names one attains *vraja-prema*. The *sādhaka* chanting *harināma* will take shelter of a specific name according to his own mood and will thus have his heart's desire fulfilled.

Text 2

A prayer for attaining attachment for the holy name is given in the fifth verse of *Nāmāṣṭaka*:

aghadamana-yaśodā-nandanau nanda-sūno
kamala-nayana-gopī-candra-vṛndāvanendrāḥ
praṇata-karuṇa-kṛṣṇāv ity aneka-svarūpe
tvayi mama ratir uccair vardhatāṁ nāmadheya

O Nāma Bhagavān, possessor of inconceivable glories, may my affection for You continue to increase, day and night. O Aghadamana! O Yaśodā-nandana! O Nanda-sūnu! O Kamala-nayana! O Gopīcandra! O Vṛndāvanendra! O Praṇata-karuṇa! O Kṛṣṇa! You have innumerable forms; may my attachment to them always increase.

Bhajana-rahasya-vṛtti

As the *rāgānuga-sādhaka* chants the holy name under the guidance of pure devotees, he prays to Nāma Prabhu in great distress, "O Nāma Prabhu! Please manifest in my heart along with Your pastimes that relate to each name."

Aghadamana – "He who protected His friends by killing the demon Agha." The word *agha* means "sin" and *damana* means "to destroy". He destroys the sins in the heart of the *sādhaka*, making it pure, and then He Himself comes to reside there. In relation to *mādhurya-rasa*, Aghadamana has another meaning: "He whose *darśana* destroys the *gopīs'* feelings of separation and thus bestows great joy upon them." During the day Śrī

Kṛṣṇacandra goes to the forest, causing the *vraja-sundarīs* to burn in the fire of separation from Him. During the night, when He is in their midst, He makes their burning separation go far away, and He appears as pleasant as the cool moon as He sports in the pastimes of *rāsa* with them. Thus He tastes *mādhurya-prema-rasa.*

Yaśodā-nandana – "The son of Yaśodā." All the good qualities of Kṛṣṇa's affectionate mother are also found in Him. Therefore one of His names is Yaśodā-nandana. *Yaśo dadāti iti yaśodā* – this means that Mother Yaśodā is famous for her *vātsalya-bhāva.* The mood of this verse is, "May the compassionate Yaśodā-nandana, who possesses the same qualities as His mother, appear in my heart."

Nanda-sūnu – "The son of Nanda." *Śrīmad-Bhāgavatam* (10.8.46) states:

nandaḥ kim akarod brahman
śreya evaṁ mahodayam
yaśodā ca mahā-bhāgā
papau yasyāḥ stanaṁ hariḥ

[Mahārāja Parīkṣit inquired:] What most auspicious activity did the very fortunate Nanda Bābā perform, and what kind of austerity did the supremely fortunate Yaśodā perform that Bhagavān Himself drank her breast milk with His lotus mouth?

By chanting this name of Kṛṣṇa, the *sādhaka* prays, "May the son of the supremely munificent and most fortunate Nanda Mahārāja, Nanda-nandana Śrī Kṛṣṇa, shower His mercy upon me."

Kamala-nayana – "Lotus-eyed one." "May Kamala-nayana Śrī Kṛṣṇa, whose half-closed eyes resemble a red lotus due to His nocturnal amorous pastimes with His beloved *vraja-devīs* in the *nikuñjas,* manifest within my heart."

Gopīcandra – "The moon of the *gopīs*." When Śrī Kṛṣṇa sees the rising full moon, remembrance of the moon-like faces of the *vraja-devīs* awakens in His heart.

Vṛndāvanendra – "The Lord of Vṛndāvana." This refers to He who makes the inhabitants of Vṛndāvana blissful by His unique quality of *prema-mādhurya.*

Praṇata-karuṇa – "He who is merciful to the surrendered." Śrī Kṛṣṇa displays His mercy and compassion to those who are surrendered to Him by making them taste His *caraṇāmṛta.* Remembering the mercy Kāliya-nāga received when Kṛṣṇa placed His lotus feet on Kāliya's heads, the *gopīs* sing, "*praṇata-dehināṁ pāpa-karṣaṇam* – Your lotus feet destroy the past sins of all souls who surrender unto them."

Kṛṣṇa – This name is derived from the verbal root *kṛṣ* meaning "to attract". Kṛṣṇa attracts everyone with His *prema-mādhurya*, and in this way bestows the bliss of divine love upon them.

Devotees pray according to their transcendental sentiments; thus Bhagavān appears to them according to their prayers and makes them joyful. The *sādhaka* chants a specific name of Bhagavān to increase his attachment to Nāma Prabhu.

Text 3

Kṛṣṇa has invested all potencies in His name. The *Skanda Purāṇa* states:

dāna-vrata-tapas-tīrtha-yātrādīnaś ca yāḥ sthitāḥ
śaktayo deva-mahatāṁ sarva-pāpa-harāḥ śubhāḥ
rājasūyāśvamedhānāṁ jñānasyādhyātma-vastunaḥ
ākṛṣya hariṇā sarvāḥ sthāpitāḥ sveṣu nāmasu

Whatever potency to nullify sins or bestow auspiciousness found in charity, vows, austerities, pilgrimage, the *rājasūya-* and *aśvamedha-yajñas*, knowledge of transcendental objects, and so forth, has been invested by Śrī Kṛṣṇa in His holy names (that is, the primary names).

dharma-yajña-yoga-jñāne yata śakti chila
saba harināme kṛṣṇa svayaṁ samarpila

Bhajana-rahasya-vṛtti

The glories of the holy name are described in this Text. Nāma Prabhu easily bestows sense enjoyment (*bhukti*) and liberation (*mukti*). The mass of sins that are nullified by the performance of charity, vows, austerities, fire sacrifices, horse sacrifices and so forth, are destroyed by the mere semblance of Nāma Prabhu. The results obtained by those desiring liberation and by those desiring sense enjoyment are the secondary results of *nāma-saṅkīrtana.* The main result given by Nāma Prabhu is the qualification to relish Bhagavān's sweetness, or the nectar of *prema*, through pure *prema-bhakti.* Pure devotees do not pray to obtain the secondary results of *bhakti.* Moreover, if these results are involuntarily obtained, they do not accept them; rather, paying respect from a distance, they disregard them. The lives of Śrīla Rūpa Gosvāmī and Śrīla Raghunātha dāsa Gosvāmī are exemplary in this regard.

Text 4

In the performance of *nāma-bhajana*, there is no consideration of cleanliness or uncleanliness, nor of proper or improper time. This is corroborated in the *Vaiśvānara-saṁhitā*:

na deśa-kāla-niyamo
na śaucāśauca-nirṇayaḥ
paraṁ saṅkīrtanād eva
rāma rāmeti mucyate

In chanting the holy name, there is no rule concerning place and time, nor is there one regarding cleanliness or uncleanliness. By repeating the name "Rāma", or in other words by performing *saṅkīrtana* of the *mahā-mantra*, the topmost liberation – namely *prema-bhakti* – is obtained.

deśa kāla-śaucāśauca-vidhi nāme nāi
hare kṛṣṇa rāma nāme sadya tare yāi

Bhajana-rahasya-vṛtti

When chanting the eternally perfect, transcendental holy name, there are no rules regarding place, time and so forth. In the performance of austerities and fire sacrifices one has to follow rules prescribed by the Vedas, but the holy name can be chanted under any circumstance, whether one is in a pure or impure state. By His own strength Nāma Prabhu purifies the heart of the *sādhaka*.

The story of Gopāla-guru is noteworthy in this context. A young boy named Gopāla was staying with Śrīman Mahāprabhu and serving Him. One day, as Mahāprabhu was going to the latrine, He caught hold of His tongue with His hand. When Gopāla asked why He was doing this, Mahāprabhu replied, "My tongue never gives up chanting *harināma*, so when I am in an impure condition I must restrain it." The boy Gopāla then asked, "If someone were to die at such a moment, what would happen to him?" Hearing this, Mahāprabhu praised the boy and said, "What you say is true. One should not consider cleanliness, uncleanliness and so forth in chanting the immeasurably powerful names of Hari. From today, your name is Gopāla-guru."

Text 5

The characteristics of misfortune are described in *Śrīmad-Bhāgavatam* (3.9.7):

daivena te hata-dhiyo bhavataḥ prasaṅgāt
sarvāśubhopaśamanād vimukhendriyā ye
kurvanti kāma-sukha-leśa-lavāya dīnā
lobhābhibhūta-manaso 'kuśalāni śaśvat

Those persons who refrain from the hearing and chanting of Your glories, which destroys all misfortune, and instead always engage in inauspicious activities, being obsessed with a desire for a particle of material sense enjoyment, are certainly wretched, for fate has stolen away their intelligence.

tomāra prasaṅga sarva, aśubha karaye kharva,
durdaiva prabhāve mora mana
kāmasukha-leśa āśe, lobha akuśalāyāse,
se prasaṅge nā kaila yatana

Bhajana-rahasya-vṛtti

Glorifying Bhagavān, Brahmā says here, "Those persons who are averse to hearing narrations about Bhagavān and *bhakti*, and who continuously perform inauspicious activities, being engrossed in worthless sense gratification, are unfortunate and bereft of good intelligence." Prahlāda Mahārāja also says, "A *jīva* who is attached to his home because of his undisciplined senses enters the deepest of hells. The intelligence of one who again and again chews the happiness and distress that has already been chewed can never become pure." One who is absorbed in *karma-kāṇḍa* by following the honey-filled statements prescribed in the Vedas will be bound by the long rope of the Vedas. The only means for the lustful living entities to become liberated is to immerse themselves in the dust of the lotus feet of a great *niṣkiñcana*, *paramahaṁsa* Vaiṣṇava.

Text 6

In *Śrīmad-Bhāgavatam* (1.7.4–6) it is stated:

bhakti-yogena manasi
samyak praṇihite 'male
apaśyat puruṣaṁ pūrṇaṁ
māyāṁ ca tad-apāśrayām

yayā sammohito jīva
ātmānaṁ tri-guṇātmakam
paro 'pi manute 'narthaṁ
tat-kṛtaṁ cābhipadyate

anarthopaśamaṁ sākṣād
bhakti-yogam adhokṣaje
lokasyājānato vidvāṁś
cakre sātvata-saṁhitām

With a pure heart Śrī Kṛṣṇa-dvaipāyana Vedavyāsa became absorbed in meditation through the process of *bhakti-yoga*. He thus saw the Supreme Person, Śrī Kṛṣṇa, along with His external energy (*māyā*), which was far away from Him but under His control. Due to this *māyā*, the conditioned living entity (*baddha-jīva*) forgets his service to Kṛṣṇa and becomes affected by *anarthas*. Although transcendental to the three modes of material nature, the living entity who is bewildered by *māyā* considers himself a material product. He thus identifies himself with this body and considers that which is related to it to be his. The infinitesimal living entity can only be delivered by *kṛṣṇa-bhakti-yoga*, but the mass of people in the material world are ignorant of this fact. Understanding this, Śrī Vyāsa manifested *Bhāgavatam* through *bhakti-yoga*.

kṛṣṇa, kṛṣṇa-māyā, jīva ei tina tattva
māyā-mohe māyā-baddha jīvera anartha

citkaṇa jīvera kṛṣṇa-bhakti-yoga-bale
anartha vinaṣṭa haya kṛṣṇa prema-phale

ei tattva nāma-samādhite pāile vyāsa
bhāgavate bhakti-yoga karila prakāśa

Bhajana-rahasya-vṛtti

Śrī Kṛṣṇa-dvaipāyana Vedavyāsa manifested all the Vedas, Upaniṣads, Purāṇas and so forth. Even though he had realisation of the Supreme Absolute Truth and His sound incarnation (*śabda-brahma*), he remained dissatisfied, feeling an inner lack. He enquired from Śrī Nārada about this, who answered, "You have not described Śrī Kṛṣṇa's sweet pastimes and spotless glories. You should do so, and by this your heart will become satisfied." By the mercy of Śrī Nārada and by the means of *bhakti-yoga*, Vedavyāsa, with a pure heart, became absorbed in meditation and received *darśana* of all Bhagavān's pastimes. He then manifested the *Bhāgavatam*, the fully ripened fruit of the desire tree of Vedic literature.

The essential teaching of this incident is that when the mind of the living entity becomes pure through the practice of *bhakti*, then by the combined mercy of the *saṁvit-* and *hlādinī-śaktis*, he can experience Kṛṣṇa, Kṛṣṇa's internal potency (Yogamāyā) and his own constitutional nature (*svarūpa*). The object of *bhajana* will manifest in the heart naturally through *bhakti-yoga*. Those who desire liberation through *jñāna* and *karma* are deprived of realisation of the complete, eternally conscious object.

The words *puruṣaṁ pūrṇam* in this Text refer to Svayam Bhagavān Vrajendra-nandana Śyāmasundara, who is the possessor of all potencies (*sarva-śaktimān*), and to all the residents of Vraja, including the *gopīs*.

By means of *bhakti-yoga*, Śrīla Vyāsadeva saw Bhagavān's various manifestations and His three *śaktis*: *svarūpa-śakti*, *māyā-śakti* and *jīva-śakti*. Through His *svarūpa-śakti*, Bhagavān is performing eternal transcendental pastimes. *Māyā-śakti* has two functions to control the *jīvas* who are averse to Bhagavān: *āvaraṇātmikā* (to cover real knowledge) and *vikṣepātmikā* (to hurl the living entity down into the ocean of material existence). Those *jīvas* who are controlled by material activities are moved by the desire to gratify their senses, and Māyā-devī makes them dance like puppets.

An argument can be raised in this connection. When Vyāsadeva received *darśana* of Bhagavān's form, qualities, pastimes and so forth, what was the purpose of his also having received *darśana* of *māyā*? The answer is that Vyāsadeva was not an ordinary living being, so he had no familiarity with the suffering of conditioned souls ensnared by *māyā*. How, then, could he help them? For this reason he also received *darśana* of the illusory energy.

The *ācāryas* write that the living entities who are controlled by *māyā* are absorbed in the three modes, devoured by the great disease of material existence and unable to taste the sweetness of Bhagavān. The liberation of the living entities bound by *māyā* is possible only when *māyā's* coverings are removed. Śrīla Viśvanātha Cakravartī Ṭhākura explains in his commentary on this Text that to cure a sick patient, an expert doctor prescribes both medicine and a good diet. The remedial measure for the conditioned living entities is the process of *bhakti*. The medicine is hearing *hari-kathā* and chanting *harināma*, and the diet is to stay in the association of devotees and avoid offences.

After receiving the above-mentioned *darśana*, Śrīla Vyāsa manifested *Śrīmad-Bhāgavatam*, the eternal authoritative scripture that is filled with all truths. He did this for the benefit of ignorant people who are devoured by the great disease of material existence. By hearing *Śrīmad-Bhāgavatam*, the living entities can become free from their *anarthas* and ignorance, and thus obtain *kṛṣṇa-prema*. Śrī Kṛṣṇa's transcendental pastimes with the *vraja-devīs*, which are filled with *prema*, are described in *Śrīmad-Bhāgavatam*. By hearing these narrations with faith, the living entities can again become established in their eternal *dharma*.

Śrīmad-Bhāgavatam (10.33.36) states: "*yāḥ śrutvā tat-paro bhavet* – upon hearing such pastimes, one becomes dedicated to Him." To become established in service to Rādhā and Kṛṣṇa, which consists of the mellows of *prema* that are saturated with sweetness, is the purpose of life. This is achieved following the removal of one's *anarthas* through the process of *bhakti-yoga*, the essence of all truths.

Text 7

Anarthas, or misfortune, are of four kinds. This is described in the *Āmnāya-sūtra*:

māyā-mugdhasya jīvasya
jñeyo 'narthaś catur-vidhaḥ
hṛd-daurbalyaṁ cāparādho
'sat-tṛṣṇā tattva-vibhramaḥ

The *anarthas* of the living entities enchanted by *māyā* are of four kinds: (1) illusion about one's real identity (*svarūpa-bhrama*), (2) hankering for that which is temporary (*asat-tṛṣṇā*), (3) offences (*aparādha*) and (4) weakness of heart (*hṛdaya-daurbalya*). They bind the living entity to the material world and entangle him in its miseries.

māyā-mugdha jīvera anartha catuṣṭaya
asat-tṛṣṇā, hṛdaya-daurbalya viṣamaya

aparādha svarūpa-vibhrama ei cāri
yāhāte saṁsāra-bandha vipatti vistāri

Bhajana-rahasya-vṛtti

The living entities seized by *māyā* and derailed from pure *dharma* wander in this material existence, falsely thinking they are its enjoyers. Four *anarthas* are noticed in these living entities: *svarūpa-bhrama, asat-tṛṣṇā, aparādha* and *hṛdaya-daurbalya.* The word *anartha* means "to collect that which has no purpose". The *jīva's* only goal is service to Kṛṣṇa, but in this material existence he is engaged in *māyā's* service – hence, this is an *anartha.*

Svarūpa-bhrama – The pure living entity is a tiny transcendental particle (*cid-aṇu*) and the eternal servant of Kṛṣṇa. Just as the conditioned living entity experiences form, taste, smell, touch and so on through his material senses, the pure living entity experiences transcendental form, taste and so forth through his transcendental senses. Forgetting that "I am an infinitesimal particle of spiritual consciousness and Kṛṣṇa's servant", the *jīva* becomes conditioned and wanders about in this material existence. The primary *anartha* of the living entity is his failure to realise his true *svarūpa.*

Asat-tṛṣṇā – To consider the material body to be "me", to consider perishable objects in relation to the body to be "mine", and to desire happiness from perishable objects, is called *asat-tṛṣṇā.*

Aparādha – *Apagata-rādho yasmād ity aparādhaḥ. Rādha* means affection (*prīti*), so that action which causes affection to vanish is called *aparādha* (offence). *Aparādha* at the lotus feet of Bhagavān and at the lotus feet of His devotees decreases *prīti.* One should avoid the ten *nāma-aparādhas,* the thirty-two *seva-aparādhas* and all the *dhāma-aparādhas.*

Hṛdaya-daurbalya – When the heart experiences illusion and distress upon the attainment or loss of that which is perishable, it is called *hṛdaya-daurbalya,* weakness of heart. This *anartha* appears naturally in the living entity due to ignorance, and it vanishes by the cultivation of Kṛṣṇa consciousness in the association of pure devotees.

Text 8

Svarūpa-bhrama is of four types, as stated in the *Āmnāya-sūtra*:

sva-tattve para-tattve ca
sādhya-sādhana-tattvayoḥ
virodhi-viṣaye caiva
tattva-bhramaś catur-vidhaḥ

The conditioned living entity is subject to four kinds of *bhrama*, illusion: (1) *jīva-svarūpa-bhrama*, (2) *paratattva-bhrama*, (3) *sādhya-sādhana-tattva-bhrama* and (4) *bhajana-virodhi-viṣaya-bhrama.*

tattva-bhrama catuṣṭaya baḍai viṣama
svīya-tattve bhrama āra kṛṣṇa-tattve bhrama
sādhya-sādhanete bhrama, virodhī viṣaye
cārividha tattva-bhrama baddha-jīva-caye

Bhajana-rahasya-vṛtti

Jīva-svarūpa-bhrama – The *jīva* cannot realise his own transcendental form due to ignorance of it. He has forgotten his real *svarūpa*, that he is the servant of Kṛṣṇa, because he thinks himself to be the enjoyer.

Paratattva-bhrama – Who is *paratattva*, the Absolute Truth? Not knowing this, the living entity becomes illusioned. Sometimes he worships Śiva, sometimes Brahmā and sometimes another demigod or goddess. The inability to correctly ascertain the Absolute Truth is called *paratattva-bhrama.*

Sādhya-sādhana-bhrama – According to the scriptures, *kṛṣṇa-prema* is the only goal (*sādhya*) and *bhakti* the only practice (*sādhana*). The conditioned living entity, however, is unable to decide which is his goal among sense enjoyment, liberation and *kṛṣṇa-prema*, and which is his practice among *karma*, *jñāna* and *bhakti*. This is *sādhya-sādhana-bhrama*, illusion about the goal and the process to attain it. If one cannot ascertain the goal, it is not possible to ascertain the practice, and without the practice it is not possible to attain the goal. It is only by the mercy of Vaiṣṇavas that one can obtain the fortune to understand that *bhakti* is the only auspicious *sādhana*, and *prema* is the only *sādhya*. *Prema* is of two kinds: *aiśvarya-para* (full of opulence) and *mādhurya-para* (full of sweetness). The *ācāryas* have determined that the topmost goal is sweet, loving service to Rādhā-Kṛṣṇa under the guidance of the *vraja-gopīs*.

Bhajana-virodhi-viṣaya-bhrama – Doctrines other than Vaiṣṇavism oppose *bhajana* and cause bewilderment (*virodhi-bhrama*). This especially applies to impersonalism (*māyāvāda*), which contaminates the heart and thus renders the living entity unable to discriminate.

Text 9

Asat-tṛṣṇā is of four kinds, as described in the *Āmnāya-sūtra*:

aihikeṣvaiṣaṇā pāra-
trikeṣu caiṣaṇā 'śubhā
bhūti-vāñchā mumukṣā ca
hy asat-tṛṣṇāś catur-vidhāḥ

The four types of *asat-tṛṣṇā* are: (1) desire for objects of this material world, (2) desire for heavenly pleasures, like those of Svarga, (3) desire for mystic powers and (4) desire for liberation.

pāra-trika aihika eṣaṇā bhūti-kāma
mukti-kāma ei cāri asat-tṛṣṇā nāma

Bhajana-rahasya-vṛtti

The desire to obtain that which is unrelated to Kṛṣṇa is known as *asat-tṛṣṇā*. This desire is of four kinds: (1) Desire for worldly, material objects and the various endeavours to obtain them. *Śrīmad-Bhāgavatam* (11.3.18) states: "*karmāṇy ārabhamāṇā duḥkha-hatyai sukhāya ca* – the conditioned living entity endeavours to obtain pleasure for the senses but receives only misery." (2) Desire to obtain the pleasures of the heavenly planets and the worship of various demigods and goddesses. (3) Desire to obtain mystic powers in order to bewilder people by material wonders and thereby attain wealth, worship, prestige and so forth. Human beings are attracted to *aṣṭāṅga-yoga* and to mystic powers like *aṇimā* and *laghimā*. (4) Desire for liberation.

These four desires are all opposed to *bhajana*, and therefore devotees of Bhagavān never accept them.

Text 10

Aparādha is of four kinds, as mentioned in the *Āmnāya-sūtra*:

kṛṣṇa-nāma-svarūpeṣu
tadīya-cit-kaṇeṣu ca
jñeyā budha-gaṇair nityam
aparādhāś catur-vidhāḥ

The four kinds of *aparādha* are: (1) offences to Kṛṣṇa's name (*nāma-aparādha*); (2) offences to Kṛṣṇa's deity form (*seva-aparādha*); (3) offences to that which belongs to Kṛṣṇa, or in other words to Girirāja-Govardhana, the Gaṅgā, the Yamunā, the *dhāma* or the lotus feet of the devotees; and (4) offences to other living entities, who are all infinitesimal particles of spirit belonging to Kṛṣṇa.

kṛṣṇa-nāme, svarūpe o bhakte, anya nare
bhrama haite aparādha catuṣṭaya smare

Text 11

Hṛdaya-daurbalya is of four kinds, as stated in the *Āmnāya-sūtra*:

tucchāsaktiḥ kuṭīnāṭī
mātsaryaṁ sva-pratiṣṭhatā
hṛd-daurbalyaṁ budhaiḥ śaśvaj
jñeyaṁ kila catur-vidham

Scholars consider *hṛdaya-daurbalya* to be of four types: (1) attachment to worthless objects; that is, objects unrelated to Kṛṣṇa; (2) hypocrisy and deceit (*kuṭīnāṭī*); (3) envy upon seeing the prosperity of others; and (4) desire for prestige and position (*pratiṣṭhā*).

kṛṣṇetara viṣaye āsakti, kuṭīnāṭī
para-droha, pratiṣṭhāśā ei ta' cāriṭi
hṛdaya-daurbalya bali' śāstre nirdhārila
chaya ripu, chaya ūrmi ihāte janmila
yata dina e saba anartha nāhi chāḍe
tata dina bhakti-latā kabhu nāhi bāḍhe

Bhajana-rahasya-vṛtti

Hṛdaya-daurbalya gives birth to six enemies: lust (*kāma*), anger (*krodha*), greed (*lobha*), delusion (*moha*), pride (*mada*) and envy (*mātsarya*); and their waves result in distress (*śoka*), bewilderment (*moha*), hunger (*kṣudhā*), thirst (*pipāsā*), old age (*jarā*) and death (*mṛtyu*).

The creeper of devotion cannot grow as long as one does not give up these *anarthas*.

Text 12

All *anarthas* are nullified by *nāma-saṅkīrtana*. *Śrīmad-Bhāgavatam* (1.1.14) states:

āpannaḥ saṁsṛtiṁ ghorāṁ
yan-nāma vivaśo gṛṇan
tataḥ sadyo vimucyeta
yad bibheti svayaṁ bhayam

If a living entity who is caught in the whirlpool of material existence even once chants the name of Kṛṣṇa, he can be freed immediately. Even fear personified trembles upon hearing the name of Bhagavān.

e ghora saṁsāre paḍi' kṛṣṇa-nāma laya
sadya mukta haya āra bhaya pāya bhaya

Bhajana-rahasya-vṛtti

The far-sighted sages, reflecting on the terrible distress of the living entities in the frightful age of Kali, asked Sūta Gosvāmipāda, "O Saumya, how can the conditioned living entities, who are attached to material existence, become liberated?" Sūta replied, "Association with devotees of Bhagavān is the only means. Bathing in the Gaṅgā destroys sins, but all sins are nullified solely by having *darśana* of a devotee who is dedicated to the holy name. The direct result of associating with Bhagavān's devotees and serving them is the attainment of *prema*. If a living entity merely utters the holy name at the time of death, Nāma Prabhu will bestow *prema* upon him."

Text 13

Śrīmad-Bhāgavatam (11.2.37) states:

bhayaṁ dvitīyābhiniveśataḥ syād
īśād apetasya viparyayo 'smṛtiḥ
tan-māyayāto budha ābhajet taṁ
bhaktyaikayeśaṁ guru-devatātmā

The *jīva* who is averse to Bhagavān forgets his own constitutional nature because of his association with *māyā*. Due to this forgetfulness, he becomes absorbed in the conception that he is the material body and thus thinks "I am a demigod", "I am a human being". In this state of bodily identification, he fears old age, disease and so forth. Therefore those who know the truth should consider their own *guru* as *īśvara*, the Supreme. In other words they should see him as their master who is non-different from Bhagavān and who is very dear to Him. Through exclusive devotion they should perform one-pointed worship of that *īśvara*, their *guru*.

kṛṣṇa chāḍi' jīva kaila anyābhiniveśa
tāi tāra viparyaya-smṛti āra kleśa

sad-guru āśraya kari' kṛṣṇakṛpā-āśe
ananya-bhajana kare yāya kṛṣṇa-pāśe

Bhajana-rahasya-vṛtti

When the *jīvas* are averse to Bhagavān, they become absorbed in *māyā* and thus become materially conditioned. Māyā-devī, through her two functions of *āvaraṇātmikā* and *vikṣepātmikā*, makes the living entities wander in the prison-like material existence, suffering its torment by thinking they are the "experiencers" of happiness and distress. A person who is resolute takes shelter of the lotus feet of a bona fide *guru* and is thus able to cross over this material existence. By accepting the guidance of a *guru* who has realised Bhagavān and by being absorbed in intimate service (*viśrambha-sevā*) to him, one attains the mercy of Bhagavān and material identification goes far away. One will attain knowledge of one's own *svarūpa*, Bhagavān's *svarūpa*, and the *svarūpa* of the illusory energy by understanding the spiritual master to be near and dear like his own soul and by serving him. By the *guru's* mercy the living entity will ultimately be engaged in eternal service in Bhagavān's abode.

Text 14

The characteristics of *bhakti-yoga* are described in *Śrīmad-Bhāgavatam* (1.2.12 and 1.2.7):

tac chraddadhānā munayo
jñāna-vairāgya-yuktayā
paśyanty ātmani cātmānaṁ
bhaktyā śruta-gṛhītayā

vāsudeve bhagavati
bhakti-yogaḥ prayojitaḥ
janayaty āśu vairāgyaṁ
jñānaṁ ca yad ahaitukam

A faithful person, after hearing *Śrīmad-Bhāgavatam*, automatically acquires *bhakti* endowed with knowledge and renunciation. By such *bhakti* he realises Bhagavān's *svarūpa* in his heart and he realises his relationship with Him. Thus he obtains service to the Lord.

When the relationship between the Lord and the living entity is established, *bhakti-yoga* for Bhagavān Vasudeva appears.

śraddhā kari' nāma bhaje sādhu-kṛpā pāñā
itare virāga nitya-svarūpa bujhiyā

ihākei bali bhakti-yoga anuttama
bhakti-yoge sarva-siddhi yadi dhare krama

Bhajana-rahasya-vṛtti

Sādhana of the non-dual Absolute Truth (*advaya-jñāna-para-tattva*) is of three kinds: *jñāna, yoga* and *bhakti.* The *jñānīs* realise Bhagavān as Brahman on the strength of their cultivation of knowledge. They see *tat-padārtha,* Bhagavān, within their souls (*ātmās*), they see their own souls in Īśvara and they also see *taṁ-padārtha,* all living entities, in Him. The *yogīs* realise the non-dual object as Paramātmā. All attempts made by the *jīvas* to attain renunciation through the cultivation of dry knowledge are useless. Renunciation (*vairāgya*) is an inherent result of *bhakti* and is easily attained through the practice of *bhakti-yoga.* The *bhakti-sādhaka* relishes the direct sweetness of the non-dual object on the strength of his devotion. The process of *bhakti* is to hear *kṛṣṇa-kathā* from the lotus mouth of the spiritual master. Knowledge endowed with a sense of one's relationship with Kṛṣṇa appears through the process of *bhakti* by the means of hearing and chanting. The *ācāryas* have ascertained that the mood of service appears by hearing from authorities. The impersonalists do not follow this path of hearing, which is the descending path. Rather, they endeavour to take shelter of the doctrine of the ascending path. Their attempts are compared to trying to reach the sky by climbing on falling raindrops. When the living entity is absorbed in service to the object of *bhajana* and not in any other object, pure *bhakti* and proper renunciation (*yukta-vairāgya*) will arise.

Text 15

The fourth verse of the *catuḥ-ślokī* of *Śrīmad-Bhāgavatam* (2.9.36) states:

etāvad eva jijñāsyaṁ
tattva-jijñāsunātmanaḥ
anvaya-vyatirekābhyāṁ
yat syāt sarvatra sarvadā

One who is inquisitive about the truth of the self (*ātma-tattva*) inquires through direct (*anvaya*) and indirect (*vyatireka*) means of deliberation about that object, which is always eternal.

anartha-nāśera yatna dui ta' prakāra
anvaya-mukhete vyatireka-mukhe āra

anvaya-mukhete vidhi bhajana-viṣaye
vyatireka-mukhete niṣedha nānāśraye

Bhajana-rahasya-vṛtti

After Brahmā took birth, he asked Śrī Bhagavān four questions, which Bhagavān answered through the *catuḥ-ślokī*. These four verses are famous as *catuḥ-ślokī Bhāgavata* because they are the seed of *Śrīmad-Bhāgavatam*. They contain the very essence of the Vedas, Vedānta and so forth.

Philosophical knowledge of Bhagavān, the eternal form of Bhagavān, His qualities, pastimes and so on, are all described in the first verse in the form of aphorisms (*sūtras*). In the second verse, *māyā-tattva*, which is separate from Bhagavān's eternal form, is discussed, as is the material world (*jaḍa-jagat*). The *sambhanda-jñāna* found in these two verses should be understood. The third verse describes the existence of Bhagavān's eternal *svarūpa*, separate from His relationship of inconceivable difference and non-difference (*acintya-bhedābheda*) with the living entities and matter. It also describes how the living entities, by taking shelter of Bhagavān's lotus feet, attain the treasure of the most elevated *prema.*

This Text 15 is the fourth verse of *catuḥ-ślokī Bhāgavata*, and it describes *sādhana-bhakti*, the means for obtaining the above-mentioned supreme goal. Direct following, or *anvaya*, means to accept the rules of *sādhana-bhakti* with a favourable mood. The word *vyatireka* is used in regard to avoiding those actions that are unfavourable and that cause obstacles in obtaining the desired goal. The path of *sādhana* is known as *abhidheya* (the process). In other words, that instruction which is obtained from the scriptures through direct interpretation (*abhidhā-vṛtti*) is known as *abhidheya.* This is described in this Text. *Sādhana-bhakti*, which is none other than *abhidheya*, is not dependent on time, place, performer or circumstance. The duty of all living entities is to perform *sādhana-bhakti* in all places, at all times and under all circumstances. The *sādhaka* should inquire and hear from the spiritual master about *sādhana-bhakti.*

In this Text the confidential meaning of "direct" and "indirect" indicates the union (*saṁyoga*) and separation (*vipralambha*) found in Vrajendra-nandana Śyāmasundara's amorous pastimes (*śṛṅgāra-rasa*) with His most beloved *vraja-sundarīs.* To deceive the conditioned living entities, all these priceless jewels are kept well protected in a box that the *jñānīs* and *aiśvarya-bhaktas* are unable to open. That *guru* who is adept at relishing the *rasa* of Vraja displays its contents only to his qualified disciples.

Text 16

The six urges unfavourable to *bhakti* and the *anarthas* related to them (i.e. *hṛdaya-daurbalya*, *asat-tṛṣṇā* and *aparādha*) are explained in the first verse of *Upadeśāmṛta*:

vāco vegaṁ manasaḥ krodha-vegaṁ
jihvā-vegam udaropastha-vegam
etān vegān yo viṣaheta dhīraḥ
sarvām apīmāṁ pṛthivīṁ sa śiṣyāt

A wise and self-composed person who can tolerate the impetus to speak, the agitation of the mind, the onset of anger, the vehemence of the tongue, the urge of the belly and the agitation of the genitals can instruct the whole world. In other words, everyone becomes a disciple of such a self-controlled person.

vākya-vega mano-vega krodha-jihvā-vega
udara upastha-vega bhajana udvega
bahu-yatne nitya saba karibe damana
nirjane karibe rādhā-kṛṣṇera bhajana

Bhajana-rahasya-vṛtti

In this Text, Śrīla Rūpa Gosvāmī has given the instruction to reject that which is unfavourable to *bhakti*. The acceptance of that which is favourable and rejection of that which is unfavourable are not direct limbs of pure *bhakti*. Rather, they are aspects of *śraddhā* that are characterised by surrender (*śaraṇāgati*) and that bestow the eligibility for *bhakti*. A person who is capable of tolerating the six urges mentioned in this verse can instruct the entire world.

The purport is that lust (*kāma*), anger (*krodha*), greed (*lobha*), delusion (*moha*), pride (*mada*) and envy (*matsaratā*) always appear in the mind and cause agitation to the living entity. These six enemies appear in the mind of the living entity due to weakness of heart, *hṛdaya-daurbalya.*

Three kinds of urges (*vegas*) are seen in the living entity attached to enjoyment of material objects in this worldly existence: the impetus to speak, agitation of the mind and agitation of the body. It is very difficult for a person who has fallen into the strong current of these three urges to be rescued.

The impetus to speak (*vākya-vega*) refers to talks that are unfavourable to *bhakti,* and to the use of words that cause distress to others. However, one should not consider talk that is useful in the service of Bhagavān to be *vākya-vega.* Rather, one should consider such talk to be the result of disciplining the impetus to speak. Agitation of the mind is born from the various desires of the heart. If these desires are not fulfilled, anger arises. The three mental urges of speech, the mind and anger will be pacified by remembering Kṛṣṇa's pastimes.

The bodily urges are also of three types: the vehemence of the tongue, the urge of the belly and the agitation of the genitals. Vehemence of the tongue appears when the desire to enjoy any of the six distinct tastes impels one to eat prohibited foods and to take intoxicants. A *bhakti-sādhaka* must never indulge in these things. One should carefully keep the urge of the tongue at bay by taking the remnants of Bhagavān and the devotees. The urge of the belly will also be pacified by taking *bhagavat-prasāda* as needed, by regularly observing Ekādaśī and by serving Kṛṣṇa.

It is possible to fall into varieties of bad behaviour and bad association just to satisfy the desires of the tongue. *Śrī Caitanya-caritāmṛta* (*Antya-līlā* 6.227) states: "*jīhvāra lālase yei iti uti dhāya, śiśnodara-parāyaṇa kṛṣṇa nāhi pāya* – one who runs here and there trying to satisfy his tongue and who is always devoted to the desires of the genitals and belly cannot attain Kṛṣṇa." Also (*Antya-līlā* 6.236): "*bhāla nā khāibe āra bhāla nā paribe* – do not eat delicious food and do not dress opulently." Many troubles come from overeating. A person who eats too much becomes a servant of his agitated genitals. In other words, he becomes devoid of character. The agitation of the genitals, or the desire to meet with the opposite sex, drags the mind towards material sense objects and therefore renders one incapable of cultivating pure *bhakti*.

Rūpa Gosvāmī composed this verse to make the heart of a person who is endeavouring to perform *bhajana* inclined towards the path of *bhakti*. It is not that the endeavour to escape these six urges is itself the practice of *bhakti*; rather, this endeavour is the path to attain the qualification to enter the realm of *bhakti*. When *bhakti* appears, these six urges automatically become pacified of their own accord. This is because *bhakti* is a self-manifesting function of Bhagavān's *svarūpa-śakti*.

Text 17

The six impediments to *bhakti* are described in the second verse of *Upadeśāmṛta*:

atyāhāraḥ prayāsaś ca
prajalpo niyamāgrahaḥ
jana-saṅgaś ca laulyaṁ ca
ṣaḍbhir bhaktir vinaśyati

The following six kinds of faults destroy *bhakti*: (1) eating too much or collecting more than necessary; (2) endeavouring for that which is opposed to *bhakti*; (3) engaging in useless mundane talk; (4) failing to adopt essential rules and regulations, or fanatically adhering to rules and regulations; (5) taking bad association; and (6) being greedy or restless in the mind to adopt worthless opinions.

atyāhāra prayāsa prajalpa jana-saṅga
niyama-āgraha laulye haya bhakti bhaṅga

Bhajana-rahasya-vṛtti

The six impediments to *bhakti* are *atyāhāra, prayāsa, prajalpa, niyamāgraha, jana-saṅga* and *laulya.*

Atyāhāra is formed by the words *ati,* meaning "too much" or "excessively", and *āhāra,* "to grasp or consume for one's own enjoyment". It means either excessive enjoyment of any sense object or collecting more than necessary. While renunciants are forbidden to accumulate objects, householder Vaiṣṇavas may collect and save what is necessary to maintain their life. However, over-accumulating is *atyāhāra.* It is not proper for those desiring to perform *bhajana* to accumulate like materialists. *Prayāsa* is the endeavour to enjoy material objects or the engagement in activities opposed to devotion. *Prajalpa* means to spend time uselessly gossiping about mundane things. *Niyamāgraha* means enthusiastic adherence to those rules that yield the lowest results, such as attaining Svarga, while abandoning the endeavour for the topmost attainment of service to Bhagavān. It also refers to indifference towards the rules and regulations that nourish *bhakti.* The word *jana-saṅga* refers to giving up the association of pure devotees and keeping company with others, especially materialistic people. *Laulyam* refers to the fickleness of the mind to accept varieties of false doctrines, and the restlessness of the mind to enjoy insignificant material sense enjoyment. The tendency for *bhakti* will be destroyed if one wanders like a promiscuous woman, sometimes on the path of *karma,* sometimes on the path of *yoga,* sometimes on the path of *jñāna* and sometimes on the path of *bhakti. Prajalpa* leads to criticism of devotees, and *laulya* awakens a taste for many temporary, uncertain conclusions. Both of these will lead to *nāma-aparādha.* Therefore one should carefully give them up.

Text 18

The six kinds of association that nourish *bhakti* are described in the fourth verse of *Upadeśāmṛta*:

dadāti pratigṛhṇāti
guhyam ākhyāti pṛcchati
bhuṅkte bhojayate caiva
ṣaḍ-vidhaṁ prīti-lakṣaṇam

Offering pure devotees items in accordance with their requirements and accepting *prasāda*, remnant items given by pure devotees; revealing to devotees one's confidential realisations concerning *bhajana* and inquiring from them about their confidential realisations; eating with great love the *prasāda* given by devotees and lovingly feeding them *prasāda* – these are the six kinds of association that symptomise love and affection.

ādāna pradāna prīte, gūḍha ālāpana
āhāra bhojana chaya saṅgera lakṣaṇa

sādhura sahita saṅge bhakti-vṛddhi haya
abhakta asat-saṅge bhakti haya kṣaya

Bhajana-rahasya-vṛtti

This verse describes the visible symptoms of the affection that nourishes devotion, or in other words, affection for pure devotees. *Bhakti* manifests by associating with Bhagavān's devotees, but one should be careful to associate only with pure devotees. One should never keep the company of and reciprocate with gross sense enjoyers, persons who desire liberation or those who want to enjoy the fruits of their actions. *Bhakti* will be destroyed by the fault of associating with them. One should also not hear anything from them about the confidential aspects of *bhakti*, and one should not accept food that has been touched by them. *Śrī Caitanya-caritāmṛta* (*Antya-līlā* 6.278) confirms this:

viṣayīra anna khāile malina haya mana
malina mana haile nahe kṛṣṇera smaraṇa

[Śrī Caitanya Mahāprabhu said:] When one eats food offered by a materialist one's mind becomes contaminated, and when the mind is contaminated one is unable to think of Kṛṣṇa properly.

On the other hand, loving exchanges with devotees who are like-minded, more advanced than oneself and affectionate to oneself (*svajātīya-snigdhāśaya*) enhance one's devotion.

Text 19

In *Śrī Caitanya-candrodaya-nāṭaka* (8.88) Śrīman Mahāprabhu has prohibited one from even seeing a sense enjoyer or a woman:

niṣkiñcanasya bhagavad-bhajanonmukhasya
pāraṁ paraṁ jigamiṣor bhava-sāgarasya
sandarśanaṁ viṣayiṇām atha yoṣitāṁ ca
hā hanta hanta viṣa-bhakṣaṇato 'py asādhu

[Śrī Caitanya Mahāprabhu greatly lamented, saying:] Alas, for a renunciant who is devoted to *bhagavad-bhajana* and who desires to cross the ocean of material existence, it is worse to see sense enjoyers and women than it is to drink poison.

niṣkiñcana bhajana unmukha yei jana
bhava-sindhu uttīrṇa haite yāṅra mana
viṣayī-milana āra yoṣit sammilane
viṣa-pānāpekṣā tāṅra viruddha-ghaṭana

Bhajana-rahasya-vṛtti

Persons who desire to cross the ocean of material existence, as well as renunciants intent on *bhagavad-bhajana*, should avoid those who are attached to sense enjoyment and the association of women. The company of people in these two categories is more fearsome than drinking poison. Śrī Raghunātha dāsa understood Śrī Caitanya Mahāprabhu's hint and thereafter refused to accept the wealth his father had sent him, understanding that it was more auspicious to accept alms. Śrī Mahāprabhu abandoned Choṭa Haridāsa for life because he associated with a woman. Therefore in *Prema-vivarta* Jagadānanda Paṇḍita says:

yadi cāha praṇaya rākhite gaurāṅgera sane
choṭa haridāsera kathā thāke yena mane

If you want to associate with Caitanya Mahāprabhu, you must always remember the incident of Choṭa Haridāsa and how he was rejected by the Lord.

Text 20

It is forbidden to judge a transcendental Vaiṣṇava from a material viewpoint. *Upadeśāmṛta* (6) states:

dṛṣṭaiḥ svabhāva-janitair vapuṣaś ca doṣair
na prākṛtatvam iha bhakta-janasya paśyet
gaṅgāmbhasāṁ na khalu budbuda-phena-paṅkair
brahma-dravatvam apagacchati nīra-dharmaiḥ

Devotees who are in this material world should not be considered material; that is, one should not consider them ordinary *jīvas*. Imperfections seen in their natures, such as birth in a low caste, harshness or lethargy, and imperfections seen in their bodies, such as ugly features, disease or deformities, are precisely like the appearance of bubbles, foam and mud in the Gaṅgā. Despite such apparent pollution of her water, the Gaṅgā retains her nature as liquefied transcendence. Similarly, one should not attribute material defects to self-realised Vaiṣṇavas.

svabhāva-janita āra vapu-doṣe kṣaṇe
anādara nāhi kara śuddha-bhakta-jane

paṅkādi julīya doṣe kabhu gaṅgā-jale
cinmayatva lopa nahe, sarva-śāstre bale

aprākṛta bhakta-jana pāpa nāhi kare
avaśiṣṭa pāpa yāya kichu dina pare

Bhajana-rahasya-vṛtti

The instruction of this Text is that it is improper to consider pure devotees to be material or to see material defects in them. It is possible that they may have defects in their bodies or natures, but it is impossible for pure devotees to fall into bad association or commit *nāma-aparādha*. The water of the Gaṅgā is considered to be pure despite the appearance of bubbles, foam, mud and so forth within it, for its nature as liquefied transcendence is never lost. Similarly, self-realised Vaiṣṇavas are not contaminated by the birth of the material body nor by its deterioration. Therefore one who is intent on performing *bhajana* should never disrespect a pure Vaiṣṇava even if these defects are apparent in him. The remaining imperfections of a Vaiṣṇava are quickly removed, and if someone even looks for them he becomes an offender.

Text 21

Śrīla Raghunātha dāsa Gosvāmī states in *Manaḥ-śikṣā* (7) that one should give up the desire for prestige and the wickedness of deceit and hypocrisy:

pratiṣṭhāśā dhṛṣṭā śvapaca-ramaṇī me hṛdi naṭet
kathaṁ sādhu-premā spṛśati śucir etan nanu manaḥ
sadā tvaṁ sevasva prabhu-dayita-sāmantam atulaṁ
yathā tāṁ niṣkāśya tvaritam iha taṁ veśayati saḥ

[Why does deceit not go away even after one has given up all material sense enjoyment? This verse has been composed in order to remove this doubt.] O mind, tell me, how can pure divine love appear in my heart (you, O mind, are my heart) as long as the shameless outcaste woman of the desire for prestige is audaciously dancing there? Therefore without delay remember and serve the immeasurably powerful commanders of Śrī Kṛṣṇa's army, the very dear devotees of Bhagavān. They will quickly chase away this outcaste woman and initiate the flow of pure *vraja-prema* in my heart.

Bhajana-rahasya-vṛtti

The desire (*āśā*) for prestige (*pratiṣṭhā*) is called *pratiṣṭhāśā*. Although all other *anarthas* may be dispelled, the desire for *pratiṣṭhā* is not easily removed. The desire for prestige is the root of all *anarthas*; all kinds of deceit and hypocrisy arise from it and are gradually nourished by it. The *svaniṣṭha-sādhaka*[1] yearns to be recognised as a virtuous, benevolent and sinless devotee of Bhagavān, who is detached from the world, scholarly and so on. Therefore as long as the desire for prestige remains in the heart, one is unable to drive away deceit. And until one becomes free from deceit, one cannot obtain immaculate divine love. In other words, if deceit remains, one does not attain *prema* for Śrī Kṛṣṇa, which is endowed with a sense of great possessiveness (*mamatā*) and which makes the heart melt.

Service to pure Vaiṣṇavas is the only means to dispel *anarthas* like wickedness, deceit and hypocrisy. The rays of the *hlādinī-śakti* are to be seen in the hearts of pure Vaiṣṇavas. These rays are transmitted into the heart of a faithful *sādhaka*, where they dispel these *anarthas* and manifest *vraja-prema*. Always serve the immeasurably merciful and powerful commanders of Śrī

[1] This term is explained in the commentary to Text 22.

Nanda-nandana's army, His beloved devotees! The embrace of pure Vaiṣṇavas, the dust from their lotus feet, the remnants of their *prasāda*, the water that has washed their feet, their instructions, and so forth are all fully competent to transmit *hlādinī-śakti* into the heart. This is confirmed in *Śrī Caitanya-caritāmṛta* (*Antya-līlā* 6.60–1):

bhakta-pada-dhūli āra bhakta-pada-jala
bhakta-bhukta-avaśeṣa – tīna mahā-bala

ei tina-sevā haite kṛṣṇa-premā haya
punaḥ punaḥ sarva-śāstre phukāriyā kaya

Text 22

Manaḥ-śikṣa (6) states:

are cetaḥ prodyat-kapaṭa-kuṭināṭī-bhara-khara-
kṣaran mūtre snātvā dahasi katham ātmānam api mām
sadā tvaṁ gāndharvā-giridhara-pada-prema-vilasat
sudhāmbhodhau snātvā svam api nitarāṁ māṁ ca sukhaya

[In spite of having subdued the enemies of lust and anger, one may not have conquered the great enemy of deceit. This verse instructs how to gain victory over this powerful enemy.] O wicked mind, although you have adopted the path of *sādhana*, still you imagine yourself purified by bathing in the trickling donkey urine of an obvious abundance of deceit and hypocrisy. By doing so you are burning yourself and at the same time scorching me, a tiny *jīva*. Stop this! Eternally delight yourself and me by bathing in the nectarean ocean of *prema* for the lotus feet of Śrī Rādhā-Kṛṣṇa Yugala.

pratiṣṭhāśā kuṭīnāṭī yatne kara dūra
tāhā haile nāme rati pāibe pracura

Bhajana-rahasya-vṛtti

The abundance of deceit and hypocrisy that are clearly evident in a *sādhaka*, even though he has adopted the path of *sādhana*, are compared to the urine of a donkey. Considering oneself intently engaged in *bhajana* while remaining devious and hypocritical is like considering oneself pure after bathing in the filthy, burning urine of a donkey. The duty of a *sādhaka* is to carefully abandon these bad qualities.

There are three kinds of *bhakti-sādhakas*: *svaniṣṭha*, *pariniṣṭhita* and *nirapekṣa*. The hypocrisy that can be demonstrated by each is described below.

The *svaniṣṭha-sādhaka* is a householder devotee who serves Śrī Hari and completely abandons the rules and prohibitions prescribed within *varṇāśrama*. The deceits of such *sādhakas* are to indulge in sense enjoyment on the pretext of *sādhana-bhakti*; to serve wealthy and influential materialists instead of unpretentious devotees; to accumulate more wealth than necessary; to be enthusiastic for futile, temporary enterprises; to indulge in false doctrines; and to adopt the dress of a renunciant in order to obtain material prestige.

The *pariniṣṭhita-sādhaka* is a householder devotee who serves and attends Bhagavān according to rules and regulations. His deceit is that externally he makes a show of strict adherence to rules and regulations (*pariniṣṭhita*), but inwardly he remains attached to material objects. He also prefers the association of *jñānīs*, *yogīs*, philanthropists and materialists to that of resolute, loving devotees.

The deceit of the *nirapekṣa-sādhaka* (the renunciant) is that he maintains pride by thinking himself to be the topmost Vaiṣṇava; he adopts the dress of a renunciant and due to false ego regards other *sādhakas* as inferior; he collects wealth and other material assets; he associates with women and materialistic people; he collects wealth in the name of *bhajana*; he weakens his affection towards Kṛṣṇa by being overly attached to the external dress and rules of the renounced order; and so forth.

A person should give up all this deceit and immerse himself in the nectarean ocean of pure transcendental pastimes that is born of *prema* for the lotus feet of the Divine Couple. The prayers expressed in the writings of Rūpa Gosvāmipāda and others in our disciplic succession (*guru-varga*) point the *sādhaka* in the proper direction. One should take guidance from these prayers and perform *sādhana* while remembering within the heart Śrī Yugala's eternal eightfold daily pastimes (*aṣṭa-kālīya-līlā*).

Text 23

The ten kinds of offence to the holy name, which should be given up without fail, are described in the *Padma Purāṇa*:

(1–2) *satāṁ nindā nāmnaḥ paramam aparādhaṁ vitanute*
yataḥ khyātiṁ yātaṁ katham u sahate tad vigarhām
śivasya śrī-viṣṇor ya iha guṇa-nāmādi-sakalaṁ
dhiyā bhinnaṁ paśyet sa khalu hari-nāmāhita-karaḥ

(3–7) *guror avajñā śruti-śāstra-nindanaṁ*
tathārtha-vādo hari-nāmni kalpanam
nāmno balād yasya hi pāpa-buddhir
na vidyate tasya yamair hi śuddhiḥ

(8–9) *dharma-vrata-tyāga-hutādi-sarva-*
śubha-kriyā-sāmyam api pramādaḥ
aśraddadhāne vimukhe 'py aśṛṇvati
yaś copadeśaḥ śiva-nāmāparādhaḥ

(10) *śrute 'pi nāma-māhātmye*
yaḥ prīti-rahito naraḥ
ahaṁ-mamādi-paramo
nāmni so 'py aparādha-kṛt

(1) To criticise the devotees of Bhagavān is a grievous offence to the holy name. How can Śrī Nāma Prabhu tolerate criticism of those great souls who are deeply devoted to Him and who spread His glories throughout the world? Therefore the first offence is criticism of *sādhus* and devotees.

(2) In this world a person who by mundane intelligence distinguishes between the all-auspicious, transcendental holy name, form, qualities and pastimes of Śrī Viṣṇu and the possessor of the holy name (*nāmi-viṣṇu*), considering them to be independent of or different from Him as is the case with material objects, commits an offence against the holy name. Furthermore, one who thinks that Lord Śiva and other demigods are independent of Viṣṇu, or similar to Viṣṇu, certainly commits *nāma-aparādha.*

(3) *Guror avajñā* – To disregard the *guru* who is established in all the truths regarding the holy name, considering him to be an ordinary man possessing a perishable body composed of material elements.

(4) *Śruti-śāstra-nindanam* – To find fault with the Vedas, the eternal Purāṇas and other scriptures. All the Vedas and Upaniṣads illuminate the glories of the holy name. To find fault with the *mantras* in which the holy name is glorified is *nāma-aparādha.* Due to misfortune, some persons neglect the *śruti-mantras* in which the glories of *nāma* are indicated and give more honour to other instructions of the Śrutis. This is also *nāma-aparādha.*

(5) *Tathārtha-vādaḥ* – To consider the glories of *harināma* to be exaggerated. The scriptures state that all of Bhagavān's potencies are contained within His name, and that the holy name is completely transcendental and therefore capable of destroying one's bondage to the material world. All these glories of the holy name are the supreme truth. One should never associate with those

who have no faith in them and who say that *śāstra* exaggerates the glories of the holy name. If such an unfaithful person appears before one's eyes, one should take bath still wearing the clothes he has on. This is the teaching of Śrī Caitanya Mahāprabhu.

(6) *Hari-nāmni kalpanam* – To consider Bhagavān's name to be imaginary. *Māyāvādīs* and materialistic *karmavādīs* consider Brahman, which is without name and form, to be the supreme truth, and they say that the *ṛṣis* manufactured names like Rāma and Kṛṣṇa thinking such names would perfect their activities. These people are *nāma-aparādhīs*. The name of Hari is not imaginary; it is eternal and transcendental. It only manifests upon the transcendental senses, and only through *bhakti*. This is the teaching given by the bona fide *guru* and *śāstra*. Therefore one should acknowledge that the glories of *harināma* are the supreme truth. One who considers these glories to be imaginary will never be able to receive the mercy of the holy name.

(7) One who has a tendency to commit sinful and material activities on the strength of the holy name cannot be purified even if he performs superficial *yoga* processes such as *yama*, *niyama*, *dhyāna* or *dhāraṇā*. This is certain.

(8) To consider religiosity, vows, renunciation, fire sacrifices and other ordinary pious activities to be equal with or comparable to the transcendental name of Bhagavān is a sign of inattentiveness and carelessness, and is thus an offence.

(9) To instruct the glories of the holy name to faithless persons who are averse to hearing and chanting is also *nāma-aparādha*.

(10) Those who, in spite of hearing the astonishing glories of the holy name, maintain the conception that "I am this material body" and that "wordly objects of sense gratification are mine", and who show no persistence in or love for the utterance of *śrī nāma*, are also *nāma-aparādhīs*.

sādhu-anādara āra anye īśa-jñāna
guruke avajñā, nāma-śāstre apamāna

nāme arthavāda, nāma-bale pāpāndhatā
anya śubha-karma saha nāmera samatā

śraddhā-hīne nāma dāna, jaḍāsakti-krame
māhātmya jāniyā nāme śraddhā nahe bhrame

ei daśa aparādha yatne parihari'
harināme kara bhāi bhajana cāturī

Bhajana-rahasya-vṛtti

Skilfulness in *nāma-bhajana* is to perform *bhajana* in association of devotees while carefully avoiding these ten offences.

Text 24

False renunciation (*phalgu-vairāgya*) is prohibited. *Bhakti-rasāmṛta-sindhu* (1.2.126) states:

prāpañcikatayā buddhyā
hari-sambandhi-vastunaḥ
mumukṣubhiḥ parityāgo
vairāgyaṁ phalgu kathyate

When *sādhakas* who desire liberation renounce that which is related to Hari, such as the scriptures, the deity, the holy name, *mahā-prasāda*, the spiritual master and Vaiṣṇavas, considering them material, their renunciation is called futile renunciation, *phalgu-vairāgya*. This is unfavourable to *bhakti*.

prāpañcika jñāne bhakti sambandha viṣaya
mumukṣu-janera tyāga phalgu nāma haya

Text 25

One who is qualified to chant the holy name gives up all fruitive activities. *Śrīmad-Bhāgavatam* (11.5.41) says:

devarṣi-bhūtāpta-nṛṇāṁ pitṝṇāṁ
na kiṅkaro nāyam ṛṇī ca rājan
sarvātmanā yaḥ śaraṇaṁ śaraṇyaṁ
gato mukundaṁ parihṛtya kartam

One who has taken complete shelter of Bhagavān Mukunda, who is affectionate towards the surrendered, is not indebted to the demigods, to his forefathers, to ordinary living entities, or to relatives and guests. He is not subordinate to anyone other than Mukunda, nor is he their servant.

ekānta haiyā nāme ye laya śaraṇa
devādira ṛṇā tāra nahe kadācana

Bhajana-rahasya-vṛtti

The performance of the *śrāddha* ceremony and other material activities meant to absolve one's debts to the forefathers, as presented in the *karma-kāṇḍa* section of the Vedas, is not for devotees surrendered to Bhagavān. The only injunction for these devotees is to worship Bhagavān, offer *bhagavat-prasāda* to the forefathers and accept *bhagavat-prasāda* with friends and relatives. The ultimate purport of the entire *Bhagavad-gītā* is that Bhagavān will liberate from all sins those who have surrendered unto Him and given up their reliance on all other *dharmas.* When a person acquires the qualification for exclusive devotion, he is not obliged to follow the rules of the *jñāna-* and *karma-śāstras,* for he will attain all perfection simply by cultivating *bhakti.* Therefore one should understand that Bhagavān's promise in *Bhagavad-gītā* (9.31), "*na me bhaktaḥ praṇaśyati* – My devotee never perishes", is placed above all.

Text 26

The *Padma Purāṇa* (quoted in *Bhakti-rasāmṛta-sindhu* (1.2.8)) states that one should give up *niyamāgraha* and follow the essence of all injunctions:

smartavyaḥ satataṁ viṣṇur
vismartavyo na jātucit
sarve vidhi-niṣedhāḥ syur
etayor eva kiṅkarāḥ

One should always remember Viṣṇu and never forget Him. All other rules and prohibitions are subservient to these two principles.

yāhe kṛṣṇa-smṛti haya, tāi vidhi jāni
kṛṣṇa-vismāraka kārya niṣedha bali' māni

Bhajana-rahasya-vṛtti

All of the various rules and prohibitions of *śāstra* are established on the basis of the above-stated main rule and prohibition. The main injunction is that throughout one's whole life one should always remember Bhagavān Viṣṇu. *Varṇāśrama* and other arrangements that are made to maintain one's life are subordinate to this rule. The main prohibition is that one should never forget Bhagavān. To abandon sinful activities, to give up indifference to Bhagavān and to atone for sins are subordinate to this principal injunction and this principal prohibition.

Hence all the rules and prohibitions mentioned in the scriptures are perpetual servants of the rule to always remember Bhagavān and of the prohibition to never forget Him. From this, one can understand that among all the rules regarding *varṇāśrama* and so forth, that rule which calls for remembering Bhagavān is eternal.

Text 27

Do not endeavour to perform activities such as atoning for sins through *karma* and *jñāna*. The *Padma Purāṇa* says:

harer apy aparādhān yaḥ
kuryād dvi-pada-pāṁśalaḥ
nāmāśrayaḥ kadācit syāt
taraty eva sa nāmataḥ
nāmno 'pi sarva-suhṛdo
hy aparādhāt pataty adhaḥ

nāmāparādha-yuktānāṁ
nāmāny eva haranty-agham
aviśrānta-prayuktāni
tāny evārtha-karāṇi ca

That wretched person who commits *seva-aparādha* at the lotus feet of Śrī Hari can become freed from his offence if he takes shelter of the holy name. Every kind of *aparādha* is nullified by service to the holy name. All perfection is attained by chanting the holy name without *anarthas* and with a sense of one's relationship with the Lord, continuously and uninterruptedly, like an unbroken stream of oil.

kṛṣṇera śrī-mūrti prati aparādha kari'
nāmāśraye sei aparādhe yaya tari'

nāma aparādha yata nāme haya kṣaya
aviśrānta nāma laile sarva-siddhi haya

Text 28

Everyone should endeavour to attain knowledge of Kṛṣṇa (*kṛṣṇa-svarūpa*) and oneself (*ātma-svarūpa*). One first attains knowledge of Kṛṣṇa's form and qualities, and then of His pastimes. *Catuḥ-ślokī Bhāgavata* (2.9.33) states:

aham evāsam evāgre
nānyad yat sad-asat param
paścād ahaṁ yad etac ca
yo 'vaśiṣyeta so 'smy aham

[Bhagavān said to Brahmā:] Before the creation of this world, only I existed. The gross and the subtle, up to the indefinable Brahman – in other words the cause (*sat*) and the effect (*asat*) – did not exist. Nothing other than I existed. What is manifested in the form of creation is also I, after creation it is also I, and after annihilation only I will remain.

cid-ghana-svarūpa kṛṣṇa nitya sanātana
kṛṣṇa-śakti pariṇati anya saṅghaṭana
sakalera avaśeṣe kṛṣṇa cid-bhāskara
avicintya-bhedābheda tattva kṛṣṇetara

Bhajana-rahasya-vṛtti

In this Text the words *aham eva*, meaning "certainly I", are used three times. This is because Bhagavān is eternally present since time immemorial in His form possessed of all opulence. Bhagavān has used these words "certainly I" three times to refute the doctrine of persons who consider Parabrahma to be without form. The implied meaning is, "Now I am present before you as a great ocean of supremely captivating beauty, qualities and sweetness. I was also present before this creation, in other words at the time of the *mahā-pralaya* (annihilation of the universe at the end of Brahmā's life)." At that time, except for creating the world consisting of the five elements, Bhagavān was performing all His activities. Bhagavān's eternal, confidential pastimes were also present with Him, as were His associates, who are assistants in His pastimes. At the time of the *mahā-pralaya* the material universes are destroyed, but Bhagavān's transcendental pastimes and His various forms, abodes and intimate associates are all eternally existent.

Bhagavān is present both before and after the creation. The entire material world is the manifestation of Bhagavān's *bahiraṅga-śakti* and the living entity is His *taṭastha-śakti.* Therefore this material world is not separate from Bhagavān. Bhagavān is situated in unlimited Vaikuṇṭha planets in His form complete with six opulences. In the material world He is present as the Supersoul (*antaryāmī*), and He appears as Matsya and other incarnations when needed.

According to the impersonalists (*nirviśeṣavādīs*), only the impersonal Brahman existed at first. To defeat this doctrine, Śrī Bhagavān says to Brahmā, "Beyond the cause (*sat*) and the effect (*asat*) is the supreme entity, Brahman. That Brahman is nothing other than Me. Few can realise My personal form replete with transcendental pastimes; they can only realise the impersonal form (*nirviśeṣa-svarūpa*). You, however, can realise My form full of transcendental beauty and all qualities, by My blessings and mercy."

Text 29

Knowledge of the intrinsic natures of *jīva-śakti* and *māyā-śakti* is found in *Śrīmad-Bhāgavatam* (2.9.34):

ṛte 'rthaṁ yat pratīyeta
na pratīyeta cātmani
tad vidyād ātmano māyāṁ
yathābhāso yathā tamaḥ

The Supreme Absolute Truth (*parama-tattva*, or *svarūpa-tattva*) is the only real truth. One should understand that which is seen to be separate from this truth, or not existing within it, to be the product of the Supreme Absolute Truth's illusory energy (*māyā*).

The following example demonstrates this. *Parama-tattva* can be compared to the sun, which is an object consisting of light. The sun is experienced in two other forms, namely its reflection and darkness. Similarly, in regards to the Absolute Truth, reflection pertains to the living entities (*jīva-śakti*) and darkness to the material world (*māyā-śakti*).

kṛṣṇa-śakti māyā, kṛṣṇa haite bhedābheda
cic-chakti svarūpāśritā cij-jyoti-sambheda

jaḍākāre māyā-śakti chāyā tamo-dharma
prapañca pratīti yāhe vinaśvara-karma

Bhajana-rahasya-vṛtti

Although the *jīva* and *māyā* are both dependent on Bhagavān, a person does not experience them while he is directly experiencing Bhagavān. And while having experience of the *jīva* and *māyā*, one will not have experience of Bhagavān.

The intrinsic nature of the Supreme Absolute Truth was ascertained in the previous Text. The *jīva* and *māyā* are separate from *parama-tattva*. When a *jīva* can realise *parama-tattva* it is known as realised knowledge, *vijñāna*. This Text 29 elaborates upon *māyā-tattva*. *Parama-tattva* is the only real truth, and that which is experienced outside *parama-tattva* and not within it, is the product of the illusory energy of the Absolute Truth.

An example of this is seen in the sun, its reflection and darkness. A semblance of the sun is the reflection of the sun on water or on other things at dawn. This semblance does not exist without the sun. Similarly, *māyā* is only perceived when the creative energy of Bhagavān is manifest, and its existence is destroyed at the time of annihilation (*mahā-pralaya*). Without Bhagavān, *māyā* is not manifest. Where there is light there can be no darkness, but darkness is also perceived through the eyes. In the same way, *māyā* cannot be perceived on its own without the help of Bhagavān. The transcendental world (*cid-jagat*) is herein compared with the rays of the sun, Bhagavān. Using the same analogy, the *jīvas* are compared to the reflection of Bhagavān and the material world (*māyā-jagat*) is compared with darkness. The material realm is very far from Bhagavān, the transcendental truth (*cit-tattva*).

There are two kinds of relationship between *parama-tattva* and *māyā-tattva*. That which is experienced as separate from the Absolute Truth is *māyā*, and that which is very far from the Absolute Truth and in ignorance of it is also *māyā*. In this way, by carefully explaining the inherent nature of Himself, the *jīva* and *māyā*, Śrī Bhagavān explained *sambandha-tattva* to Brahmā.

Text 30

The relationship between Kṛṣṇa on one side, and the living entity and the material world on the other, is one of inconceivable difference and non-difference, *acintya-bhedābheda*. Nevertheless, Kṛṣṇa is separately situated in His eternal *svarūpa*. *Śrīmad-Bhāgavatam* (2.9.35) states:

yathā mahānti bhūtāni
bhūteṣūccāvaceṣv anu
praviṣṭāny apraviṣṭāni
tathā teṣu na teṣv aham

The five great elements of material creation enter into the bodies of all living entities, high and low, from the demigods to the sub-human species. But at the same time, these elements exist independently. Similarly, I have entered into all living entities as the Supersoul, but at the same time I am situated independently in My own *svarūpa*, and I appear to My surrendered devotees both internally and externally.

mahābhūta uccāvaca-bhūte avasthita
haiyā o pūrṇa-rūpe mahābhūte sthita

sei rūpa cid-aṁśa jīve kṛṣṇāṁśa vyāpita
haiyā o pūrṇa kṛṣṇa svarūpāvasthita

Bhajana-rahasya-vṛtti

After describing His own *svarūpa*, Śrī Bhagavān says, "I am situated inside and outside every living entity." Bhagavān dwells in every living entity as the Supersoul, but not all living entities are able to perceive Him. Only His devotees can realise Him. Not only that, Bhagavān is present everywhere, in all places, and the devotees can also realise this. According to the gradation of their *bhakti*, devotees relish the existence of Bhagavān and the nectar of His sweetness and beauty. The affection of the devotees for Śrī Bhagavān is called *prema*, and this is *prayojana-tattva*, the ultimate objective. The *premi-bhakta* sees Śrī Kṛṣṇa everywhere, both within his heart and outside. This is the intrinsic characteristic (*svarūpa-lakṣaṇa*) of *prema*, as described by Śrī Kṛṣṇa Himself:

bhakta āmā preme bāndhiyāche hṛdaya-bhitare
yāhāṅ netra paḍe tāhāṅ dekhaye āmāre

Śrī Caitanya-caritāmṛta (*Madhya-līlā* 25.127)

The devotees keep Me bound in their hearts with the ropes of *prema*. And outside their hearts, they see only Me wherever they look.

Bhagavān resides affectionately in the hearts of the devotees, considering them His own; and He resides in the hearts of the other *jīvas* in a detached way. Bhagavān is supremely independent, yet His quality of being controlled is that He resides in the hearts of devotees and has possessiveness (*mamatā*) towards them. Bhagavān is made a prisoner by the loving devotion of His *premi-bhaktas*. The essence of spiritual knowledge is *prema-bhakti*, and the wonderful, confidential secret of *prema-bhakti* is that Bhagavān becomes controlled by His loving devotees.

Text 31

Knowledge of the intrinsic nature of the holy name is given in *Bhakti-rasāmṛta-sindhu* (1.2.233, quoted from the *Padma Purāṇa*):

nāma cintāmaṇiḥ kṛṣṇaś
caitanya-rasa-vigrahaḥ
pūrṇaḥ śuddho nitya-mukto
'bhinnatvān nāma-nāminoḥ

The holy name is a transcendental wish-fulfilling gem (*cintāmaṇi*), for there is no difference between Kṛṣṇa's name (*nāma*) and Kṛṣṇa Himself (*nāmī*). In other words the holy name is the bestower of the supreme goal (*parama-puruṣārtha*). This name is the very form of transcendental mellows (*caitanya-rasa-svarūpa*). It is completely pure; that is, it is unlimited and eternally liberated, devoid of any connection with *māyā*.

harināma cintāmaṇi cid-rasa-svarūpa
pūrṇa jaḍātīta nitya kṛṣṇa-nija-rūpa

Bhajana-rahasya-vṛtti

Nāma and *nāmī* are qualitatively non-different in principle. Therefore in the name "Kṛṣṇa" all the transcendental qualities of the possessor of the name are present. The holy name is always the complete Absolute Truth, unaffected by material matter. He is eternally liberated because He is never bound by the illusory energy. The holy name is Kṛṣṇa Himself and therefore the personification of the aggregate wealth of transcendental mellows. The holy name is a wish-fulfilling gem, able to give whatever one desires. *Śrī-nāma-saṅkīrtana*, which is the practice (*sādhana*), is non-different in every respect from Śrī Kṛṣṇa, who is the goal (*sādhya*). The one Absolute Truth, who is imbued with transcendental mellows consisting of eternity, knowledge and bliss (*sac-cid-ānanda*), is eternally present in these two manifested forms, *nāma* and *nāmī*.

Text 32

Bhakti-rasāmṛta-sindhu (1.2.234) states:

ataḥ śrī-kṛṣṇa-nāmādi
na bhaved grāhyam indriyaiḥ
sevonmukhe hi jihvādau
svayam eva sphuraty adaḥ

The material senses, such as the tongue, cannot perceive Śrī Kṛṣṇa's name, which appears automatically only on the transcendental senses of one in whose heart the desire to serve Kṛṣṇa has arisen.

nāma, rūpa, guṇa, līlā indriya-grāhya naya
sevā-mukhe kṛpā kari' indriya udaya

Bhajana-rahasya-vṛtti

It is a natural tendency of one who has the desire to serve Kṛṣṇa (*sevonmukha*) to be engaged in chanting Bhagavān's holy name, which is His intrinsic form. The holy name Himself appears and begins to dance on the tongue and other senses of one who has a tendency towards *śrī-nāma-sevā*, in other words, an inclination for chanting. Bhagavān's name can appear even on the tongues of animals. Examples of this are Bharata Mahārāja when he was leaving his deer body, and the elephant Gajendra when he was being pulled into the water by the crocodile.

Text 33

Śrīmad-Bhāgavatam (11.21.2) states:

sve sve 'dhikāre yā niṣṭhā
sa guṇaḥ parikīrtitaḥ
viparyayas tu doṣaḥ syād
ubhayor eṣa nirṇayaḥ

To have unyielding steadiness on the path of *dharma*, according to one's own qualification, is a virtue; conversely, to make endeavours that do not accord with one's qualification is a fault.

adhikāra susammata kārye haya guṇa
viparīta kārye doṣa bujhibe nipuṇa

Bhajana-rahasya-vṛtti

The purport of this verse is that virtue and fault are determined according to one's qualification, and not by any other criteria.

Text 34

Qualification for chanting the holy name is given in *Śrīmad-Bhāgavatam* (11.20.27–8):

jāta-śraddho mat-kathāsu
nirviṇṇaḥ sarva-karmasu
veda duḥkhātmakān kāmān
parityāge 'py anīśvaraḥ

tato bhajeta māṁ prītaḥ
śraddhālur dṛḍha-niścayaḥ
juṣamāṇaś ca tān kāmān
duḥkhodarkāṁś ca garhayan

If a person whose faith in hearing narrations of Me has been awakened is unable to give up sense enjoyment and the desire for it, even though he knows it gives misery, he should with a sincere heart condemn his inability to give it up. All the while, he should continue worshipping Me with firm faith, conviction and love.

kṛṣṇa-kathā śraddhā-lābha tyaje karmāsakti
duḥkhātmaka kāma-tyāge tabu nahe śakti

kāma-sevā kare tāhā kariyā garhaṇa
sudṛḍha-bhajane kāme kare vidhvaṁsana

puṇyamaya kāma-mātra uddiṣṭa ethāya
pāpa-kāme śraddhadhānera ādara nā haya

Bhajana-rahasya-vṛtti

By the influence of association with devotees (*sat-saṅga*), a person develops a taste for hearing *hari-kathā*. At that time he will have no interest in any other activity, and with firm faith he will chant the name of Bhagavān continually. However, if due to his previous habits someone is unable to give up sense enjoyment or the desire for it, in his heart he condemns his inability to give it up.

Here, in these two verses, the intrinsic nature of *bhakti* is described by mentioning the first symptoms of the qualification for *bhakti*. *Sarva-karmasu* means sadness that comes as a result of performing all material Vedic activities and from their results; in other words, being distressed by a miserable mind. *Kāmān* means realising the miseries that result from the desires arising from associating with the opposite sex. If a person is unable to give up these desires, he should, from the beginning, have the following firm conviction: "If my attachment to household life is destroyed or if it increases, if my *bhajana* is full of millions of obstacles or if I go to hell because of offences, I will accept it all; but I will never give up devotion, even if Brahmā himself tells me to." A person who performs *bhajana* with such firm conviction will certainly be successful. Even if desires causing misery arise from association with wife, children and so forth, a person should condemn the desires and continue fulfilling his worldly responsibilities. However, he should never give up *bhakti.* The desire for enjoyment will gradually diminish by hearing, chanting and so on, and one will ultimately attain *bhakti.*

Text 35

The six vows favourable for *bhakti* are described in the third verse of *Upadeśāmṛta*:

utsāhān niścayād dhairyāt
tat-tat-karma-pravartanāt
saṅga-tyāgāt sato vṛtteḥ
ṣaḍbhir bhaktiḥ prasidhyati

Perfection in *bhakti* can be achieved by the following six kinds of practices: (1) to be enthusiastic in following the rules which nourish devotion; (2) to have firm faith in the statements of the scriptures and in *śrī gurudeva*, whose words are fully in line with the scriptures; (3) to be patient in the practice of *bhakti*, even in the midst of obstacles or when there is a delay in attaining one's desired success; (4) to follow the limbs of *bhakti*, such as *śravaṇa* and *kīrtana*, and to give up one's material sense enjoyment for the pleasure of Kṛṣṇa; (5) to give up association that is opposed to *bhakti*, like illicit connection with women, the association of those who are overly attached to women and the association of *māyāvādīs*, atheists and pseudo-religionists; and (6) to adopt the good behaviour and character of devotees.

utsāha, dṛḍhatā, dhairya bhakti kārye rati
saṅga-tyāga, sādhu-vṛtti chaye kara mati

Bhajana-rahasya-vṛtti

To maintain one's existence and to cultivate *bhakti* are both necessary for devotees. The first half of this verse indicates the activities that nourish *bhakti* and the second half describes how a devotee should conduct his life. Enthusiasm (*utsāha*), conviction (*niścaya*), patience (*dhairya*), executing activities that nourish devotion (*tat-tat-karma-pravartana*), renouncing bad association (*saṅga-tyāga*) and adopting the good behaviour and character of pure devotees (*sad-vṛtti*) are the means to attain perfection in *bhakti*.

Utsāha means to remain indifferent in every respect to the practices related to *jñāna*, *karma* and *anyābhilāṣa* (desires other than to serve Kṛṣṇa), and also to one's preferred variety of material enjoyment, while steadily executing the limbs of *sādhana-bhakti*. "*Bhagavad-bhakti* is the only ultimate objective for all living entities" – such firm faith is called *niścaya*, conviction. Straying to the paths of *karma*, *jñāna* and so forth makes one's mind restless, and following their practices only produces suffering in the end. Therefore the firm resolve that the path of *bhakti* is the only constitutional path for sincere living entities is called *dhairya*, fortitude.

Śrī Haridāsa Ṭhākura took a vow never to give up chanting and he strictly adhered to it:

khaṇḍa-khaṇḍa hai deha yāya yadi prāṇa
tabu āmi vadane nā chāḍi harināma

Śrī Caitanya-bhāgavata (*Ādi-khaṇḍa* 16.94)

Even if my body is cut to pieces and my life air exits, I will never abandon the chanting of *harināma*.

This is the ideal in the realm of *bhakti*.

To cultivate the practices of *bhakti* such as hearing *hari-kathā*, performing *kīrtana* of Bhagavān's name, and meditating on Bhagavān's name, form and pastimes with firm conviction like Haridāsa Ṭhākura, is *tat-tat-karma-pravartana.*

Only the association of Bhagavān's devotees is desirable. One should never associate with *karmīs, jñānīs* or those filled with desires other than to serve Kṛṣṇa. One should know such people to be less intelligent and indulgent. *Karma, jñāna, aṣṭāṅga-yoga* and so forth, which are devoid of the desire to please Bhagavān, are not steps on the path of *bhakti.* The path of *bhakti* is characterised by saintly conduct (*sādhu-vṛtti*), because all virtuous qualities certainly reside within a person who possesses devotion.

Enthusiasm for serving Kṛṣṇa, conviction in service, being steadfast in *kṛṣṇa-sevā,* ensuring that all endeavours are solely for service to Kṛṣṇa, renouncing the company of all others except Kṛṣṇa's devotees and following in the footsteps of Kṛṣṇa's devotees are the six practices that enhance *bhakti.*

Text 36

The gradual development of *bhakti* through the association of genuine *sādhus* is described in *Śrīmad-Bhāgavatam* (3.25.25):

satāṁ prasaṅgān mama vīrya-saṁvido
bhavanti hṛt-karṇa-rasāyanāḥ kathāḥ
taj-joṣaṇād āśv apavarga-vartmani
śraddhā ratir bhaktir anukramiṣyati

In the association of pure devotees, there are powerful discussions that illuminate My heroic deeds and that are pleasing to both the ears and the heart. By hearing these narrations, one quickly proceeds along the path of the removal of ignorance (*avidyā-nivṛtti*), which is the sequential development of *śraddhā, rati* and *prema-bhakti.*

sādhu-saṅge haya kṛṣṇa-kathā rasāyana
tāhe śraddhā rati bhakti krame uddīpana

Bhajana-rahasya-vṛtti

By great fortune the living entity wandering throughout material existence may attain that kind of *sukṛti* which bestows *bhakti*. When this *sukṛti* accumulates over many births, it gives rise to faith (*śraddhā*) in exclusive devotion. When *śraddhā* arises, the desire to associate with pure devotees and true saints manifests, and by this association one will gradually develop a taste for *sādhana* and *bhajana*. When *anarthas* are removed and this *śraddhā* becomes pure, it transforms into *niṣṭhā*, which in turn, when pure, transforms into *ruci*. The beauty of *bhakti* makes this *ruci* very fixed, and thus turns it into *āsakti*. Gradually this *āsakti* gains perfection and transforms into *bhāva*. When *bhāva* combines with its corresponding components in the right proportion, *rasa* appears. This is the gradual development leading to the appearance of *prema*.

Text 37

A *madhyama-bhakta* renders service to the three kinds of Vaiṣṇavas. *Upadeśāmṛta* (5) states:

kṛṣṇeti yasya giri taṁ manasādriyeta
dīkṣāsti cet praṇatibhiś ca bhajantam īśam
śuśrūṣayā bhajana-vijñam ananyam anya-
nindādi-śūnya-hṛdam īpsita-saṅga-labdhyā

That person who utters Kṛṣṇa's name by just once calling out "O Kṛṣṇa!" is a *kaniṣṭha-adhikārī*, and one should offer him respect within one's mind. That person who fully understands the principle of *dīkṣā*, has accepted *dīkṣā* from a qualified *guru* and performs *bhajana* of Bhagavān in accordance with Vaiṣṇava conventions, is a *madhyama-adhikārī*. One should respect such a devotee, who is endowed with the correct understanding of reality and illusion, by offering obeisances unto him and so forth. That person who properly understands the science of *bhajana*, as described in *Śrīmad-Bhāgavatam* and other Vaiṣṇava scriptures, and performs exclusive *bhajana* of Śrī Kṛṣṇa is a *mahā-bhāgavata*. Due to his undeviating absorption in Kṛṣṇa, the pure heart of such a devotee is free from faults, such as the tendency to criticise others. He is expert in *bhajana*, which means he is skilled in the method of remembering Rādhā-Kṛṣṇa's eternal eightfold daily pastimes through *mānasī-sevā*, service performed within the mind. Knowing him to be a *mahā-bhāgavata* whose heart is established in the particular mood of service to Śrī Rādhā-Kṛṣṇa for which one aspires (*svajātīya*) and who is affectionately disposed towards oneself (*susnigdha*), one should seek his association, considering it to be topmost. One should honour him by offering prostrated obeisances, making relevant inquiry and rendering service unto him with great love.

akaitave kṛṣṇa-nāma yāra mukhe śuna
manete ādara tāre kara punaḥ punaḥ

bhakti sampradāya labhi' yei kṛṣṇa bhaje
ādara karaha paḍi' tāra pada-raje

svīya para-buddhi-śūnya ananya-bhajana
yāṅhāra, tāṅhāra sevā kara anukṣaṇa

Bhajana-rahasya vṛtti

Because the *mahā-bhāgavatas* see everything as related to Kṛṣṇa, they look upon all with equal vision. They are devoted to *kṛṣṇa-bhajana* like the *madhyama-adhikārī*, and intent on chanting the holy name like the *kaniṣṭha-adhikārī*.

The *madhyama-adhikārīs* have *prema* for Śrī Kṛṣṇa. They offer appropriate respect to the three levels of devotees (by rendering service, offering obeisances and offering respect mentally). They always endeavour to turn the conditioned living entities towards Kṛṣṇa and they are indifferent towards those who are averse to Kṛṣṇa. However, they do not possess equal vision like the *uttama-adhikārī mahā-bhāgavata*, and if they deceitfully imitate him they will very quickly fall down.

The *kaniṣṭha-adhikārī* knows that the name of Śrī Kṛṣṇa is supremely auspicious, and therefore he takes shelter of chanting the holy name. He does not understand, however, that the position of the *madhyama-adhikārī* is high and that he should strive to reach that level in the future. Sometimes the *kaniṣṭha-adhikārī* considers himself a *guru* and consequently falls down. Therefore, by carefully offering appropriate respect to those Vaiṣṇavas who are more advanced than him, he should take shelter of the holy name.

Text 38

One should chant the holy name while maintaining one's life by *yukta-vairāgya*, the mood of appropriate renunciation. *Bhakti-rasāmṛta-sindhu* (1.2.125) states:

anāsaktasya viṣayān
yathārham upayuñjataḥ
nirbandhaḥ kṛṣṇa-sambandhe
yuktaṁ vairāgyam ucyate

Appropriate renunciation is to accept objects favourable to one's service while being detached from that which is unrelated to Kṛṣṇa and attached to that which is related to Kṛṣṇa.

yathāyogya viṣaya bhoga anāsakta hañā
suyukta-vairāgya bhakti-sambandha kariyā

Text 39

Śrīmad-Bhāgavatam (7.11.32) further states:

vṛttyā sva-bhāva-kṛtayā
vartamānaḥ sva-karma-kṛt
hitvā sva-bhāva-jaṁ karma
śanair nirguṇatām iyāt

One who maintains his occupational duty (*svadharma*) by taking shelter of his innate propensity will gradually become detached from these activities and become situated beyond the material modes.

svabhāva-vihita-vṛtti kariyā āśraya
niṣpāpa jīvane kara kṛṣṇa-nāmāśraya

Text 40

Śrīmad-Bhāgavatam (11.7.39) also says:

prāṇa-vṛttyaiva santuṣyen
munir naivendriya-priyaiḥ
jñānaṁ yathā na naśyeta
nāvakīryeta vāṅ-manaḥ

I have taken a lesson from the way in which the vital force within the body operates, that one should eat and drink only as much as is required to sustain the body. A *sādhaka* should also eat only what is needed to maintain his life. A *sādhaka* should not enjoy sense objects merely for his own gratification; otherwise his intelligence will become corrupted, his mind restless and his speech engaged in topics unrelated to Kṛṣṇa.

aprajalpe kara prāṇa-vṛtti aṅgīkāra
indriyera priya-vṛtti nā kara svīkāra

vāg-indriya mano-jñāna yāhe svāsthya pāya
ei rūpa āhāre yukta-vairāgya nā yāya

Text 41

Hari-bhakti-sudhodaya (8.51) explains that one should be careful about whom he associates with:

yasya yat-saṅgatiḥ puṁso
maṇivat syāt sa tad-guṇaḥ
sva-kularddhyai tato dhīmān
sva-yuthāny eva saṁśrayet

A person develops the qualities of the company he keeps, just as a crystal reflects the colour of those objects which are brought into its proximity. Therefore, by associating with pure devotees, one can himself become pure.

svayūthera maṅgala o anye rākhi' dūra
yathā saṅga yathā phala pāibe pracura

Bhajana-rahasya-vṛtti

Association with devotees (*sādhu-saṅga*) is the source of all auspiciousness. Where the scriptures give the instruction to be solitary (*niḥsaṅga*), it refers to keeping only *sādhu-saṅga*.

Text 42

With great effort one should follow the path delineated by the *mahājanas*. This is described in the *Skanda Purāṇa*:

sa mṛgyaḥ śreyasāṁ hetuḥ
panthaḥ santāpa-varjitaḥ
anavāpta-śramaṁ pūrve
yena santaḥ pratasthire

Only by following the path upon which previous great personalities (*mahājanas*) have easily traversed can we find ultimate auspiciousness and freedom from all suffering.

Text 43

Acquiring knowledge by hearing from scriptural authorities is the real path of *bhakti*. The *Brahma-yāmala* states:

śruti-smṛti-purāṇādi-
pañcarātra-vidhiṁ vinā
aikāntikī harer bhaktir
utpātāyaiva kalpate

One can only attain the one-pointedness, or *aikāntika-bhāva*, of pure *bhakti* by adopting the path of the previous *mahājanas*. It cannot be attained by leaving the path of the *mahājanas* and creating another path. Because Dattātreya, Buddha and later preachers were unable to understand pure *bhakti*, they accepted only a semblance of this transcendental sentiment. Dattātreya mixed it with *māyāvāda* and Buddha with atheism, and thus they set forth useless paths, describing them as one-pointed devotion (*aikāntikī-hari-bhakti*). In reality, however, the paths promoted by these people are not *hari-bhakti*; they are simply a disturbance.

pūrva-mahājana pathe cale anāyāse
nava-pathe utpāta āsiyā jīve nāśe

anartha-nāśera yatna kabhu nāhi yāra
nāma-kṛpā nāhi pāya durdaiva tāhāra

nāma-kṛpā vinā koṭi koṭi yatna kare
tāhāte anartha kabhu nāhi chāḍe tāre

niṣkapaṭe yatne kāṅde nāmera caraṇe
dūra haya anartha tāhāra alpa dine

anartha chāḍiyā kara śravaṇa-kīrtana
ekānta-bhāvete lao nāmera śaraṇa

Bhajana-rahasya-vṛtti

In *rāga-mārga-bhajana* there is no consideration of the rules of the Śruti, Smṛti, Purāṇas, *Nārada-pañcarātra* and so forth. The only consideration is to follow the inhabitants of Vraja. But for *sādhakas* eligible only for *vidhi-mārga*, it is necessary to adopt the path of devotion as given by the *mahājanas* such as Dhruva, Prahlāda, Nārada, Vyāsa and Śuka. Hence there is no other means for the *vaidha-bhaktas* except to follow the path of saintly persons.

Without the mercy of Nāma Prabhu, those who perform *bhajana* will be unable to give up their *anarthas*, even after millions of attempts. But if one sincerely weeps at the lotus feet of Nāma Prabhu, all one's *anarthas* will vanish within a few days. Giving up one's *anarthas* in this way, one should take exclusive shelter of the holy name and thereby hear and chant.

Text 44

Endeavours made in performing resolute *bhajana* are described in *Hari-bhakti-vilāsa*:

evam ekāntināṁ prāyaḥ
kīrtanaṁ smaraṇaṁ prabhoḥ
kurvatāṁ parama-prītyā
kṛtyamanyan na rocyate

bhāvena kenacit preṣṭha-
śrī-mūrter aṅghri-sevane
syād icchaiṣāṁ sva-mantreṇa
sva-rasenaiva tad-vidhiḥ

vihiteṣv eva nityeṣu
pravartante svayaṁ hite
sarva-tyāge 'py aheyāyāḥ
sarvānartha-bhuvaś ca te

kuryuḥ pratiṣṭhā-viṣṭhāyāḥ
yatnam asparśane varam
prabhāte cārdharāte ca
madhyāhne divasa-kṣaye
kīrtayanti hariṁ ye vai
na teṣām anya-sādhanam

If a one-pointed devotee (*aikāntika-bhakta*) chants and contemplates the glories of his Prabhu, Śrī Viṣṇu, with great affection and according to his transcendental sentiments, he will have no taste for any other activity. With whatever mood he desires to serve the lotus feet of his beloved deity, he performs *arcana* through his particular *mantra* and his particular mellow of devotion. That same service later transforms into his eternal service. Even if one has given up everything else, something still remains to be given up before this can happen – this is the desire for name and fame, *pratiṣṭhā*, the root cause of all *anarthas*. The prime duty is to give up this *pratiṣṭhā*, which is compared to stool. What to speak of touching this *pratiṣṭhā*, do not see it, even from a distance! For one who chants the name of Śrī Hari in the morning, noon, evening and midnight, no other *sādhana* is needed.

ekānta bhaktera mātra kīrtana-smaraṇa
anya parve ruci nāhi haya pravartana

bhāvera sahita haya śrī-kṛṣṇa-sevana
svārasikī-bhāva krame haya uddīpana

ekānta bhaktera kriyā-mudrā-rāgodita
tathāpi se saba nahe vidhi-viparīta

sarva-tyāga karileo chāḍā sukaṭhina
pratiṣṭhāśā tyāge yatna pāibe pravīṇa

prabhāte gabhīra rātre madhyāhne sandhyāya
anartha chāḍiyā lao nāmera āśraya

ei-rūpe kīrtana smaraṇa yei kare
kṛṣṇa-kṛpā haya śīghra, anāyāse tare

śraddhā kari sādhu-saṅge kṛṣṇa nāma laya
anartha sakala yāya niṣṭhā upajaya

prātaḥ-kāle nitya-līlā karibe cintana
cintite cintite bhāvera haibe sādhana

Text 45

Govinda-līlāmṛta (2.1) describes the early morning pastimes (*prātaḥ-līlā*) as follows:

rādhāṁ snāta-vibhūṣitāṁ vrajapayāhūtāṁ sakhībhiḥ prage
tad-gehe vihitānna-pāka-racanāṁ kṛṣṇāvaśeṣāśanām
kṛṣṇaṁ buddham avāpta-dhenu-sadanaṁ nirvyūḍha-go-dohanaṁ
susnātaṁ kṛta-bhojanaṁ saha-carais tāś cātha tāś cāśraye

After the *kuñja-bhaṅga-līlā*, or *niśānta-līlā* (pastimes at night's end), Śrī Rādhā-Śyāmasundara return to Their respective abodes and lay down on Their beds. The condition of Śrī Kiśorī in Jāvaṭa is indescribable as She burns in separation from Her beloved. Śrī Rūpa and Rati Mañjarīs are absorbed in their service to Her, and give Her encouragement as if again infusing Her with life. Sometimes Jaṭilā, sometimes Mukharā and sometimes Paurṇamāsī enter Śrī Kiśorī's quarters, and at this time Śyāmalā also comes. Kiśorī and Śyāmalā are immersed in a joking conversation. In this way the pastime develops in newer and newer ways. Rūpa, Rati and other *mañjarīs* ornament Śrīmatī by cleansing Her body, decorating Her and so forth, and at the same time they remind Her of Śrī Kṛṣṇa's pastimes.

rādhā snāta vibhūṣita, śrī-yaśodā-samāhuta,
sakhī-saṅge tad gṛhe gamana
tathā pāka-viracana, śrī-kṛṣṇāvaśeṣāśana,
madhye-madhye duṅhāra milana

kṛṣṇa nidrā parihari, goṣṭhe go-dohana kari,
snānāśana sahacara saṅge
ei līlā cintā kara, nāma-preme garagara,
prāte bhakta-jana-saṅge raṅge

ei līlā cinta āra kara saṅkīrtana
acire pāibe tumi bhāva-uddīpana

Bhajana-rahasya-vṛtti

Śrī Kiśorī and Her *sakhīs* depart for Nanda-bhavana. On the way they meet Śrī Śyāmasundara and many pastimes full of *rasa* take place. Our Gosvāmīs have revealed these pastimes in their writings. Upon reaching Nanda-bhavana, Kiśorī starts to cook in the midst of countless stoves, and prepares many tasty dishes.

Śyāmasundara is sleeping in His home. Yaśodā-maiyā awakens Him and, seeing the nail-marks on the body of her dear son (*lālā*), she becomes sad and says, "The limbs of my *lālā* are as soft as the petals of a blue lotus. Why have the boys hurt Him in their wrestling matches? And so much *dhātu-rāga* (colour from minerals) is on His limbs. Alas, alas! What to do? I do not know how to put an end to this."

Kundalatā jokingly says, "Your *lālā* is performing *rāsa* at night." But the word *rāsa* is unknown to Yaśodā-maiyā. Then, after expressing affection for His mother, Śyāmasundara jumps up from bed and goes to milk the cows. Upon His return He bathes, eats and then leaves for cowherding. Kiśorī shyly accepts some of Her *priyatama's* remnants and returns to Jāvaṭa with Her *sakhīs*.

Many other pastimes take place amidst all these *līlās*, and it would be very difficult to describe them all. A *premi-bhakta* performs *bhajana* while remembering these pastimes, which are alluded to here, and tastes their *rasa* even in the stage of *sādhana.*

Thus ends the *Dvitīya-yāma-sādhana,*
Prātaḥ-kālīya-bhajana, of *Śrī-Bhajana-rahasya.*

3

Tṛtīya-yāma-sādhana

Pūrvāhna-kālīya-bhajana – niṣṭhā-bhajana

(from six *daṇḍas* until two *praharas*:
approximately 8.30 A.M. – 11.00 A.M.)

Text 1

The third verse of *Śikṣāṣṭaka* describes the qualification for *nāma-saṅkīrtana* and the process for chanting the holy name:

tṛṇād api sunīcena
taror api sahiṣṇunā
amāninā mānadena
kīrtanīyaḥ sadā hariḥ

Thinking oneself to be even lower and more worthless than insignificant grass that has been trampled beneath everyone's feet, being more tolerant than a tree, being prideless and offering respect to everyone according to their respective positions, one should continuously chant the holy name of Śrī Hari.

ye rūpe laile nāma prema upajaya
tāra lakṣaṇa-śloka śuna, svarūpa-rāmarāya

uttama hañā āpanāke māne tṛṇādhama
dui prakāre sahiṣṇutā kare vṛkṣa sama

vṛkṣa yena kāṭileha kichu nā bolaya
śukāiñā maileha kāre pānī nā māgaya

yei ye māgaye, tāre deya āpana dhana
gharma-vṛṣṭi sahe, ānera karaye rakṣaṇa

uttama hañā vaiṣṇava ha'be nirabhimāna
jīve sammāna dibe jāni 'kṛṣṇa'-adhiṣṭhāna

Bhajana-rahasya-vṛtti

Four symptoms are observed in *sādhakas* who chant the holy name of Śrī Kṛṣṇa free from all offences: (1) natural humility born of complete detachment from sense objects, (2) pure compassion devoid of envy, (3) purity of heart and freedom from false ego, and (4) an attitude of respect towards everyone according to their position.

Taror api sahiṣṇunā refers to the tolerance of a tree. A tree is so tolerant that it does not forget to show kindness by offering its cool shade and sweet fruits even to the person who comes to cut it down. Since Kṛṣṇa's devotees are even more merciful than a tree, they show kindness to all, both friend and enemy. This is compassion completely free from envy. Although such devotees are topmost in the kingdom of *bhakti*, they remain free from pride. They know that Kṛṣṇa resides in the hearts of all living entities, and therefore give all living entities appropriate respect. Such persons are truly eligible to perform *śrī-kṛṣṇa-nāma-kīrtana*, and only performers of *śrī-kṛṣṇa-nāma-kīrtana* attain *kṛṣṇa-prema*.

Text 2

The features of surrender (*śaraṇāgati*) are given in the *Vaiṣṇava-tantra* (*Hari-bhakti-vilāsa* (11.676)):

ānukūlyasya saṅkalpaḥ
prātikūlyasya varjanam
rakṣiṣyatīti viśvāso
goptṛtve varaṇaṁ tathā
ātma-nikṣepa-kārpaṇye
ṣaḍ-vidhā śaraṇāgatiḥ

The six types of surrender are: (1) to accept that which is favourable to *kṛṣṇa-bhakti*; (2) to reject that which is unfavourable; (3) to have the strong faith "Bhagavān will protect me"; (4) to have dependence, thinking "Bhagavān will take care of me"; (5) to be fully self-surrendered (*ātma-samarpaṇa*); and (6) to be humble.

bhakti-anukūla yāhā tāhāi svīkāra
bhakti-pratikūla saba kari parihāra

kṛṣṇa vai rakṣā-kartā āra keha nāi
kṛṣṇa se pālana more karibena bhāi

āmi āmāra yata kichu kṛṣṇe nivedana
niṣkapaṭa dainye kari jīvana-yāpana

Bhajana-rahasya-vṛtti

The symptom of *śaraṇāgati* in one-pointed devotees is that they perpetually engage in service to their Prabhu and accept whatever He arranges. Such devotees accept whatever punishment is given by Bhagavān as His mercy. They know that every action takes place only due to the desire of Kṛṣṇa; therefore they unite their desire with Kṛṣṇa's and thus remain peaceful. A devotee does not think that Kṛṣṇa has sent him to this world to suffer miseries, but that he chose the miseries of the world by misusing his independence. The symptom of *śaraṇāgati* is that one gives up the false conception of being the doer and takes shelter of *guru* and Vaiṣṇavas. The intrinsic characteristic (*svarūpa-lakṣaṇa*) of surrender is acceptance of Śrī Kṛṣṇa as one's maintainer (*goptṛtve varaṇam*). The remaining five symptoms are the marginal characteristics (*taṭastha-lakṣaṇa*) of *śaraṇāgati*.

Firm faith that "Śrī Kṛṣṇa will always maintain me" is the meaning of *goptṛtve varaṇam*. In *Bhagavad-gītā* Śrī Kṛṣṇa says: "*teṣāṁ nityābhiyuktānāṁ yoga-kṣemaṁ vahāmy aham* – for those who are always absorbed in thoughts of Me, and who worship Me by every means and with one-pointed devotion, I Myself preserve what they have and carry what they lack." He also says, "My devotees will never be destroyed."

In the second and third verses of his *Upadeśāmṛta*, Śrīla Rūpa Gosvāmī has explained two of the marginal characteristics of *śaraṇāgati*: to accept what is favourable for *bhakti* (*ānukūlyasya saṅkalpaḥ*) and to give up what is unfavourable (*prātikūlyasya varjanam*). These two verses were explained in detail in the second chapter of this book.

Text 3

One must first give up the false identification with this material body (*deha-abhimāna*). The *Mukunda-mālā* (37) states:

idaṁ śarīraṁ śata-sandhi-jarjaraṁ
pataty avaśyaṁ pariṇāma-peśalam
kim auṣadhaṁ pṛcchasi mūḍha durmate
nirāmayaṁ kṛṣṇa-rasāyanaṁ piba

This frail body, which is made of five elements and connected by hundreds of joints, is certain to decline. Consequently, the body will be burnt to ashes or will become food for worms and transformed into excrement. O foolish and wicked mind, you have decorated such a disgusting body with a senseless attachment. The elixir of *śrī-kṛṣṇa-nāma* is the only powerful medicine to cure this disease of material existence. You should constantly drink it by incessantly chanting Kṛṣṇa's holy name.

śata sandhi-jara-jara, tava ei kalevara,
patana haibe eka-dina
bhasma, kṛmi, viṣṭhā ha'be, sakalera ghṛṇya tabe,
ihāte mamatā arvācīna

ore mana, śuna mora e satya-vacana,
e rogera mahauṣadhi, kṛṣṇa-nāma niravadhi,
nirāmaya kṛṣṇa-rasāyana

Bhajana-rahasya-vṛtti

One should endeavour to serve Govinda and not painstakingly try to protect this short-lived temporary body. No matter how much one tries to protect this body, which is made of five elements, its destruction is inevitable. Therefore this Text says, "O wicked mind, give up performing *aṣṭāṅga-yoga*, physical exercises and so forth to keep this body fit, and only drink the nectar of Kṛṣṇa's holy name. Only this nectar can liberate you from the cycle of birth and death. By the mercy of *nāma* you will attain the eternal abode of Kṛṣṇa and a transcendental body suitable for rendering service there. Then you will be engaged in your *nitya-sevā*."

Text 4

One should be tolerant like a tree and compassionate to all *jīvas*. In *Śrīmad-Bhāgavatam* (3.9.12) Śrī Brahmā says:

nātiprasīdati tathopacitopacārair
ārādhitaḥ sura-gaṇair hṛdi baddha-kāmaiḥ
yat sarva-bhūta-dayayāsad-alabhyayaiko
nānā-janeṣv avahitaḥ suhṛd antar-ātmā

O Bhagavān, You are situated in the hearts of all living entities as the supremely benevolent Supersoul. Because of Your compassionate nature, You always remain pleasing to everyone, but You cannot be attained by the non-devotees.

bahu upacārārpaṇe, pūji' kāmī deva-gaṇe,
prasannatā nā la'bhe tomāra
sarva-bhūte dayā kari', bhaje akhilātmā hari,
tāre kṛpā tomāra apāra

Bhajana-rahasya-vṛtti

Śrī Brahmā is praying at the lotus feet of Bhagavān, "O Bhagavān, You are situated as the Supersoul in all living entities. You are everyone's friend and, despite being unattainable for the non-devotees, You are always merciful to everyone. The demigods worship You so that You will be pleased and fulfil their various material desires. Due to Your merciful nature, You grant their wishes, for You have said in *Bhagavad-gītā* (4.11): '*ye yathā māṁ prapadyante tāṁs tathaiva bhajāmy aham* – as all surrender unto Me and worship Me, I reciprocate accordingly.' However, You always give special mercy to Your devotees. Although Your mercy is distributed everywhere, You have special affection for Your devotees. This is not a mixture of contradictory qualities."

According to *Bhagavad-gītā* (9.29):

samo 'haṁ sarva-bhūteṣu
na me dveṣyo 'sti na priyaḥ
ye bhajanti tu māṁ bhaktyā
mayi te teṣu cāpy aham

I am equal to all living beings and am neither inimical nor partial to anyone. But as those who serve Me with devotion are attached to Me, so I too am bound by affection for them.

Text 5

The glory of the virtue of giving respect to devotees is described in the *Mukunda-mālā* (35):

śṛṇvan sato bhagavato guṇa-kīrtanāni
dehe na yasya pulakodgama-roma-rājiḥ
notpadyate nayanayor vimalāmbu-mālā
dhik tasya jīvitam aho puruṣādhamasya

If upon hearing the *kīrtana* of Hari's name, form, qualities and pastimes from the mouths of *guru* and Vaiṣṇavas, one's bodily hairs do not stand erect in ecstasy, his heart does not melt, and tears do not flow from his eyes, alas! the life of such a wretched person is condemned.

sādhu-mukhe yei jana, kṛṣṇa-nāma-guṇa-gaṇa,
śuniyā nā haila pulakita
nayane vimala jala, nā vahila anargala,
se vā kena rahila jīvita

Bhajana-rahasya-vṛtti

Sādhakas performing *bhajana* condemn their lives and repent in this way: "Alas! Even though I have heard *hari-kathā* from the mouths of saintly persons, my hard heart does not melt. This is the result of my offences. The heart of one who just once hears the glories of Kṛṣṇa's name melts immediately. But my heart has not realised this truth, and thus my life is condemned."

There is a story in this regard. There was a person who would come to hear *hari-kathā* in an assembly of *sādhus*. Upon hearing the *hari-kathā*, everyone present would be saturated with bliss, but the heart of this man bore no change. He became very remorseful about this. The next day, while hearing *hari-kathā*, he rubbed red chilli powder in his eyes, which then poured forth a shower of tears. The Vaiṣṇava giving the *hari-kathā* noticed this. When the narrations were finished, he called him over and praised him by saying, "The scriptures say those senses that refuse to perform *kṛṣṇa-bhajana* should be punished, and today you have put this into practice. *Śrīmad-Bhāgavatam* says, 'It is useless to keep those senses that are not engaged in the service of Bhagavān.'" When the man heard this, a stream of real tears flowed from his eyes.

Text 6

Knowledge of Kṛṣṇa's glories is described in the *Mukunda-mālā* (43):

kṛṣṇo rakṣati no jagat-traya-guruḥ kṛṣṇo hi viśvambharaḥ
kṛṣṇād eva samutthitaṁ jagad idaṁ kṛṣṇe layaṁ gacchati
kṛṣṇe tiṣṭhati viśvam etad akhilaṁ kṛṣṇasya dāsā vayaṁ
kṛṣṇenākhila sad-gatir-vitaritā kṛṣṇāya tasmai namaḥ

Śrī Kṛṣṇa, the *guru* of the three worlds, protects us. Viśvambhara Kṛṣṇa maintains the entire universe in all ways. This world is manifested by Kṛṣṇa – that is, by His external potency (*bahiraṅga-śakti*) – and at the proper time (during *pralaya*) the entire creation again merges into Him. Kṛṣṇa pervades the entire world; the entire world is situated within Him. Śrī Kṛṣṇa manifests all wealth and opulence. We are all Kṛṣṇa's eternal servants. I offer my respects unto this Śrī Kṛṣṇa.

jagad-guru kṛṣṇa sabe karena rakṣaṇa
kṛṣṇa viśvambhara viśva karena pālana

kṛṣṇa haite ei viśva hañāche udaya
avaśeṣe ei viśva kṛṣṇe haya laya

kṛṣṇe viśva avasthita, jīva kṛṣṇadāsa
sad-gati-pradātā kṛṣṇe karaha viśvāsa

janama layecha kṛṣṇa-bhakti karibāre
kṛṣṇa-bhakti vinā saba mithyā e saṁsāre

Bhajana-rahasya-vṛtti

As *sādhakas* chant Kṛṣṇa's names, they repeatedly sing the glories of those names. They offer Him obeisances and pray at His lotus feet: "O Kṛṣṇa, save my life by giving me Your *darśana.* You are the provider and maintainer of the entire world, and thus Your name, Viśvambhara, has become meaningful. Since I am also residing in this world, please protect me. From You come the creation, maintenance and destruction of this world. Millions of universes are situated in each and every pore of Your body. Because I am present in this world, I am also Your insignificant servant, so please bestow Your mercy upon me. Prabhu, by Your causeless mercy, You have arranged that the living entities take birth in human bodies only so they can perform *bhagavad-bhajana,* without which this entire universe is useless. As this *bhakti* cannot be received without Your mercy, please bestow that mercy upon me."

Furthermore *Śrī Caitanya-bhāgavata* (*Madhya-khaṇḍa* 2.202) states:

jagatera pitā kṛṣṇa je nā bhaje bāpa
pitṛ-drohī pātakīra janme-janme tāpa

Śrī Kṛṣṇa is the father of the universe. Although a person may perform duties to his mother, father, wife, children and so on, if he does not perform *bhajana* of his original eternal father, he is offensive to that father (*pitṛ-drohī*) and he will be scorched by the threefold miseries of *māyā,* birth after birth.

Śrī Caitanya-caritāmṛta (*Ādi-līlā* 6.85) states:

keha māne, kehā nā māne, saba taṅra dāsa
ye nā māne, tāra haya sei pāpe nāśa

Some accept Him whereas others do not, yet everyone is His servant. One who does not accept Him, however, will be ruined by his sinful activities.

The scriptures also state:

daśāśvamedhī punar eti janmani
kṛṣṇa-praṇāmī na punar bhavāya

Even a person who performs ten horse sacrifices takes birth again in this world. But he who offers obeisances to Kṛṣṇa just once does not return.

O Kṛṣṇa, I eternally offer my constant obeisances at Your lotus feet, which bring one fearlessness.

Text 7

Great eagerness in *kṛṣṇa-bhajana* is described in the *Mukunda-mālā* (33):

kṛṣṇa tvadīya-pada-paṅkaja-pañjarāntam
adyaiva me viśatu mānasa-rāja-haṁsaḥ
prāṇa-prayāṇa-samaye kapha-vāta-pittaiḥ
kaṇṭhāvarodhana-vidhau bhajanaṁ kutas te

O Kṛṣṇa, my request is that the swan of my mind be confined in the cage of Your lotus feet and dwell there in the ocean of *rasa.* At the time of death the throat will be choked up with mucus, air and bile. Under such conditions, how will it be possible to remember Your name?

vṛthā dina yāya more majiyā saṁsāre
e mānasa-rāja-haṁsa bhajuka tomāre

adyai tomāra pāda-paṅkaja-pañjare
baddha ha'ye thākuka haṁsa rasera sāgare

e prāṇa prayāṇa-kāle kapha vāta pitta
karibeka kaṇṭharodha apraphulla citta

takhana jihvāya nā sphuribe tava nāma
samaya chāḍile kise ha'be siddhakāma

Bhajana-rahasya-vṛtti

As a person who is inclined to perform *nāma-bhajana* increases his chanting of the holy name, feelings of repentance increase in his aching heart. Even though he is chanting *harināma* day and night, he thinks, "Alas, my mind has dwelled on material objects and thus my days have passed in vain. My mind is not fixed at the lotus feet of Nāma Prabhu. O Prabhu, how will I be delivered? It is my request at Your lotus feet that my swan-like mind be confined in the cage of Your lotus feet and always drink nectar. At the time of death, when mucus, air, bile and so forth choke my throat, how will I drink the nectar of Your name? If at that time Your name does not appear on my tongue, how will I be able to attain perfection? O Prabhu, I pray at Your lotus feet that at the time of death, I will give up my body while constantly chanting Your holy name."

Text 8

The following six verses of the *Yāmuna-stotra* (which comprise Texts 8–13) illustrate the poet Yāmunācārya's own humility:

na dharma-niṣṭho 'smi na cātma-vedī
na bhaktimāṁs tvac-caraṇāravinde
akiñcano 'nanya-gatiḥ śaraṇya
tvat-pāda-mūlaṁ śaraṇaṁ prapadye

I am not devoted to *dharma*, nor do I have any knowledge of the soul, and my heart has no devotion for Your lotus feet. O protector, being destitute, I take shelter of You. I have no shelter other than You. You have come as the saviour of the fallen to deliver such a wretched fallen soul as me. I am Your eternal servant and You are my eternal master.

hari he!
dharma-niṣṭhā nāhi mora, ātma-bodha vā sundara,
bhakti nāi tomāra caraṇe
ataeva akiñcana, gati-hīna duṣṭa-jana,
rata sadā āpana-vañcane

patita-pāvana tumi, patita adhama āmi,
tumi mora eka-mātra gati
tava pāda-mūle painu, tomāra śaraṇa lainu,
āmi dāsa tumi nitya-pati

Bhajana-rahasya-vṛtti

The *sādhaka* prays to Bhagavān in a meek and destitute mood, "O Prabhu, I have no devotion to *dharma*, no *bhakti* and no *jñāna*, so how can I remember Your lotus feet? You are the saviour of the fallen (*patita-pāvana*); You even give those who are poor and lowly a place at Your lotus feet. Therefore please deliver me, this degraded soul. Then Your name, Patita-pāvana, will become meaningful."

Text 9

na ninditaṁ karma tad asti loke
sahasraśo yan na mayā vyadhāyi
so 'haṁ vipākāvasare mukunda
krandāmi sampraty agatis tavāgre

O Prabhu! O Hari! There is no wicked or sinful activity I have not performed thousands and thousands of times, and I will suffer for them. O Mukunda, I see that besides You there is no other shelter. I am constantly crying, praying before You. If You so desire, punish me; for You are the ruler of this destitute body.

hena duṣṭa karma nāi, yāhā āmi kari nāi,
sahasra-sahasra bāra hari
sei saba karma-phala, peye avasara bala,
āmāya piśiche yantropari

gati nāhi dekhi āra, kāndi hari ānivāra,
tomāra agrete ebe āmi
yā' tomāra haya mane, daṇḍa deha akiñcane,
tumi mora daṇḍa-dhara svāmī

Bhajana-rahasya-vṛtti

"O Lord, birth after birth I have performed innumerable sinful and contemptible activities. To describe them all to You is not even possible; but as You are omniscient, You know of them anyway. So now I come before You, clasping a piece of straw between my teeth, humbly requesting You to please deliver me, even by giving me punishment. O Prabhu, as a result of my numerous offences, *māyā* crushes me just as one crushes a stick of sugar cane. My tearful request to You is to please purify this destitute person by punishing him. Since You give liberation to the *jīvas*, one of Your names is Mukunda. Therefore please liberate me from these sins and bestow upon me service to Your lotus feet."

Śrīla Kṛṣṇadāsa Kavirāja Gosvāmī says in *Śrī Caitanya-caritāmṛta* (*Ādi-līlā* 5.205, 207):

jagāi mādhāi haite muñi se pāpiṣṭa
purīṣera kīṭa haite muñi se laghiṣṭa

emana nirghṛṇṇā more kebā kṛpā kare
eka nityānanda vinā jagata bhitare

I am more sinful than Jagāi and Mādhāi and even lower than a worm in stool. Who in this world but Nityānanda could show His mercy to such an abominable person as me?

Text 10

nimajjato 'nanta bhavārṇavāntaś
cirāya me kūlam ivāsi labdhaḥ
tvayāpi labdhaṁ bhagavann idānīm
anuttamaṁ pātram idaṁ dayāyāḥ

O Ananta, since time immemorial I have been drowning in this unlimited ocean of material existence. The hope of one day attaining Your lotus feet is the shore of this ocean. Immersed in this material existence, I am tearfully praying to You with a distressed voice to please appear as *guru* and deliver me.

nija-karma-doṣa-phale, paḍi' bhavārṇava jale,
hābu ḍubu khāi kata kāla
sāṅtāri sāṅtāri yāi, sindhu anta nāhi pāi,
bhava-sindhu ananta viśāla
nimagna haiyā yabe, ḍākinu kātara rave,
keha more karaha uddhāra
sei kāle āile tumi, tava pada-kūla-bhūmi,
āśā-bīja haila āmāra
tumi hari dayāmaya, pāile more suniścaya,
sarvottama bhājana dayāra

Bhajana-rahasya-vṛtti

"O Lord, as a result of my previous activities I am submerged in the ocean of material existence, where many kinds of reactions are rising as huge waves, tormenting me with happiness and distress. This path of *karma* has no beginning and no end. I do not know how to swim in this vast ocean, and the crocodiles of lust, anger and so forth are eating my body. O Lord, please rescue me! You are my only hope. I now relinquish dependence on my own strength, and instead am taking shelter of Your lotus feet. I have heard from the *mahājanas* that You give mercy according to the extent of a person's fallen condition. As You protected the elephant Gajendra with Your disc, please save me from this crocodile-like ocean of material existence. Prabhu, I have also heard that You are the pinnacle of compassion. Please understand that I am fallen and wretched. Even if someone searches the entire universe, he will not find any better object for this compassion than I. Knowing this, kindly bestow Your mercy upon me."

Text 11

bhavantam evānucaran nirantaraḥ
praśānta-niḥśeṣa-mano-rathāntaraḥ
kadāham aikāntika-nitya-kiṅkaraḥ
praharṣayiṣyāmi sanātha-jīvitam

All mental creations and desires are alleviated and the mind pacified by uninterrupted service to You. When will I be designated as Your eternal servant? When will I be radiant with joy, having obtained such a competent master as You?

āmi baḍa duṣṭamati, nā dekhiyā anya-gati,
tava pade la'yechi śaraṇa
jāniyāchi ebe nātha, tumi prabhu jagannātha,
āmi tava nitya parijana

sei dina kabe habe, aikāntika-bhāve yabe,
nitya-dāsya-bhāva pāba āmi
manorathāntara yata, niḥśeṣa haibe svataḥ,
sevāya tuṣiba ohe svāmi

Bhajana-rahasya-vṛtti

While chanting, the *sādhaka* prays as follows: "O Prabhu, You are the Lord of the universe and I am Your servant, but because of being opposed to serving You, I have gone far away from You. Now I am tormented by the three kinds of afflictions of Your *māyā*. Please bestow the mercy of Your lotus feet upon this unfortunate person. Prabhu, when will that auspicious day come when illusory desires leave my heart and I become Your unalloyed servant? At that time I will please You by fulfilling Your inner desire (*manobhīṣṭa-sevā*)."

Text 12

aparādha-sahasra-bhājanaṁ
patitaṁ bhīma-bhavārṇavodare
agatiṁ śaraṇāgataṁ hare
kṛpayā kevalam ātmasāt-kuru

O Hari, I am an offender, guilty of thousands of offences and therefore punishable. I am drowning in this fearsome ocean of material existence. Lost, I take shelter of Your lotus feet; please make me Your own. You have promised that You will definitely deliver anyone who has taken shelter of You. Please therefore deliver me also.

āmi aparādhī jana, sadā daṇḍya durlakṣaṇa,
sahasra-sahasra doṣe doṣī
bhīma bhavārṇavodare, patita viṣama-ghore,
gati-hīna gati-abhilāṣī

hare tava pada-dvaye, śaraṇa lainu bhaye,
kṛpā kari' kara ātmasāt
tomāra pratijñā ei, śaraṇa laibe yei,
tumi tāre uddhāribe nātha

Bhajana-rahasya-vṛtti

"O Lord, I am suffering punishment for my thousands and thousands of offences. As a fallen soul amidst the towering waves of the fearful ocean of material existence, I am without shelter. Sometimes the waves in this ocean submerge me, and sometimes they lift me up and knock me down again. In this condition, You who deliver persons from the ocean of material existence are my only friend. Please be merciful to me and make me Your own. I have heard from the mouths of *sādhus* that You certainly deliver those who have surrendered unto You. This is Your promise. Therefore, O Lord, I am situated at Your lotus feet with the hope and faith that You will surely deliver me."

Text 13

na mṛṣā paramārtham eva me
śṛṇu vijñāpanam ekam agrataḥ
yadi me na dayiṣyase tato
dayanīyas tava nātha durlabhaḥ

O Hari, I am submitting at Your lotus feet a petition in which there is not the slightest untruth. You may or may not be merciful to me, but my complete prayer, which is full of meaning, is that if You are not merciful to me, then it will be impossible for You to find a more suitable candidate for Your mercy in this entire material existence. Your name is Dayāmaya, "one who is full of mercy". Therefore, if You do not make me the object of Your merciful sidelong glance, Your name will be disgraced.

agre eka nivedana, kari madhunisūdana,
śuna kṛpā kariyā āmāya
nirarthaka kathā naya, nigūḍhārthamaya haya,
hṛdaya haite bāhirāya

ati apakṛṣṭa āmi, parama dayālu tumi,
more dayā tava adhikāra
ye yata patita haya, tava dayā tata tāya,
tāte āmi supātra dayāra

more yadi upekṣibe, dayā-pātra kothā pā'be,
dayāmaya nāmaṭi tomāra

Bhajana-rahasya-vṛtti

"O merciful Madhusūdana, I have a prayer to present before Your lotus feet that comes from the core of my heart. Do not neglect my prayer, thinking it meaningless, because in this whole material existence You will not find a more wretched person than I. If You neglect me, whom will You accept as a fit candidate for Your mercy? Make Your compassionate name successful by bestowing Your mercy upon me."

Text 14

Freedom from pride is described in the *Yāmuna-stotra*:

amaryādaḥ kṣudraś cala matir asūyā-prasava-bhūḥ
kṛta-ghno durmānī smara-para-vaśo rakṣaṇa-paraḥ
nṛśaṁsaḥ pāpiṣṭhaḥ katham aham ito duḥkha-jaladher
apārād uttīrṇas tava paricareyaṁ caraṇayoḥ

I am disrespectful, vile, fickle-minded, full of envy, ungrateful, dependent on others, cruel and most sinful. In this condition, how can I cross this impassable ocean of material existence and attain the service of Your lotus feet?

ami ta' cañcala-mati, amaryāda kṣudra ati,
asūyā prasava sadā mora
pāpiṣṭha kṛta-ghna mānī, nṛśaṁsa vañcane jñānī,
kāma-vaśe thāki sadā ghora

e hena durjana ha'ye, e duḥkha-jaladhi va'ye,
calitechi saṁsāra-sāgare
kemane e bhavāmbudhi, pāra ha'ye niravadhi,
tava pada-sevā mile more

Bhajana-rahasya-vṛtti

"O Lord, I am a disrespectful, vile *jīva* wandering in this material existence. I am fickle-minded, full of envy, ungrateful and dependent on others. Please save this wretched person from this condition! Without Your mercy there is no other means of rescue from this ocean that is so difficult to cross. I offer millions and millions of obeisances at Your feet. Please save me and engage me in service to Your lotus feet."

Text 15

Respect for devotees is described in the *Yāmuna-stotra*:

tava dāsya-sukhaika-saṅgināṁ
bhavaneṣv astv api kīṭa-janma me
itarāvasatheṣu mā sma bhūd
api janma catur-mukhātmanā

O Bhagavān, if I take birth again due to my past activities, or by Your desire, please let it be in the home of a devotee, even if that birth is in the body of an insect. I have no desire to take birth in a household devoid of devotion to You, even if it has the opulence of Brahmā. O Puruṣottama, this is my earnest prayer unto You.

veda-vidhi-anusāre, karma kari' e saṁsāre,
jīva punaḥ punaḥ janma pāya
pūrva-kṛta karma-phale, tomāra vā icchā-bale,
janma yadi labhi punarāya

tabe eka kathā mama, śuna he puruṣottama,
tava dāsa saṅgi-jana-ghare
kīṭa-janma yadi haya, tāhāte o dayāmaya,
rahiba he santuṣṭa antare

tava dāsa-saṅga-hīna, ye gṛhastha arvācīna,
tā'ra gṛhe caturmukha-bhūti
nā cāi kakhana hari, kara-dvaya yoḍa kari',
kare tava kiṅkara minati

Bhajana-rahasya-vṛtti

"O Lord, I have heard from *guru* and Vaiṣṇavas that the living entity is wandering in the cycle of birth and death according to his past activities. Prabhu, even if according to my auspicious and inauspicious *karma* I take birth in this material world, there is no cause for grief. However, my earnest petition at Your lotus feet is that even if I have to take the low birth of an insect or dog as a result of my *karma*, please let it be in the home of a devotee so that I will have the association of the saintly Vaiṣṇavas. I have no desire to take birth in a very rich family that is opposed to You, even though its wealth may be compared to that of Brahmā. I have heard from the scriptures that *bhakti* is born of *sādhu-saṅga*:

kṛṣṇa-bhakti-janma-mūla haya 'sādhu-saṅga'
kṛṣṇa-prema janme, teṅho punaḥ mukhya aṅga

Śrī Caitanya-caritāmṛta (*Madhya-līlā* 22.83)

The root cause of *kṛṣṇa-bhakti* is *sādhu-saṅga*. Even when one's dormant *kṛṣṇa-prema* awakens, *sādhu-saṅga* is still most essential.

"O Merciful One, whether I live in heaven, hell or anywhere else, I will hear about Your lotus feet, sing their glories and meditate upon them."

Text 16

Humility that is full of self-surrender is described in the *Yāmuna-stotra* (52):

vapur-ādiṣu yo 'pi ko 'pi vā
guṇato 'sāni yathā-tathā-vidhaḥ
tad ayaṁ tava pāda-padmayor
aham adyaiva mayā samarpitaḥ

O Bhagavān, in this material existence there are the bodily distinctions of male and female, and according to the three modes of material nature (*sattva, rajas* and *tamas*) there are the divisions of the four *varṇas* and four *āśramas*. In this way humanity is unlimitedly variegated. O Prāṇeśvara, let me take birth in any kind of body or in any condition; it does not matter, because now I am completely surrendered unto Your lotus feet and there is nothing I consider mine.

strī-puruṣa-deha-gata, varṇa-ādi-dharma yata,
tāte punaḥ deha-gata bheda
sattva-rajas-tamo-guṇa, āśrayete bheda punaḥ,
ei rūpa sahasra prabheda

ye kona śarīre thāki, ye avasthā guṇa rākhi,
se ahaṁtā ebe tava pāya
sampilāma prāṇeśvara, mama bali' ataḥpara,
āra kichu nā rahila dāya

Bhajana-rahasya-vṛtti

Here humility that is full of self-surrender is expressed. While chanting the holy name, the *sādhaka*, in a mood of distress, submits a humble petition at the lotus feet of Bhagavān: "O Bhagavān, giving up this false identification with the material male or female body, with social classification and so on, I surrender this body at Your lotus feet. Prāṇeśvara, You only are my life."

As long as the *jīva* falsely identifies with the gross and subtle body, he cannot enter pure *bhajana*. When the living entity is established in the mood of the verse taught by Śrīman Mahāprabhu – *nāhaṁ vipro na ca nara-patir nāpi*[1] – or in other words, when he has become free from all material designations, the door to the realm of *bhajana* opens.

[1] This verse, from Rūpa Gosvāmī's *Padyāvalī* (74), is found on p. 248.

Text 17

An ideal example of sincere humility is given in *Kṛṣṇa-karṇāmṛta* (30):

nibaddha-mūrdhāñjalir eṣa yāce
nīrandhra-dainyonnati-mukta-kaṇṭham
dayā-nidhe deva bhavat kaṭākṣaṁ
dākṣiṇya-leśena sakṛn niṣiñca

O Deva! O Ocean of Mercy! With folded hands raised to my head, I humbly offer this prayer to You: please, just once, shower me with Your merciful sidelong glance.

mastake añjali bāndhi' ei duṣṭa-jana kāndi,
niṣkapaṭa dainya mukta-svare
phūkāri', phūkāri' kaya, ohe deva dayāmaya,
dākṣiṇya prakāśi' antaḥpare

kṛpā-dṛṣṭi ekabāra karaha siñcana
tave e-janera prāṇa haibe rakṣaṇa

Bhajana-rahasya-vṛtti

In this verse Līlāśuka Bilvamaṅgala Ṭhākura prays in a distressed voice, induced by the humility caused by the feelings of separation (*viraha*) felt by Śrī Rādhā. When Śrī Kṛṣṇa left for Mathurā, He was separated from Rādhā and lived far away (*sudūra-pravāsa*). Śrīmatī Rādhikā, agitated by extreme separation, spoke with great humility to a bumblebee (*Śrīmad-Bhāgavatam* (10.47.21)): "*smarati sa pitṛ-gehān* – O bumblebee, does *ārya-putra* (the son of a noble person) remember us?" She also asked, "Upon happily returning from Ujjain, will He come to Vṛndāvana?" When Kṛṣṇa disappeared from the *rāsa* dance, She cried out (*Śrīmad-Bhāgvatam* (10.30.40)): "*dāsyāste kṛpaṇāyā me sakhe darśaya sannidhim* – O Lord! I am Your maidservant. Please show Yourself and make Me satisfied."

Desirous of this kind of humility, Śrī Līlāśuka is saying, "O Kṛṣṇa, make me a traveller on the pathway of Your eyes. Please give me service to You. Only by Your mercy can I serve in Your intimate, secret *nikuñja-līlās*. Upon attaining this service, the *jīva* becomes forever successful. If I am unqualified for this service, then let me worship You, immersed in these sentiments. I am an offender; nonetheless, You are an ocean of mercy. I beg You, therefore, do not pay attention to my faults, and please make the creeper of my desire bear fruit. This is my prayer unto You."

Text 18

Kṛṣṇa-karṇāmṛta (29) states:

mayi prasādaṁ madhuraiḥ kaṭākṣair
vaṁśī-ninādānucarair vidhehi
tvayi prasanne kim ihā parair nas
tvayy aprasanne kim ihā parair naḥ

O Kṛṣṇa, kindly bestow Your mercy upon me through Your sweet sidelong glances, which are accompanied by the sound of Your flute. When You are pleased with me, there is no harm if others are not. But if You become displeased, even if others are pleased, what is the use?

madhura kaṭākṣa-vaṁśī-ninādera saha
āmāke prasāda kari' tava pade laha

prasanna haile tumi anya-prasannatā
prayojana kivā mora, ei mora kathā

tava prasannatā vinā anyera prasāde
ki kārya āmāra bala kahinu avādhe

ei rūpa niṣṭhā saha karile kīrtana
acire haibe ruci, pābe prema-dhana

pūrvāhna-kālera līlā ei rūpa haya
nāmāśrāya-kāle cintā kara mahāśaya

Bhajana-rahasya-vṛtti

Remembering Her previous amorous sports (*vilāsa*) with Śrī Kṛṣṇa in the *kuñjas*, Śrī Rādhikā becomes restless in separation from Him (*Śrīmad-Bhāgavatam* (10.47.21)): "*kvacid api sa kathā naḥ kiṅkarīṇāṁ gṛṇīte bhujam aguru-sugandhaṁ mūrdhny adhāsyat kadā nu* – will Kṛṣṇa again place His cooling hand, which is more fragrant than *aguru*, on our heads?" In this *viraha-pralāpa* (incoherent talk filled with lamentation, which is caused by separation from Kṛṣṇa), Rādhikā says, "O Prāṇanātha, please enter the *kuñja*, casting the same sidelong glance as You did before." What is the nature of this glance? As Kṛṣṇa plays on His flute, His sidelong glance indicates to Rādhā to enter the *kuñja*. For this reason, the flute is a giver of bliss. Someone may question: "At the time of *rāsa-līlā*, if Muralīvadana's sidelong glance signals to Śrī Rādhā alone, what about the other *gopīs*?" The answer is that by the inconceivable potency (*acintya-śakti*) contained within His flute and sidelong glance, Kṛṣṇa signals Śrī Rādhā directly and the other *gopīs* indirectly.

Rādhikā says, "I am only concerned with Your happiness. If all of us *gopīs* become unhappy but You are happy, then that is My cherished desire. If it pleases You to not appear before Me, then even the *gopīs'* endeavours to find You cannot please Me."

By resolutely performing *bhajana* with the sentiments described in this third chapter, the stage of *ruci* will arise and gradually the *sādhaka* will attain *prema*.

Text 19

The mid-morning pastimes (*pūrvāhna-līlā*) are described in *Govinda-līlāmṛta* (5.1):

pūrvāhne dhenu-mitrair vipinam anusṛtaṁ goṣṭha-lokānuyātaṁ
kṛṣṇaṁ rādhāpti-lolaṁ tad abhisṛti-kṛte prāpta-tat-kuṇḍa-tīram
rādhāṁ cālokya kṛṣṇaṁ kṛta-gṛha-gamanām āryayārkārcanāyai
diṣṭāṁ kṛṣṇa-pravṛttyai prahita-nija-sakhī vartma-netrāṁ smarāmi

I remember Śrī Kṛṣṇa, who in the forenoon goes to the forest with the cows and His *sakhās.* Śrī Nanda, Yaśodā and other Vrajavāsīs follow Him for some distance. Restless and hankering to meet with Śrī Rādhā, Kṛṣṇa arrives at the bank of Rādhā-kuṇḍa for Their rendezvous (*abhisāra*). I remember Śrī Rādhā, who after taking Kṛṣṇa's *darśana* at Nanda-bhavana, returns to Her home. Jaṭilā orders Her to worship the Sun-god. Desiring to learn of Śrī Kṛṣṇa's whereabouts, Rādhā sits and looks down the road, waiting for the return of Her *sakhī*, whom She has sent to gather this information.

dhenu sahacara saṅge, kṛṣṇa vane yāya raṅge,
goṣṭha-jana anuvrata hari
rādhā-saṅga-lobhe punaḥ, rādhā-kuṇḍa-taṭa-vana,
yāya dhenu saṅgī parihari'

kṛṣṇera iṅgīta pāñā, rādhā nija-gṛhe yāñā,
jaṭilājñā laya sūryārcane
gupte kṛṣṇa-patha lakhi', katakṣaṇe āise sakhī,
vyākulitā rādhā smari mane

Bhajana-rahasya vṛtti

In *pūrvāhna-līlā*, after Śrī Kṛṣṇa has eaten, He prepares to go to the forest, wearing the attire of a cowherd boy; and Śrī Vṛṣabhānu-nandinī, decorated with cloth and ornaments given by Śrī Yaśodā, returns to Jāvaṭa. They meet halfway. Upon seeing Śrī Rādhā, Kṛṣṇa's peacock feather falls from His head and the flute slips from His hand. This pastime is described in the following verse from *Śrī Rādhā-rasa-sudhā-nidhi* (39):

veṇuḥ karān nipatitaḥ skhalitaṁ śikhaṇḍaṁ
bhraṣṭaṁ ca pīta-vasanaṁ vrajarāja-sūnoḥ

Kṛṣṇa arrives at the bank of Rādhā-kuṇḍa for another meeting with Śrīmatī Rādhikā. Not finding Her there, He becomes extremely eager, full of desire and restless. In Jāvaṭa, meanwhile, Jaṭilā encourages Rādhikā to go and worship the Sun-god (*sūrya-pūjā*). The way in which Rādhikā performs *pūjā* to Kṛṣṇa at the place where *sūrya-pūjā* is performed is the wealth that is attained by the performance of *bhajana*.

Thus ends the *Tṛtīya-yāma-sādhana*,
Pūrvāhna-kālīya-bhajana, of *Śrī Bhajana-rahasya*.

4

Caturtha-yāma-sādhana

Madhyāhna-kālīya-bhajana – ruci-bhajana

(from the second *prahara* until three-and-a-half *praharas*: approximately 11.00 A.M. – 3.30 P.M.)

Text 1

A *nāma-sādhaka* has no desire other than unadulterated devotional service to Kṛṣṇa (*ahaitukī-kṛṣṇa-bhakti*). The fourth verse of *Śikṣāṣṭaka* states:

na dhanaṁ na janaṁ na sundarīṁ
kavitāṁ vā jagadīśa kāmaye
mama janmani janmanīśvare
bhavatād bhaktir ahaitukī tvayi

O Jagadīśa, I do not desire wealth, nor followers, nor do I desire beautiful poetry (here meaning "knowledge"). O Prāṇeśvara, my only desire is to have unalloyed devotion unto Your lotus feet birth after birth.

gṛha-dravya-śiṣya-paśu-dhānya-ādi dhana
strī-putra dāsa-dāsī kuṭumbādi jana

kāvya-alaṅkāra-ādi sundarī kavitā
pārthiva-viṣaya madhye e saba vāratā

ei saba pāivāra āśā nāhi kari
śuddha-bhakti deha more, kṛṣṇa kṛpā kari'

premera svabhāva, yāhā premera sambandha
sei māne kṛṣṇa mora nāhi bhakti-gandha

Bhajana-rahasya-vṛtti

Bhakti only appears in the heart when one performs *harināma-kīrtana* with firm faith (*śraddhā*). But the *sādhaka's* perfected body (*śuddha-svarūpa*) will not arise unless he gives up all connection with sensual happiness in this material world. This renunciation of sensual happiness takes place in two ways: positive (*anvaya*) and negative (*vyatireka*). Here *anvaya* refers to the prominent characteristic of devotion, which is the cultivation of activities favourable to Kṛṣṇa (*ānukūlya-maya-kṛṣṇānuśīlana*). *Vyatireka* refers to the two secondary characteristics of devotion, which are: (1) the absence of desire for anything other than the pleasure of Kṛṣṇa (*anyābhilāṣitā-śūnya*) and (2) the absence of the coverings of *karma* and *jñāna* (*jñāna-karmādy-anāvṛta*).

The words *na dhanaṁ na janam* in this Text clearly explain the symptoms of *vyatireka*. The word *dhana* refers to wealth and articles collected for enjoyment and entertainment, and *jana* indicates women, children, servants, maidservants, subjects, friends and relatives. *Sundarī-kavitā* means ordinary knowledge expressed in mundane poetry and literature.

"O Kṛṣṇa, Lord of my life, I am not praying to You for all these things. My only prayer is that I may have unalloyed devotion unto Your lotus feet birth after birth."

Text 2

Misusing material wealth and so forth is opposed to *bhakti*. *Śrīmad-Bhāgavatam* (3.9.6) states:

tāvad bhayaṁ draviṇa-deha-suhṛn-nimittaṁ
śokaḥ spṛhā paribhavo vipulaś ca lobhaḥ
tāvan mamety asad-avagraha ārti-mūlaṁ
yāvan na te 'ṅghrim abhayaṁ pravṛṇīta lokaḥ

As long as a person does not take shelter of Your lotus feet, which remove all kinds of fear, he will be tormented by anxiety, sorrow, hankering, wretchedness, extreme greed and so forth caused by wealth, home, friends and relatives. He will maintain the misconception of "I" and "mine", which is the sole cause of unhappiness.

dravya-deha-suhṛn-nimitta śoka bhaya
spṛhā parābhava āra lobha atiśaya

āmi mama ārti-mūla asat-āśaya
yata dina nahe tava pāda-padmāśraya

Bhajana-rahasya-vṛtti

Persons who have never heard *hari-kathā* are not inclined to serve Hari. They use their time, wealth and strength in mundane activities and they maintain the misconception that "I am the enjoyer". They will suffer due to their inclination to enjoy. In other words, although they are in distress, they still endeavour to obtain that which is unrelated to Kṛṣṇa. The sole cause of this is illusion. Forgetting that Kṛṣṇa is their only near and dear friend, they establish friendship with persons averse to Kṛṣṇa and remain fearful of the devotees. It is only by the merciful disposition of Hari, Guru and Vaiṣṇavas that the living entity can be delivered from these sufferings and the desire to serve Bhagavān can arise in his heart. In other words the inclination to serve Bhagavān (*bhagavat-sevā-vṛtti*) will manifest in his heart. The living entity then realises his own intrinsic nature, as well as the instrinsic natures of Bhagavān and the illusory energy, and engages all his senses in serving Hari, Guru and Vaiṣṇavas. Śrīla Bhaktivinoda Ṭhākura sings in *Śaraṇāgati* (*Ātma-nivedana*, song 8):

ātma nivedana, tuyā pade kari,
hainu parama sukhī
duḥkha dūre gela, cintā nā rahila,
caudike ānanda dekhī

By surrendering myself to Your lotus feet I have become supremely happy. All suffering has gone far away and I have no more worries. Now I see happiness in all directions.

Text 3

Śrī Kṛṣṇa is the supreme Lord of all lords, and by worshipping Him, all others are worshipped. *Śrīmad-Bhāgavatam* (4.31.14) states:

yathā taror mūla-niṣecanena
tṛpyanti tat-skandha-bhujopaśākhāḥ
prāṇopahārāc ca yathendriyāṇāṁ
tathaiva sarvārhaṇam acyutejyā

By watering the root of a tree, all its parts, such as the trunk, branches and sub-branches, are nourished, and by satisfying the life-airs through eating, all of the senses are nourished. Similarly, only by worshipping Śrī Kṛṣṇa are the demigods, forefathers and so forth worshipped.

taru-mūle dile jala, bhuja-śākhā-skandha
tṛpta haya anāyāse, sahaja nirbandha
prāṇera tarpaṇe yathā indriya sabala
kṛṣṇārcane tathā sarva-devatā śītala

Bhajana-rahasya vṛtti

By watering the root of a tree, all of its parts, such as the trunk, branches, leaves and fruits, obtain nourishment. By putting food in the stomach all the different bodily limbs are satisfied and nourished. Similarly, by performing exclusive worship of Acyuta, all the demigods and goddesses are also worshipped. This is because Acyuta is the root cause of all consciousness, and all conscious and unconscious matter is dependent on Him. Svayam Bhagavān is the only one who is infallible (*acyuta*), and He can never become fallible (*cyuta*). Here someone may ask, "What harm is there in worshipping both Bhagavān and the demigods and goddesses at the same time?" The answer is that such worship signifies a lack of firm faith in Bhagavān. The demigods and goddesses are ruled by material qualities, while the process of serving Bhagavān is transcendental. It is improper to disrespect the demigods and goddesses, but it is also incorrect to elevate them to the same level as Kṛṣṇa. The scriptures state that one who gives up *śrī-kṛṣṇa-bhajana* to worship the demigods and goddesses is like one who gives up his mother to worship an outcaste woman, or like one who gives up nectar to drink poison.

Text 4

Unalloyed devotees have no other duty than serving Kṛṣṇa. The *Padma Purāṇa* states:

harir eva sadārādhyaḥ
sarva-deveśvareśvaraḥ
itare brahma-rudrādyā
nāvajñeyāḥ kadācana

The Lord of all demigods, Śrī Hari, is always the only worshipful object, but it is improper to disrespect Brahmā, Rudra and other demigods.

ādau sarveśvara-jñāna kṛṣṇete haibe
anya deve kabhu nāhi avajñā karibe

Text 5

One should not increase the number of his unqualified disciples on the pretext of spreading *bhakti*. *Śrīmad-Bhāgavatam* (7.13.8) states:

na śiṣyān anubadhnīta
granthān naivābhyased bahūn
na vyākhyām upayuñjīta
nārambhān ārabhet kvacit

One should not make many disciples for material gain, nor study many books, nor give discourses on *śāstra* to earn one's livelihood. One should also give up large undertakings.

bahu-śiṣya-lobhete ayogya śiṣya kare
bhakti-śūnya śāstrābhyāse tarka kari' mare

vyākhyāvāda-bahvārambhe vṛthā kāla yāya
nāme yāra ruci sei e saba nā cāya

Bhajana-rahasya-vṛtti

While explaining the duty of a *sannyāsī*, Devarṣi Nārada said to Yudhiṣṭhira Mahārāja, "A *sannyāsī* should roam about, be devoted to Nārāyaṇa and be the well-wisher of all living entities. He should not engage in any occupation to maintain his life, nor should he engage in discussions only for the sake of debate. He should only accept objects that come through begging (*bhikṣā*). He should not be attached to literature that discusses temporary, material subject matters, nor should he, for material benefit, give *mantras* to unqualified persons to increase his number of disciples. He should not show his scholarly talent, but rather he should study literature on *bhakti* and put these teachings into practice. It is unfavourable to pure devotion, and also a waste of time, to establish and maintain large temples to make a show of opulence. Many kinds of unqualified persons will take shelter of such temples, and their devious activities will defame the society of *sādhus*. Saintly persons should perform *bhajana* under the guidance of their superiors, following the path designated by the disciplic succession (*paramparā*). Only a *sādhaka* on the platform of *bhāva* is qualified to make disciples, and he does so only for the welfare of society and the protection of the *sampradāya*. The scriptures forbid unqualified persons from making many disciples."

Text 6

Exclusive and unmotivated devotional service, known as *aikāntikī-ahaitukī-bhakti*, is described in *Śrīmad-Bhāgavatam* (1.2.14):

tasmād ekena manasā
bhagavān sātvatāṁ patiḥ
śrotavyaḥ kīrtitavyaś ca
dhyeyaḥ pūjyaś ca nityadā

With an attentive mind, one should constantly hear about, glorify, meditate upon and worship Bhagavān, who is loving towards His devotees (*bhakta-vatsala*). All the while, one should endeavour to remove his *anarthas*. Then his creeper of devotion will very quickly bestow its fruit in the form of *prema*.

ananya-bhāvete kara śravaṇa-kīrtana
nāma-rūpa-guṇa-dhyāna-kṛṣṇa-ārādhana

saṅge saṅge anartha-nāśera yatna kara
bhakti-latā phala-dāna karibe satvara

Bhajana-rahasya-vṛtti

All religious duties are observed for the pleasure of Śrī Hari. Therefore the living entity's only duty is to single-mindedly engage in *kṛṣṇa-bhajana* while giving up the desire for *karma* and *jñāna*. For the pleasure of Śrī Hari, he should reside in the *dhāma* with a resolute mind and hear narrations about Hari from *śrī guru* and Vaiṣṇavas. The method of cultivating pure *bhajana* is that after hearing *hari-kathā*, one should perform *kīrtana* and *smaraṇa* of those narrations. By this method *anarthas* are nullified and pure *bhajana* arises. This is the essence of all instruction for *sādhakas*.

Text 7

One should not be disturbed by the loss of acquired assets. In this regard *Bhakti-rasāmṛta-sindhu* (1.2.114) quotes the *Padma Purāṇa*:

alabdhe vā vinaṣṭe vā
bhakṣyācchādana-sādhane
aviklava-matir bhūtvā
harim eva dhiyā smaret

One who is devoted to *hari-bhakti* should remain undisturbed and continue remembering Hari, even if he is unsuccessful in obtaining food and clothing, or if what he has obtained is lost.

bhakṣya-ācchādana yadi sahaje nā pāya
athavā pāiyā kona gatike hārāya
nāmāśrita bhakta aviklava-mati haiyā
govinda śaraṇa laya āsakti chāḍiyā

Bhajana-rahasya-vṛtti

When the living entity attains taste (*ruci*) for *śrī-bhagavat-kathā* and *harināma*, he no longer has an attachment to worldly things. He is satisfied with only the cloth and food necessary to protect and sustain the body. If he gains or loses anything, his mind remains steady. His mood is that whatever is obtained or lost is the Lord's desire. He knows that gain, loss and so forth come according to one's previous *karma*. Detached from worldly matters, he remembers Śrī Bhagavān's name with a steady mind.

Text 8

Bhakti-rasāmṛta-sindhu (1.2.113), quoting from the *Padma Purāṇa*, mentions the necessity of giving up distress:

śokāmarṣādibhir bhāvair
ākrāntaṁ yasya mānasam
kathaṁ tatra mukundasya
sphūrtiḥ sambhāvanā bhavet

How can Mukunda manifest in the heart of a person who is filled with lamentation, anger and so forth?

putra kalatrera śoka, krodha, abhimāna
ye hṛdaye tāhe kṛṣṇa sphūrti nāhi pāna

Bhajana-rahasya-vṛtti

Mukunda never manifests in a heart that becomes agitated by pleasure upon obtaining something temporary or distressed upon losing it. In this way the living entity remains oblivious to Bhagavān. One should follow the character of Śrīman Mahāprabhu's devotees and, guided by their mood, remain peaceful and steady in every situation. In this regard one should follow the example of Śrīvāsa Paṇḍita. Once Śrīman Mahāprabhu and His devotees were performing *kīrtana* in Śrīvāsa Paṇḍita's home when, inside the house, Śrīvāsa's son left his body. Śrīvāsa remained calm and strictly forbade the ladies and other persons in the house to cry, to ensure that Mahāprabhu's *kīrtana* would not be disturbed. He did not even relate the news of his son's death to Mahāprabhu. With such a fixed and peaceful mind one should remember and meditate upon Bhagavān. This is the purport of *śāstra*.

Text 9

One should accept only as much wealth as is necessary to maintain his life. The *Nāradīya Purāṇa* states:

yāvatā syāt sva-nirvāhaḥ
svīkuryāt tāvad arthavit
ādhikye nyūnatāyāṁ ca
cyavate paramārthataḥ

A *sādhaka* who needs to maintain himself will collect only as much wealth and other material necessities as are required to maintain his *bhakti*; to accept too much or too little will surely make him deviate from his goal.

sahaje jīvana-yātrā-nirvāhopayogī
dravyādi svīkāra kare bhakta nahe bhogī

Bhajana-rahasya-vṛtti

A person qualified for *vaidhī-bhakti* should earn money to maintain his life through prescribed virtuous means; that is, according to *varṇāśrama-dharma*. It is auspicious to accept assets only according to one's needs. Craving to accept more than necessary creates attachment, which will gradually destroy one's *bhajana*. Accepting less than necessary is also harmful, as this will create an insufficiency, which in turn will weaken one's *bhajana*. Therefore as long as a person is not indifferent to material things, he should cultivate pure *bhakti* and accept only those assets that are required to maintain his life.

Text 10

The symptoms of advancement in unmotivated devotional service are given in *Śrīmad-Bhāgavatam* (11.2.42):

bhaktiḥ pareśānubhavo viraktir
anyatra caiṣa trika eka-kālaḥ
prapadyamānasya yathāśnataḥ syus
tuṣṭiḥ puṣṭiḥ kṣud-apāyo 'nu-ghāsam

With each morsel of food that a hungry person eats, he simultaneously experiences satisfaction, nourishment and relief from hunger. Similarly a surrendered devotee, who is engaged in the performance of *bhakti*, simultaneously realises his worshipful deity, strengthens his relationship with that deity and becomes detached from this temporary world and material relationships.

bhakta-jane samamāne yugapad udaya
bhakti, jñāna, virakti, tina jānaha niścaya

cid-acid-īśvara sambandha-jñāne jñāna
kṛṣṇetare anāsakti virakti-pramāṇa

ye rūpa bhajane tuṣṭi puṣṭi pratigrāse
kṣudhāra nivṛtti ei tina anāyāse

Bhajana-rahasya-vṛtti

The symptoms observed in a *sādhaka* who has directly experienced the sweetness of Bhagavān are described in this Text. In such devotees, three symptoms are simultaneously visible: attainment of service to the Lord, realisation of all knowledge related to *bhakti* and detachment from matters unrelated to Kṛṣṇa. The *sādhaka* develops detachment from those items of enjoyment that are not useful in the service of Śrī Kṛṣṇa, but he does not develop detachment from that which can be used in His service. Because he does not consider using such objects for his own pleasure, there is no need for him to renounce them.

When, due to humility, Śrīla Sanātana Gosvāmī resolved to give up his life by throwing his body under the wheel of Lord Jagannātha's chariot, Śrī Gaurasundara, who resides in everyone's heart as the Supersoul, told him that a person cannot attain Kṛṣṇa merely by giving up his body. Kṛṣṇa is only attained through *bhajana*; that is, through fulfilling the inner desire of one's *guru* (*manobhīṣṭa-sevā*).

When the *sādhaka* surrenders to *śrī guru's* lotus feet, the *guru* becomes the owner of the *sādhaka's* body. Therefore, when one acknowledges his body to be his *guru's* property, it is necessary to take care of it. In the same mood, the *vraja-devīs* decorate their bodies with clothes, ornaments, cosmetics and so forth – only for service to Śrī Kṛṣṇa.

Indifference to material objects develops according to the extent of one's realisation of Bhagavān. This indifference gives one the qualification to attain the direct service of Bhagavān. Śrīla Raghunātha dāsa Gosvāmī states in *Vilāpa-kusumāñjali* (6):

vairāgya-yug bhakti-rasaṁ prayatnair
apāyayan mām anabhīpsum andham
kṛpāmbudhir yaḥ para-duḥkha-duḥkhī
sanātanaṁ taṁ prabhum āśrayāmi

I surrender to the lotus feet of my master, Śrī Sanātana Gosvāmī, who is the bestower of *sambandha-jñāna*. He is an ocean of mercy and his heart always becomes distressed upon seeing the suffering of others. Although due to the darkness of ignorance I had no desire to taste *bhakti-rasa* imbued with renunciation, he forced me to taste it and thereby gave me knowledge of my relationship with Kṛṣṇa.

Ignorant people honour artificial renunciation and praise those who accumulate dry knowledge. Such knowledge and renunciation, being devoid of the inclination to serve, simply result in mundane talk and deception of the public. There is no pure *bhakti* in them.

Text 11

The following verse is a petition made at the stage of humility described in the previous Texts. Prahlāda Mahārāja (*Śrīmad-Bhāgavatam* (7.9.39)) prays:

naitan manas tava kathāsu vikuṇṭha-nātha
samprīyate durita-duṣṭam asādhu tīvram
kāmāturaṁ harṣa-śoka-bhayaiṣaṇārtaṁ
tasmin kathaṁ tava gatiṁ vimṛśāmi dīnaḥ

O Vaikuṇṭhanātha, my mind is polluted by the desire to sin. How can I explain to You the suffering of my mind, which is constantly afflicted by desires? My mind, strongly attached to these desires, is sometimes overpowered by happiness and sometimes by distress and fear. It is always engaged in collecting wealth and material assets, and it finds no taste in the narrations of Your pastimes. How, then, can I remember and meditate upon You?

durita-dūṣita mana asādhu mānasa
kāma-harṣa-śoka-bhaya eṣaṇāra vaśa
tava kathā-rati kise haibe āmāra?
kise kṛṣṇa tava līlā kariba vicāra?

Bhajana-rahasya-vṛtti

When steady devotion arises in the heart of a *sādhaka*, a mood of natural humility manifests. Out of greed to constantly relish the sweetness of Bhagavān he repents, "Alas, alas, I have not performed any *sādhana-bhajana*. My heart is sinful and my mind is wicked, and therefore I left the merciful Lord and am drowning in the ditch of material enjoyment. How will I be able to relish the nectar of Svāminī's lotus feet? O Lord, how can I develop affection for Your form, qualities and pastimes? How can I obtain a taste for *bhajana*? Firmly bound by many kinds of illicit desires, I am drowning in the ocean of material existence. Oh, how can I protect myself from all this? O Bhagavān, I have become a servant of the six enemies. How can I, who am unintelligent and devoted to material desires, understand the boundless, eternal and deep truth about You?" This kind of humility arises when *bhakti* is fully ripe. In reality, fully mature *prema* is humility. Considering himself to be extremely fallen and wretched, the *sādhaka* always offers Bhagavān various humble and grief-stricken prayers.

Text 12

Śrīmad-Bhāgavatam (7.9.40) explains how life is completely destroyed by attraction to the form, taste and so on of material objects:

jihvaikato 'cyuta vikarṣati māvitṛptā
śiśno 'nyatas tvag-udaraṁ śravaṇaṁ kutaścit
ghrāṇo 'nyataś capala-dṛk kva ca karma-śaktir
bahvyaḥ sapatnya iva geha-patiṁ lunanti

O Acyuta, my tongue is pulling me towards very relishable flavours, my genitals towards beautiful women, my stomach towards foodstuffs that are harmful, my ears towards sweet songs and useless talk, my nose towards pleasant fragrances, my eyes towards beauty and my sense of touch towards soft things. In this way all my sense organs are pulling me towards their respective sense objects. O Nanda-nandana, my situation is like that of a man with many wives, each dragging him towards her own bedroom. In such a condition how can I remember You and Your form, qualities and pastimes?

jihvā ṭāne rasa prati, upastha kadarthe
udara bhojane ṭāne viṣama anarthe

carma ṭāne śayyādite, śravaṇa kathāya
ghrāṇa ṭāne surabhite, cakṣu dṛśye yāya

karmendriya karme ṭāne, bahu-patnī yathā
gṛhapati ākarṣaya, mora mana tathā

emata avasthā mora śrī-nanda-nandana
ki rūpe tomāra līlā kariba smaraṇa?

Bhajana-rahasya-vṛtti

The *sādhaka* is praying to Bhagavān with great humility, "O Lord, let my mind always be completely attached to Your lotus feet and engaged in glorifying You. But, O Acyuta, although I am trying to control my senses by innumerable endeavours, I have not been successful. Alas, alas, what shall I do? My unsatisfied tongue, genitals, belly, ears, nose, restless eyes and sense of touch are drawing me in the direction of their respective sense objects – sound, form, taste, smell and touch – and are thus destroying me. O Prabhu, although I have tried my best to subdue them, I have not succeeded. My condition is like that of a man who, controlled by lust, has married several wives. Now all these wives are dragging him in their own direction, each wanting her lustful desires fulfilled. He is not able to pacify the fire of their lust nor do they leave him alone. The more this lusty man tries in various ways to satisfy the desires of these ladies, the less successful he is. Similarly, I endeavoured in many ways, but all in vain. O protector of the helpless, now You are my only shelter. I have faith in You alone. By the power of Your mercy, please deliver me from the entanglement of this material existence and thus make Your name, Patita-pāvana, meaningful."

Text 13

A prayer for obtaining the association of *vraja-bhaktas* is spoken by Lord Brahmā in *Śrīmad-Bhāgavatam* (10.14.30):

tad astu me nātha sa bhūri-bhāgo
bhave 'tra vānyatra tu vā tiraścām
yenāham eko 'pi bhavaj-janānāṁ
bhūtvā niṣeve tava pāda-pallavam

O Bhagavān, may I be so fortunate as to attain the association of Your devotees and, under their guidance, obtain service to Your lotus feet; be it in this or any other human birth, or in a birth such as an animal, bird, worm or moth.

ei brahma janmei vā anya kona bhave
paśu-pakṣī ha'ye janmi tomāra vibhave
ei mātra āśā tava bhakta-gaṇa-saṅge
thāki' tava pada-sevā kari nānā-raṅge

Bhajana-rahasya-vṛtti

Lord Brahmā became perplexed when he saw Śrī Kṛṣṇa playing with the other cowherd boys. So, in order to see more of Śrī Kṛṣṇa's pastimes, he stole the cowherd boys and calves. Śrī Kṛṣṇa, however, assumed the forms of as many cows and cowherd boys as Brahmā stole, and for one year He continued His pastimes as before. Finally, He showed Brahmā His four-armed form. Upon seeing Bhagavān's opulence, Brahmā deeply regretted his actions. He praised Śrī Kṛṣṇa in various ways and begged forgiveness for his offence: "O Lord, I have directly received Your mercy. O fulfiller of all kinds of desires, my fortune is not in having obtained this post as Brahmā. Rather, if I take birth in Vraja from the womb of an animal, bird, worm, moth or any other sub-human species, I will consider myself most fortunate. Even the mercy available to the deer in Vraja is not easily obtained in this birth as Brahmā. The deer cleanse the dust from Your limbs with their tongues, and You caress them with Your hands. I want to take birth in any species, high or low, where I can serve Your lotus feet under the guidance of Your devotees. This is my earnest desire and will be my good fortune."

Text 14

It is useless to be anxious about attaining the four goals of life. Śrī Uddhava explains in *Śrīmad-Bhāgavatam* (3.4.15):

ko nv īśa te pāda-saroja-bhājāṁ
sudurlabho 'rtheṣu caturṣv apīha
tathāpi nāhaṁ pravṛṇomi bhūman
bhavat-padāmbhoja-niṣevaṇotsukaḥ

O Lord, it is not difficult for one who has taken shelter of Your lotus feet to achieve the four goals of life (religiosity, economic development, sense gratification and liberation); nevertheless, such a person does not desire them. O Great One, he is not concerned with anything other than rendering service to Your lotus feet.

kṛṣṇa! tava pāda-padme bhakti āche yāṅra
catur-varga-madhye kivā aprāpya tāṅhāra
tathāpi tomāra pada-sevā mātra cāi
anya kona arthe mora prayojana nāi

Bhajana-rahasya-vṛtti

The inherent *dharma* of the living entity is the tendency to serve (*sevā-vṛtti*). The devotee therefore desires the fifth goal of human life, *pañcama-puruṣārtha*, which is *prema-sevā*. He does not accept the threefold designations of religiosity (*dharma*), economic development (*artha*) and sense gratification (*kāma*), nor does he accept liberation (*mokṣa*), which is free from material designations. The impersonalists strive for *sāyujya-mukti*, which the devotee always completely rejects. The *Nārada-pañcarātra* (1.1.34) states:

hari-bhakti-mahādevyāḥ
sarvā muktādi-siddhayaḥ
bhaktaś cādbhutās tasyāś
ceṭikāvad anuvratāḥ

All kinds of liberation are automatically accomplished by devotees who perform pure devotional service to Hari. Not only are they accomplished, but they follow the devotees like maidservants, always ready to serve them.

Devotees reject the five kinds of *mukti*: *sāyujya*, *sārūpya*, *sāmīpya*, *sālokya* and *sārṣṭi*. Excluding *sāyujya*, however, the other four are not entirely opposed to *bhakti*. They are of two kinds: *sukhaiśvaryottarā* (liberation tainted with the desire to enjoy the Lord's opulence) and *prema-sevottarā* (liberation in which the dominant desire is to serve the Lord for His pleasure). Because there is some desire for personal happiness in both of these, those who are devoted to unalloyed service to Bhagavān consider them opposed to loving service and do not accept them.

Text 15

One should endeavour to attain pure unalloyed devotion (*śuddha-ahaitukī-bhakti*). *Śrīmad-Bhāgavatam* (1.5.18) states:

tasyaiva hetoḥ prayateta kovido
na labhyate yad bhramatām uparyadhaḥ
tal labhyate duḥkhavad-anyataḥ sukhaṁ
kālena sarvatra gabhīra-raṁhasā

[Śrī Nārada said:] In the course of time I have been wandering from the seven higher planets to the seven lower, such as Sutalaloka, but I have not attained eternal, transcendental happiness, which wise persons endeavour to taste. Just as misery comes without endeavour, by the influence of grave, quickly-moving time, happiness also comes without any endeavour. What, therefore, is the use of endeavouring for worldly happiness?

vinā yatne duḥkhera ghaṭanā yena haya
sei rūpe kāla-krame sukhera udaya

ataeva caudda-loke durlabha ye dhana
sei bhakti-janya yatna kare budha-gaṇa

Bhajana-rahasya-vṛtti

A devotee understands that any pleasure within the material universe is insignificant compared to even the slightest experience of the nectar and fragrance of Bhagavān's lotus feet. One who has only tasted molasses will give it up when he tastes fragrant sugar candy. Similarly, before actually cultivating devotion to Bhagavān in the association of pure devotees, the living entity who is allured by the flowery words of the Vedas desires to enjoy nectar, nectarean food and the other heavenly pleasures of Svarga. Alternatively, by the influence of association with *jñānīs*, the living entity desires liberation. Pure devotees do not accept either of these – they only desire the happiness of loving service to Bhagavān through *bhakti*. This Text tells us that those who are genuinely wise search only for that constant, eternal, transcendental happiness that is only obtained in Hari-dhāma (Vaikuṇṭha). This transcendental happiness is not available to the *jīva* who wanders throughout the fourteen worlds searching for mundane enjoyment.

Material happiness is even obtained in the body of a hog. According to his *karma* the living entity sometimes tastes sorrow and difficulties, and sometimes he effortlessly tastes happiness. Therefore the scriptures unanimously instruct that one should not endeavour to obtain that which is temporary and material. The *jīva's* goal is neither to prevent his material suffering nor to be successful in endeavours for happiness. Such attempts are simply childish fickleness. The wise give up searching for these temporary things and endeavour to attain service to Śrī Hari, which is the soul's eternal *dharma*.

Text 16

The desire for liberation is made insignificant by *ahaitukī-bhakti*. *Śrīmad-Bhāgavatam* (4.9.10) states:

yā nirvṛtis tanu-bhṛtāṁ tava pāda-padma-
dhyānād bhavaj-jana-kathā-śravaṇena vā syāt
sā brahmaṇi sva-mahimany api nātha mā bhūt
kiṁ tv antakāsi-lulitāt patatāṁ vimānāt

O Lord, a drop of the bliss received from meditating on Your lotus feet, from hearing about Your pastimes – which flow from the mouths of Your devotees who are expert in relishing *vraja-rasa* – and from hearing descriptions of Your devotees' pastimes, is not available in the bliss of merging into Brahman. What to speak of being available to others, it is not even available to the demigods of the heavenly planets, who fall down again, being cut by the sword of time.

tava pada-dhyāne bhakta-mukha tava kathā
śravaṇe ye sukha tāhā māgiye sarvathā

brahma-sukha nāhi bhāla lāge mora mane
ki chāra anitya loka-sukha-saṅghaṭane

Bhajana-rahasya-vṛtti

In this prayer Dhruva Mahārāja describes the happiness he experienced after receiving *darśana* of Bhagavān: "O Master, the happiness found in hearing narrations of Your pastimes in the association of Your devotees is not available anywhere else. In the presence of the devotees' sun-like *premānanda*, the pleasure of the impersonalists' *brahmānanda* is like a firefly. The demigods' heavenly enjoyment (*svargānanda*) is insignificant and also temporary, subject to being ultimately cut by the sword of time. The living entity can enjoy this pleasure only as long as the accumulated credit of his pious activities is not exhausted." This is confirmed in *Bhagavad-gītā* (9.21):

te taṁ bhuktvā svarga-lokaṁ viśālaṁ
kṣīṇe puṇye martya-lokaṁ viśanti
evaṁ trayī-dharmam anuprapannā
gatāgataṁ kāma-kāmā labhante

Having enjoyed immense celestial pleasures, they again return to the mortal world when their pious merit is exhausted. In this way, those who perform fruitive activities as described in the three Vedas repeatedly come and go from this world.

Therefore only devotion to Bhagavān, which is devoid of the attraction to hear about the enjoyment available on Svarga and other higher planets, is supremely beneficial for the *jīva*. The wise spend their lives hearing and speaking *hari-kathā* in the company of pure devotees.

Text 17

The glory of hearing the holy name from the mouth of a *sādhu* is described in *Śrīmad-Bhāgavatam* (4.20.24):

na kāmaye nātha tad apy ahaṁ kvacin
na yatra yuṣmac-caraṇāmbujāsavaḥ
mahattamāntar-hṛdayān mukha-cyuto
vidhatsva karṇāyutam eṣa me varaḥ

O Lord, I do not want liberation. I receive no pleasure in hearing any topic other than the glorious narrations of the nectar of Your lotus feet. This nectar emanates from the mouths of saintly persons from deep within their hearts. I beg only for the boon that You will give me ten thousand ears with which I can always hear the sweetness of Your pastimes.

yāhāte tomāra pada-sevā-sukha nāi
sei rūpa vara āmi nātha kabhu nāhi cāi
bhaktera hṛdaya haite tava guṇa-gāna
śunite ayuta karṇa karaha vidhāna

Bhajana-rahasya-vṛtti

Pṛthu Mahārāja prays to the lotus feet of Bhagavān to be able to hear and glorify the auspicious narrations of His pastimes only in the association of devotees. He says, "I offer my obeisances from far away to the topics of liberation and any other kind of talk that does not proclaim the glories of the nectar of Your lotus feet. My only treasured wish is to drink the nectar of Your *līlā-kathā*, which is filled with *prema* and which flows from the mouths of devotees. I do not even desire to hear about Your sweet pastimes from the mouths of non-devotees. Even fragrant water mixed with honey should be abandoned if it is salty.

"O Lord, I pray to You to please give me tens of thousands of ears to hear the sweet narrations of Your pastimes from the lotus mouths of devotees who are adept at relishing *vraja-rasa.* In other words, I pray that I may hear descriptions of Your pastimes with intense eagerness, and that the desire for impersonal liberation never arises in my heart. Drops of nectar from Your lotus feet in the form of pollen are carried by the breeze emanating from the mouths of great personalities, thus transmitting the potency of *bhakti* to us and making our lives successful. I am always ready to do anything to hear this *kathā.* May a spark of the mood of such personalities enter my heart and submerge me in an ocean of *prema.*"

Text 18

Residence in the heavenly planets, residence in Brahmaloka, sovereignty over the Earth and lower planetary systems, the perfections of *yoga* and the eighteen mystic perfections are all insignificant from the perspective of a devotee. This is confirmed in *Śrīmad-Bhāgavatam* (6.11.25):

na nāka-pṛṣṭhaṁ na ca pārameṣṭhyaṁ
na sārva-bhaumaṁ na rasādhipatyam
na yoga-siddhīr apunar-bhavaṁ vā
samañjasa tvā virahayya kāṅkṣe

O source of all good fortune, I have no desire to have a position of great sovereignty like that of Dhruva or Brahmā, or rulership over the Earth; nor do I desire *aṇimā* or any other mystic perfection. I do not even want liberation, if attaining it means I would have to give You up.

svarga parameṣṭhī-sthāna, sarvabhauma-pada
rasātala-ādhipatya, yogera sampada

nirvāṇa ityādi yata chāḍi' sevā tava
nāhi māgi, e mora pratijñā akaitava

Bhajana-rahasya-vṛtti

Bhagavān prevents His devotees from endeavouring for *dharma*, *artha*, *kāma* and *mokṣa*, and this infers His mercy. While His mercy is easily attained by the *akiñcana-bhaktas*, it is extremely difficult to attain for living entities who are absorbed in sense enjoyment.

This Text is a prayer by Vṛtrāsura. While fighting with Indra, Vṛtrāsura considered it better to choose death over either victory or defeat, so that he could quickly cut his bodily bondage. He would then be able to directly serve Bhagavān.

Directly perceiving Bhagavān, Vṛtrāsura expressed the moods of his heart. "O source of all good fortune, I do not want a position in Dhruvaloka or Brahmaloka, nor do I want sole rulership of the Earth. I have no desire for mystic perfections or even liberation – which is the goal of impersonalists, who perform severe practices to attain it – if I have to give You up. My life is leaving my body in the fire of separation from You. O Prabhu, how can I ever attain eternal service to Your lotus feet?"

Devotees long to attain the eternal service of Bhagavān. Only one who has factually realised the bliss of serving (*sevānanda*) knows the significance of this. By obtaining *dharma*, *artha* and *kāma*, the living entity does not stop his transmigration, and by *sāyujya-mukti*, the living entity simply remains like an inert object in the effulgent Brahman. However, devotees relish the sweetness of service in newer and newer ways in the eternal abode of Bhagavān. This is the unique characteristic of the *bhakta* and *bhakti*. Bhakti-devī disappears from the heart of that person who eagerly desires liberation, and this is confirmed in *Śrī Caitanya-caritāmṛta* (*Ādi-līlā* 1.92):

tāra madhye mokṣa-vāñchā kaitava-pradhāna
yāhā haite kṛṣṇa-bhakti haya antardhāna

The foremost process of cheating is the desire for liberation, for this causes the disappearance of *kṛṣṇa-bhakti*.

Text 19

The symptom of attachment (*āsakti*) that is developed by taking shelter of the holy name is described in *Śrīmad-Bhāgavatam* (10.29.34):

cittaṁ sukhena bhavatāpahṛtaṁ gṛheṣu
yan nirviśaty uta karāv api gṛhya-kṛtye
pādau padaṁ na calatas tava pāda-mūlād
yāmaḥ kathaṁ vrajamatho karavāma kiṁ vā

[The *gopīs* said to Kṛṣṇa:] O stealer of minds (*cittacora*), by playing on Your *vaṁśī*, You have stolen our minds, which were absorbed in household affairs. This was not difficult for You. However, having lost our minds, our working senses are not functioning, and our movements and intelligence have therefore become abnormal. Our feet do not want to leave You to go anywhere else. Please tell us then, how can we possibly return to our homes?

gṛhasukhe citta chila, gṛhakārye kara
hariyā layecha tumi prāṇera īśvara
tava pādamūla chāḍi' pada nāhi yāya
yāba kothā ki kariba balaha upāya

Bhajana-rahasya-vṛtti

With the sweet sound of His flute, Śrī Kṛṣṇacandra, the crown jewel of experts in amorous pastimes (*vidagdha-śiromaṇi*), called to the *vraja-gopīs*, who were abundantly endowed with paramour love. Forgetting everything, the *gopīs* assembled on the bank of the Yamunā at Vaṁśivaṭa, which was beautifully decorated by bright moonlight. Then Śrī Kṛṣṇacandra, concealing

His real motive (*avahitthā-bhāva*), joked with them by instructing them to return to their respective homes. His intention, however, was as follows: during His previous pastime of stealing the *gopīs'* clothes, Śrī Kṛṣṇacandra, the great connoisseur of the *rāsa-līlā*, saw the *vraja-devīs'* entire bodies, but on this day He wanted to see the inner moods of their hearts. This is one unique attribute of the ocean of *prema-rasa*.

The *rasika-ācāryas* of the amorous mellow of Vraja ascertain that when the lover (*nāyaka*) assumes a submissive mood (*dākṣiṇya-bhāva*), the beloved (*nāyikā*) exhibits a contrary mood (*vāmya-bhāva*). And when the lover assumes a contrary mood, the beloved exhibits a submissive mood. The *gopīs* who assembled at the *rāsa-maṇḍala* displayed various waves of sentiments. Some of them were *pragalbhā* (bold and outspoken), some *mṛdvī* (sweet and gentle) and some *madhyā* (with qualities halfway between *pragalbhā* and *mṛdvī*). In this way, through the combination of such different sentiments, the ocean of *rasa* was adorned with unprecedented sweetness.

Śrī Kṛṣṇa said, "A virtuous woman's only duty is to serve her husband. It is improper for her to stay, even for a moment, with a *brahmacārī* in a lonely forest at night. Therefore you should all quickly return home."

Hearing these instructions, the *gopīs*, who possessed great *anurāga*, responded with words saturated with *rasa*: "O emperor of thieves! We did not come here to reside in an uninhabited place, nor did we come to ask anything from You. Our minds were happily absorbed in household affairs, when You stole them away with Your flute. The wealth of our hearts is already looted, so how can we return home? O You who are expert in rendering a person powerless by means of great *mantras*! Please return the faculty of our minds. In their absence the activities of all our senses are disabled and also our feet will not move; so return them and we will happily go back to our homes."

One *vraja-devī* began to speak sarcastically: "O Mohana, do You think that we have come to this place because we were attracted by the sound of Your flute? No, no, this is not the case! Our minds are deeply absorbed in our happy household life; You could not steal away even the smallest part of them. Do not think that we will rest here, even for a moment. Indeed, what would we do here in this desolate place? If You ask why we have come to this lonely forest, O Śyāmasundara, it is because You were so eager to have our *darśana*. That is the only reason we have come. Now that You have seen us, we are going."

Text 20

As described in the following verse, all virtue and peacefulness appear in the devotee. Prahlāda Mahārāja explains in *Śrīmad-Bhāgavatam* (5.18.12):

yasyāsti bhaktir bhagavaty akiñcanā
sarvair guṇais tatra samāsate surāḥ
harāv abhaktasya kuto mahad-guṇā
manorathenāsati dhāvato bahiḥ

All the demigods and their exalted qualities, such as religiosity and knowledge, always dwell in the heart of a person who possesses selfless devotion to Bhagavān (*niṣkāma-bhakti*). But how can a person who is not a devotee of Bhagavān possess these qualities of great personalities? He constantly runs after insignificant and superfluous things, even after taking many different vows to renounce them.

akiñcanā bhakti yāṅra tāṅhāra śarīre
sarva-guṇa saha sarva-devatā vihare

abhakta sarvadā mano-rathete caḍiyā
asad bāhye bhrame guṇa varjita haiyā

Bhajana-rahasya-vṛtti

The *ācāryas* have ascertained that once the tendency arises in someone to serve Kṛṣṇa without selfish motive (*niṣkāma-sevā-vṛtti*), all good qualities such as religiosity, knowledge and renunciation become apparent in him. This is simply the fruit of serving Mukunda. The fifty virtuous qualities of the demigods headed by Indra reside in the hearts of devotees. They cannot manifest in a deceitful and envious heart. A person who is devoid of *hari-bhakti* is attached to maintaining his body and home, and to extraneous desires, *jñāna, karma, yoga* and so on. He always runs towards external sense enjoyment through the avenues of profit, worship, name and fame, and mental speculation. In *Prema-bhakti-candrikā* (8.8) Śrīla Narottama dāsa Ṭhākura says: "*karma-kāṇḍa jñāna-kāṇḍa kevala viṣera bhāṇḍa* – fruitive activities and mental speculation are simply pots of poison." Mundane people, who are attached to material things, obtain different births according to their *karma*. The devotees, on the other hand, are preoccupied with performing service in the association of devotees and are thereby submerged in the ocean of supreme transcendental happiness. Thus they remain satisfied.

Text 21

Bhakti destroys the egoism arising from falsely identifying the body with the self (*deha-abhimāna*). This is stated in *Śrīmad-Bhāgavatam* (4.11.30):

tvaṁ pratyag ātmani tadā bhagavaty ananta
ānanda-mātra upapanna-samasta-śaktau
bhaktiṁ vidhāya paramāṁ śanakair avidyā
granthiṁ vibhetsyasi mamāham iti prarūḍham

[Manu said to Dhruva:] By searching for Bhagavān Ananta, who possesses all potencies, who is the embodiment of supreme transcendental bliss and who resides within all living entities as the Supersoul, your devotion will become very steady. On the strength of that devotion you will be able to cut the tight knot of ignorance in the form of the false conceptions of "I" and "mine".

manu bale dhruva tumi dhṛta sarva-śakti
pratyak ānanda-rūpa kṛṣṇe kara bhakti
āmi-mama-rūpa-vidyā-granthi dṛḍhatama
chedana karite krame haibe sakṣama

Bhajana-rahasya-vṛtti

A *sādhaka* experiences his own transcendental form (*svarūpa*) by cultivating pure devotional service that is unobstructed and not personally motivated. Upon realising his *svarūpa*, he very easily cuts the knot of ignorance by which he identifies the material body as "I" and material objects as "mine". When the living entity transcends the three modes (*sattva*, *raja* and *tama*), he is able to experience *bhagavad-rasa*, which is endowed with all potencies. This takes place by the influence of association with devotees. Since he is self-realised, he searches for Bhagavān, who is beyond the material modes, who is the non-dual Absolute Truth endowed with all transcendental qualities, and who is infallible. By cultivating *bhakti* in this way, he gradually becomes eternally situated in his own *svarūpa*.

Text 22

Śrīmad-Bhāgavatam (4.22.39) states:

yat-pāda-paṅkaja-palāśa-vilāsa-bhaktyā
karmāśayaṁ grathitam udgrathayanti santaḥ
tadvan na rikta-matayo yatayo 'pi ruddha-
sroto-gaṇās tam araṇaṁ bhaja vāsudevam

[Śrī Sanat Kumāra instructed Pṛthu Mahārāja:] The devotees of Bhagavān are easily able to cut the knot in the heart in the form of desires for fruitive activities by meditating upon the splendour that emanates from the toes of Bhagavān's lotus feet. However, impersonalist *yogīs*, who are devoid of loving devotion, cannot do so even by controlling their senses. Therefore give up the endeavours of *jñāna*, *yoga* and so forth, and engage in *bhajana* of Vāsudeva-Kṛṣṇa.

pratyāhāre ruddha-mati yogeśvara-gana
kadāca karite pāre yāhā sampādana
sei karmāśaya granthi kāṭe sādhu-gaṇa
yāṅra kṛpā-bale, laha tāṅhāra śaraṇa

Bhajana-rahasya-vṛtti

Impersonalists (*nirviśeṣa-jñānīs*) are not able to control their senses even by performing severely rigid practices, but devotees can very easily control the extremely strong senses by meditating upon the lustre of the lotus-petal-like toes of the most merciful Bhagavān. In this way they become absorbed in deep meditation. This meditation (*dhyāna*), and the object of meditation (*dhyeya*), Śrī Bhagavān, are both eternal. The followers of the theory of monism (*advaitavādīs*) say: "*sādhakānāṁ hitārthāya brahmaṇi rūpaḥ kalpate* – Brahman is formless but for the benefit of *sādhakas* a form has been imagined." They say that by worshipping imaginary forms of Viṣṇu, Śiva, Durgā, Sūrya and Gaṇeśa, one's heart is purified and one then attains *sāyujya-mukti*, merging into Brahman. This conception, however, is an ignorant hypothesis that is opposed to the scriptures.

The word *vilāsa-bhaktyā* in this Text 22 means that the *sādhaka* contemplates Śrī Kṛṣṇa's body and meditates on different kinds of services, such as anointing Him with perfume, giving Him an oil-massage, bathing Him and so forth. Meditation on the toes of

Śrī Kṛṣṇa, who is clever in *vraja-rasa*, means remembering that His lotus toes have been coloured by *kuṅkuma* while He was performing intimate pastimes in the bowers of Vṛndāvana with the *vraja-devīs*. By meditating on this, all the knots of the disease in one's heart are easily and naturally destroyed. How can the impersonalists, who are covered by ignorance, obtain all these transcendental sentiments? They do not even accept the eternality of Bhagavān and His transcendental form. Although they consider themselves liberated, in reality they are not. *Śrī Caitanya-caritāmṛta* (*Madhya-līlā* 22.29) confirms this:

jñānī jīvan-mukta-daśā pāinu kari' māne
vastutaḥ buddhi 'śuddha' nahe kṛṣṇa-bhakti bine

The endeavours of the offensive *nirviśeṣa-jñānīs* to control their senses are futile. Externally their activities may look like self-control, but internally there is a flow of dirty, lusty desires likened to the Phalgu River, a river in Gayā that has no flow of water on the river bed but flows underground. Even after thousands of years of severe austerities, Saubhari Ṛṣi was not liberated from material desires. However, by serving Bhagavān in the association of the pure devotee Mahārāja Māndhātā, he was liberated from material existence very easily. On the strength of *bhakti*, the devotees are able to cut ignorance at the root. All their senses remain engaged in Bhagavān's service and they make their senses successful by relishing the nectar of Bhagavān's beauty. Therefore give up futile endeavours to subdue the senses and perform *bhajana* of Śrī Vrajendra-nandana, who is eternal and full of transcendental bliss. This is the only auspicious activity.

Text 23

An introduction to the midday pastimes (*madhyāhna-līlā*) is found in *Govinda-līlāmṛta* (8.1):

madhyāhne 'nyonya-saṅgodita-vividha-vikārādi-bhūṣā-pramugdhau
vāmyotkaṇṭhātilolau smara-makha-lalitādy-āli-narmāpta-śātau
dolāraṇyāmbu-vaṁśī-hṛti-rati-madhupānārka-pūjādi-līlau
rādhā-kṛṣṇau satṛṣṇau parijana-ghaṭayā sevyamānau smarāmi

I meditate upon Śrī Rādhā-Kṛṣṇa, who at midday enjoy each other's company while being beautifully decorated with various *bhāvas*, such as *aṣṭa-sāttvika-bhāvas* and *vyabhicāri-bhāvas.* They become extremely restless due to contrariness (*vāmya*) and yearning (*utkaṇṭhā*). In Their amorous play (*kandarpa-yajña*) the joking words of Śrī Lalitā and the other *sakhīs* give Them much pleasure. They blissfully enjoy sports like swinging (*jhūlā*), frolicking in the forest (*vana-vihāra*), playing in the water (*jala-keli*), stealing the flute (*vaṁśī-haraṇa*), amorous meeting (*rati-krīḍā*), drinking honey (*madhu-pāna*), worshipping the Sun-god (*sūrya-pūjā*) and many other kinds of pastimes while being served by Their dear ones.

rādhā-kuṇḍe sumilana, vikārādi-vibhūṣaṇa,
vāmyotkaṇṭha-mugdha-bhāva-līlā
sambhoga-narmādi-rīti, dolā-khelā vaṁśī-hṛti,
madhu-pāna, sūrya-pūja khelā

jala-khelā, vanyāśana, chala-supti, vanyāṭana,
bahu-līlānande dui jane
parijana suveṣṭita, rādhā-kṛṣṇa susevita,
madhyāhna-kālete smari mane

Bhajana-rahasya-vṛtti

After finishing Her *prasāda-sevā* at Nanda-bhavana, Śrīmatī Rādhārāṇī returns to Jāvaṭa with Her *sakhīs*, where She very eagerly waits to meet Her *prāṇa-priyatama*, Śrī Kṛṣṇa. Her mother-in-law, Jaṭilā, orders Her to worship Sūryadeva, and on this pretext she leaves Her house with Her *sakhīs* and secretly departs for Rādhā-kuṇḍa, where She is able to freely meet with Her beloved. There, His *darśana* and touch decorate Her with *aṣṭa-sāttvika*, *kila-kiñcita* and many other *bhāvas*. Śrīmatī Rādhikā's contrary mood (*vāmya-bhāva*) enables Her *prāṇeśvara* to relish the mellows of pastimes to their highest extent, and it also stimulates His ever-fresh eagerness. Then many pastimes take place with the *gopīs*, such as meeting with Kṛṣṇa (*sambhoga*), joking while playing dice (*pāśā-krīḍā*), playing hide-and-seek (*āṅkha-micaunī*), stealing the flute (*vaṁśī-corī*), drinking honey (*madhu-pāna*, or *prema-pāna*), engaging in water-sports (*jala-krīḍā*), having a picnic (*vanya-bhojana*), feigning sleep (*chala-śayana*) and worshipping the Sun-god (*sūrya-pūjā*). Absorbed in meditating on these pastimes, the *rāgānuga-sādhaka* performs *kīrtana* of Kṛṣṇa's names.

Thus ends the *Caturtha-yāma-sādhana*,
Madhyāhna-kālīya-bhajana, of *Śrī Bhajana-rahasya*.

5

Pañcama-yāma-sādhana

Aparāhna-kālīya-bhajana – kṛṣṇa-āsakti

(from three-and-a-half *praharas* of the day until dusk: approximately 3.30 P.M. – 6.00 P.M.)

Text 1

The constitutional nature of the *nāma-sādhaka* and his prayer for the eternal servitorship of Śrī Kṛṣṇa are described in *Śikṣāṣṭaka* (5):

ayi nanda-tanuja kiṅkaraṁ
patitaṁ māṁ viṣame bhavāmbudhau
kṛpayā tava pāda-paṅkaja-
sthita-dhūli-sadṛśaṁ vicintaya

O Nanda-nandana, as a result of my fruitive activities, I have fallen into this fearful ocean of material existence. Please bestow Your mercy upon this eternal servant of Yours. Consider me to be just like a speck of dust at Your lotus feet and always accept me as Your purchased servant.

tava nitya dāsa muñi, tomā pāsariyā
paḍiyāchi bhavārṇave māyā-baddha haiyā
kṛpā kari' kara more pada-dhūli-sama
tomāra sevaka, karoṅ tomāra sevana

"O Lord, I am Your eternal servant, but due to my misfortune I have abandoned You. Being bound by *māyā*, I am drowning in this bottomless ocean of material existence. Please mercifully accept me as a particle of dust at Your lotus feet. I will become Your servant and serve You eternally."

Bhajana-rahasya-vṛtti

When a devotee attains the state of *āsakti*, his prayers are filled with extreme humility and lamentation. In the fully matured stage of *āsakti* there is some appearance of his perfected body (*siddha-deha*), and attachment arises for both *bhajana* and *bhajanīya*, the object of *bhajana*. When one performs *bhajana*, *śraddhā* gradually develops through *anartha-nivṛtti* and *niṣṭhā* up to the stage of *ruci*. Kṛṣṇa, as the Supersoul situated in the heart, accepts the prayers of devotees who are in these stages. However, Kṛṣṇa Himself hears the prayers of a devotee who is endowed with *āsakti*, and His heart melts with compassion.

Text 2

When one performs *kīrtana* that is free from offences, *bhāva* will arise by Śrī Kṛṣṇa's mercy. *Śrīmad-Bhāgavatam* (1.2.17–19) states:

śṛṇvatāṁ sva-kathāḥ kṛṣṇaḥ
puṇya-śravaṇa-kīrtanaḥ
hṛdy antaḥ-stho hy abhadrāṇi
vidhunoti suhṛt satām

naṣṭa-prāyeṣv abhadreṣu
nityaṁ bhāgavata-sevayā
bhagavaty uttama-śloke
bhaktir bhavati naiṣṭhikī

tadā rajas-tamo-bhāvāḥ
kāma-lobhādayaś ca ye
ceta etair anāviddhaṁ
sthitaṁ sattve prasīdati

Both hearing and chanting the glories of Śrī Kṛṣṇa are purifying. Because Kṛṣṇa is the eternal friend of saintly persons, He situates Himself in the hearts of those who hear narrations of Him and He destroys their inauspicious passions, such as lust. By continuous service to both *Śrīmad-Bhāgavatam* and the *mahā-bhāgavata* devotee, inauspicious desires are almost completely destroyed, and irrevocable devotional service (*naiṣṭhikī-bhakti*) is awakened to Bhagavān Śrī Kṛṣṇa, who is praised with transcendental prayers. As soon as this *naiṣṭhikī-bhakti* is awakened, the qualities of the modes of passion and ignorance, such as lust and anger, become pacified, and one's heart reaches the stage of purity.

yāṅra kathā śravaṇa-kīrtane puṇya haya
sei kṛṣṇa hṛdaye vasiyā nāśe bhaya

sādhakera abhadra kramaśaḥ kare nāśa
bhaktira naiṣṭhika bhāva karena prakāśa

rajas-tama-samudbhuta kāma-lobha-hīna
haiyā bhakta-citta sattve hayata pravīṇa

Bhajana-rahasya-vṛtti

Taste for the topics of Śrī Vāsudeva will manifest only after one has sincerely accepted the shelter of the lotus feet of *śrī guru*. By the *sādhaka's* performance of the activities of *sādhana*, such as *śravaṇa* and *kīrtana*, his inauspiciousness – *anarthas* and *aparādhas* – will be removed and his heart will become pure. Bhagavān Himself enters the devotee's heart through the medium of *hari-kathā* and destroys all kinds of inauspiciousness and misfortune. In other words, the bad results of the devotee's *prārabdha-karma* are destroyed, his *hṛd-roga* (disease of the heart in the form of lust) is removed, and Bhagavān resides in his heart forever.

Bhāgavata-sevā means service to both the book *bhāgavata* (*Śrīmad-Bhāgavatam*) and the devotee *bhāgavata* (the pure Vaiṣṇava). As a result of this service, steady *bhakti* arises in the *sādhaka's* heart. *Naiṣṭhikī* means that through *niṣṭhā* the mind becomes fixed. Then gradually, by the association of devotees, one's fruitive activities, false renunciation and so on are destroyed, and the unhealthy inclination to seek the company of non-devotees, such as *māyāvādīs* and those inclined towards enjoyment with the opposite sex, does not awaken. It is impossible to be freed from these tendencies by one's own endeavour. *Naiṣṭhikī-bhakti* appears in the heart only through hearing topics of Bhagavān described in exalted verses spoken by *uttama-bhāgavatas.* By this act of devotion, passion, ignorance, lust, anger and so forth are destroyed. Moreover, even if these qualities remain, they are just like fried seeds, unable to produce any fruit. The mode of passion (*rajo-guṇa*) and the mode of ignorance (*tamo-guṇa*) cause sleep, distraction and desires unrelated to serving Kṛṣṇa to arise within the living entities. The words *etair anāviddham* in this Text mean that upon the awakening of *naiṣṭhikī-bhakti*, the heart of the *sādhaka* is not agitated by the enemies headed by lust. This is because his heart is fixed on the path of *bhakti* and he no longer has taste for the objects of sense enjoyment.

Text 3

A prayer explaining Bhagavān's mercy is given in *Śrīmad-Bhāgavatam* (10.14.8):

tat te 'nukampāṁ su-samīkṣamāṇo
bhuñjāna evātma-kṛtaṁ vipākam
hṛd-vāg vapurbhir vidadhan namas te
jīveta yo mukti-pade sa dāya-bhāk

One who accepts as Your mercy the results of his own actions as well as the happiness and distress of his *prārabdha-karma*, who endures them with an undisturbed mind, and who maintains his life by offering himself unto You by body, mind and words, is eligible to attain Your lotus feet, which are the shelter of liberation.

duḥkha bhoga kari' nija-kṛta-karma-phale
kāya-mano-vākye tava caraṇa-kamale
bhakti kari' kāṭe kāla tava kṛpā āśe
mukti-pada, tava pada pāya anāyāse

Bhajana-rahasya-vṛtti

In this prayer to Bhagavān, Brahmā instructs the *sādhaka* thus: a *sādhaka* should understand the attainment of both happiness and distress to be Bhagavān's mercy, or he should understand them to be an opportunity to completely eradicate sins and offences performed due to previous impressions (*saṁskāras*). Sometimes Bhagavān creates happiness or distress for the *sādhaka* in order to increase the eagerness in his heart. In this Text the word *mukti-pada* means the one at whose lotus feet liberation (*mukti*) takes shelter. This refers either to Bhagavān or to *bhakti*, i.e. *bhagavat-sevā*.

Text 4

Upon reaching the condition described in the following verse (*Śrīmad-Bhāgavatam* (11.2.43)), one attains supreme spiritual peace (*parā-śānti*):

ity acyutāṅghriṁ bhajato 'nuvṛttyā
bhaktir viraktir bhagavat-prabodhaḥ
bhavanti vai bhāgavatasya rājaṁs
tataḥ parāṁ śāntim upaiti sākṣāt

O king, whoever devoutly worships the lotus feet of Bhagavān will develop detachment from material existence and devotion for Him that is saturated with *prema*. All knowledge related to Bhagavān will manifest in his heart and thus he will begin to experience supreme peace.

hena anuvṛtti saha yei kṛṣṇa bhaje
subhakti, virāga, jñāna, tāṅhāra upaje
se tina sundara-rūpe ekatre bāḍhiyā
parā-śānti-prema-dhana deya ta' āniyā

Bhajana-rahasya-vṛtti

In this Text, Kavi Ṛṣi, the best of the nine Yogendras, responds to one of Nimi Mahārāja's questions by saying that besides devotion to Bhagavān, there is no means to attain eternal auspiciousness. Temporary endeavours to attain imaginary peace or freedom from material suffering are foolish and can bring no actual auspiciousness to the living entity. The only auspiciousness is to take shelter of Śrī Bhagavān's devotees and by steady practice attain *bhakti*, which is beyond the three modes of material nature. A person who has pure *bhakti*, who is established in the devotional way of life (*bhāgavata-dharma*) and who performs service with appropriate renunciation (*yukta-vairāgya*) can never be touched by ignorance. Established in the kingdom of *bhakti*, he acquires higher and higher stages of elevated devotion and thus attains transcendental peace.

Practising and following means to take exclusive shelter of Śrī Bhagavān's devotees; to remember and follow Kṛṣṇa's associates is more beneficial than to remember and follow Kṛṣṇa Himself. It is more useful for the *bhakti-sādhaka* to follow the process of devotion shown by Śrīla Rūpa Gosvāmī and Śrīla Raghunātha dāsa Gosvāmī, who themselves follow the *gopīs*, than it is to follow Śrī Caitanya Mahāprabhu directly. The method to awaken *lobha*, transcendental greed, is to remember, pray and weep for the sentiments of elevated devotees. *Sādhana* means to practise *bhakti* through the senses and with the aim of attaining *svarūpa-siddhi*. When *bhāva* appears, one's practice is no longer *sādhana-bhakti* but *bhāva-bhakti*, and when one achieves *vastu-siddhi*, he will attain *prema-sevā*.

Text 5

The nine types of *bhakti-sādhana* are described in *Śrīmad-Bhāgavatam* (7.5.23–4):

śravaṇaṁ kīrtanaṁ viṣṇoḥ
smaraṇaṁ pāda-sevanam
arcanaṁ vandanaṁ dāsyaṁ
sakhyam ātma-nivedanam

iti puṁsārpitā viṣṇau
bhaktiś cen nava-lakṣaṇā
kriyeta bhagavaty addhā
tan manye 'dhītam uttamam

A person is said to have perfectly studied the scriptures if he is completely surrendered to Bhagavān Śrī Viṣṇu, if he is free from *karma*, *jñāna*, *yoga* and other obstructions, and if he is engaged in the nine kinds of *bhakti*: hearing topics related to Bhagavān (*śravaṇam*); chanting His name (*kīrtanam*); remembering His name, form, qualities and pastimes (*smaraṇam*); serving His lotus feet (*pāda-sevanam*); performing deity worship (*arcanam*); offering prayers (*vandanam*); becoming His servant (*dāsyam*); becoming His friend (*sakhyam*); and offering one's very self (*ātma-nivedanam*). Only such a person's study of the scriptures is successful.

śravaṇa-kīrtana-ādi-bhaktira prakāra
cid-ghana-ānanda kṛṣṇe sākṣāt yāṅhāra
sarva-śāstra-tattva bujhi' kriyā-para tini
sarvārtha-siddhite tiṅha vijña-śiromaṇi

Bhajana-rahasya-vṛtti

The nine kinds of devotion, *navadhā-bhakti*, comprise *svarūpa-siddha-bhakti*, unalloyed devotion. Other types of devotional practices fall into the categories of *saṅga-siddha-bhakti*, *āropa-siddha-bhakti* and so forth. It is essential that one completely surrender to Bhagavān, for one cannot enter *svarūpa-siddha-bhakti* without surrender. This is the import of the phrase *iti puṁsārpitā viṣṇau* in this Text. According to Śrīla Sanātana Gosvāmī, the word *puṁsā* here indicates the *māyā-baddha-jīva*, conditioned living entity, who is attached to sense enjoyment. The words *bhagavaty addhā* refer to the instruction to perform service to Bhagavān that is stimulated by devotion that flows like a continuous stream of oil.

Text 6

When one cultivates this kind of devotion, *bhāva* will gradually arise and *dāsya-rati* will naturally awaken within him. This is evident in Vṛtrāsura's prayer in *Śrīmad-Bhāgavatam* (6.11.24):

ahaṁ hare tava pādaika-mūla-
dāsānudāso bhavitāsmi bhūyaḥ
manaḥ smaretāsu-pater guṇāṁs te
gṛṇīta vāk karma karotu kāyaḥ

The living entity is Your eternal servant, but by the misuse of his free will, he has forgotten his position of eternal servitude. Consequently, he is caught in the snare of *māyā* and endures many kinds of afflictions in this material existence. Moreover, the desire to become the servant of Your servant can only be fulfilled by the causeless compassion of *guru* and Vaiṣṇavas. This mood of servitorship can only be obtained by performing *bhakti*. O Lord, please bestow such mercy upon me, that in my next birth I may obtain the opportunity to exclusively serve the servants who have taken shelter of Your lotus feet. May my mind always remember Your all-auspicious qualities, my speech always chant the glories of these qualities, and my body always remain engaged in Your service.

chinu tava nitya-dāsa, gale bāṅdhi' māyā-pāśa,
saṁsāre pāinu nānā-kleśa
ebe punaḥ kari āśa, haiyā tava dāsera dāsa,
bhaji' pāi tava bhakti-leśa

prāneśvara tava guṇa, smaruk mana punaḥ punaḥ,
tava nāma jihvā karuk gāna
kara-dvaya tava karma, kariyā labhuk śarma,
tava pade saṁpinu parāṇa

Text 7

By nature the living entity is the object to be enjoyed (*bhogya-vastu*) and Śrī Kṛṣṇa is the enjoyer (*bhoktā*). By performing *bhajana* in the association of *rasika-bhaktas*, the desire to serve Śrī Rādhā, who is permeated with transcendental bliss, becomes strong, and the loving sentiments of the *gopīs* (*gopī-bhāva*) awaken. *Śrīmad-Bhāgavatam* (10.29.38) states:

tan naḥ prasīda vṛjinārdana te 'ṅghri-mūlaṁ
prāptā visṛjya vasatīs tvad-upāsanāśāḥ
tvat-sundara-smita-nirīkṣaṇa-tīvra-kāma-
taptātmanāṁ puruṣa-bhūṣaṇa dehi dāsyam

[Attracted by the sound of Śrī Kṛṣṇa's flute, the *gopīs* approached Him and said:] O You who remove suffering, we have given up our homes, family members and relatives, and we have come to Your lotus feet only because we desire to serve You. O jewel among men, be pleased with us. O best among men, Your sweet smile and attractive glances have set our hearts ablaze with a burning desire for intimate meeting with You. Every pore of our bodies burns with this desire. Please accept us as Your maidservants.

tava dāsya-āśe chāḍiyāchi ghara-dvāra
dayā kari' deha kṛṣṇa, caraṇa tomāra

tava hāsya-mukha-nirīkṣaṇa-kāmi-jane
tomāra kaiṅkarya deha praphulla-vadane

Bhajana-rahasya-vṛtti

Immersed in the mood of the *gopīs*, Śukadeva Gosvāmī uttered this verse. Hearing the sound of the flute, the *vraja-gopīs* go to the *rāsa-sthalī* where they come face to face with Kṛṣṇa. Vrajendra-nandana Śyāmasundara, the ocean of all nectarean mellows, then begins to joke with them in order to taste the sentiments hidden within their hearts. The *gopīs'* retorts are full of sarcastic humour.

The general meaning of this verse is that the *gopīs* are praying to become the maidservants of Kṛṣṇa – *dehi dāsyam.* Kṛṣṇa begins by saying, "O you who are intoxicated with your fresh youth (*nava-yauvana-pramattā*), it is extremely rare to attain service to Me."

The *gopīs* reply, "O Śyāmasundara, You fulfil the desires of those who are surrendered unto You. Your beautiful smiling glances have set intense lust ablaze in our hearts and this is tormenting us. Nevertheless, we want no kind of compensation for our suffering. Please, just give us service to Your lotus feet."

Or the *gopīs* say, "O Śyāmasundara, we are young women and we want to create happiness for You with our bodily limbs. We want to worship You through the 'paraphernalia' of accepting Your blooming smiling glances and the nectar of Your lips. O ornament amongst men (*puruṣa-bhūṣaṇa*), we are fair-complexioned (*gauraṅgī*) and You are like a sapphire (*indra-nīlamaṇi*), so You are the natural ornament for our bodily limbs."

Or the *gopīs* say sarcastically, "We are not praying to obtain the dust of Your lotus feet. You are making us suffer from moral guilt and unhappiness – You are certainly living up to Your name Vṛjina-ardana (vanquisher of distress)! We have heard from Paurṇamāsī that even Lakṣmī, who enjoys pastimes on the chest of Śrī Nārāyaṇa, comes to take shelter of Your lotus feet – *te 'ṅghri-mūlam* – but we are not Lakṣmī. We have just come here out of curiosity to view the natural beauty of Vṛndāvana on a moonlit night. So give Your shelter to Lakṣmī of Vaikuṇṭha, not to us! You should remember, though, that not even Lakṣmī and others would completely accept servitude to You. O best amongst men, You so eagerly desire to attain the young brides of

Gokula that You even adorn the *sakhās*, like Subala and others, in *gopī* dress. O ornament of men, the male gender has been defamed by this nature of Yours. Don't think we are suffering from lust. And we are not Your 'beloveds' – this is only Your imagination."

Text 8

To take shelter of the perfect sentiments of the *gopīs* (*siddha-gopī-bhāva*) is described in *Śrīmad-Bhāgavatam* (10.29.39):

vīkṣyālakāvṛta-mukhaṁ tava kuṇḍala-śrī-
gaṇḍa-sthalādhara-sudhaṁ hasitāvalokam
dattābhayaṁ ca bhuja-daṇḍa-yugaṁ vilokya
vakṣaḥ śriyaika-ramaṇaṁ ca bhavāma dāsyaḥ

[The *gopīs* said:] Priyatama, after seeing Your beautiful lotus face, decorated with glossy black curling tresses; Your beautiful cheeks, upon which enchanting earrings (*kuṇḍalas*) radiate Your boundless loveliness; Your sweet lips, whose nectar defeats all other nectar; Your charming glance, which is made radiant by Your slight smile; Your two arms, which liberally give the charity of fearlessness to surrendered souls; and Your chest, beautified by Lakṣmī who resides there as a golden line, we have all become Your maidservants.

o mukha alakāvṛta, o kuṇḍala-śobhā
adhara-amṛta-gaṇḍa-smita-manolobhā
abhaya-da bhuja-yuga, śrī-sevita-vakṣa
dekhiyā halāma dāsī, sevā-kārye dakṣa

Bhajana-rahasya-vṛtti

The *gopīs'* internal *bhāva* is present within this verse. When a transcendental revelation (*sphūrti*) of *siddha-gopī-bhāva* appears to Śrīla Bhaktivinoda Ṭhākura, he remembers and utters this verse. Vrajendra-nandana Śyāmasundara is *rasika-cūḍā-maṇi*, the crest-jewel amongst those who relish *rasa*. Concealing His own submissive mood (*dākṣiṇya-bhāva*), He expresses a mood of indifference towards the *vraja-devīs*, saying, "O *vraja-devīs*, why are you trying to attain the position of being My unpaid maidservants?"

The *gopīs* meekly reply, "O Śyāmasundara, it is impossible to describe the value of the payment You have given us."

Smiling, Śyāmasundara asks, "What was that payment?"

The *gopīs* reply, "You have given all us *ramaṇīs* the naturally perfect nectar of Your lips, the touch of Your alluring arms and other limbs, and the embrace of Your chest, which is the shelter of Śrī Lakṣmī. Our eyes, which are fickle like the movement of *khañjana* birds, have been imprisoned by the net of Your face, which is encircled by Your curly hair. Those curls are not actually hair, but a snare, and both Your earrings are traps. The nectar of Your lips is the lure for our *khañjana*-bird-like eyes and Your smiling, restless glances are well-bred and trained to capture our eyes. Your alluring arms and Your chest, which bestow *rati*, calm our hearts. O Kṛṣṇa, even before we attained our adolescence, You called us to Your *kuñja-mandira* through Your enchanting sweetness, gave us *darśana* of the wealth of Your earrings and other ornaments made of precious stones (*nīla-nidhi* and *padma-nidhi*) and of the best gold (*jāmbu-nada-svarṇa*), and fed us the nectar of Your lips. Such enticements have forced us to hanker to become Your maidservants." With loving anger the *vraja-devīs* then say, "O Kṛṣṇa, upon seeing the unequalled wealth of Your beauty, we have developed the desire to become Your maidservants, but if this desire is not fulfilled, it will change into hopelessness."

Or the *gopīs* shake a chastising finger at Kṛṣṇa and say, "O crest-jewel of religious personalities (*dhārmika-cūḍāmaṇi*), we know very well about the nature of Your *dharma*; You always flirt with the wives of other men. You also keep the *ramaṇīs* of Vaikuṇṭha upon Your chest for amorous dalliance. You can be forgiven by Nārāyaṇa, but not by us, and not by our husbands. Rather, after our husbands complain to the mighty Kaṁsa, You will be punished. We are chaste women from good, noble families, and the idea of having a paramour is extremely contemptible for us. You cannot make us into Your maidservants by showing Your beauty and sweetness."

How the *gopīs* became the maidservants of Kṛṣṇa after seeing the unprecedented beauty of His form is described by the crest-jewel of those who relish *vraja-rasa*, Śrīla Viśvanātha Cakravartī Ṭhākura:

Śyāmasundara says to the *gopīs*, "I did not purchase you with any payment, so how have you become My maidservants?"

The *vraja-ramaṇīs* reply, "You have given us a payment which is millions and millions of times more than enough. If You want to know what that priceless treasure is, then listen. Ever since the very beginning of our adolescence, You called us into Your *kuñja-mandira* and gave us *darśana* of Your beautiful face, covered with falling locks of curling hair. When You wrap a tilted turban on Your head, we get *darśana* of Your lotus face through the lattice made by Your curly tresses. Then, with Your small delicate finger, You push those curling locks into Your turban and Your beauty is thoroughly revealed. Your curling tresses also hang loose when You tie a centred turban, and when You untie Your turban to take rest, Your locks of hair fall over Your face. In this way, Your lotus face is sometimes uncovered, sometimes slightly covered and sometimes completely beautified by these curly locks. When You laugh and joke, Your earrings swing to and fro to kiss Your cheeks. By the impressions resulting from this meeting, Your most attractive cheeks emanate an unprecedented beauty. In this way, by seeing Your moonlike face, the lotuses of the *gopīs'* hearts blossom. You have purchased us, with the incomparable sweetness of Your form as payment."

Kṛṣṇa may say, "I am devoted to religious principles, and you are the wives of other men. How can I make you My maidservants?"

Upon hearing this, the *gopīs* shake a finger at Him and reply, "O best of the followers of *dharma,* You keep Lakṣmī, the wife of Nārāyaṇa of Vaikuṇṭha, upon Your chest where, in front of us, out of shame, she is present merely as a golden line. In private, though, she enjoys amorous sports with You. Can any woman in the three worlds reject You? None can. By giving us *darśana* of the priceless treasure of Yourself, You are compelled to make us Your maidservants."

Text 9

The superiority of paramour love (*parakīya-bhāva*) is described in *Śrīmad-Bhāgavatam* (10.29.33):

kurvanti hi tvayi ratiṁ kuśalāḥ sva ātman
nitya-priye pati-sutādibhir ārti-daiḥ kim
tan naḥ prasīda parameśvara mā sma chindyā
āśāṁ dhṛtāṁ tvayi cirād aravinda-netra

[The *gopīs* said:] O Paramātmā, the great personalities, who are the well-wishers of everyone's soul, direct their love to You because You are the soul of all souls. What is the use of loving or serving husbands, sons and so forth, who are temporary and sources of misery? Be pleased with us and give us Your mercy. O lotus-eyed one, please do not cut the flourishing creeper of our desire to serve You, which we have nourished for such a long time.

tumi priya ātmā, nitya ratira bhājana
ārti-dātā pati-putre rati akāraṇa

baḍa āśā kari' āinu tomāra caraṇe
kamala-nayana, hera prasanna-vadane

Bhajana-rahasya-vṛtti

After the living entity attains self-realisation, his material relationships, such as those with wife and children, do not remain. He understands the futility of material existence and naturally becomes immersed in deep attachment for Kṛṣṇa. At this stage, the *jīva* is no longer under the jurisdiction of rules and regulations. Engaged in *rāga-mārga-bhakti,* he performs exclusive *bhajana* of Śrī Rādhā-Kṛṣṇa.

At this point in the conversation between the *vraja-devīs* and Śrī Kṛṣṇa, the *gopīs* say to Him, "We have forevermore given up our relationships with husbands and everyone else, and have now come here before You. The love that appeared in our hearts as a sprout has since become a vine of desire that has grown very large. We have been attached to You since childhood and have sincere love and affection for You. Please do not cut down this creeper of affection."

Or the *gopīs* say, "Our hearts have become naturally delighted by seeing Your reddish lotus eyes, and we have already become Your unpaid maidservants."

The *vraja-devīs* say with rebuking words, "O lotus-eyed one, as lotus flowers close at night time, Your eyes are also half-closed, and You are therefore deprived of the *darśana* of our youth and bodily beauty. So Your having eyes is useless."

Or they say, "We have understood Your inner heart's desire. It is right for us to desist from taking part in Your improper activities, so we will not stay here long. Please give up whatever desire is in Your heart."

Text 10

The necessity of taking shelter of the lotus feet of Śrī Rādhā is expressed by Śrī Raghunātha dāsa Gosvāmī in his *Sva-saṅkalpa-prakāśa-stotra* (1):

anārādhya rādhā-padāmbhoja-reṇum
anāśritya vṛndāṭavīṁ tat-padāṅkām
asambhāṣya-tad-bhāva-gambhīra-cittān
kutaḥ śyāma-sindho rasasyāvagāhaḥ

How can a person become immersed in the ocean of ecstatic mellows of Śyāma (*śyāma-rasa-sindhu*) if he has never worshipped the dust of Śrī Rādhā's lotus feet; if he has never taken shelter of Her pastime-place Śrī Vṛndāvana, which is marked with the impressions of Her lotus feet; and if he has never served the devotees whose hearts are already submerged in Her profound sentiments? It will never be possible.

rādhā-padāmbhoja-reṇu nāhi ārādhile
tāṅhāra padāṅka-pūta-vraja nā bhajile
nā sevile rādhikā-gambhīra-bhāva-bhakta
śyāma-sindhu-rase kise habe anurakta?

Bhajana-rahasya-vṛtti

While remembering this *stotra*, Śrīla Bhaktivinoda Ṭhākura yearns to attain the wonderful and astonishing service of Śrī Rādhā-Mādhava.

In order to be submerged in the ocean of *śyāma-rasa* (*śṛṅgāra-rasa*, or the amorous mellow), it is absolutely essential to worship the dust of the lotus feet of Śrīmatī Rādhikā, who is the personification of *hlādinī*; to worship Śrī Vṛndāvana-dhāma, Her place of playful, amorous pastimes (*keli-vilāsa-sthala*); and to worship Her dearmost devotees. Besides this method there is no way to attain the service of Śrī Rādhā-Mādhava. Considering there to be another way is only a vain and useless hope. *Śrī Rādhā-rasa-sudhā-nidhi* (80) confirms this:

rādhā-dāsyam apāsya yaḥ prayatate govinda-saṅgāśayā
so 'yaṁ pūrṇa-sudhā-ruceḥ paricayaṁ rākāṁ vinā kāṅkṣati

Those who endeavour to attain the association of Śrī Kṛṣṇa but reject *rādhā-dāsya* are like people who endeavour to see the full moon when it is not a full moon night.

Stavāvali (*Sva-niyama-daśakam* (6)) states:

ya ekaṁ govindaṁ bhajati kapaṭī dāmbhikatayā
tad abhyarṇe śīrṇe kṣaṇam api na yāmi vratam idam

I will never go near a hypocrite who worships Govinda alone [without Rādhā]. This is my vow.

If Śyāma is directly the emperor of all transcendental mellows (*rasarāja*) and the embodiment of the amorous mellow (*śṛṅgāra-rasa*), then Śrīmatī Rādhikā is the form of *madanākhya-mahābhāva*. Śrīmatī Rādhikā, with Her *śṛṅgāra-rasa*, feeds Śyāma honey in the form of Kandarpa (Cupid):

kṛṣṇake karāya śyāma-rasa madhu-pāna
nirantara pūrṇa kare kṛṣṇera sarva-kāma

Śrī Caitanya-caritāmṛta (*Madhya-līlā* 8.180)

Śrīmatī Rādhikā makes Kṛṣṇa drink the honey of the amorous mellow (*śyāma-rasa*). She is therefore engaged in satisfying all of Kṛṣṇa's lust (*kāma*).

Śṛṅgāra-rasa is also called *śyāma-rasa*. This is the opinion of Śrī Viṣṇu-daivata, found in *Sāhitya-darpaṇa*: *śyāma-varṇo 'yaṁ viṣṇu-daivataḥ*.

Śrīla Bhaktivinoda Ṭhākura sings in his song *Rādhikā-caraṇa-padma*:

rādhikā ujjvala-rasera ācārya
rādhā-mādhava-śuddha-prema vicārya

ye dharila rādhā-pada parama-yatane
se pāila kṛṣṇa-pada amūlya ratane

rādhā-pada vinā kabhu kṛṣṇa nāhi mile
rādhikā dāsīra kṛṣṇa sarva-vede bole

Śrīmatī Rādhikā is the *ācārya* of the mellows of amorous love (*ujjvala-rasa*). The pure love between Rādhā and Mādhava is meant to be discussed and contemplated. Those who place Śrīmatī Rādhikā's lotus feet in their hearts and worship them with great care obtain the priceless jewel of Kṛṣṇa's lotus feet. Without taking shelter of the lotus feet of Rādhā, one can never meet Kṛṣṇa. The Vedic scriptures declare that Kṛṣṇa is the property of the maid-servants of Śrī Rādhā.

Vṛndāvana-dhāma is the place of Śrī Rādhā-Mādhava's various amorous pastimes (*līlā-vilāsa*). Śrī Yugala-kiśora roam here performing Their pastimes, and the land of Vṛndāvana is marked with the impressions of Their lotus feet, as Bhaktivinoda Ṭhākura sings in *Rādhikā-caraṇa-padma* – *rādhā-padāṅkita-dhāma vṛndāvana yāṅra nāma.*

Śrīmad-Bhāgavatam (10.30.28) states:

anayārādhito nūnaṁ
bhagavān harir īśvaraḥ
yan no vihāya govindaḥ
prīto yām anayad rahaḥ

[The *gopīs* said:] Most certainly She is Śrī Kṛṣṇa's worshipper. Therefore, being pleased with Her, Śyāmasundara has left us and taken Her away to a solitary place.

When Śrī Kṛṣṇa disappeared from the *rāsa-sthalī* (taking Rādhā with Him), the *gopīs* who were searching for Him saw His footprints in the forest, along with Śrīmatī Rādhikā's. Praising Her good fortune they said (*Śrīmad-Bhāgavatam* (10.30.27)): "*kasyāḥ padāni caitāni yātāyā nanda sūnunā* – here are the footprints of some *gopī* who was walking with the son of Nanda Mahārāja."

All of Vṛndāvana, including Govardhana and Rādhā-kuṇḍa, is the abode of Śrī Rādhā-Kṛṣṇa's *keli-vilāsa* and is marked with Their footprints. *Jāta-rati-sādhakas* have internal revelations (*sphūrtis*) of Śrī Rādhā-Kṛṣṇa's pastimes in Vṛndāvana's bowers. Here the meaning of taking shelter of Śrī Vṛndāvana-dhāma is to remember the various *līlās* performed there and to be absorbed in the sentiments of those *līlās*. But such realisation can only be obtained by the association and mercy of great personalities who are like-minded, affectionate towards oneself, more advanced than oneself, and who taste *vraja-rasa*.

In *Prema-bhakti-candrikā* (9.9) Śrīla Narottama dāsa Ṭhākura sings:

tāṅra bhakta saṅge sadā, rāsa-līlā prema kathā,
ye kare se pāya ghanaśyāma

By staying in the company of devotees who always discuss the sweet, nectarean pastimes of the *rāsa* dance, one is sure to attain Ghanaśyāma.

The sweetness of the *rasa* of Śrī Rādhā-Śyāmasundara's pastimes can only be relished through association with and service to the great personalities who taste *rasa* and who are submerged in the waves of this endless and eternal ocean of sweetness.

Text 11

The conception of being a maidservant of Śrī Rādhā is described in the following words of the Gosvāmīs:

abhimānaṁ parityajya prākṛta-vapur-ādiṣu
śrī-kṛṣṇa-kṛpayā gopī-dehe vraje vasāmy aham
rādhikānucarī bhūtvā pārakīya-rase sadā
rādhā-kṛṣṇa-vilāseṣu paricaryāṁ karomy aham

After giving up false identification with this material body, may I obtain the body of a *gopī* and reside in Vraja by the mercy of Śrī Kṛṣṇa. Becoming a maidservant of Śrī Rādhā, may I always serve and attend Rādhā and Kṛṣṇa, who enjoy pastimes of paramour love (*pārakīya-rasa*).

sthūla-dehādite ātma-buddhi parihari'
kṛṣṇa-kṛpa-āśraye nitya-gopī-deha dhari'
kabe āmi pārakīya rase nirantara
rādhā-kṛsna-sevā-sukha labhiba vistara

Bhajana-rahasya-vṛtti

As long as the *sādhaka* identifies himself with the material body, he cannot enter the kingdom of *bhajana*. Only after one has rejected all kinds of false identities pertaining to the body, such as, "I am a *brāhmaṇa*", "I am a *kṣatriya*", and pertaining to character, such as, "I am so qualified", "I am rich", "I am a scholar", and only after he becomes more humble than a blade of grass (*tṛṇād api sunīca*) and prays with extreme distress, is it possible to obtain Kṛṣṇa's mercy. All types of *anarthas*, *aparādhas* and *abhimānas* (false identifications) can only be eradicated by good association (*sat-saṅga*).

We should weep and pray in a distressed and humble voice, "O Śrī Kṛṣṇa! O Śrī Rādhā! *Gopī-dehe vraje vasāmy aham* – when will I obtain such mercy as to reside in Vraja and become the *dāsī* of the *dāsī* of the *dāsīs* of Rādhikā, and when will I eternally serve Your *pārakīya-rasa-vilāsa* day and night?"

By such distress-filled prayers, *gopī-bhāva* will arise in the heart by the mercy of Śrī Rādhā's *sakhīs*, the eternally perfected *gopīs* of Vraja. Without *gopī-bhāva* it is impossible to attain the land of Vṛndāvana-dhāma where Rādhā and Kṛṣṇa perform Their amorous pastimes in the solitary *nikuñjas*. This mood is attained only by following Śrī Rādhā's intimate *sakhīs*, who attend Her in Her private chambers. Only they can enter these pastimes, no one else, and only they expand these pastimes and taste them. The *ekādaśa-bhāvas* and the five *daśās*[1] are evoked by their mercy.

Śrīla Narottama dāsa Ṭhākura sings in *Prema-bhakti-candrikā* (5.8):

yugala-caraṇa sevi nirantara ei bhāvi
anurāge thākiba sadāya
sādhane bhāviba yāhā siddha-dehe pāba tāhā
rāga-pathera ei se upāya

I will constantly serve the lotus feet of Rādhā and Kṛṣṇa with loving attachment. Whatever I contemplate during *sādhana* will certainly be achieved upon attaining the perfection of a spiritual body (*siddha-deha*). This is the method of the path of *rāga*.

Pārakīya-rase sadā – The scriptures establish the pre-eminence of the *pārakīya-rasa* of Vraja. By serving Śrī Rādhā-Kṛṣṇa in the mood of wedded love (*svakīya*), one will attain Goloka Vṛndāvana, and by serving in paramour love, one will attain Vraja-Vṛndāvana, the absolute innermost chamber of Goloka-dhāma where Śrī Rādhā-Kṛṣṇa's *nikuñja-līlās* take place. There, the *mañjarī-sakhīs*, being endowed with *ullāsa-rati* (much

[1] These terms are explained on pp. 255–6.

stronger affection for Rādhā than for Kṛṣṇa), are topmost. They render service to the *rasa-keli-līlā-vilāsa* in the secluded groves without any hesitation. Śrī Raghunātha dāsa Gosvāmī says in *Vraja-vilāsa-stava* (38):

tāmbūlārpaṇa-pāda-mardana-payodānābhisārādibhir
vṛndāraṇya-maheśvarīṁ priyatayā yās toṣayanti priyāḥ
prāṇa-preṣṭha-sakhī-kulād api kilāsaṅkocitā bhūmikāḥ
kelī-bhūmiṣu rūpa-mañjarī-mukhās tā dāsikāḥ saṁśraye

I take shelter of the maidservants of Śrīmatī Rādhikā of whom Rūpa Mañjarī is prominent. Unlike the *prāṇa-preṣṭha-sakhīs*, they can perform any service without hesitation. They perpetually and affectionately satisfy Śrīmatī Rādhikā by their various services, such as offering *tāmbūla*, massaging Her feet, bringing Her water and arranging for Her trysts with Kṛṣṇa.

Text 12

The rejection of all types of *dharma*, out of the desire to serve Śrī Rādhā's lotus feet, is described in *Śrī Rādhā-rasa-sudhā-nidhi* (33):

dūrād apāsya svajanān sukham artha-koṭiṁ
sarveṣu sādhana-vareṣu ciraṁ nirāśaḥ
varṣantam eva sahajādbhuta-saukhya-dhārāṁ
śrī-rādhikā-caraṇa-reṇum ahaṁ smarāmi

The desire for the pleasure received from relationships with family and friends; for the four goals of life, namely *dharma*, *artha*, *kāma* and *mokṣa*; and for countless wealth and so forth, are the causes of *anarthas*. Knowing this, I abandoned them all. I worship the foot-dust of Śrī Rādhā, which showers natural, wonderful happiness, and I always hold this foot-dust upon my head.

svajana-sambandha-sukha, catur-varga artha
sakala-sādhana chāḍi' jāniyā anartha

sahaja-adbhuta-saukhya-dhārā vṛṣṭi kari
rādhā-pada-reṇu bhaji, śire sadā dhari'

Bhajana-rahasya-vṛtti

The first line of this Text, *dūrād apāsya sva-janān sukham artha-koṭim*, means that the desires for wealth and the happiness derived from the company of relatives cause impediments in remembering the dust of Śrīmatī Rādhikā's lotus feet; they are therefore worthy of being rejected. Pure *vairāgya*, renunciation, is actually a natural distaste for material matters and a taste for the dust of Śrī Rādhā's lotus feet. *Sādhakas* who possess exclusive faith in Śrī Rādhā (*rādhā-niṣṭhā*) are solely attached to the fragrance of Her lotus feet. Without Śrī Rādhā, they do not even have a taste for Śrī Kṛṣṇa. Material happiness seems insignificant to such *sādhakas*, who have firm attachment for Her lotus feet and who are not inclined towards any other spiritual goal (*sādhya*) or any other practice (*sādhana*) to attain it. Even other exalted *sādhanas* are obstacles on the path of *prema-bhakti*.

puṇya ye sukhera dhāma, tāra nā laio nāma,
puṇya mukti dui tyāga kari'

prema-bhakti-sudhā-nidhi, tāhe ḍūba niravadhi,
āra yata kṣāra-nidhi prāya

Prema-bhakti-candrikā (6.13–14)

Although piety is the abode of material happiness, do not strive for it. Rather, give up the desire for piety, as well as that for liberation. Loving devotional service is an ocean of nectar – always be immersed in it.

Pious activities, liberation and so forth are like a pile of ashes to the devotee on the stage of *prema*. Indeed, how can the devotee, who persistently desires to submerge himself in the nectarean ocean of loving devotional service and whose bee-like heart is attracted by the fragrance of Śrī Rādhā's foot-dust, which is full of immaculate *rasa*, go anywhere else? After receiving happiness from a supremely excellent object, can one become attracted by some trifling pleasure? Compared to the happiness of merging with Brahman (*brahmānanda*), the happiness of *bhajana* (*bhajanānanda*) is a greater source of bliss. That ecstasy is indescribable. The most condensed nature of *bhajanānanda* is *premānanda*, but it is beyond words to express the nature of *premānanda*, as it is a stage that can only be realised. Amongst all varieties of *premānanda*, the *prema* of the *gopīs* when distressed in separation crosses beyond the ultimate limit of *ānanda* and attains a state that cannot be expressed in words. From the dust of the lotus feet of the crest-jewel of all *gopīs*, Śrī Rādhā, a stream of this indescribable happiness continuously flows towards that *sādhaka* who remembers Her. This stream of *ānanda*, composed of pure sweetness and devoid of even a scent of *aiśvarya-jñāna*, is natural and filled with wonderful astonishment. This is the meaning of the words *sahajādbhuta-saukhya-dhārā* in this Text.

Śrī-rādhikā-caraṇa-reṇum aham smarāmi – In the absence of directly receiving the exceedingly rare dust of Śrī Rādhā's lotus feet, the *sādhaka* who is established in *śrī-rādhā-dāsya* remembers that dust. What this actually means is that he yearns to obtain his cherished *sevā* in Śrī Rādhā's pastimes in the *vilāsa-kuñjas*. This is the heartfelt desire of Gauḍīya Vaiṣṇavas, and their topmost *sādhana*. *Prema-bhakti-candrikā* (2.2) states: "*sādhana smaraṇa-līlā, ihāte nā kara helā, kāya mane kariyā susāra* – the *sādhana* at this stage is to remember Śrī Rādhā-Kṛṣṇa's pastimes; do not neglect this. Make this the most essential endeavour of your body and mind."

Text 13

In this way, the *sādhaka* worships the dust of Śrīmatī Rādhikā's lotus feet. In *Śrī Rādhā-rasa-sudhā-nidhi* (198) Prabodhānanda Sarasvatī prays:

āśāsya dāsyaṁ vṛṣabhānu-jāyās
tīre samadhyāsya ca bhānu-jāyāḥ
kadā nu vṛndāvana-kuñja-vīthiṣv
ahaṁ nu rādhe hy atithir bhaveyam

O Rādhā! O Vṛṣabhānu-nandinī! When will I, with the hope of becoming Your maidservant, reside on the bank of the Yamunā as a guest on the pathways of Vṛndāvana's *kuñjas*?

vṛṣabhānu-kumārīra haiba kiṅkarī
kalinda-nandinī tīre ra'ba vāsa kari'
karuṇā kariyā rādhe e dāsīra prati
vṛndāṭavī kuñja-pathe haiba atithi

Bhajana-rahasya-vṛtti

Similarly, in one place Śrīla Viśvanātha Cakravartī Ṭhākura prays, "O Vṛṣabhānu-nandinī, there is a hope growing in my heart, that You will become a guest on the path of my vision as You go to Your rendezvous (*abhisāra*) on the paths of Vṛndāvana's *kuñjas* on the bank of the Yamunā."

In an extremely restless condition, Śrīla Prabodhānanda Sarasvatīpāda has composed this Text while remembering service to Śrī Svāminī. In the absence of this service, vast pain and longing has arisen in his heart as he remembers the sweetness of these pastimes. Realising his disqualification to taste such sweetness, his life-air is agitated by an intolerable unhappiness and pain. However, a firm hope of one day attaining the eternal service of Svāminī is stirring his heart. One symptom of the *jāta-rati-bhakta* is *āśā-bandha*, a firm hope of attaining Bhagavān, and the ultimate development of this *āśā-bandha* is seen in *mahābhāva*. The resolute hope of the *vraja-devīs* is indescribable. Even in the condition of long-term separation from Kṛṣṇa, the hope of attaining Kṛṣṇa's service maintains their lives. They have faith in Kṛṣṇa's words spoken when He left for Mathurā (*Śrīmad-Bhāgavatam* (10.39.35)): "*āyāsya iti* – I will return."

With this hope the poet prays at Śrī Svāminī's lotus feet, "O Rādhā! O Vṛṣabhānu-nandinī! When will I, with the hope of becoming Your maidservant (*kiṅkarī*), be a guest on the pathways of the *kuñjas* situated on the bank of the Yamunā?

"O Rādhā, You are the daughter of King Vṛṣabhānu, the empress of Vṛndāvana and a treasury of abundant compassion. Therefore do not neglect me, a destitute and lowly person. Please engage me as a maidservant in the service of You and Your *prāṇa-priyatama* in Your pastimes within the secluded groves. Filled with *premānurāga*, You move along the bank of the Yamunā towards the *nikuñjas* of Vṛndāvana to meet with Your *prāṇanātha* – when will this destitute guest sit on the path of Your travels? My determination will be fixed; I will not move from that place without first receiving Your mercy. Upon seeing this destitute guest sitting like this, Your heart will certainly become aroused with compassion. O Svāminī, You are Kṛṣṇa's most beloved and His worshipper. Please make me successful by giving me an opportunity to perform some tiny service in the worship of Your dearmost beloved. Now, at the end of my life, I am a beggar for Your mercy. Please accept me as Your unpaid maidservant. If You deprive me of this, Your name will be defamed, and that I cannot tolerate."

Text 14

Constantly seeking Kṛṣṇa through *saṅkīrtana* in the mood of *śrī-rādhā-dāsya* is described in *Śrī Rādhā-rasa-sudhā-nidhi* (259):

dhyāyantaṁ śikhi-piccha-maulim aniśaṁ tan-nāma saṅkīrtayan
nityaṁ tac-caraṇāmbujaṁ paricaran tan-mantra-varyaṁ japan
śrī-rādhā-pada-dāsyam eva paramābhīṣṭaṁ hṛdā dhārayan
karhi syāṁ tad-anugraheṇa paramādbhutānurāgotsavaḥ

Keeping at my heart my highest aspiration of one day becoming a maidservant of Śrī Rādhā's lotus feet, I will constantly meditate on Śrī Kṛṣṇa, whose head is decorated with a peacock feather. I will constantly chant His name, eternally serve His lotus feet and always utter His most excellent *mantras*. May He bestow mercy upon me at any moment so I will attain *anurāgotsava*, the great festival of attachment to Śrī Rādhā.

nirantara kṛṣṇa-dhyāna, tan-nāma-kīrtana
kṛṣṇa-pāda-padma-sevā, tan-mantra-japana
rādhā-pada-dāsya-mātra abhīṣṭa-cintana
kṛpāya labhiba rādhā-rāgānubhāvana

Bhajana-rahasya-vṛtti

Prabodhānanda Sarasvatīpāda is expressing a desire to continuously seek Śrī Kṛṣṇa through *saṅkīrtana* in the mood of *rādhā-dāsya*. The only desire and cherished objective of Gauḍīya Vaiṣṇavas is to attain *rādhā-dāsya*. It is the only goal of their *kṛṣṇa-bhajana*. The principal *mantra* of their *kṛṣṇa-bhajana* is found in the ninth verse of *Manaḥ-śikṣā*: "*mad-īśā-nāthatve vraja-vipina-candraṁ vraja-vaneśvarīṁ tāṁ nāthatve* – always remember Vṛndāvana-candra as the *prāṇanātha* of my Svāminī, Vṛndāvaneśvarī Śrī Rādhikā."

This Text 14 describes that, upon decorating the heart with the most-cherished wealth of *rādhā-dāsya*, one will meditate upon

Śrī Kṛṣṇa, whose head is adorned with a peacock feather. Kṛṣṇa is a little late in arriving at the *kuñja*, so Rādhā, endowed with *madīya-abhimāna* (the mood that "Kṛṣṇa is Mine"), becomes *māninī*, sulky. To please His beloved, Śyāmasundara bows His head at Her lotus feet, and His peacock feather crown falls to the ground. This is described in *Gīta-govinda*: *smara-garala-khaṇḍanaṁ mama śirasi maṇḍanam.*

May the remembrance of how my Svāminī controls the *dhīra-lalita-nāyaka* Śrī Kṛṣṇa, that eminent festival of *anurāga*, manifest in my heart. May I remain submerged in this most charming *śrī-kṛṣṇa-saṅkīrtana*.

Śrīla Raghunātha dāsa Gosvāmī prays, "The name of Rādhā is unprecedented, beautiful and enchanting like nectar. The name of Kṛṣṇa is delicious like condensed milk. O my tongue, O you who are faint with hunger, please constantly drink these two unprecedented substances, which are made delightful by the ice of fragrant *anurāga*."

I will worship Śrī Svāminī by serving Śrī Kṛṣṇa's lotus feet, and then giving Her Kṛṣṇa's *prasāda* and flower remnants. The *nitya-sakhīs* and *prāṇa-sakhīs* serve Kṛṣṇa in the mood that they will offer to Svāminī whatever articles, like flower remnants, are obtained by serving Him. Upon receiving the objects used by Her *prāṇanātha*, Svāminī will become extremely pleased. The ultimate attachment for service to Śrī Kṛṣṇa will manifest in my heart because my Īśvarī is pleased.

Text 15

A prayer to attain the service of Śrī Rādhā birth after birth is given in *Śrī Rādhā-rasa-sudhā-nidhi* (40):

tasyā apāra-rasa-sāra-vilāsa-mūrter
ānanda-kanda-paramādbhuta-saukhya-lakṣmyāḥ
brahmādi-durlabha-gater vṛṣabhānu-jāyāḥ
kaiṅkaryam eva mama janmani janmani syāt

Birth after birth, may I attain the position of being a maidservant of the daughter of King Vṛṣabhānu. She is the *vilāsa-mūrti* (personification of playful pastimes) of Śyāmasundara, who is Himself the essence of limitless *rasa*. She is Śrī Kṛṣṇa's supremely wonderful pleasure-Lakṣmī, and She is most difficult to attain for Brahmā and others.

apāra-rasera sāra, vilāsa-mūrati
parama-adbhuta-saukhya-ānanda nirvṛtti
brahmādira sudurlabha vṛṣabhānu-kanyā
janme janme tāṅra dāsye hai yena dhanyā

Bhajana-rahasya-vṛtti

In a voice filled with extreme distress, the poet is praying to attain the position of a maidservant of Śrī Rādhā. This prayer can never be fulfilled in this gross body. The *sādhaka* attains his eternal identity by continuously reciting the *mantra* and *nāma* given by his spiritual master. Upon attaining his *svarūpa*, deep attachment for Svāminī, Śrī Rādhā, arises in his heart and he receives an internal vision (*sphūrti*) of Her sweetness and beauty. Śrīmatī Rādhikā is the personification of Śyāmasundara's playful pastimes (*vilāsa*). In other words, Her intrinsic nature as concentrated *rasa* manifests in the *kuñjas*, where it is tasted by Śrī Śyāmasundara, the emporium of all *rasa*. Rādhikā, the essence of all *rasa*, is the personification of *vilāsa*. She is the essence of unlimited *mādhurya-rasa*. The joy of meeting is hidden within the mind of Śrī Govinda, who is the embodiment of condensed happiness. Śrī Rādhā's *mādanākhya-prema* causes this joy to blossom, thus making Him restless and beside Himself to meet with His beloved by any means possible. Therefore, in His eagerness to meet Her, He sometimes dresses Himself as a woman, and sometimes He bows down at the feet of the *sakhīs*. The bliss of meeting (*sambhoga-rasānanda*) that Śrī Svāminī provides is indescribable, even more so than Govinda Himself can imagine.

rātri-dina kuñje krīḍā kare rādhā-saṅge
kaiśora-vayasa saphala kaila krīḍā-raṅge

Śrī Caitanya-caritāmṛta (*Madhya-līlā* 8.189)

Day and night Śrī Kṛṣṇa enjoys the company of Śrī Rādhā in the *kuñjas* of Vṛndāvana. Thus His early youth was made successful through His sports with Her.

Śrī Rādhā is the *hlādinī-svarūpa-śakti* of Vrajacandra, who is *ānanda-kanda*, the source of transcendental bliss. She is a *dhīrādhīrā-nāyikā*, a heroine who with tearful eyes speaks crooked words to her beloved, and for this reason Śrī Nanda-nandana is completely controlled by Her. As stated in *Śrī Rādhā-kṛpā-kaṭākṣa-stavarāja* (3): "*nirantaraṁ vaśī-kṛta-pratīti nanda-nandane* – She always brings Nanda-nandana into submission." Śrī Kṛṣṇa is the source of transcendental bliss and Śrīmatī is His supremely wonderful *saumya-lakṣmī*, gentle goddess of fortune. Lakṣmī-devī, who always enjoys pastimes on the chest of Nārāyaṇa, is restless and proud of her opulence, but the *prema-lakṣmī* of Vraja, Śrī Rādhā, is very sweet and endowed with a gentle, steady nature. She is *kṛṣṇa-mayī* in *prema*, which means She sees Kṛṣṇa everywhere, internally and externally; She is *gaurāṅgī* in *rasa*, which means She is so expert, so beautiful, dances so well and sings so sweetly that She becomes *gaurāṅgī* (golden-limbed), and Kṛṣṇa becomes so attracted by Her that He becomes *rādhā-mayī* and *gaurāṅga*; She is *sarva-lakṣmī-mayī* in *aiśvarya*, which means She manifests everywhere, and Kṛṣṇa sees Her everywhere; and She is the prominent *gopikā* in *mādhurya*.

Service to Vṛṣabhānu-nandinī Śrīmatī Rādhikā is very difficult to attain for Brahmā and others. Brahmā, being endowed with an awareness of Bhagavān's majesty (*aiśvarya-jñāna*), is unable to comprehend the *mādhurya-rasa* of Vraja. He could not even understand Śyāmasundara's early boyhood pastimes (*paugaṇḍa-līlā*), and he became an offender by stealing the calves and cowherd boys. How, then, can he possibly understand the profound secrets of the highly confidential adolescent pastimes (*kaiśora-līlā*)? Only the *vraja-gopīs* have the qualification to serve in these most confidential pastimes that take place in the secluded bowers. Without following in the footsteps of the *sakhīs*, it is impossible to attain this *sevā*.

sakhī vinā ei līlāya anyera nāhi gati
sakhī-bhāve ye tāṅre kare anugati

rādhā-kṛṣṇa kuñja-sevā-sādhya sei pāya
sei sādhya pāite āra nāhika upāya

Śrī Caitanya-caritāmṛta (*Madhya-līlā* 8.204–5)

Without the guidance of the *sakhīs*, one cannot enter these pastimes. One who worships Kṛṣṇa in the mood of the *sakhīs*, following in their footsteps, can attain the service of Rādhā-Kṛṣṇa in the *kuñjas* of Vṛndāvana. There is no other means to achieve this goal.

Śrī Kiśorī's maidservants (*kiṅkarīs*) are always devoted to Her service. The word *kaiṅkarya* expresses a mood of being ardent to serve and it means *kiṁ karomi*, "What may I do? What service can I do?" – this mood is expressed in pure *rādhā-dāsya*, or *mañjarī-bhāva*. May I attain this *kaiṅkarya* of Śrī Vṛṣabhānu-nandinī birth after birth.

To serve exclusively under the guidance of the *vraja-devīs* is called *tat-tad-bhāva-icchāmayī kāmānugā-bhakti*. This is the deep meaning of this Text.

Text 16

Searching for Śrī Rādhānātha while engaged in the service of Śrī Rādhā (*rādhā-dāsya*) is described in *Śrī Rādhā-rasa-sudhā-nidhi* (142):

rādhā-nāma sudhā-rasaṁ rasayituṁ jihvās tu me vihvalā
pādau tat-padakāṅkitāsu caratāṁ vṛndāṭavī-vīthiṣu
tat-karmaiva karaḥ karotu hṛdayaṁ tasyāḥ padaṁ dhyāyatāṁ
tad-bhāvotsavataḥ paraṁ bhavatu me tat-prāṇanāthe ratiḥ

May my tongue become constantly overwhelmed by relishing the nectarean *rasa* of the name Rādhā, may my feet wander on the pathways of that Vṛndāvana where Vṛṣabhānu-nandinī walks, may both my hands be engaged in Svāminī's service, and may my heart contemplate Her lotus feet. By Śrīmatī's festival of ecstatic moods (*bhāvotsava*), may one-pointed attachment manifest within me for Her *prāṇanātha*, Śrī Śyāmasundara. This is my earnest prayer.

jihvā hauka su-vihvala, rādhā-nāma gāne
vṛndāraṇye cala pada, rādhā anveṣaṇe

rādhā-sevā kara-kara, rādhā smara mane
rādhā-bhāve mati, bhaja rādhā-prāṇa-dhane

Bhajana-rahasya-vṛtti

Śrīla Gosvāmipāda is humbly praying to attain attachment to the lotus feet of Śrī Rādhā's *prāṇanātha* through Her festival of ecstatic moods (*bhāvotsava*), by engaging all his senses in *rādhā-bhajana*. When will my tongue become overwhelmed by tasting the nectarean *rasa* of Śrī Rādhā's name? There is no equal to the happiness experienced by the tongue that, with heartfelt *prema*, tastes the nectar of Śrīmatī's name. Happiness comes when one has achieved the desired perfection by performing *nāma-saṅkīrtana* of one's object of worship. The name appears primarily upon the tongue, and both the chanter and the hearer derive bliss.

nāma-saṅkīrtanaṁ proktaṁ
kṛṣṇasya prema-sampadi
baliṣṭhaṁ sādhanaṁ śreṣṭhaṁ
paramākarṣa-mantravat

tad eva manyate bhakteḥ
phalaṁ tad-rasikair janaiḥ
bhagavat-prema-sampattau
sadaivāvyabhicārataḥ

Bṛhad-bhāgavatāmṛta (2.3.164–5)

It is said that to obtain the wealth of *prema* for Śrī Kṛṣṇa, *nāma-saṅkīrtana* is the best and most powerful *sādhana*. This supremely attractive *mantra* draws Śrī Kṛṣṇa towards the *sādhaka*. Therefore *rasika* devotees of Bhagavān conclude that *saṅkīrtana* is the result of *bhakti*. It is unfailing in bestowing the wealth of *bhagavat-prema*.

Relish of the very *rasa* of Bhagavān, who is Himself an embodiment of concentrated *rasa*, is definitely contained within His name. Although there is such taste in His name, that same *nāmī*, Śrī Śyāmasundara, becomes overwhelmed when He tastes the name of Śrī Rādhā. It is the nature of *prema* that the lover will have affection for the name of the beloved.

Once, due to the vigilance of Jaṭilā, Śrī Kiśorī could not meet Śyāmasundara, who fainted in separation from Her. Madhumaṅgala went to Kiśorī, but since She was under guard, She was unable to leave the house. To pacify Kṛṣṇa's fire of separation, She wrote the two syllables *rā* and *dhā* on a leaf and sent it to Him. When He received it, Kṛṣṇa returned to His senses and He said to Madhumaṅgala, "Friend, I am completely satisfied with what you have given Me."

In the second line of this Text, Śrīpāda is praying: "*pādau tat-padakāṅkitāsu caratāṁ vṛndāṭavī-vīthiṣu* – may my feet traverse the paths of Vṛndāvana-dhāma, which is marked with the foot-prints of Śrī Rādhā. While wandering there, may this sentiment be in my heart: My Svāminī is travelling on these paths to meet with Her *prāṇanātha.* Every infinitesimal particle of Vraja is mixed with the dust from Her lotus feet and is thus perceived as *prema-makaranda*, the nectar of love. May my Īśvarī's *vilāsa-līlā* be painted on the canvas of my heart. May the dust particles that have touched Her lotus feet be the ornaments of my limbs."

Śrī Kṛṣṇa's dear associate Uddhava also desired to attain a particle of this dust by taking birth in Vraja as a blade of grass or a shrub. Such a heart's longing will only be fulfilled by remembering Śrī Kiśorī's foot-dust which lies upon the pathways of Vraja.

Śrīla Gosvāmipāda continues: "*tat-karmaiva karaḥ karotu* – may both my hands be engaged in stringing various kinds of flowers into garlands, ornaments and so forth for Śrī Svāminī. When Svāminī is fatigued from Her *vilāsa*, please allow me to attain the good fortune of massaging Her lotus feet.

"*Tad-bhāvotsavataḥ paraṁ bhavatu me tat-prāṇanāthe ratiḥ* – Śrī Rādhā's *bhāvotsava,* festival of ecstatic moods, is Her pastimes with Śrī Govinda. Sometimes, when Śrīmatī becomes *māninī*, sulky, Govinda will pray to me with clever words, 'O beautiful one! O merciful one! Please satisfy Śrī Rādhā and thereby pacify My fire of separation.' Upon hearing His petition, I will catch hold of His hand and lead Him to Svāminī. May it be my goal and all-good fortune to arrange for my Svāminī to meet with Her *prāṇa-priyatama*. Govinda will certainly give me mercy, knowing that I have taken shelter of Śrī Rādhā's lotus feet."

Text 17

A prayer to attain Śrī Rādhā's lotus feet, which are the only goal, is given in *Vilāpa-kusumāñjali* (8):

devi duḥkha-kula-sāgarodare
dūyamānam ati-durgataṁ janam
tvaṁ kṛpā-prabala-naukayādbhutaṁ
prāpaya svapada-paṅkajālayam

O Devī Śrī Rādhikā, I am in a helpless condition, drowning in the ocean of unhappiness. Please lift me into the strong boat of Your mercy and give me the shelter of Your lotus feet.

duḥkha-sindhu mājhe devi, durgata e jana
kṛpā-pote pāda-padme uṭhāo ekhana

Bhajana-rahasya-vṛtti

Feeling himself to be bereft of service, Śrī Raghunātha dāsa Gosvāmī is extremely agitated by separation from Śrī Rādhā. He feels himself to be without shelter and is drowning in the deep ocean of unhappiness. Remembering this *śloka*, he begins to glorify Śrī Svāminī in every way by using the word *devī*. The root of *devī* is *div*, which means "playful" or "sportive". In other words, She enjoys pastimes of divine love sports with Śrī Kṛṣṇa. Remembering this, Dāsa Gosvāmī uses the word *devī*. In

Śrī Caitanya-caritāmṛta (*Ādi-līlā* 4.84) it is said: "'*devī*' *kahi dyotamānā, paramā sundarī* – *devī* means 'resplendent and most beautiful'."

"O Śrīmatī Rādhikā, deprived of service to Your lotus feet, I am drowning in this ocean of material existence, which is difficult to cross. Please shelter me within the boat of Your mercy and bestow upon me the qualification to serve Your lotus feet, for apart from this service, there is no other remedy to remove the exhaustion caused by pangs of separation from You. Everything in the material world causes misery; only service to You is fully blissful."

The *mañjarīs* are firmly and resolutely fixed in the mood of being Śrī Rādhā's maidservants. The only thing on their minds is service to Śrī Rādhā's lotus feet. A desire to enjoy bodily association with Śrī Hari does not arise even in their dreams. If Śrī Kṛṣṇa forcefully catches hold of them and begins to speak to them, they say stiffly, "O Nanda-nandana! Do not dare touch this body!"

The *bhāva* that Śrī Rādhā's maidservants have towards Her is pure and completely free from the desire for self-enjoyment. They do not even have a tinge of any desire other than to serve Her.

Text 18

The inclination to be solely attached to serving Śrī Rādhā is described in *Vilāpa-kusumāñjali* (16):

pādābjayos tava vinā vara-dāsyam eva
nānyat kadāpi samaye kila devi yāce
sakhyāya te mama namo 'stu namo 'stu nityaṁ
dāsyāya te mama raso 'stu raso 'stu satyam

O Devī, I have no desire other than for the topmost attainment of servitude to Your lotus feet. I forever offer obeisances to the position of being Your *sakhī*, but may I remain firmly attached to being Your maidservant. I speak this as a solemn vow.

tava pada-dāsya vinā kichu nāhi māgi
tava sakhye namaskāra, āchi dāsya lāgi'

Bhajana-rahasya-vṛtti

In this Text, Śrīla Raghunātha dāsa Gosvāmī, absorbed in his internal *mañjarī* form, is praying in great distress to the lotus feet of his Svāminī. "O Svāminī, please make me Your maidservant by bestowing upon me the great fortune of service to Your lotus feet." This servitorship (*dāsya*) is topmost (*vara*) because Śrī Rādhā's maidservants are free from reverence and fear. Their service is devoid of hesitation and is supremely tasty and relishable. The desire for this *dāsya* is the compassionate gift of Śrīman Mahāprabhu, and its attainment is the heartfelt aim of Gauḍīya Vaiṣṇavas.

As maidservants, the *mañjarīs* are also receptacles of *mādhurya-rasa*. They can, without fear or shyness, enter the solitary *nikuñja* where amorous pastimes are taking place, and very gracefully and cleverly perform their service. They also thoroughly know the requirements of the youthful Divine Couple, as well as when and how to fulfil them. The speciality of these *mañjarīs* is performing their service while knowing the innermost feelings of the Divine Couple's hearts. Seeing the enchanting skill of the *mañjarīs'* service, a desire for such service is aroused in the mind of Śyāmasundara Himself, the crest jewel of all those who relish *rasa*.

As *svādhīna-bhartṛkā*, a heroine who controls her lover, Śrī Rādhā orders Him, "Fix My dishevelled clothes and ornaments, or the other *sakhīs* will see them and tease Me." Understanding Svāminī's mood, the *kiṅkarīs* bring clothes and cosmetics. Śrīmatī orders Śyāmasundara to apply footlac (*altā*), and upon seeing the beauty of Her lotus feet, He becomes overwhelmed with *prema*. Ecstatic transformations (*sāttvika-vikāras*) make all His limbs horripilate and tremble (*pulakita* and *kampita*), and as a result He is unable to hold the brush. Observing His condition, Śrīmatī softly and sweetly smiles and orders Rati Mañjarī to apply the *altā*. The *mañjarīs* taste various types of sweet pastimes like this in a completely unobstructed way.

Śyāmasundara has to take shelter of the *mañjarīs* in order to get the opportunity to meet with Śrīmatī or to pacify Her *māna*. While eating at the house of Nanda in the evening, Śyāmasundara becomes restless to know if He will be able to meet with Rādhikā that night or not. Through subtle gestures He inquires from Śrīmatī's maidservants about the possibility of this meeting. A maidservant indicates, "Yes, it will take place." Whatever these *mañjarīs* have is for the pleasure of the Divine Couple – they have nothing of their own. In rank, the *priya-narma-sakhīs* are superior, but from the perspective of having the most fortunate service, the *mañjarīs* are superior.

The *kāmātmikā-bhakti* of Vraja, which is exclusive to *mādhurya-rasa*, is of two kinds: *sambhoga-icchāmayī* and *tat-tad-bhāva-icchāmayī*. The *mādhurya-rasa* that Vraja's *yūtheśvarīs* (group leaders) such as Rādhā, Candrāvalī and Śyāmalā have towards Śrī Kṛṣṇa is called *sambhoga-icchāmayī*. Serving the Divine Couple in the mood of *mañjarīs* like Śrī Rūpa and Śrī Rati, whose inclination is towards Śrīmatī Rādhikā (*rādhā-snehādhikā*), is called *tat-tad-bhāva-icchāmayī* or *sakhī-bhāva* (that is, *nitya-* and *prāṇa-sakhī-bhāva*).

The *sakhīs* are of three kinds: (1) *rādhā-snehādhikā* – those more inclined towards Śrī Rādhā, (2) *kṛṣṇa-snehādhikā* – those more inclined towards Śrī Kṛṣṇa, and (3) *ubhaya-snehādhikā* – those equally disposed to both. The *sakhīs* are also of five kinds: (1) *sakhī*, (2) *nitya-sakhī*, (3) *prāṇa-sakhī*, (4) *priya-sakhī* and (5) *priya-narma-sakhī*. Both the *nitya-sakhīs* and *prāṇa-sakhīs* are *rādhā-snehādhikā* and are called *mañjarīs*. The *mañjarīs* are absorbed in the mood of service, even though they feel friendship (*sakhya*) for Śrī Rādhā. They remain exclusively intent on Śrī Rādhā's lotus feet and do not desire bodily contact with Śrī Kṛṣṇa, even in their dreams. This is confirmed in *Vṛndāvana-mahimāmṛta* (16.94):

ananya-śrī-rādhā-pada-kamala-dāsyaika-rasadhīr
hareḥ saṅge raṅga-svapana-samaye nāpi dadhatī

Single-pointed service to the lotus feet of Śrī Rādhā is an ocean of transcendental *rasa*. One who wishes to enter that ocean will never desire enjoyment with Śrī Hari, even in dreams.

The object (*viṣayālambana*) of the *mañjarīs'* love and affection is Śrī Yugala-kiśora. The *mañjarīs* experience all kinds of *rati* by beholding the Divine Couple embracing, by hearing Them conversing, by tasting Their chewed *tāmbūla* remnants, by smelling the matchlessly beautiful fragrance arising from Their amorous pastimes, by touching Their lotus feet as they massage them, and so forth. They also taste the ecstasy of Rādhā and Kṛṣṇa's most intimate union (*samprayoga*). In this regard, Śrīla Kṛṣṇadāsa Kavirāja says in *Śrī Caitanya-caritāmṛta* (*Madhya-līlā* 8.209–10):

rādhāra svarūpa – kṛṣṇa-prema-kalpa-latā
sakhī-gaṇa haya tāra pallava-puṣpa pātā

kṛṣṇa-līlāmṛta yadi latāke siñcaya
nija-sukha haite pallavādyera koṭi-sukha haya

By nature Śrī Rādhā is like a creeper of *kṛṣṇa-prema* and the *sakhīs* are the leaves, flowers and twigs of that creeper. When the nectar of Kṛṣṇa's pastimes is sprinkled on that creeper, the leaves, flowers and twigs experience a happiness millions of times greater than if they were to be directly sprinkled with this nectar.

In *Govinda-līlāmṛta* one also finds this type of description: when Kṛṣṇa touches Śrī Rādhā, *sāttvika-bhāvas* also arise on the bodies of Her *mañjarīs*. And when Kṛṣṇa drinks the nectar of Rādhā's lips, the resultant *bhāva* is also reflected in the *nitya-sakhīs* and *prāṇa-sakhīs*, who become as if intoxicated. This is described in the first verse of *Vilāpa-kusumāñjali*:

tvaṁ rūpa-mañjari sakhi! prathitā pure 'smin
puṁsaḥ parasya vadanaṁ na hi paśyasīti
bimbādhare kṣatam anāgata-bhartṛkāyā
yat te vyadhāyi kim u tac chuka-puṅgavena

My dear *sakhī* Rūpa Mañjarī, you are well known in Vraja for not even looking at the face of any man other than your husband. Therefore it is surprising that your lips, red like *bimba* fruits, have been bitten, even though your husband is not at home. Has this been done by the best of parrots?

Like Śrī Rādhā, Her *mañjarīs* also have *samartha-rati*[2]. This *rati* is causelessly present in them in a transcendental, incomprehensible and inconceivable way. *Śrī Caitanya-caritāmṛta* (*Madhya-līlā* 18.225) says: "*sunileo bhāgya-hīnera nā haya pratīti* – even though hearing of this, those devoid of good fortune cannot perceive it."

In this Text 18, Dāsa Gosvāmī prays to attain *pālyadāsī-bhāva*. Using the words *raso 'stu*, he expresses an ever-fresh heightening of *prema* and prays to Śrī Svāminī not to cheat him, either with clever words or by giving him other blessings.

[2] The word *samartha* means "capable, suitable, complete"; therefore *samartha-rati* means "capable of controlling Kṛṣṇa".

Text 19

A sincere prayer for attaining *śrī-rādhā-dāsya*, spoken in a voice choked with emotion, is found in *Stava-mālā* (*Śrī Gāndharvā-samprārthanāṣṭakam* (2)):

> *hā devi! kāku-bhara-gadgadayādya vācā*
> *yāce nipatya bhuvi daṇḍavad-udbhaṭārtiḥ*
> *asya prasādam abudhasya janasya kṛtvā*
> *gāndharvike! nija-gaṇe gaṇanāṁ vidhehi*

O Devī Gāndharvikā! Today, in utter desperation, I throw myself on the ground like a stick. Filled with great distress, I implore You with a choked voice to be merciful to this fool and count me as one of Your own.

> *bhume daṇḍavat-paḍi' bahu ārti-svare*
> *kāku-bhare gadgada-vacane yoḍa kare*
>
> *prārthanā kari go devi, e abudha jane*
> *tava gaṇe gaṇi' kṛpā kara akiñcane*

Bhajana-rahasya-vṛtti

Here Śrī Rūpa Gosvāmī is offering an extremely grief-filled prayer at the lotus feet of Śrī Svāminī: "Please also count me amongst Your intimate maidservants." Even though he is one of Śrīman Mahāprabhu's eternal associates, he considers himself an *ajāta-rati-sādhaka*. There is not a great difference between humility and *prema*. *Bṛhad-bhāgavatāmṛta* (2.5.224–5) states, "In the fully mature stage of the highest type of *prema*, natural humility arises. Similarly, when humility matures, incessant *prema* develops. Therefore, in humility and *prema* a relationship of mutual 'cause and effect' or 'producer and product' is clearly seen."

The phrase *kāku-bhara-gadgadayādya vācā* indicates melting of the heart, which is the external symptom of *prema*. The word *hā* expresses longing (*utkaṇṭhā*), and the word *gadgada*, which means "with a choked voice", indicates that his prayer is beseeching and filled with humility.

Because their longing is so intense, the *vraja-devīs* are able to reject their family members and the rules and regulations of society. Due to abundant possessiveness (*mamatā*), they are also able to cross over all obstacles and impediments. Śrī Kṛṣṇa, who is controlled by this *mamatā*, which is filled with longing, considers Himself ever-indebted to the *gopīs*.

The words *devi gāndharvike* express the glories of Śrī Rādhā's good fortune. They refer to She who is a mine of sweetness and beauty and who, by Her captivating dancing, singing, playing on musical instruments and performance of other charming arts, completely enchants the mind of Kṛṣṇa.

Attachment (*rati*) filled with longing and humility is the wealth of *rāga-mārga-sādhakas*. Śrīla Sanātana Gosvāmī defines humility as follows: "If in spite of possessing all good qualities, one considers oneself wretched, abhorrent and incompetent, this is *dainya*, humility." It is only humility that attracts the mercy of Bhagavān and makes a person a worthy recipient of Kṛṣṇa's mercy. Pretentious humility is inimical to *bhakti* and is always to be abandoned. In fact, real humility is not mere external behaviour; it manifests from the heart.

Śrīla Bhaktivinoda Ṭhākura sings in *Vimala-vaiṣṇava* (from *Kalyāṇa-kalpa-taru*):

antara bāhire, sama vyavahāra, amānī mānada ha'ba
kṛṣṇa-saṅkīrtane, śrī kṛṣṇa-smaraṇe, satata majiyā ra'ba

With a heart free from duplicity, my outer behaviour will correspond to my inner thoughts and feelings. Seeing myself as completely insignificant, I will give respect to others, seeking no honour in return. Always singing the holy names and dancing, I will remain constantly absorbed in remembering Śrī Kṛṣṇa's pastimes.

Text 20

A prayer to attain the position of a maidservant of Śrī Rādhā, who attracts the mind of Śrī Kṛṣṇa, is found in *Śrī Rādhā-rasa-sudhā-nidhi* (39):

veṇuṁ karān nipatitaṁ skhalitaṁ śikhaṇḍaṁ
bhraṣṭaṁ ca pīta-vasanaṁ vraja-rāja-sūnoḥ
yasyāḥ kaṭākṣa-śara-ghāta-vimūrcchitasya
tāṁ rādhikāṁ paricarāmi kadā rasena

When, with *rasa*, will I serve Śrī Rādhā, whose arrow-like side-long glance causes Śrī Nanda-nandana to faint, the flute to fall from His hands, the peacock-feather crown to slip from His head, and His yellow cloth to fall from His body?

yāṅhāra kaṭākṣa-śare śrī-kṛṣṇa mūrcchita
kara haite vaṁśi khase, śikhaṇḍa skhalita
pīta-vastra bhraṣṭa haya, se rādhā-caraṇa
kabe āmi rasa-yoge kariba sevana?

Bhajana-rahasya-vṛtti

Bhakti-rasāmṛta-sindhu (1.2.291) states: "*teṣāṁ bhāvāptaye lubdho bhaved atrādhikāravān* – the *anurāga* from which ever-fresh greed is born and which is displayed in a variegated way, manifests in an astonishing, unparalleled manner and reaches the stage of *mahābhāva*. Only a person who craves to attain this kind of *bhāva* is eligible to enter *rāga-mārga*."

Taste, or *ruci*, is the most important aspect of *bhāva-bhakti*. When a person has *ruci* for *rāgānuga-bhajana* in the mood of *mādhurya-rasa*, he relishes Śrī Rādhā-Mādhava's names, forms, qualities and pastimes in his hearing and chanting. By this kind of *bhajana*, one can perceive the method of service of the *nitya-siddha-mañjarīs*.

In this Text, Śrī Sarasvatīpāda is praying for the *rasa*-filled loving service of Śrī Rādhā, who enchants the mind of Kānu, or Kṛṣṇa. Concealed within this verse is the influence of *mādanākhya-mahābhāva* on the heart of Śrī Kṛṣṇa, who is the emporium of all nectarean mellows, *akhila-rasāmṛta-mūrti*.

Padmā and other *sakhīs* somehow allured Śrī Kṛṣṇa to Candrāvalī's *kuñja*, leaving Śrīmatī distressed in a state of extreme separation. The clever *kiṅkarīs*, however, skilfully brought Him from there and submitted Him to Śrīmatī. Rādhā's mood of contrariness was then set in motion. First She forbade Kṛṣṇa to touch Her; then She exhibited feigned anger and cast a crooked sidelong glance at Him.

Śrī Rādhā is the embodiment of *mahābhāva*, and the only function of *mahābhāva* is to incite happiness in Śrī Kṛṣṇa's heart. Here, *mādanākhya-mahābhāva* incited countless indescribable, transcendental sentiments in the heart of *akhila-rasāmṛta-mūrti* Śrī Kṛṣṇa, thus silencing His boastfulness. Śrī Kṛṣṇa became submerged in a swoon of bliss, pierced by the arrow of Śrīmatī's crooked sidelong glance. On a battlefield a hero faints when struck by an arrow, and his bow, arrows, crown, clothes, ornaments – everything – become scattered. Similarly, in this battle of Cupid, the strike of one arrow-like glance makes the flute fall from the hand, the peacock-feather crown fall from the head and the yellow cloth fall from the body of the transcendental young Cupid – and He faints. That person whose crooked sidelong glances strike the *vraja-sundarīs* like Cupid's arrows has now fallen to the ground. Only by Śrī Rādhā's sidelong glance does He who bewilders Cupid fall unconscious. That flute by whose very sweet sound hundreds and hundreds of *vraja-sundarīs* become stricken with restlessness, like deer struck by arrows, now falls to the ground from a trembling hand. Mādhava's peacock feather crown, which is an emblem of the pastimes of Vraja and which enamours the minds of the *gopa-ramaṇīs*, now rolls in the dust as a result of Śrī Rādhā's crooked sidelong glance. That yellow cloth (*pītāmbara*) which like a lightning bolt from a fresh thundercloud emanates splendorous beauty and upon seeing which the *vraja-ramaṇīs* gave up the honour of their lineage, has now also fallen down. This condition of the *dhīra-lalita-nāyaka* is all due to the crooked sidelong glance of Śrī Rādhā.

The embodiment of *ānanda-rasa* has fainted by the arrow of Śrī Rādhā's sidelong glance. Although Śrīmatī makes many attempts to break this swoon of bliss (*ānanda*), it cannot be broken. Now the service starts for the *rasa-kiṅkarīs*. With a sweet voice, a maidservant sings a *madana-rāga* (a melody of Cupid), which she learnt from Śrī Svāminī. The *kiṅkarī* breaks the swoon of the hero (*nāyaka*) who has fainted in *prema*, and thus facilitates Śrī Svāminī's meeting with Her beloved. This is the maidservant's *rasa-paricaryā*, her service that enhances *rasa*: to arrange for the sweet pastime of the Divine Couple to begin. Then, at the end of Their pastime, the maidservants desire to attain the good fortune of serving Them by offering cool water, betelnuts, garlands, a fan and so forth.

Text 21

Śrīmad-Bhāgavatam (11.6.46) describes the mood of a *sādhaka* who has attained attachment for *rādhā-dāsya*:

tvayopabhukta-srag-gandha-
vāso-'laṅkāra-carcitāḥ
ucchiṣṭa-bhojino dāsās
tava māyāṁ jayema hi

O Prabhu, we decorate ourselves with the garlands, sandalwood paste, cloth and ornaments worn by You. Since we are Your servants who eat Your remnants, we will certainly conquer Your illusory energy (*māyā*). [Therefore, Prabhu, we are not afraid of Your *māyā* – we are only afraid of being separated from You.]

tomāra prasāda-mālā-gandha-alaṅkāra
vastrādi pariyā dina yāya ta āmāra

tomāra ucchiṣṭa-bhojī-dāsa-paricaye
tava māyā jaya kari anāsakta ha'ye

Bhajana-rahasya-vṛtti

Persons who are not inclined to serve Kṛṣṇa are intent on their own sense enjoyment, and thus they perform various activities, such as sleeping, sitting, travelling about, staying in one place and sporting. However, if the same activities are connected to Bhagavān, the *jīva* becomes eternally blessed. If the *jīva* is eager for the service of honouring the remnants enjoyed by Śrī Kṛṣṇa, such as garlands, fragrant oils, clothes and ornaments, he will not be ensnared by the bondage of material existence. Here Uddhava is saying to Śrī Bhagavān, "By obtaining Your *prasāda*, the living entity becomes freed from the slavery of *māyā*."

Hari-bhakti-vilāsa states that a person who doubts the potency of items offered to Viṣṇu will reside in hell for eternity. One should not disrespect *mahā-prasāda*. Even *mahā-prasāda* that has fallen into the mouth of a dog is supremely pure and acceptable even for a *brāhmaṇa*. The *prasāda* offered to ancient deities or deities established by *mahāpuruṣas* is extremely pure and worthy of acceptance. But it is not proper to distribute the *prasāda* of deities who have been established here and there by persons who indulge in sense enjoyment. This is confirmed in the *Nārada-pañcarātra*:

śruti-smṛti-purāṇādi-
pañcarātra-vidhiṁ vinā
aikāntikī harer bhaktir
utpātāyaiva kalpate

Even one who practises one-pointed devotion to Hari will only create a disturbance if he abandons the rules of Śruti, Smṛti, the Purāṇas and the *Nārada-pañcarātra.*

The remnants of Śrī Kṛṣṇa are called *mahā-prasāda.* When a pure devotee honours this *mahā-prasāda,* his remnants are called *mahā-mahā-prasāda.* Śrī Kṛṣṇadāsa Kavirāja Gosvāmī says in *Śrī Caitanya-caritāmṛta* (*Antya-līlā* 16.60):

bhakta-pada-dhūli āra bhakta-pada-jala
bhakta-bhukta-avaśeṣa – ei tina mahābala

The foot-dust of a devotee, the water that has washed his feet and the remnants of food left by him are three very powerful items.

By serving these three items, *kṛṣṇa-prema-bhakti* will appear. They are extremely powerful.

It is improper for a *sādhaka-bhakta* to imitate the behaviour of pure devotees. Once, my *gurudeva,* then Śrī Vinoda-bihārī Brahmacārī, and his godbrother Śrī Narahari Prabhu went to Śrī Vaṁśīdāsa Bābājī's *bhajana-kuṭī* to take his *darśana.* Bābājī had offered tea and was distributing it. Vinoda-bihārī and Narahari Prabhu also received some tea *prasāda.* Vinoda-bihārī paid his respects to it, put it aside and did not take it. When Narahari Prabhu asked him why, Śrī Vinoda-bihārī answered philosophically, "An object which is taken by a *mahā-bhāgavata* can still be unsuitable for us. Mahādeva drank a deadly poison. He is capable of doing that, but if an ordinary person drinks poison, he is sure to die. For a *sādhaka* it is only proper to follow the rules of the *bhakti-śāstras.*"

Text 22

The late afternoon pastimes (*aparāhna-līlā*) are described in *Govinda-līlāmṛta* (19.1):

śrī-rādhāṁ prāpta-gehāṁ nija-ramaṇa-kṛte kḷpta-nānopahārāṁ
susnātāṁ ramya-veśāṁ priya-mukha-kamalāloka-pūrṇa pramodām
śrī-kṛṣṇaṁ cāparāhne vrajam anucalitaṁ dhenu-vṛndair-vayasyaiḥ
śrī-rādhāloka-tṛptaṁ pitṛ-mukha-militaṁ mātṛ-mṛṣṭaṁ smarāmi

In the afternoon, after *madhyāhna-līlā*, Śrī Rādhā goes to Her home, bathes and gets dressed and decorated. On the affectionate order of Śrī Yaśomatī, She prepares various kinds of preparations, such as *karpūra-keli* and *amṛta-keli*, for Her *prāṇanātha* Śrī Kṛṣṇa. As He returns to Vraja from the forest with the cows and *sakhās*, She has *darśana* of His lotus face and becomes filled with delight. Śrī Kṛṣṇa also becomes fully satisfied by receiving Her *darśana*. After meeting with Śrī Nanda and the other elderly *gopas*, He is bathed and dressed by the elderly *gopīs*. I contemplate this Śrī Rādhā-Kṛṣṇa.

śrī-rādhikā-gṛhe gelā, kṛṣṇa lāgi' viracilā,
nānā-vidha-khādya-upahāra
snāta ramya-veśa dhari', priya-mukhekṣaṇa kari',
pūrṇānanda pāila apāra
śrī-kṛṣṇāparāhna-kāle, dhenu-mitra laiyā cale,
pathe rādhā-mukha nirakhiyā
nandādi milana kari', yaśodā-mārjita hari,
smara mana ānandita haiyā

Bhajana-rahasya-vṛtti

The various pastimes of Śrī Rādhā-Kṛṣṇa during *madhyāhna-līlā*, such as water sports (*jala-krīḍā*), playing dice (*pāśā-khelā*), swinging (*dola-līlā*), and laughing and joking (*hāsa-parihāsa-*

līlās), are now completed. In the house of Nanda, Śrī Svāminī is not able to feed Her *priyatama* with Her own hands, but at midday, Her desire to serve in this way is fulfilled. Kṛṣṇa goes to the forest with His *sakhās* to herd the cows, and on the pretext of beholding the beauty of the forest, He separates Himself from His *sakhās* to go to Svāminī. Text 20 described Kṛṣṇa's condition when He sees Svāminī's charmingly attractive lotus face. After *madhyāhna-līlā*, Śrī Rādhā and Her *sakhīs* return to Her home in Jāvaṭa, and Śyāmasundara, along with His cows, calves and *sakhās*, also returns from the forest.

In Her home, Śrī Svāminī busily performs various activities with a restless mind, eagerly desiring to meet with Her *priyatama*. At the time of Śrī Kṛṣṇa's return, the *sakhās* accompanying Him play their horns and other instruments, making a tumultuous sound. The Vrajavāsīs become extremely blissful when they see the dust flying from the cows' hooves. The arrival of Śrī Kṛṣṇa is like the arrival of the rainy season. The sky is filled with clouds of dust raised by the cows, the song of the flute is like a shower of nectar raining from the sky, and the cows' mooing is like the rumbling of clouds. Like extremely thirsty *cātaka* birds (who only drink rainwater as it falls), the Vrajavāsīs come forward. When the cowherd boys leave to go cowherding, Kṛṣṇa walks in the front, and when they return, Baladeva Prabhu is at the front.

When Śrī Kṛṣṇa passes through Jāvaṭa-grāma, Śrī Rādhā has *darśana* of Him through the openings in the small latticed windows of Her house. Śrī Kṛṣṇa also craves the *darśana* of His beloved, and sometimes receives it directly when He begs something from Her. Before Priyājī can give Him anything, though, He steals Her heart like a snatching thief. But my Svāminī is no less. She also steals the heart of Her *priyatama*. Now each acts with the heart and mind of the other. Jīva Gosvāmipāda, in his *Śrī Yugalāṣṭakam* (6), prays:

kṛṣṇa-citta-sthitā rādhā, rādhā-citta-sthito hariḥ,
jīvane maraṇe nityaṁ rādhā-kṛṣṇau gatir mama

Rādhā is always firmly situated within the mind of Kṛṣṇa and Kṛṣṇa is always firmly situated within the mind of Rādhā. May Rādhā and Kṛṣṇa be my shelter in life or death.

My desired object is the service of this Divine Couple.

Śrī Kṛṣṇa arrives at His home, the house of Nanda. With the end of her *sārī*, Yaśodā cleans her *lālā's* face, which is covered with dust from the cows, performs *ārati* and then, placing Him on her lap, breast-feeds Him. After some time, Kṛṣṇa goes to milk the cows. Upon His return, Yaśodā bathes Him and very lovingly feeds Him the sweets sent by Śrī Rādhā. Śrī Rādhā's *kiṅkarīs* have *darśana* of all these pastimes and, returning to their Svāminī, who is restless and agitated, relate all these events to Her.

He who chants *harināma* while contemplating these pastimes will, by Śrī Svāminī's grace, become eligible to one day serve these pastimes.

Thus ends the *Pañcama-yāma-sādhana*,
Aparāhna-kālīya-bhajana, of *Śrī Bhajana-rahasya*.

6

Ṣaṣṭha-yāma-sādhana

Sāyaṁ-kālīya-bhajana – bhāva

(six *daṇḍas* after dusk: approximately 6.00 P.M. – 8.30 P.M.)

Text 1

The sixth verse of *Śikṣāṣṭaka* describes the visible manifestations of perfection:

nayanaṁ galad-aśru-dhārayā
vadanaṁ gadgada-ruddhayā girā
pulakair nicitaṁ vapuḥ kadā
tava nāma-grahaṇe bhaviṣyati

O Lord, when will tears flow from my eyes, my voice falter and all the hairs on my body stand erect as I chant Your holy names?

prema dhana vinā vyartha daridra jīvana
'dāsa' kari' vetana more deha prema-dhana

"Without the wealth of *prema*, my wretched life is useless. O Lord, please accept me as Your paid servant and grant me the wealth of *prema* as wages."

Text 2

The intrinsic nature of *bhāva* is described in *Bhakti-rasāmṛta-sindhu* (1.3.2):

premnas tu prathamāvasthā
bhāva ity abhidhīyate
sāttvikāḥ svalpa-mātrā syur
atrāśru-pulakādayaḥ

The first stage of *prema* is known as *bhāva*. In this stage *sāttvika-bhāvas*, such as hairs standing on end (*pulaka*), tears (*aśru*) and shivering (*kampa*), are slightly manifest.

premera prathamāvasthā bhāva nāma tāra
pulakāśru svalpa haya sāttvika vikāra

Bhajana-rahasya-vṛtti

Bhāva, also known as *rati*, is considered to be the sprout of *prema*, which is the fully blossomed state of *bhakti*. *Bhāva*, a special manifestation of *śuddha-sattva*, is compared to a ray of the sun of *prema* and it softens the heart by various tastes (*ruci*). In other words *bhāva* is the condition in which the heart melts as a result of cultivating activities favourable to Kṛṣṇa (*kṛṣṇānuśīlana*).

Bhāva is also described in the following verse from *Bhakti-rasāmṛta-sindhu* (1.3.1):

śuddha-sattva-viśeṣātmā
prema-sūryāṁśu-sāmyabhāk
rucibhiś citta-māsṛṇya-
kṛd asau bhāva ucyate

Bhāva-bhakti is a special manifestation of *śuddha-sattva*. In other words the constitutional characteristic of *bhāva-bhakti* is that it is a phenomenon entirely constituted of *śuddha-sattva*. It is like a ray of the sun of *prema* and it softens the heart by various tastes (*ruci*).

In his commentary to this verse Śrīla Viśvanātha Cakravartī Ṭhākura writes, "When *sādhana-bhakti* succeeds in softening the heart by various tastes (*ruci*), it is called *bhāva-bhakti*. The word *ruci* here refers to: (1) the desire to attain Bhagavān (*bhagavat-prāpti-abhilāṣa*), (2) the desire to do what is favourable for Bhagavān (*ānukūlya-abhilāṣa*) and (3) the desire to serve Bhagavān with affection (*sauhārda-abhilāṣa*). The constitutional nature of *bhāva-bhakti* is *śuddha-sattva-viṣeśātmā*, which means it is fully comprised of *śuddha-sattva*. *Śuddha-sattva* refers to the self-manifest cognitive function of Bhagavān's *svarūpa-śakti* known as *samvid-vṛtti*, the function of divine cognisance. When the word *viśeṣa* is added to *śuddha-sattva*, it indicates *hlādinī*, another great potency of *svarūpa-śakti*. One should understand from this that *mahābhāva*, which is the highest state of *hlādinī*, is included within *śuddha-sattva-viśeṣa*. Hence *śuddha-sattva-viṣeśātmā* is that supreme function of *svarūpa-śakti* which is possessed of desire favourable to Bhagavān, which is the essence of the combined *samvit-* and *hlādinī-śaktis*, and which is situated in the hearts of Bhagavān's eternal associates. It is one with the mood of their hearts (*tādātmya-bhāva*). In simple words, the eternally perfect moods situated within the eternal associates of Śrī Kṛṣṇa are called *śuddha-sattva-viśeṣātmā*. The constitutional nature of *bhāva-bhakti* is *śuddha-sattva-viśeṣātmā* and, because it is likened to the first ray of the sun of *prema-bhakti*, it is also called the sprout of *prema*.

The natural function of *bhāva* is to manifest Kṛṣṇa's inherent nature (*svarūpa*) and the inherent nature of His pastimes. *Bhāva* can arise in two ways: (1) by absorption in one's spiritual practice (*sādhana-abhiniveśa-ja*) and (2) by the mercy of Śrī Kṛṣṇa or His devotees (*śrī-kṛṣṇa-prasāda-ja* or *śrī-kṛṣṇa-bhakta-prasāda-ja*).

By the influence of associating with great personalities, one engages in the *sādhana* of *bhagavad-bhakti*. Gradually a taste (*ruci*) for *bhakti* arises within him, he develops attachment (*āsakti*) for Bhagavān, and finally he attains *bhāva*. *Bhāva* received in this way is called *sādhana-abhiniveśa-ja*.

Bhāva that suddenly arises, without any *sādhana*, is called *śrī-kṛṣṇa-prasāda-ja-bhāva* or *śrī-kṛṣṇa-bhakta-prasāda-ja-bhāva*. *Prasāda-ja-bhāva* is rare; generally the living entity attains *sādhana-abhiniveśa-ja-bhāva*.

Śrī-kṛṣṇa-prasāda-ja-bhāva is received by Kṛṣṇa's benediction, His *darśana*, or by a revelation (*sphūrti*) within the heart. Śrīla Śukadeva Gosvāmī received *bhāva* as a result of mercy manifesting in his heart. Numerous examples of these three kinds of *prasāda-ja-bhāvas* were seen during the advent of Śrīman Mahāprabhu. *Bhāva* arose in the hearts of countless people just by receiving Mahāprabhu's *darśana*. Jagāi and Mādhāi received *bhāva* as a result of a benediction, and Śrī Jīva Gosvāmī's *bhāva* manifested as a *sphūrti* within his heart.

Dhruva and Prahlāda are examples of personalities who attained *śrī-kṛṣṇa-bhakta-prasāda-ja-bhāva*, as they received *bhagavad-bhāva* by the mercy of Śrī Nārada Muni. *Bhāva* was also awakened in the hearts of countless people by the mercy of Śrī Rūpa, Śrī Sanātana and other associates of Mahāprabhu.

Text 3

The characteristics of *sthāyibhāva* are described in *Bhakti-rasāmṛta-sindhu* (1.3.25–6):

kṣāntir avyartha-kālatvaṁ
viraktir māna-śūnyatā
āśā-bandhaḥ samutkaṇṭhā
nāma-gāne sadā ruciḥ

āsaktis tad-guṇākhyāne
prītis tad-vasati-sthale
ity ādayo 'nubhāvāḥ
syur jāta-bhāvāṅkure jane

When *bhāva* arises, the following nine symptoms are observed in the *sādhaka*: forbearance, effective use of one's time, detachment, absence of pride, steadfast hope that Kṛṣṇa will bestow His mercy, intense longing to obtain one's goal, constant taste for chanting the holy name, attachment to hearing about Kṛṣṇa's qualities and affection for Kṛṣṇa's pastime-places.

kṣobhera kāraṇa sattve kṣobha nāhi haya
sadā kṛṣṇa bhaje, nāhi kare kāla-kṣaya

kṛṣṇetara-viṣaye virakti sadā raya
māna thakileo abhimānī nāhi haya

avaśya pāiba kṛṣṇa-kṛpā āśā kare
kṛṣṇa bhaje ahar ahaḥ vyākula antare

hare-kṛṣṇa-nāma-gāne ruci nirantara
śrī-kṛṣṇera guṇākhyāne āsakti vistara

prīti kare sadā kṛṣṇa-vasatira sthāne
ei anubhāva bhāvāṅkura vidyamāne

Bhajana-rahasya-vṛtti

(1) *Kṣānti* – When one remains calm and composed although there is reason to be angry or restless, it is called *kṣānti*, forbearance. A *sādhaka* naturally displays forbearance, as seen in the example of Parīkṣit Mahārāja. Even after he received the curse of imminent death by Śṛṅgī, the son of a *muni*, he did not become disturbed, but with a steady mind proceeded to hear *hari-kathā*.
(2) *Avyartha-kālatva* – This means not wasting time, and always being absorbed in *hari-bhajana*.
(3) *Virakti* – A natural distaste for material sense enjoyment is called *virakti*, detachment.

(4) *Māna-śūnyatā* – Pride arises from one's high birth, social class, stage of life, wealth, beauty, high position and so on. *Māna-śūnyatā* is the condition in which the heart remains free from pride even though one may have all these qualifications.
(5) *Āśā-bandha* – To apply one's mind very diligently to *bhajana* with the firm faith that "Śrī Kṛṣṇa will surely bestow His mercy upon me" is called *āśā-bandha*, steadfast hope.

Śrīla Raghunātha dāsa Gosvāmī has expressed his hope (*āśā*) in *Vilāpa-kusumāñjali* (102):

āśā bharair amṛta-sindhu-mayaiḥ kathañcit
kālo mayātigamitaḥ kila sāmpratam hi
tvaṁ cet kṛpāṁ mayi vidhāsyasi naiva kiṁ me
prāṇair vrajena ca varoru bakāriṇāpi

O Varoru Rādhā, it is as rare to fulfil my hope as it is to attain an ocean of nectar, but I pass my days, greatly longing to fulfil it. Now You must give mercy to this poor, unhappy person. What to speak of my life, everything – my residing in Vraja and even my service to Kṛṣṇa – is useless without Your mercy.

(6) *Samutkaṇṭhā* – Intense longing to attain one's desired object is called *samutkaṇṭhā*. This kind of eagerness is shown in the prayer of Vṛtrāsura (*Śrīmad-Bhāgavatam* (6.11.26)):

ajāta-pakṣā iva mātaraṁ khagāḥ
stanyaṁ yathā vatsatarāḥ kṣudhārtāḥ
priyaṁ priyeva vyuṣitaṁ viṣaṇṇā
mano 'ravindākṣa didṛkṣate tvām

O lotus-eyed one, as baby birds that have not yet developed their wings always look for their mother to return and feed them, as small calves tied with ropes anxiously await the time of milking when they will be allowed to drink the milk of their mothers, or as a morose wife whose husband is away from home always longs for him to return and satisfy her in all respects, I always yearn for the opportunity to render direct service unto You.

(7) *Nāma-gāne sadā ruci* – To constantly chant the name of Hari with the faith that *śrī-nāma-bhajana* is the topmost form of *bhajana*, is called *nāma-gāne sadā ruci*, taste in chanting the holy name. To have a taste for the holy name is the key to obtaining the ultimate auspiciousness.

Kṛṣṇa-nāma is both the practice (*sādhana*) and the goal (*sādhya*). The topmost name, as taught by Śrī Gaurasundara, is the Hare Kṛṣṇa *mahā-mantra*. Nowadays, non-devotees write lyrics that are imaginary and full of *rasa-ābhāsa*, overlapping of transcendental mellows. Many people understand these lyrics to be *nāma-mantras*, but such *mantras* are not mentioned in the scriptures and it is improper to chant them. Śrīman Mahāprabhu (*Śrī Caitanya-bhāgavata* (*Madhya-khaṇḍa* 13.10)) has given the order: "*ihā vai āra nā bolibā bolāibā* – ask them to chant only Hare Kṛṣṇa, nothing else."

(8) *Āsaktis tad-guṇākhyāne* – The thirst of a *bhāva-bhakta* to describe and hear the sweet pastimes of Śrī Kṛṣṇa, which are filled with all auspicious qualities, is never satiated. The more he hears, the more his attachment increases.

(9) *Tad-vasati-sthale-prīti* – The desire to reside in Śrī Vṛndāvana, Śrī Navadvīpa or other abodes of Bhagavān is called *tad-vasati-sthale-prīti*, affection for the transcendental residences of Bhagavān. Living in the *dhāma* is only beneficial when one has the association of pure devotees.

Śrīla Bhaktivinoda Ṭhākura sings in his song *Śuddha-bhakata*:

gaura āmāra ye saba sthāne karalo bhramaṇa raṅge
se saba sthāna heriba āmi praṇayi-bhakata-saṅge

In the association of loving devotees, I will go to all the places that Gaura joyfully visited.

And in the song *Kabe gaura-vane*, he sings: "*dhāma-vāsī-jane praṇati kariyā māgiba kṛpāra leśa* – when will I offer obeisances to all the residents of the *dhāma*, begging one drop of mercy from them?"

If it is not possible to physically live in the *dhāma*, then one should live there mentally, and, in the company of pure devotees, one should hear and recite *Śrīmad-Bhāgavatam* and other scriptures. This is the same as living in the *dhāma*.

If some of the symptoms of *bhāva* are observed in *karmīs*, who desire sense enjoyment, or in *jñānīs*, who aspire for liberation, one should understand that such symptoms are nothing but a reflection (*pratibimba*) of *bhāva* or a semblance of *rati* (*raty-ābhāsa*). When ignorant persons exhibit these symptoms of *bhāva* by virtue of their association with devotees, it can be called a shadow of *bhakti* (*chāyā-rūpa-bhakty-ābhāsa*).

Text 4

The *anubhāvas* that arise in a devotee when he reaches a developed stage of *bhāva* are listed in *Bhakti-rasāmṛta-sindhu* (2.2.2):

nṛtyaṁ viluṭhitaṁ gītaṁ
krośanaṁ tanu-moṭanam
huṅkāro jṛmbhaṇaṁ śvāsa-
bhūmā lokānapekṣitā
lālāsrāvo 'ṭṭa-hāsaś ca
ghūrṇā-hikkādayo 'pi ca

The external transformations that reveal the heart's emotions (*bhāvas*) are called *anubhāvas*. They are dancing (*nṛtya*), rolling on the ground (*viluṭhita*), singing (*gīta*), loud crying (*krośana*), writhing of the body (*tanu-moṭana*), roaring (*huṅkāra*), yawning (*jṛmbhaṇa*), breathing heavily (*śvāsa-bhūmā*), neglecting others (*lokānapekṣitā*), drooling (*lālāsrāva*), loud laughter (*aṭṭa-hāsa*), staggering about (*ghūrṇā*) and hiccups (*hikkā*).

nṛtya, gaḍāgaḍi, gīta, cītkāra, huṅkāra
tanu-phole, hāṅī uṭhe, śvāsa bāra bāra

lokāpekṣā chāḍe, lālāsrāva, aṭṭa-hāsa
hikkā ghūrṇā bāhya anubhāva suprakāśa

Bhajana-rahasya-vṛtti

With the development of the *sādhaka's* transcendental emotions, the above-mentioned *anubhāvas* manifest. Not caring for public opinion, the *sādhaka* chants and dances. It is impossible for worldly-minded persons to understand such activities of the devotees. The behaviour of the devotees who can taste *bhāva* (*bhāvuka-bhaktas*) is completely different from that of mundane persons. Sometimes, hypocrites, who desire material gain, worship or fame, imitate the activities of pure devotees. Once, while watching a snake dance, *nāma-ācārya* Śrīla Haridāsa Ṭhākura remembered Śrī Kṛṣṇa's pastime of subduing Kāliya-nāga (*kāliya-damana-līlā*) and started to dance. Other devotees took his foot-dust and smeared it on their heads, considering themselves very fortunate. An envious *brāhmaṇa* began to imitate Haridāsa Ṭhākura, but no devotee was attracted to him, and instead he was scolded by the snake-charmer.

Text 5

Bhakti-rasāmṛta-sindhu (2.3.16) describes the *aṣṭa-sāttvika-bhāvas* as follows:

te stambha-sveda-romāñcāḥ
svara-bhedo 'tha vepathuḥ
vaivarṇyam aśru pralaya
ity aṣṭau sāttvikāḥ smṛtāḥ

The *aṣṭa-sāttvika* transformations of *bhāva* are: (1) becoming stunned (*stambha*), (2) perspiration (*sveda*), (3) standing of the hairs on end (*romāñca*), (4) faltering of the voice (*svara-bheda*), (5) trembling (*kampa*), (6) loss of colour (*vaivarṇya*), (7) tears (*aśru*) and (8) loss of consciousness or fainting (*pralaya*).

stambha, sveda, romāñca o kampa svara-bheda
vaivarṇya, pralaya, aśru vikāra-prabheda

Bhajana-rahasya-vṛtti

In the pure consciousness (*śuddha-sattva*) of the living entity, when the action of the heart (*citta*) becomes stimulated it precipitates further action. At that time a natural wonderfulness arises, which makes the heart blossom in various ways. This externally manifests as *udbhāsvaras*, *anubhāvas* that manifest as external actions. These transformations, such as dancing and so forth, are of many varieties. When the *anubhāvas*, which nourish *vibhāva*, arise in the heart, they pervade the body as *udbhāsvaras*.

The word *sattva* refers to the heart that is directly stimulated by transcendental sentiments. The *bhāvas*, or emotions, that arise from this *sattva* are called *sāttvika-bhāvas*. Becoming stunned (*stambha*), trembling (*kampa*) and so forth are symptoms of *sāttvika* transformations. When the *sādhaka's* heart attains oneness with *sāttvika-bhāvas*, it submits itself to the life-air (*prāṇa*). Then, when the *prāṇa* is excited, it is transformed, causing excessive agitation to the body. At that time, *stambha* (becoming stunned) and other transformations arise.

In *anubhāvas* such as dancing (*nṛtya*), the *bhāva* that is manifested by *sattva* does not directly perform the activity. Rather, the activity is performed as a result of the intelligence being stimulated. In the *sāttvika-bhāvas* such as *stambha*, however, the intelligence is not needed, as the *sāttvika-bhāva* itself directly performs the activity. For this reason, *anubhāvas* and *sāttvika-bhāvas* are considered to be different.

In some conditions, the life-air (*prāṇa*) becomes present as the fifth element together with the other four elements of earth, water, fire and sky. Sometimes it consists mainly of itself – that is, it is predominated by air (*vāyu*) – and it moves throughout the body of the living entity. When the *prāṇa* comes in contact with the earth element, inertness (*stambha*) is observed; when it takes shelter of water, tears (*aśru*) manifest; when it contacts fire, perspiration (*sveda*) and change in bodily colour (*vaivarṇya*) are evident; and when it takes shelter of sky, it manifests devastation (*pralaya*) or loss of consciousness (*mūrccha*). When it consists predominately of itself, or in other words, when it takes shelter of the element air, horripilation (*romāñca*), trembling (*vepathu*) and faltering of the voice (*svara-bheda*) manifest respectively, corresponding to the *prāṇa's* mild, moderate or intense strength.

Stambha is a state in which one becomes inert, and it arises from jubilation, fear, astonishment, dejection, regret, anger and depression. Perspiration (*sveda*) arises from jubilation, fear, anger and so forth. When the bodily hairs stand on end, the condition is known as *romāñca*, and it arises from astonishment, jubilation, enthusiasm and fear. Faltering of the voice (*svara-bheda*) arises from despair, wonder, anger, jubilation and fear. Trembling (*vepathu*) is caused by fear, anger, jubilation and so forth. When the body changes colour it is called *vaivarṇya*, and it arises from despair, anger, fear and so on. Tears (*aśru*) come from the eyes through the influence of jubilation, anger, despair and so on. Tears of joy are cool, whereas tears of anger and so forth are warm. Cessation of all action, loss of consciousness, becoming motionless and falling to the ground are called *pralaya*. *Pralaya* arises from both happiness and distress.

These *sāttvika-bhāvas* manifest in five stages of intensity, according to the progressive gradation of *sattva*: (1) smouldering (*dhūmāyita*), (2) flaming (*jvalita*), (3) burning (*dīpta*), (4) brightly burning (*uddīpta*) and (5) blazing (*sūddīpta*). They are gradually reflected in the heart of a sincere pure devotee according to the level of his *sādhana*. Many people exhibit these *bhāvas* to impress others or to achieve success in their own activities in this material world, but such demonstrations are not the transcendental sentiments of pure devotion.

Text 6

In his spiritual body (*siddha-deha*) the living entity is a transcendental servant of Kṛṣṇa. When attachment to service (*dāsya-rati*) arises, the *jīva* deems his material designations insignificant. The following statement of Śrīman Mahāprabhu is found in *Padyāvalī* (74):

nāhaṁ vipro na ca nara-patir nāpi vaiśyo na śūdro
nāhaṁ varṇī na ca gṛha-patir no vanastho yatir vā
kintu prodyan-nikhila-paramānanda-pūrṇāmṛtābdher
gopī-bhartuḥ pada-kamalayor dāsa-dāsānudāsaḥ

I am not a *brāhmaṇa*, *kṣatriya*, *vaiśya* or *śūdra*, nor am I a *brahmacārī*, *gṛhastha*, *vānaprastha* or *sannyāsī*. My sole nature is that of a servant of the servants of the Vaiṣṇavas who are the servants of the lotus feet of Śrī Rādhā-vallabha, the maintainer of the *gopīs*. He is naturally effulgent and the complete ocean of bliss.

vipra, kṣatra, vaiśya, śūdra kabhu nāhi āmi
gṛhī, brahmacārī, vānaprastha, yati, svāmī
prabhūta paramānanda-pūrṇāmṛtāvāsa
śrī-rādhā-vallabha-dāsa-dāsera anudāsa

Bhajana-rahasya-vṛtti

The living entity is actually a servant of the transcendental Śrī Kṛṣṇacandra, the ocean of all nectarean mellows. This is confirmed in *Śrī Caitanya-caritāmṛta* (*Ādi-līlā* 5.142):

ekala īśvara kṛṣṇa āra saba bhṛtya
yāre yaiche nācāya, se taiche kare nṛtya

Śrī Kṛṣṇa alone is Īśvara, the supreme controller, and all others are His servants. They dance as He makes them do so.

The living entity who is bound by *māyā* identifies himself with the temporary material body of a woman or man and various other designations. However, with His own lotus mouth, Śrī Gaurasundara, the incarnation in Kali-yuga and saviour of all fallen souls, instructed the human beings tormented by Kali. He said, "We are not bound by social classes (*varṇas*), such as *brāhmaṇa, kṣatriya, vaiśya* or *sūdra*, nor by *brahmacārya* or other stages of life (*āśramas*). Our pure identity is *gopī-bhartuḥ pada-kamalayor dāsa-dāsānudāsaḥ*, that of the servant of the servant of the servant of the maintainer of the *gopīs*."

Because the living entity is conditioned, he receives a new body according to his previous life's desires and impressions (*saṁskāras*), and thus takes birth in one of the *varṇas*. The destination he attains after death is in accordance with his *karma*. This is called *karma-cakra*, the cycle of action and reaction. The living entity realises his pure form (*śuddha-svarūpa*) by taking shelter of the lotus feet of a bona fide *guru* and thereby following the path of *bhajana* as established by the previous *mahājanas*. His material identification is removed by his constant performance of *nāma-bhajana*. A pure spiritual mood then manifests, and he attains a pure, transcendental body with which he can serve Kṛṣṇa. This body is also endowed with hands, legs and so forth just like the material body.

In pure, transcendental nature, Śrī Kṛṣṇa is the only male and all *jīvas* are female. Actually, in the structure of the *jīva's* heart, male and female characteristics do not exist; yet when embodied the living entity naturally conceives of himself as being male or female. The *jīva* attains a pure body through the medium of *sādhana-bhajana*. A person who is inclined towards the amorous mellow (*mādhurya-rasa*) will perform *sādhana-bhajana* under the guidance of *rasika-bhaktas* and, according to his own desire and constitutional nature, he will attain his spiritual form, which will be the body of a *gopī*. Yogamāyā makes all arrangements for the devotee's service in a specific *rasa* by the potency that makes the impossible possible (*aghaṭana-ghaṭana-paṭīyasī-śakti*). *Prema-bhakti-candrikā* states:

sādhane bhāviba yāhā siddha-dehe pāba tāhā

Whatever one contemplates in *sādhana*, one will attain at perfection.

pakvāpakva mātra se vicāra

The only difference is that in *sādhana* it is unripe, and at perfection, ripe.

Dāsānudāsa – No one has the qualification to enter *mādhurya-sevā* to Śrī Yugala-kiśora unless he is under the guidance of the *vraja-gopīs*. By performing *bhajana* under the guidance of the *mañjarī-sakhīs* who are following those *gopīs*, one can attain the post of a maidservant. At the time of *sādhana*, one desires to have a mood of service to Śrī Kṛṣṇa according to the moods of the *vraja-gopīs*. Then, when *bhāva* arises he considers himself to be a maidservant of a *vraja-gopī* like Lalitā Sakhī and serves Śrī Rādhā-Kṛṣṇa under her guidance. In *śṛṅgāra-rasa-upāsana*, worship through the amorous mellow, one conceives of oneself as a paramour (*parakīya* or *paroḍhā*).

Some persons, although males, consider themselves to be Lalitā or Viśākhā. They adopt feminine attire, pose as *sakhīs*, and thus perform "*bhajana*". By such actions, they only destroy themselves and others. To think, "I am Lalitā" or "I am Viśākhā" is the *ahaṅgrahopāsanā* of the *māyāvādīs*, a type of worship in which one considers himself to be identical with the object of worship. Those who think like this are offenders at the lotus feet of Lalitā, Viśākhā and others, and they descend into the most dreadful hell. The living entity can never become Rūpa Mañjarī, Śrīmatī Rādhikā's eternal *kiṅkarī*, nor can he become Lalitā or any other *sakhī*. These *sakhīs* are not living entities; they are Śrī Rādhā's direct expansions (*kāya-vyūha-svarūpa*).

While performing *śṛṅgāra-rasa-upāsana* at the time of *sādhana*, the living entity should serve Śrī Rādhā-Kṛṣṇa under the guidance of Śrīmatī Rādhikā's eternal *sakhīs*. Conceiving oneself as a paramour, one's aspiration should be to take birth in the home of a *vraja-gopī*, marry a specific *gopa* and remain a childless *gopa-kiśorī*. This *kiśorī*, whose mood is *parakīya-bhāva*, is a female *sādhaka* with an intense yearning to serve Śrī Kṛṣṇa under the guidance of Śrī Rādhā. When this *bhāva* is perfected, one attains *gopī-bhāva*.

In his song *Dekhite dekhite* Śrīla Bhaktivinoda Ṭhākura sings: "*vraja-gopī-bhāva, haibe svabhāva, āna-bhāva nā rahibe* – my sole disposition and nature will be that of a *vraja-gopī*."

Text 7

In *Bhakti-rasāmṛta-sindhu* (1.2.295) it is described how the devotee in *rāga-mārga* is fixed in two kinds of service moods – one is executed with his external body (*sādhaka-deha*) and the other with his internally contemplated body (*siddha-deha*):

sevā sādhaka-rūpeṇa
siddha-rūpeṇa cātra hi
tad-bhāva-lipsunā kāryā
vraja-lokānusārataḥ

One who has intense longing to attain *rāgātmikā-bhakti* follows in the footsteps of the Vrajavāsīs [such as Rūpa Gosvāmī] who are devoted to *rāga-mārga*. With his external body (*sādhaka-rūpa*) he should chant and hear according to the practice of *rāgānuga-bhakti*, and with his internally contemplated body (*siddha-rūpa*) bestowed upon him by his *guru*, he should perform service.

śravaṇa-kīrtana bāhye sādhaka-śārīre
siddha-dehe vrajānuga-sevā abhyantare

Bhajana-rahasya-vṛtti

Rāgānuga-bhakti is performed in two ways: (1) with the external body (*sādhaka-rūpa*) and (2) with the internally contemplated body (*siddha-rūpa*) that is suitable for carrying out the *prema-sevā* for which one aspires. With the external body one should perform service like Śrī Rūpa, Śrī Sanātana and other eminent Vrajavāsīs. With an intense desire to obtain one's cherished object Śrī Kṛṣṇa, who resides in Vraja, and the sentiments of His beloved associates (in other words, their affection for Śrī Kṛṣṇa), one should execute service within the mind (*mānasī-sevā*), following eternal residents of Vraja such as Śrī Rādhā, Lalitā, Viśākhā and Rūpa Mañjarī.

Because unqualified people are unable to understand the *sādhaka's* transcendental activities and gestures, for their benefit he practises the rules and regulations of *vaidhī-bhakti* with his external body. If such unqualified people were to imitate the *sādhaka's* transcendental activities, their process of *bhajana* itself would become the cause of their entanglement in material existence. Our previous *ācāryas* personally followed rules and regulations just to instruct the *ajāta-rati-sādhakas* (those not on the platform of *bhāva*) and to enable them to enter into pure *bhakti*.

The meaning of *vidhi-mārga* is the practice of the sixty-four limbs of *bhakti*, beginning with *guru-padāśraya* (taking shelter of the lotus feet of a genuine spiritual master). By following *vidhi-mārga* in this way and by the influence of associating with devotees who are practising *rāga-mārga*, intense longing for *rāgānuga-bhakti* manifests in the heart and one attains the qualification to enter that path. Śrīla Bhaktivinoda Ṭhākura confirms this in *Kalyāṇa-kalpataru*: *vidhi-mārga-rata-jane, svādhīnatā ratna-dāne, rāga-mārge karāna praveśa.*

Day and night one should serve Śrī Rādhā-Kṛṣṇa Yugala in Vraja in one's spiritual body (*siddha-deha*) that has been revealed by the mercy of *śrī guru*. The *sādhaka*, following Śrī Kṛṣṇa's beloved associates whom he cherishes in his heart and for whose service he has developed greed (*lobha*), should constantly serve the youthful Divine Couple with an enraptured heart. By following the mood of one of Kṛṣṇa's associates who is amongst His servants, friends, parents or beloveds, and whose disposition corresponds to his own, the *sādhaka* attains affection for Śrī Kṛṣṇa's lotus feet. This affection is of the same nature as the affection of the associate whom he follows. This is the method of *rāgānuga-bhakti.*

Smaraṇa (remembrance) is the primary limb of *rāgānuga-bhakti.* In accordance with one's own internal mood, *smaraṇa*, *kīrtana* and the other limbs of devotion should be performed in relation to Kṛṣṇa, His pastimes, His abode, His specific natures and His beloved associates. Because *smaraṇa* is predominant in *rāgānuga-bhakti*, some persons, who still have *anarthas* and in whose hearts genuine attachment to Kṛṣṇa has not yet appeared, make a deceitful display of solitary *bhajana*, and considering themselves *rāgānugā* devotees, they practise what they call *aṣṭa-kālīya-līlā-smaraṇa*. However, *Bhakti-rasāmṛta-sindhu* (1.2.101) quotes from the *āgama-śāstras* as follows:

śruti-smṛti-purāṇādi-
pañcarātra-vidhiṁ vinā
aikāntikī harer bhaktir
utpātāyaiva kalpate

If a person violates the regulations mentioned in the Śruti, Smṛti, Purāṇas and the *Nārada-pañcarātra*, great misgivings (*anarthas*) are produced, even though he may be engaged in unalloyed devotion to Hari (*aikāntikī-hari-bhakti*).

The specific point to be understood in connection with *rasa* is that, upon hearing of the sweetness of *śṛṅgāra-rasa* and the other transcendental sentiments of the eternal associates in *vraja-līlā*, a greed arises to obtain those same sentiments. At that point, a person is no longer dependent on the logic of the scriptures that explain *vaidhī-bhakti* and he inquires, "How may this irresistible *vraja-bhāva* be obtained?" He must then depend on *śāstra*, because only *śāstra* describes the means by which he can attain it. The scripture that establishes the method of *bhagavad-bhajana* is *Śrīmad-Bhāgavatam*.

There are five kinds of *sādhana* in *rāgānuga-bhakti*:
(1) *Svābhīṣṭa-bhāvamaya* (composed of one's desired mood) – When *śravaṇa*, *kīrtana* and other such limbs of *bhakti* are saturated with one of the primary *bhāvas* (*dāsya*, *sakhya*, *vatsālya* or *mādhurya*), they nourish the tree of the *sādhaka's* future *prema*. At that time they are called *bhāvamaya-sādhana*. When *prema* manifests, they are called *bhāvamaya-sādhya*.
(2) *Svābhīṣṭa-bhāva-sambandhī* (related to one's desired mood) – The limbs of *bhakti*, including *śrī-guru-padāśraya*, *mantra-japa*, *smaraṇa*, *dhyāna* and so on, are known as *bhāva-sambandhī-sādhana*. Because the following of vows on holy days such as Ekādaśī and Janmāṣṭamī assists the limb of *smaraṇa*, it is considered partial *bhāva-sambandhī*.

(3) *Svābhīṣṭa-bhāva-anukūla* (favourable to one's desired mood) – Wearing neckbeads made of *tulasī*, applying *tilaka*, adopting the outward signs of a Vaiṣṇava, rendering *tulasī-sevā*, performing *parikramā*, offering *praṇāma* and so forth are *bhāva-anukūla*.

(4) *Svābhīṣṭa-bhāva-aviruddha* (neither opposed to nor incompatible with one's desired mood) – Respecting cows, the banyan tree, the myrobalan tree and *brāhmaṇas* are conducive limbs and therefore called *bhāva-aviruddha*.

The above-mentioned (1–4) kinds of *sādhana* are all to be adopted in the performance of *bhajana*.

(5) *Svābhīṣṭa-bhāva-viruddha* (opposed to one's desired mood) – *Nyāsa* (mental assignment of different parts of the body to various deities), *mudrā* (particular positions of intertwining the fingers), *dvārakā-dhyāna* (meditation on Kṛṣṇa's pastimes in Dvārakā) and other such limbs should be abandoned in the performance of *rāgānuga-bhakti* because they are opposed to the attainment of one's desired *bhāva*.

The *rāga-mārga-sādhaka* always follows the Vrajavāsīs; in other words, he follows Śrī Rūpa Gosvāmī, Śrī Sanātana Gosvāmī and Śrī Ragunātha dāsa Gosvāmī, and constantly practises the process of *bhajana* shown by them. A *rāga-mārga-sādhaka* should always reside in Vraja. If possible he should reside there physically; otherwise, mentally.

Siddha-rūpeṇa – By the mercy of the spiritual master, the *sādhaka* gains the *ekādaśa-bhāvas* and the five *daśās*. He then performs *sevā* in meditation while being internally absorbed in these sentiments; that is to say, he remains absorbed in remembrance of *aṣṭa-kālīya-līlā*.

The *ekādaśa-bhāvas* are: (1) *sambandha*, relationship; (2) *vayasa*, age; (3) *nāma*, name; (4) *rūpa*, personal form; (5) *yūtha*, group; (6) *veśa*, dress; (7) *ājñā*, specific instruction; (8) *vāsa*, residence; (9) *sevā*, exclusive service; (10) *parākāṣṭhā-śvāsa*, the utmost summit of divine sentiment, which is the aspirant's very life breath; and (11) *pālyadāsī-bhāva*, the sentiment of a maidservant.

The five *daśās* are: (1) *śravaṇa-daśā*, the stage of hearing; (2) *varaṇa-daśā*, the stage of acceptance; (3) *smaraṇa-daśā*, the stage of remembrance; (4) *bhāvāpanna-daśā*, the stage of spiritual ecstasy; and (5) *prema-sampatti-daśā*, the stage in which the highest success of *prema* is achieved.

By the mercy of the *svarūpa-śakti*, the *sādhaka* receives a spiritual body appropriate for service to Kṛṣṇa. The *Sanat-kumāra-saṁhitā* describes how a *sādhaka* in *mādhurya-rasa* is always absorbed in his internally contemplated body:

ātmānaṁ cintayet tatra
tāsāṁ madhye manoramām
rūpa-yauvana-sampannāṁ
kiśorīṁ pramadākṛtim

nānā-śilpa-kalābhijñāṁ
kṛṣṇa-bhogānurūpiṇīm
prārthitām api kṛṣṇena,
tato bhoga-parāṅmukhīm

rādhikānucarīṁ nityaṁ
tat-sevana-parāyaṇām
kṛṣṇād apy adhikaṁ prema
rādhikāyāṁ prakurvatīm

prīty anudivasaṁ yatnāt
tayoḥ saṅgama-kāriṇīm
tat-sevana-sukhāhlāda-
bhāvenāti-sunirvṛtām

ity ātmānaṁ vicintyaiva
tatra sevāṁ samācaret
brāhma-muhūrtam ārabhya
yāvat tuṣyān mahāniśi

[Sadāśiva said to Nārada:] O Nārada, contemplate your *svarūpa* in the transcendental land of Vṛndāvana amidst Kṛṣṇa's beloved damsels, who look upon Him as their paramour, in the following way: "I am a *kiśorī-ramaṇī*, whose beautiful youthful form is full of happiness. I am skilled in many fine arts that please Kṛṣṇa. I am an eternal maidservant of Śrī Rādhā, Kṛṣṇa's most beloved consort, and I will always be joyful to arrange for Her meeting with Him. Therefore, even if Kṛṣṇa prays for union with me, I will do anything to avoid that kind of meeting because it would not be for Kṛṣṇa's sense pleasure, but my own. I am always ready to serve and attend to Kṛṣṇa's beloved Śrīmatī Rādhikā, and I have more affection for Śrīmatī than I do for Kṛṣṇa. Every day I am devoted to affectionately and carefully arranging meetings between Śrī Rādhā and Śrī Kṛṣṇa. Remaining absorbed in the happiness of serving Them, I will increase Their bliss in that meeting."

In this way, attentively contemplating one's *svarūpa*, one should impeccably perform *mānasī-sevā* in the transcendental land of Vṛndāvana, from *brāhma-muhūrta* until midnight.

The word *siddha-rūpeṇa* in this Text 7 is defined by Śrīla Jīva Gosvāmī as follows: "*antaś cintita tat sevopayogī deha* – the internally contemplated body that is suitable for carrying out one's desired service." One should thus be engaged in service according to one's mood and with a body suitable for serving Śrī Kṛṣṇa. One should serve being absorbed in the ocean of sentiments of Kṛṣṇa's beloved associates in Vraja, who fulfil His innermost desires.

Śrī gurudeva, the desire-tree of the devotees, makes the *siddha-deha* appear within the heart of his dear disciple, and thereafter acquaints him with this *siddha-deha*. Having full faith in the *guru's* words, the *sādhaka* performs *bhajana* with firm *niṣṭhā*, and by the mercy of the *hlādinī-śakti*, he fully realises his ultimate state of being. The *sādhaka* then completely identifies himself with his *siddha-deha* and in this perfected form, he intently engages in the service of his most cherished Śrī Kṛṣṇa, the skilful enjoyer of pastimes (*līlā-vilāsī*).

Text 8

Śrīman Mahāprabhu (*Śrī Caitanya-caritāmṛta* (*Madhya-līlā* 1.211)) has described the public behaviour of *rāga-mārga-bhaktas* with the following words:

para-vyasaninī nārī
vyagrāpi gṛha-karmasu
tad evāsvādayaty antar
nava-saṅga-rasāyanam

When a woman is attached to a man other than her husband, she continues to carry out her many household duties, but within her heart she relishes the new pleasure of her meeting with her paramour. [Similarly, a devotee may be engaged in activities within this world, but he always relishes the *rasa* of Kṛṣṇa that he has tasted in the association of devotees.]

para-puruṣete rata thāke ye ramaṇī
gṛhe vyasta thākiyāo divasa-rajanī

gopane antare nava-saṅga-rasāyana
parama-ullāse kare sadā āsvādana

sei rūpa bhakta vyagra thākiyāo ghare
kṛṣṇa-rasāsvāda kara niḥsaṅga antare

Bhajana-rahasaya-vṛtti

In this verse, by using a mundane example, Śrī Caitanya Mahāprabhu explains both the internal and external behaviour of the *rāga-mārga-sādhaka*. A woman who is attached to her paramour very competently performs her household duties, but her mind and heart are with her lover. She remembers their laughing and loving exchanges, and she relishes the happiness of their recent meeting. Similarly, the *rāga-mārga-sādhaka* always tastes the pleasure of serving Bhagavān within his heart, even though he seems to be occupied with his various duties. The opinion of the *ācāryas* is that externally one should serve with the physical body, and internally one should remember Kṛṣṇa's form, qualities, pastimes, associates and so forth.

Śrīla Narottama dāsa Ṭhākura sings: "*gṛhe vā vanete thāke, 'hā gaurāṅga' bole ḍāke, narottama māṅge tāra saṅga* – whether a person lives in his home as a householder or in the forest as a renunciant, as long as he exclaims 'O Gaurāṅga!' Narottama dāsa begs for his association."

Text 9

In this state of *rāga-mārga-bhajana*, the devotee has affection for places that are dear to Kṛṣṇa, and he longs to stay in such places. This is described in the following verse from *Bhakti-rasāmṛta-sindhu* (1.2.156):

kadāhaṁ yamunā-tīre
nāmāni tava kīrtayan
udvāṣpaḥ puṇḍarīkākṣa!
racayiṣyāmi tāṇḍavam

O lotus-eyed Kṛṣṇa, when, upon the banks of the Yamunā, will I chant Your holy names and dance like a madman, my eyes brimming with tears of love?

Bhajana-rahasya-vṛtti

According to Śrīla Jīva Gosvāmipāda, this is an example of *lālasāmayī-vijñapti* made by a *jāta-rati-bhakta*; that is, a devotee in whom *bhāva* has appeared. *Lālasāmayī-vijñapti* is a prayer in which such a devotee prays to attain his desired *sevā*. *Samprārthanātmikā-vijñapti* is a prayer by a *sādhaka* in whom *rati* has not yet awakened. Such a prayer is also full of longing (*lālasā*), but *bhāva* is absent. This Text 9 is a prayer by a devotee on the path of *rāgānuga*.

The name Puṇḍarīkākṣa (lotus-eyed) here excites the devotee's heart with pastimes related to that name: "Śrī Kṛṣṇa's eyes have become reddish like a lotus due to sporting with the *vraja-gopīs* at night in a cottage situated in a secluded grove on the bank of the Yamunā. With extreme bliss and joy, in the society of *sakhīs* I will describe Śrī Kṛṣṇa's *rasa*, His personal beauty and so on." This is the mood that manifests. Or, "After arranging the union of Śrī Kṛṣṇa with my beloved *sakhī*, I will dance in a festival of bliss. Being satisfied, my Svāminī will bless me." Or, "When Śrīmatī Rādhikā becomes victorious in water sports (*jala-keli-vihāra*) in the Yamunā, I will dance like a madwoman, horripilating, shivering and with tears in my eyes."

Śrīla Bhaktivinoda Ṭhākura sings:

yamunā-salila-āharaṇe giyā, bujhiba yugala-rasa
prema-mugdha haye pāgalinī-prāya, gāiba rādhāra yaśa

As I go to draw water from the Yamunā, I will understand the confidential mellows of Yugala-kiśora's loving affairs. Like a madwoman captivated by *prema*, I will sing Śrī Rādhikā's glories.

Text 10

Apart from devotees, who desire to love Kṛṣṇa, everyone else's hearts are impure and stone-like due to offences. According to *Śrīmad-Bhāgavatam* (2.3.24), the emotions exhibited by such people are artificial:

tad aśma-sāraṁ hṛdayaṁ batedaṁ
yad gṛhyamānair hari-nāma-dheyaiḥ
na vikriyetātha yadā vikāro
netre jalaṁ gātra-ruheṣu harṣaḥ

When a *sādhaka* performs *harināma-saṅkīrtana*, the hairs of his body stand on end and tears of joy begin to flow from his eyes. But the heart of one in whom such *sāttvika-bhāva* transformations do not arise, is not actually a heart, but a hard thunderbolt.

harināma-saṅkīrtane roma-harṣa haya
daihika vikāra netre jala-dhārā baya

se samaye nahe yāra hṛdaya-vikāra
dhik tāra hṛdaya kaṭhina vajra-sāra

Bhajana-rahasya-vṛtti

If someone has been chanting the holy name for a long time but his heart is not melting, it is certain that he is a *nāma-aparādhī*. The holy name is all-powerful (*sarva-śaktimān*), but no immediate result takes place in a heart that is hard like stone. To criticise *sādhus* or to commit other such offences obstructs the desired transformation of the heart. If the obstruction is ordinary, the utterance of the holy name manifests as a semblance of the name (*nāma-ābhāsa*). If the obstruction is deep, however, then it manifests as *nāma-aparādha*. In other words, by offences committed at the lotus feet of a great personality (*mahāpuruṣa*), one's heart becomes hard like iron, and it is not melted by *śravaṇa*, *kīrtana* and so on.

The external symptoms of a heart that is melted by *harināma* are tears, horripilation and so forth. However, such symptoms are also seen in one whose heart is full of distress. Rūpa Gosvāmipāda says that occasionally tears, horripilation, etc. are observed in those whose hearts are naturally devious. Externally such people appear to be soft-hearted, but internally their hearts are actually hard. These symptoms can also be observed in those who believe they can acquire *sāttvika-bhāvas* by determined practice, even without *sattva-ābhāsa* (the semblance of *sāttvika-bhāvas*). Such emotions are never connected to *bhakti*.

One will definitely observe the nine symptoms of *bhāva*, such as forbearance (*kṣānti*) and not wasting time (*avyartha-kālatva*), in a fortunate person whose heart has been transformed by the appearance of pure *harināma* on his tongue, which is always engaged in service (*sevonmukha*). One should therefore understand that extraordinary forbearance and exceptional attachment to chanting the holy name are symptoms of a transformed heart. If an ordinary person, a so-called Vaiṣṇava who is actually envious, chants the holy name (*nāma-aparādha*) for a long time, his heart will not melt. He cannot perceive the sweetness of the holy name due to the offences in his heart. The nine symptoms of *bhāva*, beginning with *kṣānti*, may appear to be observed in a person whose heart is disturbed by *aparādha*, but his heart is actually hard like stone and he is worthy of reproach. However, if that person associates with devotees, he will gradually pass through *anartha-nivṛtti* and come to *niṣṭhā*, *ruci* and the other stages. Then, at the suitable time, the offences hardening his heart will be removed and his heart may melt. By receiving the mercy of Vaiṣṇavas and a pure *niṣkiñcana*, *mahā-bhāgavata guru* and practising spiritual life under their guidance, one will become free from the influence of *aparādhas* and *anarthas*. Finally he will become fixed in *vraja-bhāva*, which is filled with *rasa*, and he will attain the supreme goal, *prema*.

Text 11

In *Kṛṣṇa-karṇāmṛta* (107) it is said that when attachment (*rati*) for the holy name arises, the youthful form of Kṛṣṇa easily manifests:

bhaktis tvayi sthiratarā bhagavan yadi syād
daivena naḥ phalati divya-kiśora-mūrtiḥ
muktiḥ svayaṁ mukulitāñjaliḥ sevate 'smān
dharmārtha-kāma-gatayaḥ samaya-pratīkṣāḥ

O Bhagavān, if someone has steady devotion unto Your lotus feet, he easily perceives Your most charming divine youthful form. Thereafter, liberation stands before him with folded hands, and *dharma*, *artha* and *kāma* also wait for an opportunity to serve him.

bhakti sthiratarā yāṅra brajendra-nandana
tomāra kaiśora-mūrti tāṅra prāpya dhana

kara-yuḍi' mukti seve tāṅhāra caraṇa
dharma-artha-kāma kare ājñāra pālana

Bhajana-rahasya-vṛtti

The pure name manifests in a person's heart when he chants with pure devotees. At that stage *bhakti* that is symptomised by *prema* manifests in his heart as visions of pastimes (*līlā-sphūrtis*). When this *prema-bhakti* becomes steadfast, Śrī Kṛṣṇa's transcendental youthful form automatically appears in the heart. Although Mukti-devī is neglected by the devotee, she personally prays with folded hands for the devotee to accept her service. *Dharma*, *artha* and *kāma* also wait for the opportunity to pray to the devotee for service.

The *jāta-rati-bhakta* inclined towards *mādhurya-rasa* is greatly allured by the divine adolescent form of Śrī Kṛṣṇa, whose topmost pastimes of amorous love (*sṛṅgāra-rasa-vilāsa*) are displayed at this age. *Śrī Caitanya-caritāmṛta* (*Madhya-līlā* 8.189) states:

rātri-dina kuñje krīḍā kare rādhā-saṅge
kaiśora-vayasa saphala kaila krīḍā-raṅge

Day and night Śrī Kṛṣṇa enjoys the company of Śrī Rādhā in the *kuñjas* of Vṛndāvana. Thus, His adolescence is made successful through His pastimes with Her.

The art of amorous sport (*rati-kalā*), endowed with cleverness and other qualities, is expressed in the sweetest way during adolescence (*kaiśora*). *Bhakti-rasāmṛta-sindhu* states, "Śrī Kṛṣṇa embarrasses Śrī Rādhā by revealing to the *sakhīs* His skill and arrogance during the previous night's amorous sports by showing them how He expertly painted wonderful *keli-makarī*[1] on Her breasts. In this way Śrī Kṛṣṇa sports in the *kuñjas*, making His youth successful."

Text 12

Śrīmad-Bhāgavatam (11.3.30–1) describes the practice of chanting the holy name at the stage of *rati* in the association of pure devotees:

parasparānukathanaṁ
pāvanaṁ bhagavad-yaśaḥ
mitho ratir mithas tuṣṭir
nivṛttir mitha ātmanaḥ

smarantaḥ smārayantaś ca
mitho 'ghaugha-haraṁ harim
bhaktyā sañjātayā bhaktyā
bibhraty utpulakāṁ tanum

Bhagavān's glories are supremely purifying. Devotees discuss these glories amongst themselves and thus develop loving friendships, feel satisfaction, and gain release from material existence. They practise *sādhana-bhakti*, constantly remembering and reminding each other of the killer of Aghāsura, Śrī Hari. In this way *para-bhakti*, or *prema-bhakti*, arises in their hearts, and their bodies manifest ecstatic symptoms such as bodily hairs standing on end.

[1] A *makarī* is the female counterpart of the *makara*, a large sea creature that is considered to epitomise sensual desire.

bhakta-gaṇa paraspara kṛṣṇa-kathā gāya
tāhe rati tuṣṭi sukha paraspara pāya

hari-smṛti nije kare, anyere karāya
sādhane udita bhāve pulakāśru pāya

Bhajana-rahasaya-vṛtti

Śrī Kṛṣṇa burns up heaps of sins in a moment; therefore everyone should remember Him and also remind others about Him. In this way, by continuously following *sādhana-bhakti*, *prema-bhakti* arises in the devotee. Due to the predominance of *prema*, the devotee's body then displays ecstatic symptoms.

A *sādhaka's* duty is to increase his affection for the *svajātīya-bhaktas* (like-minded devotees who are more advanced than oneself and affectionate towards oneself) with whom he is associating, and to arrange for their happiness. It is also his duty to give up sense objects that are unfavourable to *bhakti*. The pure-hearted *svajātīya-bhakta* purifies one's heart by glorifying Śrī Kṛṣṇa's qualities. Thus, by cultivating devotion through processes such as the hearing and speaking of *kṛṣṇa-kathā*, *bhāva* arises in the heart. By hearing, speaking and remembering *hari-kathā*, which destroys all inauspiciousness, the *sādhaka* enters the perfected stage (*siddha-avasthā*).

The special meaning of this verse is that by the influence of associating with *vraja-rasika-bhaktas* who have the same mood as oneself, Bhakti-devī enters the heart. Hearing such devotees' *hari-kathā* with a pure heart matures a new *sādhaka's* impressions of *bhakti*.

In *Prema-bhakti-candrikā* it is said:

sādhane bhāviba yāhā siddha-dehe pāba tāhā

Whatever one contemplates in *sādhana*, one will attain at perfection.

pakvāpakva mātra se vicāra

The only difference is that in *sādhana* it is unripe, and at perfection, ripe.

By the mercy of a bona fide *guru*, the *sādhaka* realises his perfected form (*siddha-svarūpa*) and receives further instruction in the method of *bhajana.*

When like-minded pure devotees (*svajātīya-śuddha-bhaktas*) meet, they speak only *kṛṣṇa-kathā*, thus becoming overwhelmed by the description of Kṛṣṇa's form, qualities, etc. At Ṭera-kadamba and other places, Śrī Rūpa Gosvāmī and Śrī Sanātana Gosvāmī used to become submerged in *aṣṭa-sāttvika-bhāvas* when sharing realisations from their *bhajana.*

The *sādhaka* should be careful, though, that on the pretext of speaking *bhagavat-kathā*, he does not gratify his senses with female association, economic gain, fame, adoration and so forth. The *sādhaka* should be extremely cautious in the cultivation of his Kṛṣṇa consciousness (*kṛṣṇānuśīlana*), otherwise he will deviate from the correct path and be cheated of the wealth of Śrīman Mahāprabhu's *prema.*

Text 13

Sometimes the prideless pure devotee preaches *nāma-prema* throughout the world by the medium of *kīrtana.* As stated in *Śrīmad-Bhāgavatam* (1.6.26):

nāmāny anantasya hata-trapaḥ paṭhan
guhyāni bhadrāṇi kṛtāni ca smaran
gāṁ paryaṭaṁs tuṣṭa-manā gata-spṛhaḥ
kālaṁ pratīkṣan vimado vimatsaraḥ

[While telling his life story, Śrī Nārada said:] Not feeling shy or embarrassed, I began to chant and remember the mysterious and auspicious sweet names and pastimes of Bhagavān. My heart was already free from longing, pride and envy. Now I roamed the Earth joyfully, waiting for the right time.

lajjā chāḍi' kṛṣṇa-nāma sadā pāṭha kare
kṛṣṇera madhura-līlā sadā citte smare

tuṣṭamana, spṛhā-mada-śūnya-vimatsara
jīvana yāpana kare kṛṣṇecchā tatpara

Bhajana-rahasaya-vṛtti

Śrī Nārada engaged himself in the activities of chanting the holy names and remembering Bhagavān's confidential pastimes while he waited for his *vastu-siddhi*. Pure devotees wholly absorb themselves in chanting the holy names without a trace of hypocrisy, and they never allow criticism to enter their ears. They reveal confidential pastimes of Śrī Rādhā-Govinda, which are filled with extremely deep *prema-vilāsa*, to affectionate devotees who are of a similar disposition (*svajātīya-snigdha-bhaktas*). In his poem *Vaiṣṇava ke?*, Śrīla Bhaktisiddhānta Sarasvatī Prabhupāda states:

kīrtana prabhāve smaraṇa haibe
sei kāle nirjana bhajana sambhava

Smaraṇa, remembrance, will come as a result of performing *kīrtana*, and at that time *bhajana* in seclusion becomes possible.

Nāma and *nāmī* are non-different. Upon attaining the stage of *bhāva*, a devotee's material sentiments are destroyed and he becomes humble, respecting everyone. He does not expect honour for himself, and giving up any sense of shyness and inhibition, he performs *harināma-saṅkīrtana*. Śrī Nārada is describing this condition in this Text. Giving up all pride and shyness, he propagated the chanting of the holy names everywhere. The topmost devotees preach everywhere for the welfare of human society. Śrīla Bhaktisiddhānta Sarasvatī Prabhupāda says: "*prāṇa āche yāra se hetu pracāra* – he who has life can preach."

Smaraṇa is a limb of *bhakti* that is subservient to *śravaṇa* and *kīrtana*. According to Śrīla Jīva Gosvāmī, narrations of the deep and confidential activities of Bhagavān – that is, His pastimes of *vilāsa* with His beloveds – should not be revealed in the presence of ordinary persons. One should perform *smaraṇa* and *kīrtana* according to one's qualification.

Śrī Caitanya-caritāmṛta (*Madhya-līlā* 22.157, 159) states:

'mane' nija-siddha-deha kariyā bhāvana
rātri-dine kare vraje kṛṣṇera sevana

nijābhīṣṭa kṛṣṇa-preṣṭha pāche ta' lāgiyā
nirantara sevā kare antarmanā hañā

The perfected devotee serves Kṛṣṇa in Vṛndāvana day and night within his mind, in his original, pure, self-realised position (*nija-siddha-deha*). Actually, the inhabitants of Vṛndāvana are very dear to Kṛṣṇa. If a person wants to engage in spontaneous loving service, he must follow the inhabitants of Vṛndāvana and constantly engage in devotional service within his mind.

Text 14

Śrīmad-Bhāgavatam (11.3.32) states:

kvacid rudanty acyuta-cintayā kvacid
dhasanti nandanti vadanty alaukikāḥ
nṛtyanti gāyanty anuśīlayanty ajaṁ
bhavanti tūṣṇīṁ param etya nirvṛtāḥ

The transcendental *mahā-bhāgavata's* condition is astonishing. Sometimes he starts to worry, thinking, "So far I have not had direct audience of Bhagavān. What shall I do? Where shall I go? Whom shall I ask? Who will be able to find Him for me?" Thinking like this he begins to weep. Sometimes he receives an internal revelation (*sphūrti*) of Bhagavān's sweet pastimes, and he laughs loudly as he beholds Bhagavān, who is endowed with all opulences, hiding in fear of the *gopīs*. Sometimes he is submerged in bliss upon receiving Bhagavān's *darśana* and directly experiencing His *prema*. Sometimes, when situated in his *siddha-deha*, he speaks with Bhagavān, saying, "O Prabhu, after so long, I have attained You," and he proceeds to sing the glories of his Lord. Sometimes, when he receives Bhagavān's affection, he starts to dance, and sometimes he experiences great peace and remains silent.

bhāvodaye kabhu kāṅde kṛṣṇa-cintā phale
hāse ānandita haya, alaukika bale

nāce gāya, kṛṣṇa ālocane sukha pāya
līlā-anubhave haya, tūṣṇīm bhūta prāya

Bhajana-rahasya-vṛtti

Upon the appearance of *bhāva*, the *sādhaka's* internal and external activities become extraordinary. Due to remembering narrations of Bhagavān, sometimes he cries, sometimes he laughs, sometimes he dances, sometimes he displays delight and sometimes, becoming silent, he is grave. And at other times, in the association of like-minded devotees, he describes his transcendental realisations, which are filled with *prema*.

In the Gambhīrā, Śrīman Mahāprabhu was immersed in many transcendental sentiments and would reveal them to Svarūpa Dāmodara and Rāya Rāmānanda. Mahāprabhu's mind used to completely drown in the ocean of Śrī Rādhā's sentiments and He became as if mad (*unmatta*), sometimes losing external consciousness, and sometimes, in *ardha-bāhya-daśā* (half internal and half external consciousness), He would express some of the sentiments in His heart. While absorbed in a dream (*svapnāveśa*), He would become silent, fully absorbed in bliss. Sometimes, in *ardha-bāhya-daśā*, He saw Kṛṣṇa, and sometimes He lost Him. In *bāhya-daśā* (external consciousness), He was unhappy to be separated from the jewel He had attained but had now lost. Sometimes, like a madman, He asked animals, birds and people, "Where is Kṛṣṇa? Have you seen Him?" At night, when the atmosphere was calm and it was time for Rādhikā's rendezvous with Kṛṣṇa, He could not keep His composure. As He remembered the *rāsa-līlā*, He would become overwhelmed with *bhāva* and begin to sing and dance.

In *antar-daśā* (internal consciousness) there is only meeting and happiness. Sometimes, while thus absorbed, Mahāprabhu would say, "Today Kṛṣṇa, surrounded by the *sakhīs*, was sporting at Rādhā-kuṇḍa. One *sakhī* helped Me behold those *vilāsa* pastimes from a distance." When Mahāprabhu returned to *bāhya-daśā*, He would say, "Svarūpa! Did I just say something to you? What? Oh, I am a *sannyāsī* named Caitanya!" He then lamented in the anguish of separation. Remembering Kṛṣṇa's qualities, He would clasp the necks of Rāya Rāmānanda and Svarūpa Dāmodara, and cry with great restlessness. This would happen every day.

In the stage of *bhāva*, a *sādhaka* sometimes cries, "Alas! Alas! It is impossible for me to obtain *kṛṣṇa-prema*, so it is useless for me to remain alive." Sometimes he laughs as he remembers a pastime, and he thinks, "Śrī Kṛṣṇa, who steals the young wives of the cowherd men, passed the whole night under a tree in the courtyard. Although He was calling the *gopīs* in various intonations, He was defeated by Jaṭilā and Kuṭilā's careful guard and interrogation, and He could not attain the *gopīs'* association." Sometimes a *sādhaka* becomes silent and peaceful, concealing the wealth of *prema* in his heart. Sometimes, imitating a pastime of Hari, he dances, and sometimes he speaks in a strange and incomprehensible way.

Text 15

Attachment to beholding the beautiful form of the deity is described in *Śrīmad-Bhāgavatam* (10.23.22):

śyāmaṁ hiraṇya-paridhiṁ vanamālya-barha-
dhātu-pravāla-naṭa-veśam anuvratāṁse
vinyasta-hastam itareṇa dhunānam abjaṁ
karṇotpalālaka-kapola-mukhābja-hāsam

He is dark-complexioned like a fresh raincloud, and His yellow cloth, which defeats the splendour of gold, shimmers against His body. His head is decorated with a peacock feather, and every part of His body is ornamented with designs that are drawn with various coloured minerals. Sprigs of new leaves adorn His body, and around His neck is an enchanting forest-flower garland of five colours. Dressed in this way, He appears as a fresh, youthful, expert dancer. He rests one hand upon His *sakhā's* shoulder and with the other He twirls a pastime lotus. His ears are decorated with earrings (*kuṇḍalas*), curly locks of hair splash against His cheeks, and His lotus face blossoms with a gentle smile.

kṣaṇe-kṣaṇe dekhe śyāma, hiraṇya-valita
vanamālā-śikhi-piñcha-dhātv-ādi-maṇḍita

naṭaveśa, saṅgī-skandhe nyasta-padma-kara
karṇa-bhūṣā-alakā-kapola-smitādhara

Bhajana-rahasya-vṛtti

Upon the appearance of *rati*, attachment arises in the *sādhaka's* heart when he takes *darśana* of the deity, and he experiences the splendour of Śrī Kṛṣṇa's beauty as described in this verse. Śrī Kṛṣṇa's head is decorated with a peacock feather crown, and His neck is beautified by a garland of flowers and leaves strung by the *vraja-gopīs*. His body is decorated with pictures made with aromatic minerals from Kāmyavana. Śrī Kṛṣṇa, who attracts everyone with His smiling face, puts His left arm around the shoulder of a *priya-narma-sakhā*, and His right hand twirls a pastime lotus. The *ācāryas* explain that from His twirling of the pastime lotus it can be understood that Kṛṣṇa's heart dances like that lotus when He sees the devotees. Or, the devotees' hearts dance like the lotus when they see Kṛṣṇa. Here, by His twirling of the lotus, Śrī Kṛṣṇa expresses the sentiment, "O fortunate *brāhmaṇīs*, I am holding your lotus-like hearts in My hand." He implies, "Upon attaining *darśana* of Me, your hearts dance like this lotus." Or, "By accepting your hearts, I will make you My own."

Śrī Kṛṣṇa entices all living entities to drink nectar by attracting them with the sweetness of His beauty. By this mercy, many kinds of pastimes manifest within the *sādhaka's* heart, and he experiences the happiness of relishing these pastimes.

Text 16

Also in *Śrīmad-Bhāgavatam* (10.21.5):

barhāpīḍaṁ naṭa-vara-vapuḥ karṇayoḥ karṇikāraṁ
bibhrad vāsaḥ kanaka-kapiśaṁ vaijayantīṁ ca mālām
randhrān veṇor adhara-sudhayāpūrayan gopa-vṛndair
vṛndāraṇyaṁ sva-pada ramaṇaṁ prāviśad gīta-kīrtiḥ

[Seeing Kṛṣṇa through the eyes of *bhāva*, the *gopīs* in *pūrva-rāga* described His beauty:] Śyāmasundara is entering the forest of Vṛndāvana accompanied by His cowherd boyfriends. In His turban there is a peacock feather; over His ears, a *karṇikāra* flower; on His body, a *pītāmbara* glitters like gold; and around His neck, extending down to His knees, is a heart-stealing garland strung with five kinds of fragrant forest flowers. His beautiful dress is like that of an expert dancer on a stage, and the nectar of His lips flows through the holes of His flute. Singing His glories, the cowherd boys follow from behind. In this way, this Vṛndāvana-dhāma, which is more charming than Vaikuṇṭha, has become even more beautiful by the impressions of Śrī Kṛṣṇa's lotus feet, which are marked with the conch, disc and other symbols.

śikhicūḍa, naṭavara, karṇe karṇikāra
pītavāsa, vaijayantī-mālā-galahāra

veṇu-randhre adhara-pīyūṣa pūrṇa kari'
sakhā-saṅge vṛndāraṇye praveśila hari

Bhajana-rahasya-vṛtti

With this verse Śrī Śukadeva Gosvāmī, the crown jewel of all *paramahaṁsas*, has drawn an amazing picture of the sweet form of Kṛṣṇa that manifested in the hearts of the beautiful damsels of Vraja when they heard the sound of His *veṇu*. The *vraja-ramaṇīs*, filled with deep attachment for Kṛṣṇa, became overwhelmed upon hearing the sweet sound of His flute. As they began to describe to each other the astonishing sweetness of that sound, the image of Śrī Kṛṣṇa in His very beautiful threefold-bending form (*tribhaṅga-lalita*), with His playful way of strolling, His crooked glances, His sweet slight smile and so on, manifested within their hearts and overwhelmed them with *prema*.

Barhāpīḍam – In the middle of the locks of black curly hair on Śrī Kṛṣṇa's head there is a peacock feather crown that looks like a rainbow on a fresh raincloud. These peacock feathers were a gift from blissfully dancing peacocks. By wearing this crown on His head, the *dhīra-lalita-nāyaka* Kṛṣṇa reveals the *hāva, bhāva* and other ecstatic symptoms of His beloveds in an unprecedented way. The *nakha-candrikā*, the shining bluish-green centre of the peacock feather, is a seal of cleverness in the loving affairs (*prema-vidagdha*) that comprise the art of *rasa*. By wearing a peacock feather on His head, Kṛṣṇa proclaims the victory of His beloved Rādhā in the previous night's pastimes in the pleasure groves.

Naṭa-vara-vapuḥ – Even the art of dancing (*nṛtya-vilāsa*) is defeated by Kṛṣṇa's playful way of strolling. Śyāmasundara, the best of dancers, is the personification of the highest sweetness, which is beyond comparison. When, accompanied by His cowherd friends, He follows the cows into the Vṛndāvana forest, His lotus feet dance in His own natural style, which shames the art of dancing itself. At the same time, His jewelled anklebells, golden-coloured *pītāmbara*, waist bells and the *vaijayantī-mālā* on His chest also dance. His fingers, too, dance upon the holes of His flute in a unique manner. Kṛṣṇa's two eyes, which defeat the beauty of the restless movement of *khañjana* birds and baby deer, also dance with various expressions. His *makara*-shaped earrings, His black curling tresses and the peacock feather adorning the top of His head also start to dance. Thus, He Himself is the unequalled expert dancer (*naṭa-vara*) and every part of His body is also a *naṭa-vara*.

Karṇayoḥ karṇikāram – The yellow *kanera* flower (*karṇikāra*) that Śyāmasundara wears on His ears as He enters the forest increases the incomparable sweetness of His fresh youth. *Rasika-śekhara* Śrī Kṛṣṇa wears only one *kanera* flower, sometimes on

His right ear and sometimes on His left, thus demonstrating His carefree, intoxicated youth. He places this flower on the ear that faces the loving *gopīs* who stand on the roof-tops, thus showing them His great affection.

Bibhrad vāsaḥ kanaka-kapiśam – *Naṭa-vara* Śyāmasundara's body, whose dark complexion defeats the colour of fresh storm clouds, is adorned with a golden-yellow garment (*pītāmbara*) which resembles lightning against a thundercloud. By covering His body with the *pītāmbara*, which is similar in colour to the *vraja-gopīs'* golden complexions, He expresses how He feels when being embraced by them, thus revealing His deep love for them. On His very broad chest, a *vaijayantī-mālā*, made from five kinds of flowers, swings gently and sweetly. Seeing this, ever-fresh waves of emotion surge in the *gopīs'* hearts. These five flowers are like five arrows released by the *gopīs* that pierce each and every part of Kṛṣṇa's body.

Randrān veṇor adhara-sudhayāpūrayan – When Śrī Kṛṣṇa covers the holes of the *veṇu* with His fingers, puts it to His tender, bud-like lips that defeat the beauty of ripe *bimba* fruits, and gently blows into it, a sweet sound pours from the holes that infatuates the entire world and enchants all moving and non-moving beings. The lifeless *veṇu* becomes alive and stirs the *gopīs'* hearts, stimulating transcendental lust (*kāma*) within them. Moreover, when the *gopīs* see that the *veṇu* is enjoying their wealth of the nectar of Kṛṣṇa's lips (*adhara-sudhā*) right in front of them, even though the flute is male, the *sañcāri-bhāva* called jealousy (*īrṣyā*) arises in their hearts.

In this way, Śyāmasundara plays on His *veṇu* as He enters the most pleasant forest of Vṛndāvana. The moment a stream of the flute's sweet nectar enters the ears of the *vraja-ramaṇīs*, who are endowed with *mahābhāva*, an amazing condition arises in their hearts. They become restless with a strong desire to meet with

Kṛṣṇa, and although they try to conceal this mood, they are unsuccessful.

A *sādhaka* who aims to attain the *gopīs'* love for Kṛṣṇa will gradually develop his *bhāva-mādhurya* by performing *sādhana* under the guidance of his spiritual master. When the stage of *bhāva* arises, Śrī Kṛṣṇa's form manifests within the *sādhaka's* heart. At this stage the *sādhaka's* mood is similar to that of a *gopī*. He understands himself (in his *svarūpa*) to be a young girl (*kiśorī*), and he becomes absorbed in rendering service under the guidance of the *nitya-siddha-gopīs*.

Text 17

When the holy name fully manifests, one becomes enchanted by the deity, who enchants even Himself. In *Śrīmad-Bhāgavatam* (3.2.12) Śrī Uddhava says to Vidura:

yan-martya-līlaupayikaṁ sva-yoga-
māyā-balaṁ darśayatā gṛhītam
vismāpanaṁ svasya ca saubhagarddheḥ
paraṁ padaṁ bhūṣaṇa-bhūṣaṇāṅgam

Through His Yogamāyā potency, Bhagavān appeared in His transcendental form suitable for His pastimes as a human being. This form was so beautiful that it not only enchanted the entire world, but also amazed Bhagavān Himself. This blessed form is the ultimate summit of beauty, and His beautiful bodily lustre even embellishes His ornaments.

martya-līlā-upayogī savismaya-kārī
prakaṭila vapu kṛṣṇa cic-chakti vistāri'
subhaga-ṛddhira para-pada camatkāra
bhūṣaṇa-bhūṣaṇa-rūpa tulanāra pāra

Bhajana-rahasya-vṛtti

By the influence of His *cit-śakti*, Bhagavān Śrī Kṛṣṇa manifests a completely captivating form appropriate for His human-like pastimes. The unparalleled beauty of this form astonishes even Śrī Kṛṣṇa Himself. Śrī Kṛṣṇa has unlimited pastimes as well as unlimited manifestations, such as: His *svayaṁ-prakāśa* (personal manifestations) like Vāsudeva and Saṅkarṣaṇa; His *vilāsa-mūrti* (pastime form) Śrī Nārāyaṇa; and His *svāṁśa-rūpa* (personal expansions), which are the *puruṣa-avatāras* (Lords of creative energy – Kāraṇodakaśāyī Viṣṇu, Garbhodakaśāyī Viṣṇu and Kṣīrodakaśāyī Viṣṇu), *guṇa-avatāras* (incarnations of the three qualities of nature – Brahmā, Śiva and Viṣṇu) and *āveśa-avatāras* (empowered living entities). Of all these expansions, He Himself (*svayaṁ-rūpa*), Śrī Kṛṣṇa of Gokula – who is an ever-youthful and expert dancer, who is attired in the dress of a *gopa* and who holds a flute – is superior and the most attractive. A single particle of this sweetness fully submerges Gokula, Mathurā, Dvārakā and even Devī-dhāma.

By His Yogamāyā, Kṛṣṇa manifests Himself in such an unparalleled form in this material world along with His most confidential jewel, the eternal pastimes of Goloka Vṛndāvana. This astonishing nature amazes even Kṛṣṇa Himself, rendering Him helpless in His attempts to taste its sweetness. Śrī Kṛṣṇa, complete in the six opulences of wealth, beauty, fame, strength, knowledge and renunciation, is situated in His ultimate perfection. These six opulences are adorned with sweetness and assume an unprecedented divine beauty.

Ornaments usually beautify the body, but Śrī Kṛṣṇa's body enhances the beauty of His ornaments. His threefold-bending form (*tribhaṅga-lalita*) enhances the amazing beauty of His limbs and attracts the hearts of all. The arrow of His crooked sidelong glance joined to the bow of His eyebrows stirs the minds of Śrī Rādhā and the other *vraja-devīs*. The Lakṣmīs, proclaimed in the Vedas to be virtuous and chaste, are also attracted by His beauty and desire to serve the effulgence emanating from His toenails. Even though Śrī Rādhā and Her *sakhīs* in Vraja worship with their lives, millions of times over, the moonbeams emanating from Śrī Kṛṣṇa's toenails, they eternally keep His moon-like face in the caves of their hearts.

On the strength of His own *cit-śakti*, Bhagavān Kṛṣṇacandra manifests an extraordinary form for His pastimes in the material world. This form generates astonishment even in Nārāyaṇa, His *vilāsa-vigraha*. Even Kṛṣṇa Himself becomes mad to taste His own sweetness. *Śrī Caitanya-caritāmṛta* (*Ādi-līlā* 4.158) confirms this: *kṛṣṇera mādhurye kṛṣṇe upajaya lobha.*

Text 18

Kṛṣṇa's beauty attracts the hearts of all. *Śrīmad-Bhāgavatam* (9.24.65) describes the Vrajavāsīs' anger towards Brahmā for making eyes that blink and thus obstruct their vision of Kṛṣṇa while they drink the beauty of His form:

yasyānanaṁ makara-kuṇḍala-cāru-karṇa-
bhrājat-kapola-subhagaṁ savilāsa-hāsam
nityotsavaṁ na tatṛpur dṛśibhiḥ pibantyo
nāryo narāś ca muditāḥ kupitā nimeś ca

The *makara*-shaped earrings that swing on Śrī Kṛṣṇa's ears play in the lake of His cheeks, and this splendour increases even further the beauty of His cheeks. When He smiles with enjoyment, the bliss that is always present on His face is augmented. With the cups of their eyes, all men and women drink the nectarean beauty of His lotus face. They are never satisfied, however, so they become angry with Brahmā for creating eyes that blink and thus obstruct their relish of this sweetness.

subhaga-kapola heri' makara-kuṇḍala
savilāsa hāsya-mukha-candra niramala

nara-nārī-gaṇa nitya-utsave mātila
nimeṣa-kārīra prati kupita haila

Bhajana-rahasya-vṛtti

Śrīla Śukadeva Gosvāmī, radiant with joy, began to describe the sweetness of Śrī Kṛṣṇa's beautiful form to Mahārāja Parīkṣit. When the Vrajavāsīs see this beauty, they are overwhelmed with *prema* and their own loving attachment (*anurāga*) is unlimitedly amplified, attaining a delightfulness beyond description. The *vraja-sundarīs*, filled with *mahābhāva*, relish Kṛṣṇa's extraordinary beauty (*rūpa-mādhurya*) to its fullest extent due to their very thick and deep *anurāga*. Their sentiments are on the topmost level, and although there is no higher position, their transcendental moods keep increasing to the stage of *yāvad-āśraya-vṛtti*[2]. In this state of *anurāga*, which cannot be described in words, they experience nothing but *rasa*. They attain *sva-saṁvedya-daśā*[2], which is the ultimate stage of *mahābhāva*. This condition is the wealth of the *vraja-sundarīs* alone.

Śrī Kṛṣṇa's cheeks are surrounded by curly locks of hair and are radiant with divine earrings. An eternal festival of unprecedented beauty pervades His charming lotus face. In the centre of this eternal festival, a gentle, nectarean smile gracefully resides, like an emperor of the sweetest of all great sweetness. Because Śrī Kṛṣṇa has attained adolescence (between the ages of *paugaṇḍa* and *kiśora*), happiness, impatience, liveliness and so forth have appeared on His lotus face, revealing His restlessness. His white teeth, stained by chewing *tāmbūla*, and His reddish lips endowed with a charming smile, have reached the extreme limit of beauty.

[2] Please refer to the Glossary for an explanation of these terms.

It seems that on the full moon night, the moon rays remove the burning suffering of all living entities and give rise to greed in the hearts of the devotee-like *cakora* birds. In the same way, when the *vraja-devīs* see the unprecedented sweetness of Śrī Kṛṣṇa's beauty, their ocean of *kāma* increases. Kṛṣṇa's beauty thus destroys their consideration of family, caste, religion, patience and so forth; they become infatuated by His charm and drown in an ocean of bliss. Constantly swinging *makara*-shaped earrings dance on the cheeks of Śrī Kṛṣṇa's gentle, softly smiling face as they embrace and kiss His cheeks. When the *gopīs* see this, Śrī Kṛṣṇa appears in their hearts as *dhīra-lalita*, a hero expert in amorous sports. His intention to embrace the *vraja-sundarīs* and kiss their breasts is expressed by the *kuṇḍalas'* touching and embracing His cheeks.

The *gopīs*, however, are not thoroughly satisfied by watching the festival of Śrī Kṛṣṇa's sweetness in this way. Angry with Brahmā for creating eyelids that momentarily interrupt their *darśana*, they curse him. "Brahmā is not qualified to create. To view such a beautiful scene he has given only two eyes, and they even have doors on them in the form of eyelids! After dying, we will become Brahmā in our next lives and show how creation should be done. Two eyes alone are not sufficient to behold such elegance and beauty. The entire body should have eyes with no eyelids so that we can have unlimited *darśana* of Kṛṣṇa without blinking!"

This Text uses the words *nāryo narāś ca* to indicate that all men and women drink the nectarean beauty of Kṛṣṇa's lotus face. *Nāryaḥ* means Rādhā and the other *gopīs*, and *narāḥ* means Subala and other *priya-narma-sakhās*.

Only in Vraja are Śrī Kṛṣṇa's four unique qualities – *prema-mādhurya*, *līlā-mādhurya*, *rūpa-mādhurya* and *veṇu-mādhurya* – present in their most complete form. For this reason there is a special importance and a distinguishing virtue that Vraja-dhāma has over other *dhāmas* and that Vrajendra-nandana Śrī Rādhā-ramaṇa and the *vraja-gopikās* have over other incarnations.

Text 19

The Creator fashioned Śrī Kṛṣṇa in an unprecedented way, as described in *Śrīmad-Bhāgavatam* (3.2.13):

yad dharma-sūnor bata rājasūye
nirīkṣya dṛk-svasty-ayanaṁ tri-lokaḥ
kārtsnyena cādyeha gataṁ vidhātur
arvāk-sṛtau kauśalam ity amanyata

When the people from all three worlds who were present at Dharmarāja Yudhiṣṭhira's *rājasūya-yajña* beheld Bhagavān Kṛṣṇa's form, which is so pleasing to the eye, they thought that in fashioning this form the Creator had reached the zenith of his expertise in creating human forms.

yūdhiṣṭhira-rāja-sūye nayana-maṅgala
kṛṣṇa-rūpa loka-traya-nivāsī sakala

jagatera sṛṣti madhye ati camatkāra
vidhātāra kauśala e karila nirdhāra

Bhajana-rahasya-vṛtti

Uddhava, overwhelmed with *kṛṣṇa-prema*, is describing the beautiful form of Śrī Kṛṣṇa to Vidura. "Those who personally saw Śrī Kṛṣṇa at Yudhiṣṭhira Mahārāja's *rājasūya-yajña* praised Vidhātā's (Brahmā's) skill in creating by saying, 'Even the Creator, Brahmā, becomes wonderstruck upon seeing the splendour of this graceful body, which eclipses the lustre of a blue lotus or a sapphire.'"

This Text praises Vidhātā's creative skill, yet Śrī Kṛṣṇa's form is eternal, without a beginning. Nevertheless, for the sake of material perspective, words like "creation" have been used. Śrī Kṛṣṇa's form is perfect, eternal, human-like and beginningless. This form is manifest in Vṛndāvana and is suitable for human-like pastimes (*nara-līlā*). Among all the pastimes performed by Kṛṣṇa in His different *svarūpas* in His various abodes, such as Vaikuṇṭha, His *nara-līlā*, which He performs in Vraja like an ordinary human being, is topmost. He is glorified in three ways according to the degree to which His qualities are manifest: *pūrṇa* (complete), *pūrṇatara* (more complete) and *pūrṇatama* (most complete). His form in which all of His qualities such as beauty, sweetness and opulence are manifest in the most complete way is called *pūrṇatama*, and this form is manifest in Vṛndāvana. He appears in His most complete form of Bhagavān only there, because that is where His associates express the ultimate limit of *prema*. In all other places He manifests as either *pūrṇa* or *pūrṇatara*, according to the level to which *prema* is developed in His associates of that abode.

In Vraja, Kṛṣṇa manifests as *pūrṇatama*. In three of the *bhāvas* in which He has relationships with the Vrajavāsīs (*dāsya*, *sakhya* and *vātsalya*), there is an expectation of only one kind of relationship (for instance, in *dāsya* only servitude is expected). Also, there is some etiquette (*maryādā*) in the service rendered to Him by the devotees in these three *rasas*. But the relationship the *vraja-gopīs* have with Śrī Kṛṣṇa is that of lover and beloved (*kānta-kāntā*), and their service follows solely in the wake of their desire for Him. They do not hesitate to transgress chastity and dignity for the sake of serving Him and giving Him happiness. Therefore, *kāntā-prema* is supreme. Śrī Rādhā is the crown jewel of all these *kāntās* and Her love entirely controls Śrī Kṛṣṇa. By the influence of Śrī Rādhā's *prema*, the *pūrṇatama* beauty and sweetness of Śrī Kṛṣṇacandra increase without cessation.

Text 20

The result of having *darśana* of the deity with deep, loving attachment (*anurāga*) is described in *Śrīmad-Bhāgavatam* (3.2.14):

yasyānurāga-pluta-hāsa-rāsa-
līlāvaloka-pratilabdha-mānāḥ
vraja-striyo dṛgbhir anupravṛtta-
dhiyo 'vatasthuḥ kila kṛtya-śeṣāḥ

When the young women of Vraja were honoured by Kṛṣṇa's affectionate laughter, joking words and playful glances, their eyes would become fixed on Him. Their minds would become so absorbed in Him that they would become unaware of their bodies and homes, and they would remain standing as if lifeless – like dolls.

anurāga hāsa-rāsa-līlāvalokane
sampūjita-vraja-gopī nitya-daraśane

sarva-kṛtya-samādhāna antare māniyā
kṛṣṇa-rūpe mugdha-netre rahe dāṅḍāiyā

Bhajana-rahasya-vṛtti

Śrī Kṛṣṇa, who is controlled by *prema*, casts sidelong glances at the *gopīs* as He laughs playfully. At that time, *prema* increases in the *gopīs'* hearts, and their desire to enhance Śrī Kṛṣṇa's pleasure awakens. They make Him eager to meet them by their varieties of laughing, joking and sulkiness. In response to their love for Him, Kṛṣṇa runs with an eager heart to pacify their *māna*. Controlled by the deeply affectionate *prema* of the *gopīs*, He announces His gratitude by accepting eternal indebtedness to them.

Unlimited waves enter the ocean of *bhāva* of the *vraja-ramaṇīs*, who are endowed with *mahābhāva*, and while attending to their household duties, such as cleaning, smearing cow dung over the floor and churning yoghurt, they are always absorbed in remembering Śrī Kṛṣṇa's different pastimes. The *vraja-ramaṇīs'* hearts and senses become His dedicated followers, and their minds become imprisoned within His heart. Seeing their activities, Kṛṣṇa Himself becomes astonished, what to speak of others.

Śrī Kṛṣṇa is extremely attached to the *gopīs* in many ways. He prays to them, He spends much time trying to appease their *māna*, and He waits at the gate of a *kuñja* for permission to enter. At that time, the *gopīs* feel content and successful. They drink the splendour of His beauty and thus become motionless like statues.

Text 21

The mood of absolute opulence assuming the form of sweetness (*mādhurya*) is described in *Śrīmad-Bhāgavatam* (3.2.21):

svayaṁ tv asāmyātiśayas tryadhīśaḥ
svārājya-lakṣmy-āpta-samasta-kāmaḥ
baliṁ haradbhiś cira-loka-pālaiḥ
kirīṭa-koṭīḍita-pāda-pīṭhaḥ

Śrī Kṛṣṇa is Himself the Supreme Lord of the three potencies (*sandhinī, saṁvit* and *hlādinī*). No one is equal to Him, so who can be greater than Him? All of His desires are fulfilled by His own transcendental goddess of fortune (*rājya-lakṣmī*). Indra and innumerable other *loka-pālas*, deities presiding over different regions of the universe, bring Him varieties of offerings and pay their obeisances, touching the tops of their crowns to the footstool on which He rests His lotus feet.

samādhika-śūnya kṛṣṇa triśakti-īśvara
svarūpa-aiśvarye pūrṇa-kāma nirantara

sopāyana-lokapāla-kirīṭa-niścaya
lagna-pāda-pīṭha stavanīya atiśaya

Bhajana-rahasya-vṛtti

The general meaning of the word *tryadhīśvara* is that Śrī Kṛṣṇa has innumerable forms and incarnations. He has unsurpassed opulence. Brahmā, Viṣṇu and Mahādeva are the lords of creation, but they are under the rule of Śrī Kṛṣṇa, who is the Supreme Lord (*adhīśvara*) of everyone.

The intermediate meaning of *tryadhīśvara* is that the three *puruṣa-avatāras* – Kāraṇodakaśāyī, Garbhodakaśāyī and Kṣīrodakaśāyī – are the partial expansions of Śrī Kṛṣṇa's expansion, Baladeva Prabhu. This means that Śrī Kṛṣṇa is the Supreme Lord of them all.

The essential meaning of *tryadhīśvara* is as follows. In the scriptures, Śrī Kṛṣṇa is known to have three places of residence. One place is His inner quarters, Goloka Vṛndāvana, where He is eternally present with His mother, father, friends and beloveds. There Yogamāyā serves Him as a maidservant. Beneath this Goloka-dhāma is Paravyoma, also known as Viṣṇuloka. Śrī Kṛṣṇa's *vilāsa-mūrti*, Śrī Nārāyaṇa, and unlimited other forms reside there. This is Kṛṣṇa's intermediate place of residence. Below this Paravyoma is Śrī Kṛṣṇa's third place of residence, called *bāhyāvāsa*, His external residence. It is situated in the material realm, across the Virajā River where countless universes (*brahmāṇḍas*) are present like chambers. This place is also called Devī-dhāma, or Māyā-devī's *dhāma*, and the living entities who are bound by *māyā* reside there. The material energy (*jagat-lakṣmī*), the shadow of the transcendental goddess of fortune (*rājya-lakṣmī*), protects the wealth of this world.

Śrī Kṛṣṇa is the Supreme Lord of these three places – Goloka, Paravyoma and the material universes. Both Goloka and Paravyoma are transcendental and are the divine opulence (*vibhūti*) of the *cit-śakti*. They are therefore called *tripāda-aiśvarya*, the opulence comprising three-quarters of the Lord's energy. The *vibhūti* of *māyā*, the material universe, is called *ekapāda-aiśvarya*. The opulence in Śrī Kṛṣṇa's transcendental *dhāmas* is three times that of the material world. His *tripāda-vibhūti* (the spiritual world) cannot be glorified in words. In the unlimited universes of the *ekapāda-vibhūti* there are countless Brahmās and Śivas, and they are called *loka-pālas*, eternal maintainers of the order of creation.

Once in Dvārakā, Brahmā came for Śrī Kṛṣṇa's *darśana*. When the doorman went to inform Bhagavān that Brahmā had come to meet with Him, Śrī Kṛṣṇa asked, "Which Brahmā has come? What is his name? Go and ask him." The door-keeper went back and enquired accordingly. Brahmā became astonished and said, "Please go and tell Him that the father of the four Kumāras, Caturmukha Brahmā, has come."

When Brahmā reached the threshold of the Sudharmā assembly hall, he became stunned. The crowd was such that he could not enter. Millions and millions of Indras, Brahmās, Śivas and other *loka-pālas*, each with heads numbering from eight to thousands, were paying their prostrated obeisances in front of Śrī Kṛṣṇa's footstool. When their crowns, which were inlaid with jewels, touched the ground, loud clattering sounds arose and mixed with sounds of the *loka-pālas' jaya-dhvani* (calls of victory), which resounded in all directions. Caturmukha Brahmā was like a firefly in the midst of millions of suns. Suddenly everything disappeared and the dumbfounded Caturmukha Brahmā stood alone. He was astonished to see this magnificent opulence of Śrī Kṛṣṇa, and his pride vanished. Ashamed of his offence, he began to glorify the Lord, praying for forgiveness. Thereafter, Śrī Kṛṣṇa sent Brahmā on his way.

Tryadhīśvara has another confidential meaning. The word *tri* refers to Śrī Kṛṣṇa's three abodes – Gokula, Mathurā and Dvārakā. Another name for these abodes is Goloka. Śrī Kṛṣṇa is naturally and eternally present in these three abodes, and He Himself is their *adhīśvara* (Supreme Lord). Therefore, He is called *tryadhīśvara*. The *dikpālas*, who preside over the ten directions of the globe of the unlimited material universes, as well as all the *cira-loka-pālas* who reside in the coverings of the unlimited Vaikuṇṭhas, were paying their *daṇḍavat-praṇāmas* at Śrī Kṛṣṇa's footstool.

Svārājya-lakṣmy-āpta-samasta-kāmaḥ – *Svarājya-lakṣmī*, the transcendental goddess of fortune, fulfils all Śrī Kṛṣṇa's desires. He has unlimited pastimes in Vaikuṇṭha and other abodes, but amongst them all, His human-like pastimes (*nara-līlā*) are top-most. In His inner quarters of Śrī Goloka Vṛndāvana, His opulence (*aiśvarya*), being adorned with sweetness (*mādhurya*), is billions of times greater than His opulence in Vaikuṇṭha.

Text 22

It is stated in *Śrīmad-Bhāgavatam* (10.16.36) that Śrī Kṛṣṇa's mercy is inconceivable (*acintya*) and causeless (*ahaitukī*):

kasyānubhāvo 'sya na deva vidmahe
tavāṅghri-reṇu-sparśādhikāraḥ
yad-vāñchayā śrīr lalanācarat tapo
vihāya kāmān su-ciraṁ dhṛta-vratā

[The Nāgapatnīs prayed to Śrī Kṛṣṇa:] O Lord, we cannot understand what *sādhana* our husband has performed to become qualified to receive the touch of the dust of Your lotus feet. This dust is so rare that to attain it, even Your wife Lakṣmī gave up all forms of enjoyment for many, many days and performed austerities according to rules and regulations.

ki puṇye kāliya pāya pada-reṇu tava
bujhite nā pāri kṛṣṇa kṛpāra sambhava

jāhā lāgi' lakṣmī-devī tapa ācarila
bahukāla dhṛta-vratā kāmādi chāḍila

Bhajana-rahasya-vṛtti

The astonished wives of Kāliya-nāga are saying, "O Gokuleśvara, we cannot understand what kind of *sukṛti* resulted in this lowly Kāliya attaining Your rare foot-dust. The supremely gentle and very beautiful Lakṣmī, who plays on the chest of Śrī Nārāyaṇa, gave up the association of her husband and observed a *vrata* in which she performed severe austerities to attain this dust, but she was unsuccessful. Prabhu, it is not possible even for Lakṣmī to have the same fortune as Kāliya and receive the direct touch of Your lotus feet."

This Text describes Kāliya's great fortune. Lakṣmī desired the association of Nanda-nandana Śrī Kṛṣṇa in her body as Lakṣmī. However, Nanda-nandana does not accept any demigoddess or beautiful lady; the only way to attain Him is to follow the *vraja-devīs* and accept the body and mood of a *gopī*. Since this was impossible for Lakṣmī, she could not attain Śrī Kṛṣṇa's association. Jīva Gosvāmipāda says that the one-pointedness of the *gopīs* was absent in Lakṣmī: *aprāpti-kāraṇaṁ ca gopīvat tad-ananyatābhāva aivati ca*.

There can be two reasons why Kāliya attained Śrī Kṛṣṇa's lotus feet. The first reason is that he had the association of his wives, who were very good devotees. The second reason is his residence in the Yamunā, which is within Vṛndāvana. Due to *saṁskāras*, impressions, from his previous lives, he attained both of these, but due to his offensive inclination, he was indifferent to them.

The *dhāma* and other transcendental objects do not manifest immediately before offensive persons. When Śrī Kṛṣṇa split Kāliya's hoods with a blow from His dancing feet, Kāliya's mouths began to vomit blood. He then believed the words of his wives, that Śrī Kṛṣṇa is Bhagavān, and surrendered to Him. Kṛṣṇa had merely been waiting to bestow His mercy upon Him.

Śrī Viśvanātha Cakravartīpāda explains in his commentary to this verse that Kāliya had the seed of *bhakti* in his heart due to the association of his wives, who were devotees, but this seed could not sprout in his hard heart, which was like barren land due to his offences and cruelty. By the touch of Śrī Kṛṣṇa's feet, that barren land became fertile enough for the seed of *bhakti* to germinate.

Text 23

Śrīmad-Bhāgavatam (10.47.60) states that the *vraja-gopīs'* devotion is topmost:

nāyaṁ śriyo 'ṅga u nitānta-rateḥ prasādaḥ
svar-yoṣitāṁ nalina-gandha-rucāṁ kuto 'nyāḥ
rāsotsave 'sya bhuja-daṇḍa-gṛhīta-kaṇṭha-
labdhāśiṣāṁ ya udagād vraja-sundarīṇām

In the *rāsa* festival, Śrī Kṛṣṇa embraced the *vraja-sundarīs* around their necks with His vine-like arms, thus fulfilling their hearts' desires. Even Lakṣmī, who eternally resides on His chest, does not attain this mercy. It is also not attained by the most beautiful girls of the heavenly planets, whose bodily lustre and fragrance resemble the lotus flower, what to speak of other beautiful women.

rāse vraja-gopī skandhe bhujārpaṇa kari'
ye prasāda kaila kṛṣṇa, kahite nā pāri

lakṣmī nā pāila sei kṛpā-anubhava
anya devī kise pābe se kṛpā-vaibhava?

Bhajana-rahasya-vṛtti

With this Text, Śrī Uddhava, desirous of *vraja-bhāva* and filled with patience, meekness and humility, offers his precious *puṣpāñjali* to the lotus feet of Śrī Kṛṣṇa's beloved *vraja-gopīs*, the crown jewels amongst His devotees. These words reveal the glory of the *vraja-sundarīs' prema*. To proclaim that the *vraja-gopīs* are worshipful to the entire world, Uddhava says, "Such unprecedented mercy of Bhagavān has never been seen or received by anyone else." Uddhava's astonishment is shown in this Text by his use of the exclamation *u*. In the festival of *rāsa*, Śrī Kṛṣṇa joyfully embraced the *vraja-gopīs*, putting His arms around their necks and fulfilling their hearts' desires. This good fortune was not even attained by Lakṣmī, who is eternally situated on His chest. Nor can such fortune be attained by the beautiful heavenly women, whose excellent bodily lustre and fragrance are like lotuses, so how can it be possible for other beautiful ladies?

In his commentary on this Text, Śrīla Jīva Gosvāmī raises an argument: "In *tattva*, Śrī Kṛṣṇa and Nārāyaṇa are non-different, and the most affectionate Lakṣmī-devī, who sports on the chest of Nārāyaṇa, is His *svarūpa-śakti*. She also resides on Śrī Kṛṣṇa's chest as a golden line, and she is never separated from Him. Why, then, are the *gopīs'* moods glorified over hers?"

He then resolves this argument: "Although Śrī Kṛṣṇa and Nārāyaṇa are non-different in *tattva*, Śrī Kṛṣṇa's unique pastimes, which are filled with astonishingly excellent *rasa*, are embellished with an exceedingly splendid brilliance. Lakṣmī is only engaged in meeting (*sambhoga-rasa*), but the *gopīs* sometimes engage in meeting (*milana*) and sometimes in separation (*viraha*). Lakṣmī is Nārāyaṇa's beloved who sports on His chest (*vakṣaḥ-vilāsinī*), but the *gopīs* are not merely Śrī Kṛṣṇa's beloveds; they delight in the *rasa* of amorous pastimes endowed with paramour love (*parakīya-bhāva*), thereby expanding His *prema-mādhurya* in an unprecedented way. Vrajendra-nandana Śyāmasundara's *aiśvarya* and *mādhurya* only manifest in their topmost form when He is with the *vraja-devīs*. Eagerly desiring this *mādhurya*, Lakṣmī also desires to meet with Kṛṣṇa. However, the *gopīs'* one-pointed, steady devotion is absent in Lakṣmī. In *nara-līlā*, Śrī Kṛṣṇa belongs to the caste of *gopas*, cowherds. Because He considers Himself a *gopa*, His beloveds are naturally daughters of *gopas*, and only they can be His beloveds. Śrī Lakṣmī did not want to assume the body of a *gopī*. She was unable to take birth in the home of a *gopī*, marry a *gopa* other than Kṛṣṇa for the sake of entering *parakīya-bhāva*, associate with the *nitya-siddha-gopīs* and give up her identification as a *brāhmaṇī*. This is why she was unable to meet with Kṛṣṇa."

In *Śrīmad-Bhāgavatam* (10.47.35) it says:

yathā dūra-care preṣṭhe
mana āviśya vartate
strīṇāṁ ca na tathā cetaḥ
sannikṛṣṭe 'kṣi-gocare

When her lover is far away, a woman thinks of him more than when he is present before her.

Śrī Viśvanātha Cakravartī Ṭhākura comments on this *śloka* as follows: "The lover's heart is more attracted to the beloved when she is far from him than when she is living near him. Due to this, although Lakṣmī perpetually sports upon Nārāyaṇa's chest, the glories of her good fortune are less than those of the *gopīs'*."

The *rāsa-līlā* is the crown jewel amongst all Śrī Kṛṣṇa's pastimes. Śrī Sanātana Gosvāmī says: "*rāsaḥ parama-rasa-kadambamaya-rati-yaugikārtha* – the *rāsa* dance is the supreme *rasa*; supreme *rasa* is that in which there is a relationship with the supreme object." The *rāsa-līlā* does not take place in this world, nor does it occur in the heavenly planets. In Dvārakā, where there are 16,108 queens, the *rāsa* dance is a possibility, but it does not take place there either. Nor does it take place in Bhagavān's other abodes, such as Vaikuṇṭha. The *rāsa-līlā* only manifests in Vṛndāvana and the *vraja-ramaṇīs* are its participants. The main fountainhead of this pastime, which is filled with all the consummate mellows, is Śrī Vṛṣabhānu-nandinī. In extreme joy, Śrī Śyāmasundara both floats upon and becomes submerged in the waves of the ocean of *prema* that are found in the supreme festival of *rāsa-līlā*. To protect Himself from the towering waves of the *gopīs'* charming behaviour and sidelong glances in this vast ocean of *prema*, He clutches the *gopīs'* necks and rests Himself upon their breasts.

Being especially insightful, Uddhava foresaw the marriage of Kṛṣṇa and Rukmiṇī. Rukmiṇī is famous in the world as Hari-priyā, the beloved of Hari; nevertheless, she did not attain even a scent of the *vraja-gopīs'* good fortune. How, then, could it be possible for the other queens of Dvārakā and the heavenly goddesses? The *vraja-devīs* are capable of completely controlling Śrī Kṛṣṇa. The pinnacle of *mahābhāva*, *mādanākhya-bhāva* endowed with *samartha-rati* (that *rati* which is capable of controlling Kṛṣṇa), is the *bhāva* of Śrī Rādhā only, and She is the main source of pleasure in *mādhurya-rasa*. All the other *gopīs* are like ingredients for *rasa*. The words *vraja-sundarīṇām* in this Text allude to Śrī Rādhā's love, elegance, erudition, virtuous nature, good qualities, skill in dancing and singing, and great wealth of beauty.

Text 24

All types of devotees long for *gopī-bhāva*. This is explained in *Śrīmad-Bhāgavatam* (10.47.61):

āsām aho caraṇa-reṇu-juṣām ahaṁ syāṁ
vṛndāvane kim api gulma-latauṣadhīnām
yā dustyajaṁ sva-janam ārya-pathaṁ ca hitvā
bhejur mukunda-padavīṁ śrutibhir vimṛgyām

Aho! The *vraja-devīs* have given up everything that is difficult to renounce, such as children, family and the path of chastity, and they have taken shelter of the path of *prema-bhakti* to Śrī Kṛṣṇa that is searched for but rarely attained by the Śrutis. My prayer is that in a future birth I may acquire a form among the bushes, creepers and herbs of Śrī Vṛndāvana that receive the dust of these *gopīs'* lotus feet.

dustyajya ārya-patha-svajana chāḍi' diyā
śruti-mṛgya kṛṣṇa-pada bhaje gopī giyā
āhā! vraje gulma-latā-vṛkṣa deha dhari'
gopī-pada-reṇu ki seviba bhakti kari'?

Bhajana-rahasya-vṛtti

In the previous Text, Śrī Uddhava described the excellence of the *gopīs' prema-mādhurya*. In his heart he understands his insignificance and wretchedness, and an eager longing awakens in him for *prema* like that of the *gopīs*. The only means to attain this *prema*, which is unattainable even for Lakṣmī and the queens of Dvārakā, is to be sprinkled with the foot-dust of the *mahābhāva-vatī gopīs*. The exclamation *aho* expresses the rarity of the attainment of this *prema*. The *nitya-siddha-gopīs* have natural attachment (*anurāga*) for Kṛṣṇa, and because of this deep *anurāga*, they successfully renounced the honour given by society for following social etiquette and so forth, which is very difficult to give up. The Śrutis and Upaniṣads such as *Gopāla-tāpanī* are searching for such *kṛṣṇa-anurāga*, eagerly desiring to attain it. Uddhava began to ponder, "It will not be possible for me to attain such good fortune as the *mahābhāva-vatī gopīs*, unless

I can somehow obtain the dust of their lotus feet." He thus considers himself very fallen and insignificant, and prays to take birth in Vṛndāvana as a bush, creeper or herb.

Śrī Viśvanātha Cakravartīpāda comments on this in his *Sārārtha-darśanī ṭīkā* as follows: "It is because of their *anurāga* that the *vraja-devīs* gave up their reputation, patience and so forth, and departed in the middle of the night for a rendezvous (*abhisāra*) with Śrī Śyāmasundara. Due to the strength of their *prema*, they were helpless and could not consider whether their decision to leave their family was right or wrong. As soon as they heard the sound of Śrī Śyāmasundara's flute, they were pierced by the arrow of lust (*kāma*), and, as if mad (*unmādinī*), they moved like deer, leaving the forest path without caring for shrubs, thorns and sharp grass. At that time, the dust of their feet fell on the grass, bushes and other vegetation. I can only receive this dust by one day becoming such grass, a plant like a creeper, or a bush. Even if I were to beg humbly for a particle of that dust, they would never bestow it upon me."

Uddhava also had a doubt in this regard. "My birth and mood are not compatible with *vraja-bhāva*, so why would the *gopīs* be merciful to me?"

In this verse, the word *caraṇa-reṇu* (foot-dust) is singular, thus indicating the foot-dust of Śrīmatī Rādhikā, the crown jewel of the *gopīs*.

Mukunda-padavī means "attaining the service of Kṛṣṇa". The *gopīs* always attain this service. Śrī Jīva Gosvāmī says, "The name Mukunda comes from *muktiṁ dadāti*, which means 'He who gives liberation from one's hair plait or waist cloth'." Śrīla Sanātana Gosvāmī's purport of *mukunda-padavī* is *tad-anurakti-bhajana*, or *bhajana* imbued with the *gopīs'* affection for Kṛṣṇa. The *gopīs*, before and after Kṛṣṇa's cowherding (in *pūrvāhna-līlā* and *aparāhna-līlā*), eagerly watch for Kṛṣṇa's departure to and arrival from the pastures. Absorbed in waiting for Him, they steal His heart and mind by their bodily gestures and demeanour. Only the *gopīs* can render this special service. Actually, the path followed by the *gopīs* in serving Kṛṣṇa is the real *ārya-patha*, the path of honesty and chastity indicated in the scriptures. The Vedas enjoin that one should completely give up all kinds of mundane and transcendental rules for *aikāntika-nirupādhika-prema*, love for Śrī Kṛṣṇa that is one-pointed and free from material designations. To attain Kṛṣṇa, there is no fault in transgressing the apparent *ārya-patha*.

According to another meaning of *mukunda-padavī*, the top-most devotees on the path of devotion are none other than the *gopīs*.

Sanātana Gosvāmipāda has raised a question in *Bṛhad-bhāgavatāmṛta*: "To attain Śrī Kṛṣṇa, Rukmiṇī-devī even abandoned her own marriage ceremony, which was arranged by her father. By personally writing a letter to Śrī Kṛṣṇa, offering herself completely to Him and sending it with the son of her priest, she also abandoned the honour of being a chaste girl from a noble family. So, what is the feature that distinguishes the *vraja-devīs*, who renounced everything in order to attain Kṛṣṇa, from Rukmiṇī, who gave up her noble family for Him?"

Sanātana Gosvāmī then explains, "The *gopīs'* attachment (*rati*) to Kṛṣṇa has no cause, whereas Rukmiṇī's *prema* for Him developed after hearing about His name, form, qualities and so on. From birth the *gopīs* have natural love for Kṛṣṇa, and with an extreme eagerness to meet Him, they abandon their family members and *ārya-patha*."

In *Prīti-sandarbha* Śrī Jīva Gosvāmī says, "This eagerness reveals their *prema* as being far superior. The *gopīs'* extraordinary eagerness causes the development of an amazing power by which *ārya-patha* is naturally abandoned."

The word *mukunda* in this verse also refers to one whose enchanting lotus face is like a *kunda* flower; it also refers to the *dhīra-lalita-nāyaka* Śrī Kṛṣṇacandra, who fully manifests His sweetness in the assembly of the *gopīs*.

Text 25

In *Śrīmad-Bhāgavatam* (10.47.58) Uddhava mentions that Brahmā is also distracted upon seeing the mood of the *gopīs*:

etāḥ paraṁ tanu-bhṛto bhuvi gopa-vadhvo
govinda eva nikhilātmani rūḍha-bhāvāḥ
vāñchanti yad bhava-bhiyo munayo vayaṁ ca
kiṁ brahma-janmabhir ananta-kathā-rasasya

The *gopīs* have one-pointed *rūḍha-bhāva* towards Śrī Kṛṣṇa, who is the soul of all living entities. This is the topmost level of *kṛṣṇa-prema*, and by this, their lives are successful. This *bhāva* is hankered for, not only by fearful persons desiring liberation from this material existence, but also by great *mahāpuruṣas*, as well as devotees like ourselves; but none of us are able to attain it. For one whose mind is attached to *kṛṣṇa-kathā*, the three kinds of birth – seminal, brahminical and sacrificial – are not necessary; but for one who has no taste for hearing *kṛṣṇa-kathā*, what is the benefit of taking birth, even as Brahmā, again and again for many *mahā-kalpas*?

bhava-bhīta muni-gaṇa āra deva-gaṇa
yāṅhāra caraṇa-vāñchā kare anukṣaṇa

se govinde ruḍha-bhāvāpanna gopī dhanya
kṛṣṇa rasa-āge brahma-janma nahe gaṇya

Bhajana-rahasya-vṛtti

With this verse and others, Śrī Uddhava is praising the crown jewels of all devotees, the *gopīs*, who are worshipped by all.

Uddhava is Kṛṣṇa's dearmost friend. Seeing the extraordinary *prema* of the *gopīs*, he became astonished and reflected as follows: "Lord Brahmā is Kṛṣṇa's son, but is proud of being His son. Śaṅkara's nature is one with Kṛṣṇa's, but he thinks more about his oneness with Kṛṣṇa than he thinks of *bhakti.* Saṅkarṣaṇa has the mood of a brother, and Lakṣmī the mood of a wife, and these *bhāvas* are more prominent in them than the mood of *prema.* But the *gopīs* love Kṛṣṇa as their *prāṇa-priyatama*, and their love is *nirupādhika*, free from any other designation, and has reached the upper limit of *prema*. They have *rūḍha-bhāva* towards Gokulendra-nandana Govinda."

Rūḍha-bhāva is *prema* that is endowed with *mādhurya-bhāva* and free from any sense of awe and reverence. It is affection for Kṛṣṇa without any designation, and it is paramour *bhāva* without any expectation. *Rūḍha-bhāva* appears in the higher levels of *mahābhāva. Rūḍha-bhāva* is mentioned in this verse, but the *gopīs* actually attain *adhirūḍha-bhāva*, which is the final limit of their *mahābhāva.* To only mention *rūḍha-bhāva* limits the extent of the *gopīs' bhāvas.* The *vraja-devīs*, who are endowed with *adhirūḍha-bhāva*, in other words with *mādana*, *mohana* and all other *bhāvas*, are the very soul of Govinda. This is the meaning of the words *nikhilātmani rūḍha-bhāvāḥ.*

Uddhava starts to contemplate the following: "Govinda is the condensed form of Svayam Bhagavān Parameśvara." All *śāstras* state that the original, non-dual truth, Govinda, is the original Person (*ādi-puruṣa*). Govinda gives pleasure to the Vrajavāsīs with the sweetness of His form: "*go vindayati iti govinda* – Govinda is He who gives pleasure to the *gopas*, *gopīs* and cows." *Go* means one who pervades the senses, and the *gopīs* pervade the senses of Govinda. It is a severe offence to ascribe the moods of ordinary females to the *vraja-devīs*, who are not ordinary, but the very embodiments of concentrated *prema.*

Vāñchanti yad bhava-bhiyo munayo vayaṁ ca – Those desiring liberation, *munis* and others who have attained liberation and who are fully self-satisfied (*ātmārāma*), and even Uddhava, who lives with Govinda, as well as the Pāṇḍavas, Yādavas, Caturmukha Brahmā and others, are attracted by the *gopīs' mahābhāva* and eagerly desire it. If one has no taste for hearing narrations about Ananta-kṛṣṇa, then even birth as Brahmā is useless. There is even no gain if as Brahmā one performs the act of creation, or as a *brāhmaṇa* studies the Vedas, Upaniṣads and other scriptures, and takes vows, performs austerities and so on. Śrīla Jīva Gosvāmī says, "The life and death of a person who has no taste for hearing narrations of Śrī Kṛṣṇa's *prema-mādhurya* are insignificant and meaningless." If a person's mood is not similar to that of the *gopīs*, then Kṛṣṇa does not accept him. He therefore sent the *mathurā-brāhmaṇīs* back to their homes, as described in Chapter 23 of the Tenth Canto of *Śrīmad-Bhāgavatam*.

Bhuvi – Refers to this Earth, the heavenly planets and the spiritual world. The only success in these three worlds is to take the form of a *gopī*.

Tanu-bhṛto bhuvi – Kṛṣṇa delivers all *jīvas* from material existence, even those who are low and insignificant. He nourishes them accordingly with the *prema* of the *gopīs*, who are situated in His heart. He propagates *prema*, He relishes this extraordinary *prema* and makes others relish it, and He increases *prema* in those to whom he gives it. The name of this potency is "*gopī*".

Uddhava is profusely praising the greatness of the *vraja-devīs* in this verse. He also establishes the superiority of a married *gopī's* paramour mood in comparison to the mood of a husband and wife. This paramour mood is not possible anywhere else except Vraja. In paramour love (*parakīya-bhāva*), *rasa* is produced by unprecedented astonishment.

Text 26

Even devotees inclined towards Śrī Bhagavān's opulence (*aiśvarya*) long to attain *gopī-bhāva*. This is stated in *Śrīmad-Bhāgavatam* (10.44.14):

gopyas tapaḥ kim acaran yad amuṣya rūpaṁ
lāvaṇya-sāram asamordhvam ananya-siddham
dṛgbhiḥ pibanty anusavābhinavaṁ durāpam
ekānta-dhāma yaśasaḥ śriya aiśvarasya

Sakhī, I do not know what austerities the *gopīs* have performed to be always drinking the sweetness of Kṛṣṇa's form with their eyes. What is the nature of His form? It is the essence of bodily beauty (*lāvaṇya-sāra*)! Within this material existence or above it, there is no beauty equal to His, what to speak of a greater beauty. He is not decorated by anyone, nor is He perfected by ornaments and clothes. Rather, He is perfect in Himself. While seeing this form, one does not become satiated, because its beauty increases at every moment. All fame, beauty and opulence take shelter of it. Only the *gopīs* are fortunate enough to have such a *darśana* of Kṛṣṇa; no one else.

yaśaḥ śrī aiśvarya-dhāma durlabha ekānta
atīva-lāvaṇya-sāra svataḥ-siddha kānta

ki tapa karila gopī yāhe anukṣaṇa
nayanete śyāma-rasa kare āsvādana

Bhajana-rahasya-vṛtti

This Text was spoken by the young, beautiful women of Mathurā in Kaṁsa's wrestling arena when they had received *darśana* of Śrī Kṛṣṇa's unprecedented lustrous body. Amazed by that form, they yearned to taste it. They said, "O *sakhī*, what kind of austerities have the *gopīs* performed to be able to fill their eyes with the extraordinary beauty of Śrī Kṛṣṇa's form? They have made their birth, body and mind successful. What is this beauty like? There is no *rūpa-mādhurya* equal to or greater than this. In Paravyoma, there are so many forms of Bhagavān, but even Nārāyaṇa, Śrī Kṛṣṇa's pastime expansion (*vilāsa-mūrti-svarūpa*), does not have such *rūpa-mādhurya*, what to speak of other forms."

Śrī Kṛṣṇa's beauty is topmost. It is incomparable, perfect and natural, and it is not brought about by any kind of ornamentation. In fact, it is both the origin and treasury of all beautiful, sweet qualities. Śrī Kṛṣṇa's form, which is filled with unequalled beauty, is only present in Vṛndāvana, and Vrajabhūmi is blessed because the original Person (*purāṇa-puruṣa*) performs pastimes there in disguise. In this Vrajabhūmi, the *vraja-devīs* are especially blessed because they received *darśana* of *dhīra-lalita-nāyaka* Śrī Kṛṣṇa, who is adorned with all beauty and sweetness.

By the word *amuṣya*, the women of Mathurā note, "Today in this wrestling arena, by our insignificant piety, we are receiving Śrī Kṛṣṇa's *darśana*, but the *gopīs'* piety is complete. O omniscient *munis*, please direct us how to perform austerities like those performed by the *gopīs*, so that we also will be able to gaze at Śrī Kṛṣṇa's sweet form in Vraja."

Another woman of Mathurā said with amazement, "O *sakhī*, the good fortune of the *vraja-devīs* is not the result of any austerity; their *prema* is without cause and cannot be expressed in words." If she had said, "We can also go to Vraja and drink the nectar of Kṛṣṇa's beauty like the *gopīs*," another lady would have replied, "That is very difficult for us (*durāpam*). Only by the mercy of the *gopīs*, who possess the topmost *prema*, is it possible to drink this nectar."

Another lady started speaking. "Oh! Before the *vraja-gopīs*, Śrī Kṛṣṇa's beauty manifests in newer and newer forms, uninterruptedly, moment by moment."

The women of Mathurā glorified the good fortune of the *vraja-devīs* and eagerly desired to have a *sevā* like theirs. They used to hear from the fruit-sellers and others coming from Vraja about the sweet pastimes of Śrī Kṛṣṇa and the *vraja-devīs*. By hearing descriptions of these pastimes, a yearning for a *sevā* like that of the *gopīs* arose in their hearts.

Text 27

An introduction to the evening pastimes (*sāyaṁ-kālīya-līlā*) is found in *Govinda-līlāmṛta* (20.1):

sāyaṁ rādhāṁ sva-sakhyā nija-ramaṇa-kṛte preṣitāneka-bhojyāṁ
sakhyānīteśa-śeṣāśana-mudita-hṛdaṁ tāṁ ca taṁ ca vrajendum
susnātaṁ ramya-veśaṁ gṛham anu-jananī-lālitaṁ prāpta-goṣṭhaṁ
nirvyūḍho 'srālidohaṁ sva-gṛham anu punar bhuktavantaṁ smarāmi

I remember Śrī Rādhā who, in the evening, sends many kinds of cooked foodstuffs with Her *sakhīs* to Her lover, Śrī Kṛṣṇa, and who becomes joyful by taking Kṛṣṇa's remnants that are brought back to Her by Her *sakhīs*. I remember Śrī Kṛṣṇa, who takes bath upon returning from cowherding, who is dressed in beautiful attire, and who is fondly attended in many ways by Mother Yaśodā. He goes to the cowshed, and after milking the cows returns home for His evening meal.

śrī-rādhikā sāyaṁ-kāle, kṛṣṇa lāgi' pāṭhāile,
sakhī haste vividha miṣṭhānna
kṛṣṇa-bhukta śeṣa āni', sakhī dila sukha māni',
pāñā rādhā haila prasanna

snāta ramyaveśa dhari', yaśodā lālita hari,
sakhā-saha godohana kare
nānāvidha pakva anna, pāñā haila parasanna,
smari āmi parama ādare

Bhajana-rahasya-vṛtti

When Śrī Rādhā sees that evening has come, in Her heart She becomes very eager and thinks, "Now Kṛṣṇa must have returned from cowherding!" In the kitchen, She wears a white dress, and together with Her *sakhīs* prepares many kinds of sweets, such as *amṛta-keli, karpūra-keli, candrakānti* and *modaka*. All the preparations are put into new clay pots and covered with white cloth. She puts the pots into the hands of Her *nitya-sakhīs* and *prāṇa-sakhīs* to take to Her *priyatama* in Nanda-bhavana. The *sakhīs* depart, and Śrī Rādhā's mind goes with them. She thinks, "When My *sakhīs* reach the house of Nanda, Maiyā will embrace them to her heart, and she will remember Me and give Me her blessings. My *prāṇanātha*, surrounded by Bābā and the *sakhās*, will eat these preparations. I do not know which ones He will like and which ones He won't." In this way, with eyes of *bhāva*, Śrī Rādhā has internal *darśana* of the evening meal. The *sakhīs* offer all the preparations to Yaśodā, the queen of Vraja, who affectionately serves them to Kṛṣṇa, Balarāma and the *sakhās*. Cleverly, Dhaniṣṭhā places Śrī Kṛṣṇa's remnants in the hands of a *sakhī* and sends them to Śrī Rādhā, along with information about the location of Their *abhisāra* later that night. At that time, Śrī Rādhā anxiously awaits the *sakhīs'* return from Nanda-bhavana. When they arrive, they describe all the conversations at Nanda-bhavana and how Kṛṣṇa relished each preparation. Śrī Rādhā relishes Śrī Kṛṣṇa's remnants in the same way. The *sakhīs* are also extremely happy to take the remnants of Śrī Kṛṣṇa and Śrī Rādhā.

Thus ends the *Ṣaṣṭha-yāma-sādhana*,
Sāyaṁ-kālīya-bhajana, of *Śrī Bhajana-rahasya*.

7

Saptama-yāma-sādhana

Pradoṣa-kālīya-bhajana – vipralambha-prema

(from six *daṇḍas* of the night until midnight:
approximately 8.30 P.M. – 12.00 P.M.)

Text 1

The internal symptom of devotion at the stage of perfection (*sādhya-bhakti*) is worship of Śrī Kṛṣṇa in a mood of separation. *Śikṣāṣṭaka* (7) states:

yugāyitaṁ nimeṣeṇa
cakṣuṣā prāvṛṣāyitam
śūnyāyitaṁ jagat sarvaṁ
govinda-viraheṇa me

O *sakhī*, in separation from Govinda, even a moment seems like a millennium to Me. Tears pour from My eyes like torrents of rain in the monsoon season and this entire world seems void to Me.

udvege divasa nā yāya, 'kṣana' haila 'yuga-sama'
varṣāra meghaprāya aśru varṣe du' nayana

govinda-virahe śūnya haila tribhuvana
tuṣānale poḍe – yena nā yāya jīvana

Bhajana-rahasya-vṛtti

Śrīman Mahāprabhu is absorbed in Śrī Rādhā's feelings of intense separation from Śrī Kṛṣṇa. He says, "*Sakhī*, in My distress without Śrī Nanda-nandana My days stand still. Each and every moment seems like an entire millennium. Tears flow incessantly from My eyes, like torrents of rain from the clouds. I cannot tolerate separation from Govinda anymore. The entire universe appears void and My body constantly burns in the fire of separation from Him. It is as if My limbs have been placed in a fire of burning husks.[1] But still, My life air does not leave Me. What shall I do now?"

Both *pūrva-rāga* (attachment prior to meeting one's beloved) and *pravāsa* (separation by distance) are favourable to *bhajana* in the mood of separation. *Rati* (attachment) that is filled with eagerness and which exists prior to meeting is called *pūrva-rāga*. When the *gopīs*, who are deeply attached to Śrī Kṛṣṇa, hear the glories of His form, qualities and so forth, many types of sentiments are stimulated in their hearts and an astonishing impatience (*vyagratā*) arises that is impossible to describe. Those learned in the *rasa-śāstras* call this impatience *pūrva-rāga*. In this state of *pūrva-rāga*, various *sañcāri-bhāvas* arise, such as longing (*lālasā*), anxiety (*udvega*) and sleeplessness (*jāgaraṇa*). Texts 2–6, taken from *Śrīmad-Bhāgavatam*, describe the *pūrva-rāga* of the *gopīs*.

Text 2

The *gopīs* praise the flute, which drinks the nectar of Śrī Kṛṣṇa's lips. *Śrīmad-Bhāgavatam* (10.21.9) states:

[1] Burning husks are difficult to extinguish, burn very slowly and emit much heat. This analogy is used to describe Rādhikā's extreme suffering.

gopyaḥ kim ācarad ayaṁ kuśalaṁ sma veṇur
dāmodarādhara-sudhām api gopikānām
bhuṅkte svayaṁ yad avaśiṣṭa-rasaṁ hradinyo
hṛṣyat-tvaco 'śru mumucus taravo yathāryāḥ

What pious activities has this flute performed to relish the nectar of Kṛṣṇa's lips, which is meant for us *gopīs*? He is drinking all the *rasa* and not even leaving us one drop. *Sakhī*, upon seeing the good fortune of the *veṇu*, the Yamunā, Mānasī-gaṅgā, and other rivers and ponds manifest the ecstatic symptom of horripilation in the form of blossoming lotuses and other flowers. The trees shed tears of love, delighted to have such a descendant in their dynasty, just as noble persons are delighted that a Vaiṣṇava has taken birth in their family.

ohe sakhi! kivā tapa kaila kṛṣṇa-veṇu
gopī prāpya mukhāmṛta piye punaḥ punaḥ

avaśeṣa-jala deya taru aśru-chale
sādhu-putra-prāptye yena pitṛ-aśru gale

Bhajana-rahasya-vṛtti

One *gopī* says to another, "O *sakhī*, I do not know what kind of highly pious activities this *veṇu*, a dry piece of wood, has performed to profusely and independently relish the nectar of Śrī Kṛṣṇa's lips, which is meant to be enjoyed only by us *gopīs*. He does not leave even a drop of this nectar for us. Seeing the good fortune of this *veṇu*, Mānasī-gaṅgā and other ponds secretly display their ecstasy through their blossoming lotus flowers. When family elders see that one of their descendents is filled with love for Bhagavān, they shed tears of joy. Similarly, since the trees have a relationship with the *veṇu*, they emit streams of honey, as if shedding tears of bliss."

Now the *vraja-ramaṇīs*, already eager to meet with Kṛṣṇa, become even more restless. A vision of the sweetness of Kṛṣṇa's beauty appears in their hearts, and in this vision, they see the *veṇu* on His lips. The *gopīs* reflect on the flute's rare good fortune. "O *sakhī*, this *veṇu* always relishes the nectar of Kṛṣṇa's association, so there is no doubt about his extreme fortune. But he has now become so proud and arrogant that we find it intolerable. The nectar of Dāmodara's lips is meant for the pleasure of the *gopikās*, but the *veṇu* considers it his. Dāmodara was born in the *gopa* dynasty and so were we. From childhood we shared deep love for each other. He is our *priyatama*, so we alone have full rights to the nectar of His lips. But this impudent and shameless *veṇu* is depriving us of our birthright, and he drinks the nectar of Dāmodara's lips just as he pleases. We have taken birth in the dynasty of *gopas*, but we are deprived of the nectar of Gopendranandana Śrī Kṛṣṇa's lips. Yet the *veṇu*, who has taken birth in the dynasty of inert trees, constantly drinks that nectar. By doing so, he challenges us in a manly way.

"The day Yasodā-maiyā bound Kṛṣṇa with rope, He became famous as Dāmodara, and that very same day we *gopikās* began our loving relationships with Him. No one in Vraja knew anything about the *veṇu* then. It was when Kṛṣṇa started taking the cows out to graze that the *veṇu's* relationship with Him began. By this meagre relationship, the *veṇu* became the complete heir to the nectar of Kṛṣṇa's lips. Even though we *gopikās* have loved Kṛṣṇa since childhood, we remain deprived of this right. Therefore, I say, O *sakhī*, birth as a *veṇu* is higher and more blessed than birth as a *gopī*.

"Seeing the great fortune of the *veṇu*, the trees, unable to contain themselves, become covered with fruits and flowers and ooze honey. It is as if they become ecstatic and their hair stands on end upon seeing the supreme good fortune of their own child, and they shed tears of love due to pride. And why not? The *veṇu* is made of bamboo, and bamboo is considered to be in the family of trees. Bamboo is nourished by the water of rivers and ponds, so for the bamboo, this water is actually milk, and the rivers and ponds are the bamboo's mothers. Seeing the rare good fortune of their son, these mothers, such as the Yamunā, Mānasī-gaṅgā, Pāvana-sarovara, Māna-sarovara and Kusuma-sarovara, sometimes laugh by displaying blossoming flowers. Sometimes, in their great rapture, they express their joy through their undulating waves, and at other times they shed tears of happiness."

In this way the *gopīs*, endowed with *mahābhāva*, deliberate upon the *veṇu's* great fortune and on their own misfortune, and they display envy (*asūyā*) and other *sañcāri-bhāvas*. They say, "In his previous life, this *veṇu* must have performed some severe austerity or pious activity. If we knew what it was, we would do the same and also attain such rare good fortune. Paurṇamāsī is a perfected ascetic who knows past, present and future. Let us go and ask her! By acting according to her instruction, we will attain that rare good fortune."

According to Śrīla Sanātana Gosvāmī, this verse is spoken by Vṛṣabhānu-nandinī Herself, as She reveals Her *bhāvas* to Her dear Lalitā Sakhī. Upon analysing the various statements and indications in this *śloka*, it is apparent that this *prema* is on the level of *adhirūḍha-mahābhāva*.

Text 3

Śrīmad-Bhāgavatam (10.21.11) describes the good fortune of the does and their husbands when they hear the sound of the flute:

dhanyāḥ sma mūḍha-gatayo 'pi hariṇya etā
yā nanda-nandanam upātta-vicitra-veśam
ākarṇya veṇu-raṇitaṁ saha-kṛṣṇa-sārāḥ
pūjāṁ dadhur viracitāṁ praṇayāvalokaiḥ

O *sakhī*, when Nanda-nandana Śyāmasundara, wearing beautiful, multi-coloured attire, vibrates a sweet melody on His flute, even the does, who are foolish due to having taken birth from the wombs of ignorant animals, run towards Him along with their husbands and gaze upon Him with love-laden eyes. They are not merely gazing, *sakhī*, but they are worshipping Him with crooked sidelong glances from their large lotus-like eyes, and He is accepting their worship with His own loving sidelong glance. The lives of these deer are truly blessed. *Sakhī*, although we are *gopīs* of Vṛndāvana, we are unable to offer ourselves like this because our family members harass us. How ironic!

kṛṣṇa-citra-veśa svīya cakṣete heriyā
tāṅhāra vāṁśarī-dhvani karṇete śuniyā
pūjāra vidhāna kaila praṇaya-nayane
kṛṣṇa-sāra-saha āja dhanya mṛgī-gaṇe

Bhajana-rahasya-vṛtti

The *vraja-ramaṇīs* are always restless to meet with Kṛṣṇa. This restlessness is due to their inability to be satisfied, which is a natural characteristic of their *prema*. They are also unable to steady their minds in any way. They consider anyone who has even the slightest relationship with Kṛṣṇa to be extremely fortunate. While sitting in their homes, the *gopīs* hear the flute-song of Govinda, who steals the hearts of all beings in Vṛndāvana, and they become completely submerged in *prema-rasa*. With eyes of *bhāva*, they see the does in the forest not only abandon grazing when they hear the sound of the *veṇu*, but abandon caring for their offspring and everything else as well. These does dash towards Kṛṣṇa with great speed, stopping so close to Him that He can touch them with His hands.

The *gopīs* express their moods in a concealed way (*avahittha-bhāva*). One says, "O *sakhī*, just see the affection that these does, from the animal kingdom, have for Kṛṣṇa. Indeed they are blessed! We, on the other hand, who have taken birth as human beings, are deprived of taking such *darśana* and performing such *sevā*, which are a human being's right. This is the frustration of our lives."

In autumn Vrajendra-nandana Śrī Kṛṣṇa, beautifully decorated in marvellous attire suitable for roaming in the forest, enters Vṛndāvana to herd the cows and blissfully plays enchanting notes on His flute. At that time, the does become content by seeing the sweet form of Śyāmasundara, who steals the hearts of everyone in the universe, and by hearing the sound of His flute. One *sakhī* begins to speak, saying, "When the does hear the sound of *prāṇanātha* Śyāmasundara's flute, they become senseless and proceed towards Him, staggering and stumbling. At that time, their husbands, the *kṛṣṇa-sāra* deer, follow behind them, accepting the guidance of their wives. In this way, no obstacle prevents the does from meeting with Kṛṣṇa." *Kṛṣṇa-sāra* means that Kṛṣṇa alone is the essence of their lives.

Hearing this, another *sakhī* says, "O friend, this is really true! Where is our such fortune? We are females and the wives of other men, so we cannot abandon the fear of public opinion. When Śyāmasundara goes cowherding on the path that runs by our homes, we can only get *darśana* of Him through the holes in the latticed windows. For this only, our family members abuse us and create obstacles for us. Our husbands are also disapproving. Birth as a deer is more fruitful than birth as a human."

The *vraja-devīs'* longing to meet with Kṛṣṇa increases more and more. Eagerness (*utkaṇṭhā*) and longing (*lālasā*) to meet Kṛṣṇa are very helpful for a *sādhaka*.

Praṇayāvalokaiḥ pūjāṁ dadhau means that the does lovingly look upon Kṛṣṇa with their very beautiful eyes, which serve as lamps to perform *ārati* to Him. Kṛṣṇa reciprocates by accepting their worship.

In *Ujjvala-nīlamaṇi* Śrīla Rūpa Gosvāmī defines *praṇaya* as the state in which the hearts of both the hero (*nāyaka*) and heroine (*nāyikā*) become one. The hearts of the does are one with Kṛṣṇa's heart, and therefore the *gopīs* have used the word *praṇayāvalokaiḥ*. With these glances, the does offer their *bhāvas* as flowers and other articles to worship Kṛṣṇa. In this Text, the sweetness of the *vraja-devīs'* paramour love is expressed through metaphors.

Text 4

Hearing the sound of the *veṇu*, all the rivers stop flowing and worship Kṛṣṇa's feet with lotus flowers. *Śrīmad-Bhāgavatam* (10.21.15) states:

nadyas tadā tad upadhārya mukunda-gītam
āvarta-lakṣita-manobhava-bhagna-vegāḥ
āliṅgana-sthagitam ūrmi-bhujair murārer
gṛhnanti pāda-yugalaṁ kamalopahārāḥ

Hearing the song of Śrī Kṛṣṇa's *veṇu*, the Yamunā, Mānasī-gaṅgā and other rivers have become deluded by lust (*kāma*). Their hearts' desires for love cause many whirlpools to surface and they stop flowing. Bringing lotuses as gifts with their arm-like waves, they embrace Madana-mohana and place His lotus feet on their breasts.

āhā! nadī kṛṣṇa-gīta śravaṇa kariyā
śroto-vega phirāila mohita haiyā

urmi-chale kṛṣṇa-pada āliṅgana kaila
o pada-yugale padma upahāra dila

Bhajana-rahasya-vṛtti

Hearing the sweet sound of Kṛṣṇa's *veṇu*, the *vraja-devīs*, who are attached to Kṛṣṇa with profound love (*kṛṣṇa-anurāgiṇī*), have become overwhelmed with *prema*. They started speaking with *sakhīs* from their own groups about the effects of the sound of the flute (*veṇu-nāda*) and other such topics. With metaphors, they describe how lifeless rivers exhibit transformations of love upon hearing the sweet sound of Kṛṣṇa's *veṇu*. Although it is not possible for rivers to experience any feeling, the *vraja-ramaṇīs*, who are endowed with *mahābhāva* and controlled by its astonishing nature, do not consider whether a being is sentient or insentient, and they ascribe their own respective *bhāvas* everywhere they look. Whatever mood and relationship an *uttama-adhikārī* devotee has with his worshipful deity (*iṣṭadeva*), Śrī Bhagavān, that same mood and relationship is seen by him to exist in all living entities. This is described in *Śrī Caitanya-caritāmṛta* (*Madhya-līlā* 8.273–4):

mahā-bhāgavata dekhe sthāvara-jaṅgama
tāhāṅ tāhāṅ haya tāṅra śrī-kṛṣṇa-sphuraṇa

sthāvara-jaṅgama dekhe, nā dekhe tāra mūrti
sarvatra haya nija iṣṭa-deva-sphūrti

While roaming in the charming Vṛndāvana forest, Nanda-nandana Śrī Kṛṣṇa arrives at the banks of the Yamunā or Mānasī-gaṅgā, where he hears the sweet murmur of water, sees the beautiful lotus flowers floating on high waves, hears the sounds of cuckoo birds on the river banks, and is pleasantly touched by a gentle, fragrant breeze. Overwhelmed with immense elation, He plays a sweet melody on His *muralī*. Upon hearing it, the river stops flowing, and on the still waters of her breast, unlimited whirlpools appear. Gradually the water of the river rises to the height of Śrī Kṛṣṇa's chest. The repeated crashing of waves causes the lotus flowers to break from their stems and present themselves at Kṛṣṇa's lotus feet.[2]

Upon seeing these whirlpools in the rivers, the *gopīs* are unable to conceal their own *bhāvas*. One says, "O *sakhī*, hearing our *prāṇakānta's* flute-song, this river is affected by lust (*kāma*) and has become senseless. His face is all-pleasing. It is radiant, fragrant, soft, sweet and attractive to the heart, like a *kunda* flower. This is why He is called Mukunda. With His soft, delicate lotus face, He relishes kissing, the biting of lips and other transcendental mellows of union. When these mellows are relished, all kinds of obligations are cut and, due to an increase in *kāma*, He observes with an agitated heart the *gopīs'* lotus-navels, which look like whirpools."

Another *vraja-devī* says, "When the rivers see Mukunda's sweet beauty and hear the ascending and descending waves of sound from His *veṇu*, both of which enchant the whole universe, their hearts become afflicted with *kāma*. Now they have reversed their flow with great force, and instead of moving towards their husband, the ocean, they flow towards Kṛṣṇa. Their arm-like waves rise up higher and embrace Murāri's chest."

There is a reason why the *gopīs* call Kṛṣṇa "Murāri". They say, "We have taken shelter of Śrī Nanda-nandana, who has all the qualities of Nārāyaṇa, the destroyer of the Mura demon. It is very sad, however, that we are always tormented by *kāma*, or Cupid. Although the killer of Mura is aware of this, He makes no arrangement to punish *māra*, or *kāma* (lust). Śrī Nārāyaṇa has become famous as Murāri by killing the demon Mura, thus making the demigods fearless. In the same way, if Kṛṣṇa destroys *māra*, He will become famous as Murāri and will be recognised

[2] Śrīla Cakravartipāda explains that the river, after trying to embrace Kṛṣṇa, became ashamed and withdrawn, and instead presented lotus flowers at Kṛṣṇa's feet.

as having the same qualities as Nārāyaṇa, otherwise not. With *māra* destroyed, we *vraja-ramaṇīs* will also breathe a sigh of relief."

Āliṅgana-sthagita – The waves of the rivers move closer and closer to Kṛṣṇa's chest and upon reaching it, they fall to ripple at His lotus feet. Seeing this, the *gopīs,* whose hearts are filled with loving attachment for Kṛṣṇa, say, "O *sakhī*! Look, look! At first these *anurāgī* rivers were trying to bind Śyāmasundara in the bond of their embrace, but seeing His indifference, they have become ashamed. They have stopped trying to embrace Him and are again offering lotus flowers at His feet with their arm-like waves."

Upon observing the behaviour of the Yamunā and other rivers, the *vraja-ramaṇīs* express various *bhāvas.* Seeing how the moods of Śrī Yamunā and Mānasī-gaṅgā are one with those of the *gopa-ramaṇīs* is an unprecedented *darśana.*

Text 5

Giri-Govardhana becomes blissful by the touch of Śrī Kṛṣṇa's and Śrī Balarāma's lotus feet, and he worships them with various articles. *Śrīmad-Bhāgavatam* (10.21.18) states:

hantāyam adrir abalā hari-dāsa-varyo
yad rāma-kṛṣṇa-caraṇa-sparśa-pramodaḥ
mānaṁ tanoti saha-go-gaṇayos tayor yat
pānīya-sūyavasa-kandara-kandamūlaiḥ

O *sakhīs,* this mountain, Govardhana, is the crown jewel of Hari's servants. Blessed is his fortune! By the touch of the lotus feet of our *prāṇa-vallabha* Śrī Kṛṣṇa and Baladeva Prabhu, who is most pleasing to the eyes, Govardhana is blossoming with delight and supplying crystal-clear water, soft grass, wonderful caves and varieties of roots. By thus serving Śrī Kṛṣṇa and

Balarāma, who are surrounded by the cowherd boys and cows, he highly honours them.

haridāsa-varya ei giri-govardhana
rāma-kṛṣṇa pada-sparśe sukhe acetana
sakhā-dhenu-saha kṛṣṇe ātithya karila
pānīya-kandara-kandamūla nivedila

Bhajana-rahasya-vṛtti

The *vraja-devīs*, who are the embodiments of *mahābhāva*, say, "If anyone can be said to be the topmost devotee, it must be Girirāja. In a variety of ways he serves our *prāṇa-vallabha* and the cowherd boys and cows who accompany Him. We do not have the strength of *kṛṣṇa-prema*, and therefore we are weak (*abalā*). This Girirāja, however, is the proprietor of *kṛṣṇa-prema*. Let us go, *sakhī*. We should bathe in Mānasī-gaṅgā, do *parikramā* of Girirāja, take *darśana* of his presiding deity, Śrī Harideva, and worship him. Then the desires we have long held in our hearts will be fulfilled. Even though attainment of the wealth of *prema* is extremely rare, Girirāja will give some of it to us. O sister, we want to touch *priyatama* Śyāmasundara's chin and talk to Him. It is so frustrating that we are unable to talk with Him, what to speak of render direct service to Him.

"Just look! Girirāja becomes ecstatic by the touch of Kṛṣṇa's limbs as Kṛṣṇa climbs upon his body, and one can easily see his ecstatic sentiments, such as tears, horripilation and perspiration. The appearance of grass is horripilation, the humidity is his perspiration and the waterfalls are his tears. Moreover, Kṛṣṇa also receives pleasure by sporting on Govardhana's body and performing pastimes there. Having seen all this, we do not have even the slightest doubt that Girirāja-Govardhana is *haridāsa-varya*, the topmost servant of Śrī Hari."

That servant who delights Śrī Hari with his service, and who receives the greatest happiness by rendering that service to Him, is topmost among Śrī Hari's servants. In *Śrīmad-Bhāgavatam*, three great personalities are called *haridāsa*: Mahārāja Yudhiṣṭhira, Śrī Uddhava and Śrī Girirāja-Govardhana. Mahārāja Yudhiṣṭhira accepts Śrī Kṛṣṇa, who is the Supreme Absolute Truth and fully independent, as his intimate friend, and he serves Him lovingly in the mood of a servant (*dāsya*), a friend (*sakhya*) and a parent (*vātsalya*).

Śrī Uddhava, the second *haridāsa*, became Śrī Kṛṣṇa's messenger and went to Vraja to console Kṛṣṇa's parents as well as the *vraja-ramaṇīs* and other Vrajavāsīs. Upon seeing the symptoms of the *gopīs'* high class of *prema*, Śrī Uddhava became astonished. He not only realised the glories of the *gopīs'* foot-dust, he also expressed a desire to take birth in Vraja as grass, a shrub or a herb. He fulfilled this desire at the most magnanimous Girirāja-Govardhana, by taking birth in Girirāja's lap near Kusuma-sarovara as a blade of grass, but still he was unable to serve the Vrajavāsīs as Girirāja does.

Girirāja is *haridāsa-varya*, the topmost servant of Hari. Why? Because he fulfils all the needs of Kṛṣṇa and the Vrajavāsīs. He serves Kṛṣṇa and His companions, the cowherd boys and cows, with his body, mind, wealth and very life, sacrificing everything to satisfy all of their inner hearts' desires. He offers them the pure, cool, sweet drinking water of Mānasī-gaṅgā and other *sarovaras*, very tasteful fruits and roots to eat, varieties of flowers and red minerals for decoration, jewelled seats and beds, precious stones to use for lamps and mirrors, and well-adorned caves and *kuñjas* for resting and playing. And he offers nutritious grass and plants to the cows. Śrī Kṛṣṇa and His beloveds relish very confidential pastimes in the beautifully decorated groves and caves of Girirāja, who is expert in performing the topmost service in *śṛṅgāra-rasa*. Because Rādhā and Kṛṣṇa's confidential *nikuñja-līlās* take place inside and upon his body, so as to not disturb these confidential pastimes he has permanently assumed the stationary form of stone.

In this way, the *gopīs* lavishly praise Girirāja-Govardhana upon seeing the many kinds of services he renders to Kṛṣṇa.

Text 6

Upon hearing the sound of Kṛṣṇa's flute, moving living entities acquire the nature of the non-moving, and non-moving entities acquire the nature of the moving. *Śrīmad-Bhāgavatam* (10.21.19) states:

gā gopakair anu-vanaṁ nayator udāra-
veṇu-svanaiḥ kala-padais tanu-bhṛtsu sakhyaḥ
aspandanaṁ gati-matāṁ pulakas tarūṇāṁ
niryoga-pāśa-kṛta-lakṣaṇayor vicitram

O *sakhīs*, the elegance and charm of the two brothers, our Śyāmasundara and Gaurasundara Balarāma, are quite unique and wonderful. When Śyāmasundara, together with His cowherd friends, leads the cows from one forest to another by sweetly playing a melody on His *veṇu*, He binds the top of His turban with the *niryoga* rope, which is used for binding the legs of calves, and from His shoulders (like His *pītāmbara*) hangs a rope known as *pāśa*. Upon seeing that sweet, unparalleled beauty and hearing the sound of the *veṇu*, moving living entities, such as animals and birds, as well as rivers – and what to speak of human beings – become inert like stone. And ecstatic symptoms like horripilation are displayed in non-moving entities, such as trees. *Sakhī*, how can I describe the magical sound of that flute?

sakhā-dhenu-saṅge kṛṣṇa udāra-svabhāva
muralīra gāne sabe deya sakhya-bhāva

jaṅgame karila spandahīna, tarugaṇe
pulakita kaila aho! vicitra lakṣaṇe

hena kṛṣṇa nā pāiyā prāṇa pheṭe yāya
kabe sakhi! vidhi kṛṣṇa dibena āmāya

Bhajana-rahasya-vṛtti

The beautiful women of Vraja, being filled with *mahābhāva*, reflect, "All the moving and non-moving entities of Vṛndāvana are blessed. Their lives are successful because, regardless of their form, they have attained the touch of Kṛṣṇa's lotus feet, or else they have attained some kind of relationship with Him. In the whole of Vraja, only we are unfortunate." As the *vraja-ramaṇīs* speak, the pastime of Kṛṣṇa taking the cows to graze in the forest and the melodious sound of His *veṇu* manifest in their hearts. Now they become completely immersed in ecstatic rapture, as if seeing Kṛṣṇa directly.

Overwhelmed with *prema*, they say, "Look *sakhī*! How sweet are the movements of Śyāmasundara, the best of dancers, as He gracefully roams from one forest to the other. The sweet sound of His flute causes all moving and non-moving living entities to become overwhelmed with the ecstasy of *prema*, and they visibly manifest *aṣṭa-sāttvika* transformations."

Furthermore, the *gopīs* say, *niryoga-pāśa-kṛta-lakṣaṇayor vicitram*. "*Aho*! What a beautiful sight are the two brothers, Rāma and Kṛṣṇa, as They walk into the forest wearing the *niryoga* and *pāśa* on Their bodies." While the cows are being milked, with a rope their restless calves are tied before them to a post in the ground. In this way, their mothers can see them. This rope is called *niryoga*. Another rope, *pāśa*, binds the two hind legs of a restless cow to keep her calm while being milked. The *niryoga* and *pāśa* used by Śrī Kṛṣṇa are made of soft, yellow threads of jute, tied at either end with clusters of pearls. Like the other *gopas*, Kṛṣṇa ties the *niryoga* to the top of His turban and lets the *pāśa* hang from His shoulders onto His chest. His attire is so fascinating that anyone who sees it cannot help being charmed, and the mere sight of it renders the *prema*-filled *gopa-ramaṇīs* unconscious.

They continue, "O *sakhī*, in Vidhātā's creation there is no living entity who will not be charmed by the sight of the sweetness of Rāma's and Kṛṣṇa's beauty, which attracts the entire universe. When Kṛṣṇa plays a melody on His enchanting *muralī* to gather together the cows who are far away, the condition He creates is difficult to describe. When the tinkling of the ankle bells on Kṛṣṇa's lotus feet mixes with the inexpressibly melodious sound of His captivating *muralī*, the sweetness of that sound increases even more. Is there any person who can remain composed upon hearing this?"

While discussing Kṛṣṇa's enchanting cowherd attire and the sound of His flute, the *vraja-ramaṇīs*, who are helplessly immersed in *prema*, say, "*Sakhī*, upon seeing Kṛṣṇa's *niryoga* and *pāśa*, it seems that they really are *niryoga-pāśa* – through them, *yoga* (meeting) is certain to take place uninterruptedly, for one's whole life. Even continuous *samādhi-yoga* is insignificant compared to this. Kṛṣṇa's *niryoga-pāśa* are really *prema-pāśa*, ropes of love. The Vrajavāsīs and the *vana-vāsīs* (forest entities) are rendered helpless by His *niryoga-pāśa*. This demonstrates the amazing effect of these 'ropes of love'." In this way, the *gopīs* consider Śrī Kṛṣṇa's *niryoga-pāśa* to be a trap of love.

Hearing the sound of Kṛṣṇa's flute, all the moving living entities of the forest, such as the deer and birds, are overwhelmed by *prema* and become inert. The trees, creepers and other non-moving living entities give up their natures and adopt the characteristics of moving beings. They become jubilant and experience ecstatic symptoms. Furthermore, the Yamunā,

Mānasī-gaṅgā and other rivers stop flowing, and the stones on Govardhana and other mountains melt and flow like streams.

Text 7

The sentiments of Śrī Rādhā in *pravāsa* (separation by being out of sight) are most favourable to meditate upon for the *sādhaka* who, immersed in these sentiments, should read chapters from *Śrīmad-Bhāgavatam* such as *Bhramara-gīta*. Śrī Mādhavendra Purī has expressed Śrī Rādhikā's *bhāvocchvāsa*, outburst of feeling that expresses the *bhāva* hidden in the heart, at the time of *pravāsa* (*Padyāvalī* (334)):

ayi dīna-dayārdra nātha he
mathurā-nātha kadāvalokyase
hṛdayaṁ tvad-aloka-kātaraṁ
dayita bhrāmyati kiṁ karomy aham

O You whose heart is most merciful to the wretched! O Master! O Lord of Mathurā! When will I have Your *darśana*? O Lord of My life, because I cannot see You, My heart has become agitated. What shall I do now?

he dīna-dayārdra-nātha, he kṛṣṇa mathurā-nātha,
kabe punaḥ pāba daraśana
nā dekhi' se cāṅdamukha, vyathita hṛdaye duḥkha,
he dayita! ki kari ekhana?

Bhajana-rahasya-vṛtti

As the Kaustubha jewel is the topmost of all jewels, this verse is foremost among *rasa* poetry. Śrī Svāminī spoke it in the state of *divyonmāda* (divine madness), when She was deeply aggrieved in separation from Kṛṣṇa, and by Her mercy it manifested in the speech of Śrī Mādhavendra Purīpāda. Then, accepting the mood of Śrī Rādhā, Śrī Kṛṣṇacandra relished this verse as Śrī

Gauracandra. No fourth person has ever tasted its inner moods. Uttering this verse, Śrīman Mahāprabhu would become overwhelmed by *prema* and faint. Thus maddened by *prema*, sometimes He would run here and there, sometimes He laughed and sometimes He danced. He was unable to utter more than "*ayi dīna, ayi dīna*" due to absorption in ecstatic love (*premāveśa*). Tears would flow from His eyes, and *sāttvika*, *vyabhicārī* and other *bhāvas* appeared in His body in their blazing state (*sūddīpta*). (This is described by Śrī Kṛṣṇadāsa Kavirāja Gosvāmī in *Śrī Caitanya-caritāmṛta* (*Madhya-līlā* 4.191–203).)

Śrīman Mahāprabhu is the gardener of the desire tree of *kṛṣṇa-prema*. He distributes the fruits of this tree and also relishes them Himself. Śrī Mādhavendra Purī, whose heart was saturated with *kṛṣṇa-prema*, was the very first sprout of this desire tree. With Śrī Īśvara Purī, this sprout of *prema-rasa* grew. The gardener, Śrī Caitanya Himself, also manifested as the trunk. Previous to Śrī Mādhavendra Purīpāda there was no *rasamayī-upāsanā*, devotional service in amorous love, in the Madhva *sampradāya*. Through the ideas expressed by the Tattvavādīs whom Śrīman Mahāprabhu met while travelling in South India, one can understand that worship in the Madhva *sampradāya* used to be performed only in a mood of awe and reverence (*aiśvaryamayī-upāsanā*).

Various *sañcāri-bhāvas* manifest in the state of separation (*viraha*) and agitate the ocean of *prema*. Humility (*dainya*), envy (*asūyā*) and contrariness (*māna*) due to jealousy appear in the heart and nourish the *sthāyibhāva*. Many kinds of *sañcāri-bhāvas* arise in Śrī Rādhā's heart when She is submerged in the ocean of separation from Śrī Kṛṣṇa. *Bhāva-utpatti* (the generation of a *bhāva*), *bhāva-sandhi* (the meeting together of two *bhāvas*, either of the same or different types), *bhāva-śābalya* (the clashing of many *bhāvas*, in which one *bhāva* suppresses another and becomes prominent) and *bhāva-śānti* (pacification of an extremely powerful *bhāva*) create waves in this ocean of separation.

Rādhā, who is mad in separation (*viraha-unmādinī*), addressed Kṛṣṇa in extreme humility: "*Ayi dīna-dayārdra-nātha*! O Kṛṣṇa, You are very simple-hearted and affectionate. It is You who remove the sorrows of the residents of Vraja, so please bestow Your mercy upon Me. You give mercy to all living entities, thus protecting them from all distress, so why will You not give mercy to Me, who am separated from My master? If You do not bestow Your mercy upon Me, Your reputation as 'He who removes the distress of the residents of Vraja' will become disgraced. Only You are My beloved." This is why the word *nātha*, meaning "master", is used in this *śloka*.

In this ocean of separation, though, there is a towering wave that represses this feeling of humility (*dainya*) and manifests the mood of envy (*asūyā*) and contrariness (*māna*) due to jealousy. Now Śrī Rādhā addresses Śyāmasundara as Mathurānātha, "the Lord of Mathurā". "O Mathurānātha, why would You be merciful to us now? How can You remember us while You are in Mathurā, where hundreds of affectionate, beautiful ladies serve You? Surely You have forgotten us milkmaids. Since You are receiving so much honour from the fabulously opulent kings of Mathurā, how can You have time to remember us wretched persons? By the association of Mathurā's Yādavas, Your heart has also become hard. Why would it melt upon seeing the condition of us *gopīs*, who are distressed in separation?"

Speaking thus, Śrī Rādhā becomes momentarily stunned, and the *sañcāri-bhāva* of *dainya* again appears. She says, "O beloved (*dayita*)! O Śyāmasundara, You are more dear to us than our own lives. How can we forget Your loving dealings? When we would become tired during the *rāsa* dance, You would wipe away our drops of perspiration with Your own *pītāmbara*. And if our *kuṅkuma* stained the *pītāmbara*, You would lovingly hold it to Your heart. When You left us You said, 'I will return.' With this assurance we remain alive. But having to wonder whether You will return or not confuses us, so please give us some consolation. Our hearts are intensely restless to see Your moon-like face."

Śrīla Bhaktivinoda Ṭhākura writes that the topmost *bhajana* is to follow the *vraja-devīs'* moods of separation from Śrī Kṛṣṇa.

Text 8

Agitated by separation from Śrī Kṛṣṇa, the *gopīs* blame Vidhātā (Providence). *Śrīmad-Bhāgavatam* (10.39.19) describes:

aho vidhātas tava na kvacid dayā
saṁyojya maitryā praṇayena dehinaḥ
tāṁś cākṛtārthān viyunaṅkṣy apārthakaṁ
vikrīḍitaṁ te 'rbhaka-ceṣṭitaṁ yathā

O Vidhātā, you are the arranger of everything, but there is not even a trace of mercy in your heart. First you unite living entities in this world in friendship and love, but before they can fulfil their desires and hopes, you pointlessly separate them while they are still unsatisfied. The truth is that, like the play of a child, this whimsical behaviour of yours is useless.

vidhātaḥ he! nāhi dayā kichu-i tomāra
maitra-bhāve praṇayete, dehī-dehī-saṁyogete,
kena eta kaile avicāra?
akṛtārtha-avasthāya, viyoga karile hāya,
bālakera ceṣṭā e vyāpāra

Bhajana-rahasya-vṛtti

The *vraja-devīs*, whose hearts have been seized by Śrī Kṛṣṇa, are distressed in fear of impending separation from Him. They have heard that Akrūra has come with a chariot to take their *prāṇakānta* Śyāmasundara to Mathurā. Tormented by the fear of future separation, the *vraja-devīs*, speaking to like-minded *gopīs*, express their own special sentiments of love and afflictions of separation, and in doing so reveal the helplessness of their *prema*.

"Śrī Kṛṣṇa is going to Madhupurī!" Hearing this, the lustre of Bhadrā's lotus face and the lotus faces of the other *taṭasthā-gopīs*[3] withered and became dejected. Śyāmalā's and other *suhṛt-pakṣā-gopīs'* dresses, belts, hair and so on loosened. In *samādhi*, Candrāvalī, who is *vipakṣā*, began to see Śrī Govinda in her heart, which was lost in meditation. The crown jewel of all the *vraja-gopīs*, *mahābhāva-vatī* Śrīmatī Rādhikā, other *svapakṣā-gopīs* like Lalitā and Viśākhā, and other beloveds of Śrī Kṛṣṇa, envisioned in their hearts their *prāṇa-priyatama's* various *prema-vilāsa* – His behaviour, dealings, laughter, glances and so forth. Then, overwhelmed by the deep pain of separation from Him, they began to weep.

In different groups the *gopīs* express their own innermost feelings according to their *prema*. Together in each group, they voice the deep pain of separation: "If our life-airs leave our bodies due to the pain of separation from Śrī Kṛṣṇa, Vidhātā is solely responsible. O Vidhātā, you rule the entire universe very well, but is there no arrangement for compassion in your kingdom? If you had ever just once contemplated justice or injustice,

[3] The four groups of *gopīs* are as follows: (1) *taṭastha-pakṣā*, those who are neutral towards Śrī Rādhā; (2) *suhṛt-pakṣā*, those who are friendly to Śrī Rādhā; (3) *vipakṣā*, Śrī Rādhā's rivals; and (4) *svapakṣā*, those who belong to Śrī Rādhā's personal party.

you would not be so harsh. You arrange for the meeting and separation of living beings according to a mere whim. You also establish affectionate friendships between *jīvas*, but only for a moment do you let them relish the happiness of meeting before You again submerge them in an ocean of separation. You are heartless and cruel, and we are witness to this. Your behaviour is like that of an ignorant child who makes toys and then afterwards destroys them. Therefore, O Vidhātā, you are not only merciless, unscrupulous and inconsiderate, you are also wicked. Your present behaviour is highly contemptible. First, you created the form of our *prāṇakānta* Mukunda, who embodies all beauty, sweetness and charm, and who charms the entire universe, and then you granted us *darśana* of that form, by which our hearts experienced boundless love. However, after placing this unprecedented form before our eyes, you again removed it and took our *prāṇakānta* far away. Such deceit is not proper; only a wicked person acts like this. Why do you behave sinfully even though you are so wise and learned? Are you not committing the sin of taking back that which you have given?"

Text 9

For a person attached to Kṛṣṇa, even a moment of separation from Him is intolerable. *Śrīmad-Bhāgavatam* (10.39.29) states:

yasyānurāga-lalita-smita-valgu-mantra-
līlāvaloka-parirambhaṇa-rāsa-goṣṭhyām
nītāḥ sma naḥ kṣaṇam iva kṣaṇadā vinā taṁ
gopyaḥ kathaṁ nv atitarema tamo durantam

Sakhīs, by His captivating, affectionate smile, sweet, intimate conversations, playful glances and loving embraces, the long, long nights of the *rāsa-līlā* passed in a moment. Indeed, how can we now overcome the boundless anguish of separation from Him?

anurāga-vilokita, valgu-mantra-sulalita,
smita-āliṅgana rāsa-sthale
brahma-rātra kṣane gela, tabu tṛpti nā haila,
ebe kṛṣṇa-viraha ghaṭila

gopīra emana dina kemane yāibe
duḥkhera sāgare ḍūbe prāṇa hārāibe

Bhajana-rahasya-vṛtti

When Śrī Kṛṣṇa was about to depart for Mathurā, the *vraja-gopīs*, who were distressed by the fear of imminent separation from Him, began to lament and reproach Vidhātā (Providence) in various ways. They said, "Today cruel (*krūra*) Vidhātā has arrived in Vraja, bearing the name Akrūra (not cruel). We gave up our families and religious principles, and offered our everything unto the lotus feet of our *prāṇakānta* Śyāmasundara. Now what will happen to us? Oh! Destiny is unfavourable to us! There is no means of protection from this."

Another *gopī* said, "O *sakhī*, today we shall give up all shame and hesitation; we will somehow put a stop to Govinda's journey. Seeing our boldness and independence, all of our relatives will be displeased, our family elders will not tolerate our shamelessness and our family friends will punish us, threaten us with death, or forcibly evict us from our homes. But *sakhī*, we have already given up the attachment to home and bodily relationships. If we are put out of our homes, it will be auspicious for us, because then we will easily attain the company of Govinda. We shall give up our homes and roam here and there with Him. Even if they punish us with death there will be no loss, because it is better to die than be separated from Govinda. If they lock us in our homes we will die happily, meditating on Govinda. Therefore *sakhī*, why wait? Go quickly! Do not delay in putting a stop to Govinda's journey."

While Śrī Kṛṣṇa's beloveds lamented in the burning heat of

separation, they fell unconscious. At that time, happy memories of meeting began to awaken in their hearts, where the previous night of *rāsa* manifested. Śrī Kṛṣṇa's gentle, sweetly smiling and loving lotus face, His affectionate, charming conversations and His affectionate, strong embrace manifested on the screen of their hearts, and that night seemed to pass very slowly. The thought of being deprived of Śrī Kṛṣṇa's sweet company, the pain of separation, seemed like countless forest fires. The *gopīs* lamented, "How can we cross this ocean of suffering? How can we remain alive in separation from our *prāṇakānta*? In the afternoon, when Śrī Kṛṣṇa, surrounded by the cowherd boys, returns home from the forest, the beauty of His face is unprecedented. The indescribable sound of the *muralī* and His sidelong glances stir our hearts. His face, which is covered by the dust that has been raised by the cows' hooves, His curly locks of hair, the extraordinarily beautiful garland of forest flowers around His neck, and His sidelong glances all reveal His love-filled desires. How can we forget all our loving exchanges?"

That day Śrī Kṛṣṇa prepared to go to Mathurā, leaving the *gopīs* behind. Who can express their deep anguish? When the time for departure came, the barrier of their patience broke and they all assembled, loudly expressing the great pain in their hearts by incessantly wailing, "O Govinda! O Dāmodara! O Mādhava!"

Text 10

Śrī Rādhā's strong expressions of separation from Śrī Kṛṣṇa are described in *Haṁsadūta* (2):

yadā yāto gopī-hṛdaya-madano nanda-sadanān
mukundo gāndhinyās tanayam anurundhan madhu-purīm
tadāmāṅkṣīc cintā-sariti ghana-ghūrṇāparicayair
agādhāyāṁ bādhāmaya-payasi rādhā-virahiṇī

Upon the request of Akrūra, Śrī Kṛṣṇacandra, who gladdens the *gopīs'* hearts, departed Nanda-bhavana for Mathurā. Now separated from Her lover, Śrī Rādhikā became greatly agitated and was completely submerged in a river of anxiety, which was full of deep whirlpools of unlimited suffering.

gopikā-hṛdaya-hari, vraja chāḍi' madhupurī,
akrūra-sahita yabe gelā
tabe rādhā virahiṇī, ghana-ghūrṇa-taraṅgiṇī,
cintā-jale agādhe paḍilā

Bhajana-rahasya-vṛtti

In his book *Haṁsadūta*, Śrī Rūpa Gosvāmipāda gives an incomparable description of the *vraja-ramaṇī's* feelings of separation (*vipralambha-rasa*) that resulted from Śrī Kṛṣṇa's residing in a distant place (*sudūra-pravāsa*). In *śṛṅgara-rasa*, *vipralambha-rasa* is most relishable. Śrī Rūpa Gosvāmipāda has enabled *rasika* devotees to dive deep into the ocean of *vipralambha-rasa* by writing about the waves of separation that arose in all the limbs of Śrī Rādhā's body, Her incoherent conversations in *divyonmāda*, and Her sorrowful speech, which were all due to blazing (*sūddīpta*) *sāttvika* transformations.

The very bliss of the *vraja-gopīs'* hearts, Śrī Nanda-nandana, was taken to Mathurā by Akrūra, whose name means "not cruel". Actually, however, Akrūra was supremely cruel, and as a consequence, all the *gopīs* drowned in a bottomless ocean of separation (*viraha*).

One day the crown jewel of the *gopīs*, the personification of *mahābhāva*, Śrī Rādhā, overwhelmed by feelings of separation from Kṛṣṇa, went to the bank of the Yamunā with Śrī Lalitā and other *sakhīs* to soothe Her affliction. However, just by again seeing the *kuñjas* where Their playful pastimes took place, Śrī Rādhā fainted, distressed by the burning fire of that separation.

The *sakhīs* lifted Her up and laid Her on a bed of lotus petals. Śrī Lalitā fanned Her with the end of her veil and the *sakhīs* chanted the names of Kṛṣṇa. By fanning Her and anointing Her with cooling sandalwood paste, they tried to bring Her back to consciousness.

Impatient, Śrī Lalitā went to bring Her cool water from the Yamunā. There, she saw an extremely beautiful, white, male swan. An inspiration arose in her to send a message to *prāṇa-vallabha* Śrī Kṛṣṇa about the incidents that were destroying the life of her dear *sakhī*, Śrī Rādhā. She understood that this male swan (*haṁsa*) would be a suitable messenger (*dūta*), and she politely petitioned him to go to Mathurā. While describing the main road, she remembered previous pastimes with Kṛṣṇa. She mentioned these pastimes to the swan, thus making him thoroughly understand all the sufferings in Śrī Rādhā's heart, which was overwhelmed by separation from Kṛṣṇa.

After Śrī Kṛṣṇa departed for Mathurā with Akrūra, Śrī Rādhā became submerged in a fathomless ocean of anxiety. She began to think, "Shall I protect this life-air, which is burning in the fire of agony, by binding it with the rope of hope? Or, shall I liberate My body from this rope? As Prāṇanātha left Vṛndāvana, He said, '*Āyāsya iti dautyakai* – I will return the day after tomorrow.' But the day after tomorrow has been replaced with many years, and we still have not received news that He is coming. Shall I give up that hope and choose death by entering fire or the waters of the Yamunā?"

Śrī Rādhikā further reflected, "When *prāṇakānta* Śyāmasundara returns from Mathurā and does not find Me here, He will become so distressed. So what shall I do? My intelligence is perplexed. If My *prāṇanātha* cannot see Me, He also will be unable to remain alive. What shall I do? If I die, I will not see My *priyatama's* soft, delicate lotus face which resembles a *kunda* flower. But I am unable to remain alive, as I am burning in separation. That Lord of our lives has not abandoned us; therefore, it is only right that I protect My life." In this way, Śrī Rādhā was submerged in the boundless ocean of separation, in whirlpools of thoughts filled with pain. The *vraja-sundarīs'* yearning to meet Kṛṣṇa is a transformation of their *prema*. It increases unlimitedly, exuding a wonderful sweetness.

Śrī Rūpa Gosvāmipāda follows Śrī Rādhā's *bhāvas* and becomes one with them. He taunts Akrūra by using the word *gāndhinī-tanaya*, the son of Gāndhinī, which has a double meaning. Akrūra took birth from the womb of Gāndhinī, the daughter of the king of Kāśī. He stayed in her womb for twelve years, which caused her much pain. His father asked, "O child, why are you not taking birth? Why are you making your mother suffer like this?"

The child in the womb replied, "Father, if you give one cow to each *brāhmaṇa* every day, I will take birth after one year." His father gave the cows as requested, and after one year, the child took birth. The Purāṇas state that a son who is named after his father or his paternal grandfather is blessed, but that son who is known by his mother's name is wretched. In this Text, Śrī Rūpa Gosvāmipāda indicates Akrūra's cruel nature by making him known through his mother, not his father. The *Viṣṇu Purāṇa* describes that Akrūra's mother gave her family suffering, anxiety and worry. Consequently, Akrūra, having the same qualities as his mother, threw the *gopīs* and Vrajavāsīs into a limitless ocean of grief.

This Text expresses *cintā* (anxious consideration) aroused in the state of *udghūrṇā* in *mohana-mahābhāva*. *Cintā* is one of the ten stages of *pravāsa-vipralambha*.

Text 11

The ten conditions of *viraha*, separation, are described in *Ujjvala-nīlamaṇi*:

cintātra jāgārodvegau
tānavaṁ malināṅgatā
pralāpo vyādhir unmādo
moho mṛtyur daśā daśa

Ten conditions arise in *viraha*: (1) *cintā* (anxious consideration), (2) *jāgara* (sleeplessness), (3) *udvega* (agitation), (4) *tānava* (emaciation of the body), (5) *malināṅgatā* (discolouring of bodily limbs), (6) *pralāpa* (incoherent speech), (7) *vyādhi* (being stricken with a tormenting ailment), (8) *unmāda* (madness), (9) *moha* (bewilderment) and (10) *mṛtyu* (death, or being unconscious for a long time). At the stage of *mohana*, an extraordinary condition manifests in Śrī Rādhā, in which She experiences extreme anguish of separation from Kṛṣṇa.

jāgara, udvega, cintā, tānavāṅga-malinatā,
pralāpa, unmāda āra vyādhi
moha, mṛtyu, daśā daśa, tāhe rādhā suvivaśa,
pāila duḥkha-kulera avadhi

Text 12

While Śrī Rādhā suffers from the scorching poison of *viraha*, She expresses Her transcendental emotions, as described in *Jagannātha-vallabha-nāṭaka* (3.9):

prema-ccheda-rujo 'vagacchati harir nāyaṁ na ca prema vā
sthānāsthānam avaiti nāpi madano jānāti no durbalāḥ
anyo veda na cānya-duḥkham akhilaṁ no jīvanaṁ vāśravaṁ
dvi-trīṇy eva dināni yauvanam idaṁ hā hā vidhe kā gatiḥ

Śrī Hari does not understand the pain of separation in *prema*. In fact, *prema* does not know anything about who is deserving of itself and who is not. Kāmadeva also torments us, knowing us to be weak. It is impossible for anyone to understand another's misery. Life is so fleeting – it has no certainty – and youth remains only two or three days. Alas! Alas! What kind of arrangement of Vidhātā (the Creator) is this?

sakhī bale dhairya dhara, āsibe nāgara-vara,
vyākula haile kivā phala
rādhā bale ohe sakhi, patha āra nāhi lakhi',
prema-ccheda roga ye bāḍila

latā vāñcāite hari, nā āsila madhupurī,
prema nā bujhila sthānāsthāna
niṭhura kānura preme, pa'ḍe gelāma mahābhrame,
madana tāhāte hāne bāṇa

duḥkha nā bujhila sakhi, jīvana cañcala lakhi,
tāte e yauvana-śobhā yāya
āra ki nāgaramaṇi, e braje āsibe dhani,
hā hā vidhi! ki habe upāya

Bhajana-rahasya-vṛtti

Śrī Rāya Rāmānanda gives the following description in his *Jagannātha-vallabha-nāṭaka*. Once Śrī Rādhā and Her *sakhīs* entered the Vṛndāvana forest. The *sakhīs* began to describe the sweetness of Śrī Kṛṣṇa's beauty with verses appropriate for *pūrva-rāga*, such as *so 'yaṁ yuvā yuvati-citta-vihaṅga-śākhī* (*Jagannātha-vallabha-nāṭaka* (1.50)). Śrī Kṛṣṇa spotted Rādhā from a distance and They both became extremely restless to meet each other. Rādhā sent a love-letter to Śrī Kṛṣṇa through Śaśimukhī Sakhī. Although Śrī Kṛṣṇa became overwhelmed with emotion upon reading it, He concealed His emotion and disrespected Rādhā and the *gopīs* with words of indifference: "It is improper for women from good families to forsake their family honour to love Me like this."

Śaśimukhī returned to Śrī Rādhikā, and relating all this to Her, advised Rādhā to place Her attention elsewhere. This made Śrī Rādhā attain an unbearably severe state of *viraha*, and She conveyed Her sentiments in this Text 12. Śrī Rādhā said to the *gopī* Madanikā, "Attracted by the incomparably beautiful form of Śrī Kṛṣṇa, I was unable to remain patient, so I sent a letter to Him. O *sakhī*, what was My fault in doing that? He is certainly crooked, as His sole intention was to give Me a punishment equal to death. First He attracted Me with the sweetness of His form and now He is rejecting Me. O *sakhī*, you may ask, 'Why do You feel affection for Śrī Kṛṣṇa when He is very competent in killing women?' but what can I say? *Hā hā vidhe kā gatiḥ*. It is very difficult to understand why Vidhātā gives a particular punishment to a particular person. I loved Kṛṣṇa for pleasure, but instead of Vidhātā giving Me pleasure, he gave Me sorrow, and because of this My life-air is now leaving Me." This is also described in *Śrī Caitanya-caritāmṛta* (*Madhya-līlā* 2.20) as follows:

sakhi he, nā bujhiye vidhira vidhāna
sukha lāgi' kailuṅ prīta, haila duḥkha viparīta,
ebe yāya, nā rahe parāṇa

O *sakhī*, I do not understand the regulative principles given by the Creator. I loved Kṛṣṇa for happiness, but the result was just the opposite. I am now in an ocean of distress. It must be that I am now going to die, for My vital force no longer remains. This is My state of mind.

Śrī Rādhā continues, "Sakhī Madanikā, the movement of *prema* is crooked, like that of a snake, and it is foolish. It does not consider whether the place is suitable or unsuitable, or if the object is fit or unfit. This *prema* moves in a crooked way and has tied My hands, feet and neck with the ropes of that wicked one's beauty and virtues. I am unable to untie that knot."

Śrī Rādhā is so captivated by Śrī Kṛṣṇa's qualities that it is impossible for Her to abandon the hope of meeting Him. Her condition is similar to that of a person who relishes the sweetness of hot sugarcane so much that he cannot give up chewing it, even if his mouth is burning. Moreover, She says, "Observing My helpless condition, Madana (Cupid) torments Me with his five arrows, thus exhausting My entire body."

The *sakhī* says, "O Rādhā, take revenge on Kāmadeva (Cupid)."

Rādhā answers, "O *sakhī*, Kāmadeva has no body, so how can I retaliate? He tears My body asunder with His five arrows, causing Me agony, but these arrows do not take away My life."

"Svāminī, since Śrī Kṛṣṇa is an ocean of mercy, He will certainly bestow mercy upon You. Have patience."

Śrī Rādhā replies, "*Dvi-trīṇy eva dināni yauvanam idam*. Life is momentary. Who can remain alive until then? The life-span of the living entity in a human body is one hundred years, but youth only lasts a few days. Without youth, how will I serve Him? My youth only is the cause of His happiness."

In reality, Śrī Rādhā is the eternal beloved of Śrī Kṛṣṇa. She is not an ordinary *māninī*, a woman who has been offended by Her lover – She is the personification of *viśuddha-sattva*. By her power, Yogamāyā has manifested these pastimes on the surface of the Earth for the purpose of accomplishing Kṛṣṇa's *nara-līlā*. *Śrī Caitanya-caritāmṛta* (*Ādi-līlā* 4.29–30) confirms this with the following words:

mo-viṣaye gopī-gaṇera upapati-bhāve
yoga-māyā karibeka āpana-prabhāve

āmiha nā jāni tāhā, nā jāne gopī-gaṇa
duṅhāra rūpa-guṇe duṅhāra nitya hare mana

The influence of Yogamāyā will inspire the *gopīs* with the sentiment that I am their paramour. Neither the *gopīs* nor I shall notice this, for our minds will always be entranced by one another's beauty and virtues.

Text 13

Śrī Rādhā's condition of *udvega*, anxiety, in separation from Śrī Kṛṣṇa is described in *Kṛṣṇa-karṇāmṛta* (42):

kim iha kṛṇumaḥ kasya brūmaḥ kṛtaṁ kṛtam āśayā
kathayata kathām anyāṁ dhanyām aho hṛdayeśayaḥ
madhura-madhura-smerākāre mano-nayanotsave
kṛpaṇa kṛpaṇā kṛṣṇe tṛṣṇā ciraṁ bata lambate

What shall I do now? To whom shall I speak? What is the purpose of holding on to the futile hope of receiving His *darśana*? Please speak about something better. *Aho*! But how can I possibly stop talking about He who is contained within My heart? His gentle, sweet smile is a festival for the mind and eyes. My longing to see this form of Śrī Kṛṣṇa increases moment by moment.

ebe bala ki kariba, kāre duḥkha jānāiba,
deha dhari kṛṣṇera āśāya
kaha anya kathā dhanya, yāte citta suprasanna,
sakhi! tāhā nā haibe upāya

kṛṣṇa hṛde śu'ye āche, mṛdu madhu hāsiteche,
mano-nayanera mahotsava
kṛṣṇa lakhibāra āśā, mane kaila cira vāsā,
se āśā kṛpaṇā asambhava

Bhajana-rahasya-vṛtti

A variety of sentiments are arising in Śrī Rādhā's heart. While in this state of *bhāva-śābalya* (the clashing and jostling of many different *bhāvas*, in which one *bhāva* suppresses another and becomes predominant), Śrī Rādhā says, "O *sakhīs*, what shall I do in this state of misfortune? I do not know how I will attain the *darśana* of Śrī Kṛṣṇa. To whom shall I express this heart-breaking anguish? In this state of separation from Kṛṣṇa, your condition is similar to Mine, so who in Vraja can I tell about the condition of My heart?"

A moment later, Śrī Rādhā conceals Her *bhāva-śābalya* and says (*Śrīmad-Bhāgavatam* (11.8.44)): "'*Āśā hi paramaṁ duḥkham* – hope itself is the consummate giver of sorrow.' For many days I have sat and waited, hoping that Kṛṣṇa would soon come, but so far He has not arrived. Now it is appropriate to give up that hope." Here the *sañcāri-bhāva* called *mati* (resolve or wisdom) has arisen, after which *amarṣa* (intolerance or indignation) appears. Śrī Rādhā then says, "O *sakhīs*, abandon talk about ungrateful Kṛṣṇa! Please tell Me about something else." As She says this, Kṛṣṇa manifests to Her internal vision. Wounded by the arrow of *kāma*, She becomes restless like a deer pierced by an arrow, and the *bhāva* of *amarṣa* becomes covered by the appearance of *trāsa* (fear). Distressed, She cries, "Oh, what suffering! Kṛṣṇa is lying in My heart and looking at Me with His sidelong glance, which is imbued with a sweet, gentle smile. This glance, full of laughter, is a great festival for the eyes and minds of all *vraja-ramaṇīs*."

Suddenly this *bhāva* disappears, and great distress and remorse are aroused in Her heart. Again She laments, saying, "*Sakhī*, what shall I do? You tell Me to be patient, but how can I be patient? The hope of receiving Kṛṣṇa's *darśana* resides in My mind, but this seems to be merely a vain hope that is fit to be abandoned." While lamenting in this way, *autsukya-bhāva* (ardent desire) again arises. Restless in separation from Kṛṣṇa, Śrīmatī says, "Understanding that her hope was extremely distressful, the prostitute Piṅgalā[4] abandoned it and became happy. I should also give up the hope of attaining Kṛṣṇa, but it is so difficult to stop talking about Him. Alas! The thirst for Śrī Kṛṣṇa's *darśana* is increasing in My heart moment by moment. That thirst is also increasing *madana* (*kāma*), which is sweeter than sweet."

Text 14

The *divyonmāda* (transcendental madness) of Śrī Rādhā, who is restless in the intense fire of separation from Śrī Kṛṣṇa, is described in *Kṛṣṇa-karṇāmṛta* (41):

amūny-adhanyāni dināntarāṇi
hare! tvad-ālokanam antareṇa
anātha-bandho! karuṇaika-sindho!
hā hanta! hā hanta! kathaṁ nayāmi

Alas! Alas! O Hari! O friend of the helpless! O You who are the only ocean of mercy! How can I pass these miserable days without Your *darśana*?

nā heriye tava mukha, hṛdaye dāruṇa, duḥkha,
dīna-bandho, karuṇā-sāgara
e adhanya divā-niśi, kemane kāṭābe dāsī,
upāya balaha ataḥpara

Bhajana-rahasya-vṛtti

Without the *darśana* of Śrī Kṛṣṇa, a moment seems like hundreds of *yugas* for Śrī Rādhā, who is burning in the fire of separation, and Her days stand still. "These days and nights, in which I cannot serve You, are not blessed."

[4] The story of Piṅgalā is narrated in *Śrīmad-Bhāgavatam*, Eleventh Canto, Chapter 8.

The word *hā* (meaning "alas") in this verse expresses a distress that is full of grief. Kṛṣṇa may say (*Śrīmad-Bhāgavatam* (10.29.20)), "*patayaś ca vaḥ, vicinvanti* – O Rādhā, Your body, which is pierced by the arrows of Anaṅga (Cupid), burns in the fire of *kāma*, so You should search for Your husband."

Then Śrī Rādhā will reply, "O Śyāma, I am searching for My *prāṇa-priyatama* Vrajendra-nandana. What need have I for a husband who gives distress? O friend of the helpless, having abandoned My husband, I have come to My *priyatama* (You)."

If somebody says, "Why have You come to Your *priyatama*?" then Śrīmatī would answer, "He is the friend of the helpless and destitute. I am helpless, so He is also My friend."

If Kṛṣṇa says (*Śrīmad-Bhāgavatam* (10.29.24)), "*bhartuḥ śuśrūṣaṇaṁ strīṇāṁ paro dharmaḥ* – the supreme duty of women is to serve their husbands," then, in reply, She will say (*Śrīmad-Bhāgavatam* (10.29.34)), "*cittaṁ sukhena bhavatāpahṛtam* – our minds and senses were satisfied engaging in household duties, but You stole them. O Hari, we have come to You in search of the great wealth of our hearts and senses. If there is anything wrong with this, it is Your fault."

If Kṛṣṇa says, "You are liars! When did I steal your *dharma* and your hearts?" then She will reply (*Śrīmad-Bhāgavatam* (10.29.38)), "*tan naḥ prasīda* – be pleased with us, O You who are the only ocean of mercy, kindly give us a mere drop from that ocean."

Text 15

Kṛṣṇa-karṇāmṛta (40) describes Śrī Rādhā's longing to meet Śrī Kṛṣṇa:

he deva! he dayita! he bhuvanaika-bandho!
he kṛṣṇa! he capala! he karuṇaika-sindho!
he nātha! he ramaṇa! he nayanābhirāma!
hā hā kadā nu bhavitāsi padaṁ dṛśor me

O Lord! O dearest one! O only friend of the three worlds! O Kṛṣṇa! O restless one! O only ocean of compassion! O Deva! O lover (*ramaṇa*)! O You who delight the eyes! Oh! When will You again be visible to My eyes? When will I receive Your *darśana*?

he deva, he prāṇapriya, ekamātra bandhu iha,
he kṛṣṇa, capala, kṛpā-sindhu
he nātha, ramaṇa mama, nayanera priyatama,
kabe dekhā dibe prāṇa-bandho

Bhajana-rahasya-vṛtti

The *sakhīs* are consoling Śrī Vṛṣabhānu-nandinī, who is suffering in separation from Kṛṣṇa. Suddenly, Śrī Rādhā looks here and there and says, "O *sakhī*, listen! It is the sound of Śrī Kṛṣṇa's ankle-bells! But why is He not coming before My eyes? Surely that rogue is sporting with some beautiful girl in a nearby *kuñja*." While speaking like this, Śrī Rādhā becomes mad (*unmādinī*) and in that maddened condition, She sees that Śrī Kṛṣṇa has come. On His body, though, are signs that He has been sporting with another woman. Upon seeing the marks, Śrī Rādhā becomes indignant (*amarṣa*) and, even though Śrī Kṛṣṇa is present before Her, She does not speak to Him but turns Her face away. Śrī Kṛṣṇa then disappears and Rādhā eagerly begins to search for Him here and there.

Restlessness resulting from a delay in seeing and attaining the desired object is called *autsukya*, ardent desire. When *bhāvas* overlap, it is known as *bhāva-śābalya*. When *autsukya* and *asūyā* (envy) awaken simultaneously, Śrī Rādhā sometimes criticises Kṛṣṇa, and sometimes She praises Him. Sometimes She goes into *māna*, sometimes She becomes proud and sometimes She praises Him sarcastically.

She says, "O Deva, because You sport with other women, You are called Deva[5]." Due to this disrespect, Kṛṣṇa leaves. Repentant, Śrī Rādhā begins to speak out of an eager longing to again have His *darśana*. "O beloved (*dayita*), You are the most dear of My life. Why did You abandon Me? Please, grant Me Your *darśana*."

Hearing this, Śrī Kṛṣṇa again appears. As soon as Śrī Rādhā sees Him, the *bhāvas* of *amarṣa* (indignation) and *asūyā* (envy) arise in Her, and She sarcastically derides Him. "O only friend of the three worlds (*bhuvanaika-bandho*), by playing on Your enchanting flute, You bring all women under Your control, and for this reason You are the friend of the entire world. You are the friend of all *gopīs*, therefore You stay near them. Isn't it Your own fault then, that You do not come to Me?"

Hearing this, Kṛṣṇa again disappears. Not seeing Him, Śrī Rādhā says, "O Kṛṣṇa! O Śyāmasundara! You attract the hearts of the entire universe. After stealing My heart, where have You gone? Please, kindly give Me Your *darśana*, just once."

Hearing this, Śrī Kṛṣṇa again comes and says, "O Priyā, I was just outside the *kuñja*. Please, be satisfied with Me."

Upon hearing Śrī Kṛṣṇa's entreaty, which is mixed with fickleness, Rādhā says, "O fickle one (*capala*)! O snake of the cowherd maidens! Please, go away from here, stealer of other men's wives! I have no need for You. Go back where You came from."

Kṛṣṇa hears this and pretends to leave. Śrī Vṛṣabhānu-nandinī understands that Her *prāṇanātha* has gone and offers a supplication. "O only ocean of mercy, I know that I am an offender, but You are the ocean of compassion and Your heart is soft, so please, give Me Your *darśana*. O lover (*ramaṇa*), You are always sporting with Me, so please come to the *kuñja*."

[5] Deva means "someone who sports or plays".

Within Her mind, She understands that Kṛṣṇa has again arrived. Thus absorbed, She holds out Her arms to embrace Him but is unable to do so. Coming to external consciousness, She begins speaking in extreme distress, "O You who delight the eyes (*nayanābhirāma*)! O You who give joy to the eyes! My eyes are very thirsty to have Your *darśana*. Alas! When will You appear before them?"

Text 16

Kṛṣṇa-karṇāmṛta (68) describes an internal vision (*sphūrti-darśana*) of Kṛṣṇa:

mārah svayaṁ nu madhura-dyuti-maṇḍalaṁ nu
mādhuryam eva nu mano-nayanāmṛtaṁ nu
veṇī-mṛjo nu mama jīvita-vallabho nu
kṛṣṇo 'yam abhyudayate mama locanāya

Is this Cupid himself, or is it a halo of sweet effulgence? Is this the personification of sweetness, or the life-giving nectar of the mind and eyes? Is this the lover who loosens My braid, the beloved of My life, the youthful Kṛṣṇa, who has manifest before My eyes?

svayaṁ kandarpa eki, madhura-maṇḍala nāki,
mādhurya āpani mūrtimāna
mano-nayanera madhu, dūra ha'te āila bandhu,
jīvana-vallabha vraja-prāṇa

āmāra nayana-āge, āila kṛṣṇa anurāge,
dehe mora āila jīvana
saba duḥkha dūre gela, prāṇa mora juḍāila,
dekha sakhi! pāinu hārādhana

Bhajana-rahasya-vṛtti

When Śrī Kṛṣṇa disappears from the *rāsa-līlā*, the *gopīs* sing a piteous *kīrtana* filled with the mood of separation from Him. At that time, Kṛṣṇa, who is *manmatha-manmatha*, the bewilderer of the mind of Cupid, appears before them. In *Śrīmad-Bhāgavatam* (10.32.2) Śrīla Śukadeva Gosvāmī describes that unprecedentedly beautiful form of Kṛṣṇa: "*tāsām āvirabhūc chauriḥ smayamāna-mukhāmbujaḥ* – with a smile on His lotus face, Kṛṣṇa appeared before the *gopīs*. Wearing a flower garland and a yellow garment, He appeared directly as one who can bewilder the mind of Cupid, who himself bewilders the minds of ordinary people."

Śauri Śrī Kṛṣṇa, who defeats even Cupid, appears before the *gopīs*. Upon seeing His beauty, Rādhā becomes perplexed and wonders, "Is Kṛṣṇa really present before us?" Confused, She says to Her *sakhīs*, "O *sakhīs*, is He who is standing before us Cupid incarnate, whose invisible form attacks everyone?" Here in this Text, the word *nu* (meaning "whether") is used in the sense of reasoning. Again perceiving His sweetness, She says with astonishment, "That Cupid cannot be so sweet, so is this a halo of sweet beauty? This is also astonishing. No, no it is not merely a halo of beauty, it is some kind of embodied sweetness. No other kind of sweetness can satisfy our eyes, but our eyes are satisfied with this *darśana*." With great pleasure, She says, "Is this nectar itself? But *sakhī*, nectar does not have a form and this does, so it cannot be nectar." Again She says, "Is it our beloved, who loosens our braids, who has come to us out of love?" Looking very carefully at Kṛṣṇa, She blissfully says, "O *sakhīs*, it is the love of our lives, the fresh, youthful dancer (*nava-kiśora-naṭavara*). It is He who gives pleasure to the eyes and who is our *prāṇakānta*."

Text 17

A description of the direct *darśana* of Śrī Kṛṣṇa is given in *Śrīmad-Bhāgavatam* (10.32.2):

tāsām āvirabhūc chauriḥ
smayamāna-mukhāmbujaḥ
pītāmbara-dharaḥ sragvī
sākṣān manmatha-manmathaḥ

Just then, Śrī Kṛṣṇa appeared in the midst of the *gopīs*. His lotus face blossomed with a mild, gentle smile. Hanging from His neck was a garland of forest flowers, and He wore a golden-yellow garment (*pītāmbara*). What was the nature of His beauty? That beauty stirs the mind of Kāmadeva (Cupid), who himself stirs the minds of everyone.

gopīra sammukha hari, dāṅḍāila veṇu dhari',
smayamāna-mukhāmbuja-śobhā
vanamālī pītāmbara, manmathera manohara,
rādhikāra deha-mano-lobhā

Bhajana-rahasya-vṛtti

Śrī Kṛṣṇa, who is ever-skilful in increasing His devotees' *prema*, disappeared from the *rāsa-līlā*. Devastated by separation from Him, weeping, the *gopīs* arrived at the bank of the Yamunā. There they performed *kīrtana*, having exhausted all alternatives in their search for Him. Their voices were full of extreme feeling and they used metaphors with multiple meanings to express their sentiments. Restless in the pain of separation, the *vraja-ramaṇīs'* tears, full of *prema*, flowed freely and continuously from their eyes. At that time, Śrī Kṛṣṇacandra, who was in the dense, dark forest, heard their weeping and suddenly appeared in their midst, manifesting His lustre.

In this Text, Śrīla Śukadeva Gosvāmī is thoroughly absorbed in *mañjarī-bhāva* and in anger, he has used the word *śauri* as an insult. Śrī Kṛṣṇa appeared in a *kṣatriya* family within the Śūra dynasty, whose hearts were deceitful and hard. Śukadeva Gosvāmipāda was unable to tolerate Svāminī's agony of separation from Kṛṣṇa, and he therefore saw Śrī Kṛṣṇa's hiding as a defect. He thought, "The young girls of Vraja are simple lovers (*premikās*), and You become joyful by making them unhappy. Seeing the *gopīs* afflicted by grief, You display Your prowess (*śaurya*)." Śrīla Śukadeva Gosvāmī felt that such so-called prowess was a disgrace: "If Your heart were truly honest, You would not have done such a thing." These are examples of the defamatory remarks used in *prema*; only one whose *prema* is deep can speak like this.

Śrī Kṛṣṇacandra, the crown jewel of all those skilled in amorous pastimes (*vidagdha-cūḍāmaṇi*), appeared in the midst of the *vraja-devīs*, displaying His unparalleled beauty. This beauty is described in this Text by the use of three adjectives: *smayamāna*, *sragvī* and *sākṣān-manmatha-manmathaḥ*.

Smayamāna – Although His face was radiant and smiling, Śrī Kṛṣṇa's heart was remorseful. Smiling is a characteristic of *bhagavattā* (the quality of being Bhagavān), but Kṛṣṇa's smile before the *gopīs* was caused by the *bhāvas* He experienced upon seeing them. He smiled to remove their distress and console them. *Darśana* of His extremely enchanting lotus face removes all the *gopīs'* sorrow. When Śrī Kṛṣṇa, wearing a *pītāmbara* (golden-yellow garment), heard the distress-filled cry of the *vraja-devīs*, He came swiftly, holding His *pītāmbara* around His neck, so that it would not slip off.

Śrī Kṛṣṇa had charmed the *gopīs* with the sound of His flute. All those *gopīs* had abandoned their families, morality, patience and shyness to arrive at Kṛṣṇa's side. But on that day, Kṛṣṇacandra had abandoned the *gopīs* and disappeared. Upon His return, He held His yellow cloth around His neck as a gesture, in order to show that He was praying for forgiveness. Conscious that He had given great suffering to His dear ones, Kṛṣṇa admitted that He Himself was an offender, and He held His *pītāmbara* with His hands to beg forgiveness for His offence. Just as an offender clasps a piece of straw between his teeth, Kṛṣṇa humbly put His cloth around His neck, thus begging forgiveness. His hands held His *pītāmbara*, which He used to carefully wipe away the tears from the eyes of the *vraja-devīs*, who were grief-stricken in separation from Him. Vrajendra-nandana is also relating the following mood to the *gopīs*: "You are of golden complexion, so I have covered My body, heart and mind with the *pītāmbara*; My inner heart is also coloured by your golden *anurāga*."

Sragvī – Leaving aside all other ornaments, Kṛṣṇa wore a fresh, radiant garland of forest flowers around His charming neck. He wore this garland of cooling lotuses only to remove the *gopīs'* fire of separation. In doing so, He expressed the sentiment, "You are like the garland's flowers; you are like My very heart. By embracing you, I am praying for forgiveness and beg you to soothe the heat of My feelings of separation from you. You strung this very garland yourself and garlanded Me with it. I am displaying My eternal gratitude by wearing it upon My heart."

Sākṣān-manmatha-manmathaḥ – Śrī Kṛṣṇa's extremely charming beauty, embellished by His being in the midst of the *gopīs*, churned the mind of Cupid. *Vyaṣṭi-kāmadeva* and *samaṣṭi-kāmadeva* are concealed in *sākṣāt-manmatha*, the original Kāmadeva. The *vyaṣṭi-kāmadevas* are the Kāmadevas that exists in different universes, *samaṣṭi-kāmadeva* is Pradyumna, and the original Kāmadeva is Nanda-nandana Himself. The material Madana (Kāmadeva) intoxicates all *jīvas*, but when this material Madana receives *darśana* of Śrī Kṛṣṇa's form, which enchants the three worlds, he falls unconscious. *Sākṣāt-manmatha-manmatha*

Kṛṣṇa, who is the transcendental Kāmadeva, manifested such a form to decrease the *gopīs'* suffering.

Śrīla Jīva Gosvāmī writes in the *Krama-sandarbha* that *manmatha-manmatha* signifies that person who infatuates even Madana. Śrī Kṛṣṇacandra displayed His Mohinī-mūrti and even bewildered Mahādeva in his form as Rudra.[6] But actually, Śrī Kṛṣṇa's form as *sākṣāt-manmatha-manmatha* is only displayed in the *rāsa-maṇḍala.* This is confirmed in *Śrī Caitanya-caritāmṛta* (*Ādi-līlā* 5.212–3):

vṛndāvana-purandara śrī-madana-gopāla
rāsa-vilāsī sākṣāt brajendra-kumāra

śrī-rādhā-lalitā-saṅge rāsa-vilāsa
manmatha-manmatha-rūpe yāṅhāra prakāśa

Madana-gopāla, the Lord of Vṛndāvana, is the enjoyer of the *rāsa* dance and is directly the son of the King of Vraja. He enjoys the *rāsa* dance with Śrīmatī Rādhikā, Śrī Lalitā and others. He manifests Himself as the Cupid of Cupids.

Text 18

Śrī Rādhā's meeting with Kṛṣṇa in Nava-Vṛndāvana, Dvārakā, and an expression of a desire for *vraja-bhāva,* is described in *Lalita-mādhava* (10.260):

cirād āśā-mātraṁ tvayi viracayantaḥ sthira-dhiyo
vidadhyur ye vāsaṁ madhurima gabhīre madhu-pure
dadhānaḥ kaiśore vayasi sakhi tāṁ gokula-pate
prapadyethās teṣāṁ paricayam avaśyaṁ nayanayoḥ

[Śrī Rādhā said:] O Śrī Kṛṣṇa, for a long time, persons with fixed intelligence have sustained their lives with the hope that You will

[6] The story of how Mahādeva became bewildered by Śrī Kṛṣṇa's Mohinī-mūrti form is narrated in *Śrīmad-Bhāgavatam,* Eighth Canto, Chapter 12.

one day return. You reside in Madhupurī, which is filled with profound sweetness. O master of Gokula, the adolescent *sakhās* are patiently gazing at Your return path. Therefore, You must give us Your *darśana* without fail.

gabhīra-mādhurya-maya, sei vraja-dhāma haya,
tathā yata sthira-buddhi jana
cira-āśā hṛde dhari', tomāra darśane hari,
basiyāche se saba sajjana

tomāra kaiśora-līlā, hṛdaye varaṇa kailā,
ebe se savāre kṛpā kari'
nayana-gocara haiyā, līlā kara tathā giyā,
ei mātra nivedana kari

Text 19

Suffering pangs of separation from Śrī Kṛṣṇa, Rādhā desires to bring Him back to Vṛndāvana, which is filled with sweet memories. *Lalita-mādhava* (10.261) states:

yā te līlā-rasa-parimalodgāri-vanyā-parītā
dhanyā kṣauṇī vilasati vṛtā māthurī mādhurībhiḥ
tatrāsmābhiś caṭula-paśupī-bhāva-mugdhāntarābhiḥ
saṁvītas taṁ kalaya vadanollāsi veṇur vihāram

Near the highly praised Mathurā is that land of Vṛndāvana, which is full of forests that emit the sublime fragrance of the mellows of Your pastimes (*līlā-rasa*), and which is made splendid with sweetness and beauty. With a smiling face and playing the flute, please sport in that Vṛndāvana with those whose hearts are infatuated with capricious and unpredictable *gopī-bhāva*.

mathurā-maṇḍala majhe, mādhurī-maṇḍita sāje,
dhanya-dhanya vṛndāvana-bhūmi
tāhe tava nitya-līlā, parimala prakāśilā,
acintya-śaktite kṛṣṇa tumi

gopī-bhāve mugdha yata, tomāra śṛṅgāra-rata,
āmā ādi praṇayī-nicaya
āmā-sabe la'ye punaḥ, krīḍā kara anukṣaṇa,
vaṁśī-vādye brajendra-tanaya

Bhajana-rahasya-vṛtti

In his *Lalita-mādhava*, Śrīla Rūpa Gosvāmī gives the following narration. In one *kalpa* Śrī Rādhā was so unable to tolerate the affliction of separation from Kṛṣṇa after He had left for Mathurā, that She jumped into the Yamunā. Yamunā, the daughter of Sūryadeva, then took Śrī Rādhā to her father. Sūryadeva entrusted Her to his friend and devotee, Satrājit, who was childless, and told him, "Her name is Satyabhāmā. Consider Her to be your daughter." Later, upon the instruction of Nārada, King Satrājit sent Satyabhāmā to Śrī Kṛṣṇa's inner quarters in Dvārakā. The wife of Sūrya, Saṁjñā, was the daughter of Viśvakarmā. Through her father, Saṁjñā had previously created the captivating Nava-Vṛndāvana for Satyabhāmā (Śrī Rādhā) in Dvārakā. Rukmiṇī, Śrī Kṛṣṇa's principal queen, kept the extraordinarily charming and beautiful Satyabhāmā hidden in Nava-Vṛndāvana, so that Kṛṣṇa would not see Her. In due course, however, Satyabhāmā did meet with Kṛṣṇa, and the secret that Satyabhāmā is actually Rādhā and Rukmiṇī is actually Candrāvalī was revealed. Thereafter, Rukmiṇī arranged for Satyabhāmā's marriage to Śrī Kṛṣṇa. At the time of the wedding, Yaśodārāṇī, Paurṇamāsī, Mukharā and other Vrajavāsīs were present in Dvārakā.

One day, in this Nava-Vṛndāvana, Kṛṣṇa said to Rādhā, "O Dearest, what more can I do to make You happy?"

Śrī Rādhā replied, "Prāṇeśvara, all the *sakhīs* of Vraja, My cousin-sister Candrāvalī, Mother Vrajeśvarī and everyone else came here, and I met with them. Nonetheless, My earnest request to You is to please leave this abode of opulence, Dvārakā, and in

Your form as a fresh, youthful, expert dancer, wearing the attire of a cowherd boy, sport with Me in the *kuñjas* of Vraja-dhāma, the renowned land of eternal pastimes."

Text 20

Anguished that their blinking prevented them from seeing Kṛṣṇa when they were taking His *darśana*, the *gopīs* curse the person who created eyelids. *Śrīmad-Bhāgavatam* (10.82.39) describes this condition of the *gopīs* at their meeting with Kṛṣṇa in Kurukṣetra:

gopyaś ca kṛṣṇam upalabhya cirād abhīṣṭaṁ
yat-prekṣaṇe dṛśiṣu pakṣma-kṛtaṁ śapanti
dṛgbhir hṛdī-kṛtam alaṁ parirabhya sarvās
tad-bhāvam āpur api nitya-yujāṁ durāpam

[Śrīla Śukadeva Gosvāmī, who was experiencing the mood of the *gopīs* when they saw Śrī Kṛṣṇa at Kurukṣetra, said:] The *vraja-sundarīs*, who cursed the Creator for making eyelids that obstructed their *darśana* of Śrī Kṛṣṇa, now saw Śrī Kṛṣṇa again after a very long time. They took Him from the path of their eyes into their hearts and tightly embraced Him there. They attained that rare absorption that cannot be attained either by *yogīs* or by Rukmiṇī and the other queens of Dvārakā, who are always with Him.

cira-dina kṛṣṇa-āśe, chila gopī vraja-vāse,
kurukṣetre prāṇanāthe pāiyā
animeṣa-netra-dvāre, āni' kṛṣṇe premādhāre,
hṛde āliṅgila mugdha haiyā

āhā se amiya bhāva, anya jane asambhava,
svakīya-kāntāya sudurlabha
gopī vinā ei prema, yena viśodhita hema,
lakṣmī-gaṇe cira asambhava

Bhajana-rahasya-vṛtti

At the time of the solar eclipse, all the Vrajavāsīs arrived at Kurukṣetra, eager to see and meet with Śrī Kṛṣṇa. When the *vraja-ramaṇīs* saw Kṛṣṇa after being separated from Him for so long, they became radiant with bliss, and their hearts and eyes did not move. Those *vraja-gopīs* had been unable to tolerate even a moment's separation caused by the blinking of their eyes, and had thus cursed the creator of eyelids. Who can describe their ecstasy when they again saw Śrī Kṛṣṇa after burning in a raging fire of separation from Him?

The Śrutis say it is impossible to describe in words the happiness derived from merging into Brahman (*brahmānanda*); no one is able to determine the extent of it. This *brahmānanda*, however, is like a firefly before *rasānanda*, the bliss attained by the *mahābhāva-vatī gopīs* in their *prema*-filled service to Kṛṣṇa. The *gopīs'* bodies are composed of *anurāga*, which is caused by the great depth of their relationship with Kṛṣṇa. *Anurāga* is a function of the *hlādinī-śakti* when it is endowed with *saṁvit*. This state is called *sva-saṁvedya*, which means that it can only be known by the person who experiences it.

According to the intensity of *anurāga*, *prema* is determined as perfect (*pūrṇa*), more perfect (*pūrṇatara*) or most perfect (*pūrṇatama*). Compared to the *pūrṇatama anurāga* of the *gopīs*, the bliss of the service performed by Lakṣmī, who sports on the chest of Nārāyaṇa, and also the skill of the queens of Dvārakā in the art of various loving sports, are bland and insipid. Although they exhibit various extraordinary moods, enchanting and beautiful smiles, and so on, they cannot bring Kṛṣṇa's heart under their control. The *vraja-gopīs*, however, who are coloured with dense *anurāga*, as well as with *prema* imbued with *madīya-bhāva* (a feeling that "Kṛṣṇa belongs to me"), control Śrī Kṛṣṇa's heart through their crooked, sidelong glances. Śrīla

Śukadeva Gosvāmipāda's reference to the *gopīs'* extraordinary *prema* in this Text is a sharp cue meant for the *jñānīs*, who meditate on Brahman. In effect he is saying, "O *jñānīs* performing arduous *sādhana*! Fie on you! If you want to make your lives successful, then surrender at the lotus feet of these *gopīs*, who are endowed with *prema*."

Darśana of the *vraja-gopīs' prema-mādhurya* also makes Uddhava yearn to attain it: *vāñchanti yad bhava-bhiyo munayo vayaṁ ca* (*Śrīmad-Bhāgavatam* (10.47.58)). Enchanted by this *prema-mādhurya*, the queens of Dvārakā, who always accompany Kṛṣṇa, pray to attain the fragrance of Śrī Kṛṣṇa's lotus feet, which are coloured with *kuṅkuma* from the *gopīs'* breasts.

One unprecedented experience of ecstasy in separation is called *divyonmāda*. This ocean of *prema* stirs enormous waves that inundate every universe. Its current bewilders the heavenly damsels, whose lustre is like the lotus. It stirs the hearts of earthly beings, invades Satyaloka, and even rebukes the beauty of the land of Vaikuṇṭha. Uddhava, Nārada and others are astonished to see the *prema* engendered by the *gopīs' mahābhāva*, which even stuns the hearts of Rukmiṇī and Satyabhāmā. Despite performing several arduous practices, the *yogīs* are unable to establish in their hearts so much as the effulgence of the nails of Śrī Kṛṣṇa's lotus feet. The *gopīs*, however, very easily and directly adorn their breasts with the lotus feet of youthful Kṛṣṇa, who is the essence of all beauty and lustre, and thus they pacify His fire of lust. Blessed are these masterful *gopīs*.

Text 21

The *gopīs'* intense longing to receive Śrī Kṛṣṇa in their own home, Vṛndāvana, is described in *Śrīmad-Bhāgavatam* (10.82.48):

āhuś ca te nalina-nābha padāravindaṁ
yogeśvarair hṛdi vicintyam agādha-bodhaiḥ
saṁsāra-kūpa-patitottaraṇāvalambaṁ
gehaṁ juṣām api manasy udiyāt sadā naḥ

[At the meeting in Kurukṣetra, Śrī Rādhikā and the prominent *gopīs* said:] O Kamalanābha (You whose navel is like a lotus), great *yogīs* who possess profound intelligence meditate upon Your lotus feet in their hearts. Your lotus feet are the only means of escape for those who have fallen into the well of material existence. O Lord, please give us the benediction that, even when we perform household work, Your lotus feet shall always reside in our hearts and we shall never forget them, even for a moment.

kṛṣṇa he!
agādha-bodha-sampanna, yogeśvara-gaṇa dhanya,
tava pada karuṇa cintana
saṁsāra-patita jana, dharu tava śrī-caraṇa,
kūpa haite uddhāra kāraṇa

āmi vraja-gopa-nārī, nāhi-yogī, na-saṁsārī,
tomā lañā āmāra saṁsāra
mama mana vṛndāvana, rākhi' tathā o'caraṇa,
ei vāñchā pūrāo āmāra

Bhajana-rahasya-vṛtti

At the time of their meeting in Kurukṣetra, Śrī Kṛṣṇa tried to console the *vraja-gopīs*, who had been agitated in separation from Him, by instructing them on *brahma-jñāna* and *yoga*. He said, "I am all-pervading; I am never separated from you all. Endeavour to see Me in your hearts through devout meditation."

Hearing their *priyatama's* instructions on *brahma-jñāna* and *yoga*, the *gopīs* became somewhat angry and said, "O shining sun of *tattva-ācāryas*! Give these instructions on *jñāna-yoga* somewhere else; we very simple and ignorant *gopīs* cannot understand them. It is commendable to give an instruction that is suitable to the listener. When we hear these instructions, our hearts begin to burn. Prāṇanātha, it is true that the hearts of others are the same as their minds, but our hearts are the same as Vṛndāvana, so if You go to Vṛndāvana, we shall consider that You have entered our hearts. Only this will be Your complete mercy, nothing else. Vraja is not only our heart, it is also our home. Unless we meet You there, our life-airs will certainly leave our bodies.

"First, You sent Uddhava to instruct us on *yoga* and *jñāna*, and today You are personally giving us this same instruction. You are *rasika* and supremely compassionate, and You also understand the feelings in our hearts, so why do You speak like this? You know we want to remove our affection for You and place it in worldly enjoyment, but even after a hundred thousand such attempts, we have been unable to do so. Now You are instructing us to meditate upon You. Can You not even slightly consider the persons You are instructing? We *gopīs* are not great *yogīs*, and we can never be satisfied by meditating on Your lotus feet. Hearing You talk like this makes us very angry. O simpleton, where is the possibility of a well of material existence, and desire for deliverance from it, for those who cannot even recall their own bodies? We are always drowning in the deep waters of separation from You, where the crocodiles of lust swallow us. O Prāṇanātha, please save us!

"O wealth of our lives, have You forgotten Vṛndāvana, Govardhana, the banks of the Yamunā, and the *rāsa-līlā* and other pastimes that took place in the *kuñjas*? *Aho*! It is surprising that You have forgotten the *sakhās*, Your parents and all the other Vrajavāsīs. It is our misfortune. We are not unhappy for ourselves; we are unhappy for Vrajeśvarī Yaśodā-maiyā. It tears our hearts apart to see her so forlorn. We may or may not have a relationship with You, but You are related to Yaśodā-maiyā by blood, as Your body is made of her blood. You may forget that relationship, but it cannot be removed. Whether You come to Vṛndāvana or not is up to You, but why have You kept the Vrajavāsīs alive? Is it just to make them suffer again and again? Yes, if You want to keep them alive, then quickly come to Vṛndāvana. This royal attire of Yours, the elephants and horses, Your association with the officers of the king of this place, and this foreign land, do not slightly befit the Vrajavāsīs. Although we are unable to abandon Vṛndāvana, we could not remain alive without seeing You. You are the life of Vraja, the wealth of Vrajarāja's life and also the very life of our lives. Quickly return to Vṛndāvana and protect the lives of everyone."

Text 22

Śrīmad-Bhāgavatam (10.82.40) describes Śrī Kṛṣṇa's conversation with the *gopīs* that occurred in a solitary place:

bhagavāṁs tās tathā-bhūtā
vivikta upasaṅgataḥ
āśliṣyānāmayaṁ pṛṣṭvā
prahasann idam abravīt

When Śrī Kṛṣṇa saw that the *gopīs* had attained oneness (*tādātmya*) with Him, He went with them to a secluded place. After embracing them to His heart and inquiring about their well-being, He laughed and spoke as follows.

vivikte laiyā, gopī āliṅgiyā,
preme marma-kathā kaya
kṛṣṇa gopī prīti, mahiṣīra tati,
dekhiyā āścarya haya

Bhajana-rahasya-vṛtti

When Śrī Kṛṣṇa heard Śrī Rādhā's anguished talks of separation, He remembered His unlimited, honest love for the Vrajavāsīs and became very restless. Considering Himself indebted to them, He began to console them by addressing Śrī Rādhā. "Priyatamā, accept the following as truth. Remembering You, I burn day and night in a fire of separation. No one knows the extent of My unbearable pain. The Vrajavāsīs, My parents and the *sakhās* are My very life, and among them, the *gopīs* are directly My life. And You are the life of My life. What more can I say? I am always subservient to Your unconditional love. Misfortune is very strong, and no one can do anything about it. This misfortune has separated Me from You, keeping Me in a distant country.

"It is true that the beloved cannot remain alive without the association of the lover, and that the lover cannot live without the beloved, but neither will die because each thinks, 'If I die, his condition of separation will be the same as mine.' *Aho*! The faithful beloved and the truly affectionate lover think of each other's welfare even in separation. They never think of their own sorrows and sufferings, but always want their beloved to be happy. This kind of loving couple meet each other again very quickly.

"You do not know that daily I worship Bhagavān Śrī Nārāyaṇa to protect Your life. By His potency, I come to Vṛndāvana from this distant country every day to meet with You and sport with You in various ways, but You think this is only a vision. Beloved Rādhā, it is My good fortune that Your love for Me is unlimited and incomparable. This *prema* will quickly pull Me back to You in Vṛndāvana. In just a few days, after killing the remaining enemies of the Yādavas, I will return to Vṛndāvana. Consider that I have already come."

Text 23

Śrī Kṛṣṇa spoke the following words to give the *gopīs* consolation. *Śrīmad-Bhāgavatam* (10.82.44) states:

mayi bhaktir hi bhūtānām
amṛtatvāya kalpate
diṣṭyā yad āsīn mat-sneho
bhavatīnāṁ mad-āpanaḥ

Sakhīs, it is greatly fortunate that you have developed *prema* for Me, by which one can attain Me. Loving devotional service unto Me qualifies living entities to attain My supremely blissful eternal abode.

āmāte ye prema-bhakti parama amṛta
tava snehe niravadhi tava dāsye rata

Bhajana-rahasya-vṛtti

After a long separation, the *gopīs* met with Śrī Kṛṣṇa at Kurukṣetra. There, in a solitary place, Śrī Kṛṣṇa consoled the beautiful, lotus-eyed women of Vraja by embracing and kissing them, wiping the tears from their eyes, and inquiring about their health and well-being. He said, "O *sakhīs*, in this long separation you have remembered Me! You are convinced that I am ungrateful, but you do not consider Me cruel, do you? Without doubt, Bhagavān is the cause of the living entities' meeting and separating. Just as blades of grass, cotton fluff and granules of dust meet and again separate due to the wind, similarly everyone meets and separates according to the desire of Īśvara, the Supreme Controller. If you say that I am that Īśvara who arranges meeting and separation, then there is no reason for your sorrow, because by good fortune you have achieved that *prema* by which I can be attained. Devotion performed unto Me is capable of giving living entities the eternal supreme abode, but your loving affection for

Me makes Me unable to remain far away from you. Rather, it attracts Me to you."

In his *Krama-sandarbha* commentary, Śrīla Jīva Gosvāmipāda says, "Through the practice of *sādhana-bhakti*, the living entity can attain the *dhāma* of Bhagavān according to his desire and constitutional nature. Being pleased with such devotees, Śrī Kṛṣṇa accepts their service. The *sneha*, *rāga*, *anurāga* and *mahābhāva* of the *vraja-devīs* assume the highest excellence and therefore Śrī Kṛṣṇa is controlled by the *gopīs*. Pure devotional service and affection etc., which are endowed with possessiveness, attract Śrī Kṛṣṇa. One should understand that affection for Bhagavān is the topmost way to attract Him."

Śrī Kṛṣṇa again speaks. "The sky and the other four primary elements are in all material objects in their beginning, middle and end stages. Similarly, I exist in the beginning and end of all objects, and inside and outside of them also. I am not, therefore, separated from you in any way. You are suffering from a false pain of separation – due to a simple lack of discrimination. Your bodies and life-airs are all situated in My *svarūpa*. Try to realise this truth and meditate in your hearts as *yogīs* do, then your pain of separation will be removed."

Upon hearing this spiritual teaching from the lotus mouth of their *prāṇa-vallabha* Śrī Kṛṣṇa, the *gopīs* began to speak, their lips quivering in anger born of affection. "O Nalinanābha (one with an extremely beautiful lotus-like navel), You want to please our hearts by instructing us in knowledge of *bhagavat-tattva*, but this knowledge does not enter our ears. We are already engaged in relishing the nectar of Your beauty through our eyes. Where is the time to hear these *tattvas*?"

Or by use of the word *nalinanābha* the *vraja-devīs* insinuate, "O Kṛṣṇa, a lotus has grown from Your navel. This is a good thing, but just as the root of the lotus is connected with water and mud, Your intelligence has also become soiled. Please give these instructions to ignorant persons only, not to us. Does one give the food of animals to human beings? Now You are claiming Yourself to be Bhagavān. If the Vrajavāsīs hear this, You will become a laughing stock. *Agādha-bodhair yogeśvarair hṛdi vicintya.* Please give this *jñāna-yoga* to profoundly intelligent *yogīs*, endowed with *tattva-jñāna*, who are unable to meditate on Your feet."

Or the *gopīs* speak reproachfully, saying, "O Kṛṣṇa, we have heard from Paurṇamāsī that Brahmā was born from the lotus emanating from Your navel. By the association of that *jñānī*, Brahmā, Your intelligence has also greatly decreased." ("*Yasya yat-saṅgatiḥ puṁso maṇivat syāt sa tad-guṇaḥ* – a person develops the qualities of the company he keeps, just as a crystal reflects the colour of those objects which are brought into its proximity.")

Or the *gopīs* angrily say, "O Kṛṣṇa, only great *yogīs* endowed with profound intelligence are capable of meditating on Your lotus feet. We are ignorant cowherd girls with restless minds, and it is impossible for us to meditate on Your lotus feet."

Or the *gopīs* reveal the inner feelings of their hearts to Śrī Kṛṣṇa: "O Kṛṣṇa, what to speak of meditating on Your lotus feet, now the mere memory of them distresses us. We fear placing Your lotus feet, which are softer than a newly-blossomed lotus, on our hard breasts.

yat te sujāta-caraṇāmburuhaṁ staneṣu
bhītāḥ śanaiḥ priya dadhīmahi karkaśeṣu
tenāṭavīm aṭasi tad vyathate na kiṁ svit
kūrpādibhir bhramati dhīr bhavad-āyuṣāṁ naḥ

Śrīmad-Bhāgavatam (10.31.19)

[The *gopīs* said:] A fear has arisen in our minds that Your very soft lotus feet may be pained by being placed on our hard breasts. Our minds are agitated by such thoughts, as if tormented by a stinging scorpion.

Or they say, "O Kṛṣṇa, the nineteen signs marked on Your lotus feet have appeared on the screen of our hearts, reminding us of our previous pastimes in the *kuñjas.* The flag on Your lotus feet reminds us of Your defeat by Śrī Rādhā in amorous sports (*keli-vilāsa*). You said that You would take Her victory flag on Your shoulder and wander here and there. The sign of the goad on Your feet reminds us that Śrī Rādhā, who is likened to an elephant-driver, brings such an intoxicated elephant as You under Her control with Her goad of *prema.* You Yourself have admitted, '*Na pāraye 'haṁ niravadya-saṁyujām* – O *gopīs,* I cannot repay you.' "

Or the *gopīs* say, "You assumed Your form of Mohinī to cheat the demons out of nectar, and then You arranged for the demigods to relish it. Similarly, by instructing the *yogīs* on meditation, You deprive them of the secret of love. But we are not like the demon or *yogī* who is deprived of the confidential secret of *prema-tattva.*"

Saṁsāra-kūpa-patitottaraṇāvalambaṁ te padāravindam – With affectionate anger, the *gopīs* say, "O Kṛṣṇa, You also sent Uddhava to Vraja with Your collection of *tattva-jñāna,* but instead of alleviating our pain of separation, Your message simply increased it. And now You again are giving us that same ridiculous instruction, which is suitable for a child. Brahmā and other great *yogīs* can be delivered from this material existence by meditating on Your lotus feet, but we have not fallen into the well of material existence. Rather, we have fallen into the ocean of separation from You and cannot even recollect our own bodies. We gave up attachment to our homes for Your happiness.

How, then, is it possible for us to have fallen into the well of material existence? Rather, we have fallen into the ocean of separation, and the *timiṅgila* fish of lust wants to swallow us. Therefore, O crown jewel of experts in amorous sports (*vidagdha-śiromaṇi*), do not instruct us on *jñāna-yoga*. Please just give us the pleasure of Your association to deliver us from this ocean of separation. Our hearts run towards Vṛndāvana, because Vṛndāvana's trees, creepers, fruits, flowers and every particle of dust are inseparably studded with memories of You. If Your lotus feet appear in Vṛndāvana, they will also appear in our hearts."

Gehaṁ juṣām api manasy udiyāt – Distressed, the *vraja-devīs* say, "O Kṛṣṇa, we have again met with You here at Kurukṣetra, and our meeting with You is like a first meeting, but our minds are stolen away by memories of Vṛndāvana. Here there is *lokāraṇya*, a "forest" of people, and the uproarious sounds of elephants, horses and chariots. In Vṛndāvana there is *puṣpāraṇya*, a forest of flowers, where only the sweet sounds of bumblebees and cuckoos are heard. Vṛndāvana is very pleasant and filled with music and song. It resounds with the sweet sounds of *śukas*, *sārīs*, peacocks and cuckoos. Here in Kurukṣetra, You are dressed in royal attire and are accompanied by *kṣatriya* warriors who are adorned with a variety of weapons. In Vṛndāvana, however, where You wore the attire of a *gopa*, You held a beautiful flute to Your lips. On Your head was a peacock feather crown, on Your ears were earrings made from the buds of *campa* flowers, and You were decorated with creepers, leaves and minerals like *gairika* (red ochre)."

Śrī Rādhā says, "O lotus-eyed one, the hearts of others are non-different from their minds, and they are unable to separate their hearts from their minds. But My mind *is* Vṛndāvana. They are one; there is no difference between them. Being Vṛndāvana, My mind is the sporting ground for My *prāṇakānta*. Previously, as the topmost connoisseur of mellows (*rasikendra-śiromaṇi*), You performed playful pastimes, filled with the sweetness of *rasa*, with Me there. My mind is eager to meet with You again in that Vṛndāvana."

prāṇanātha, śuna mora satya nivedana
vraja – āmāra sadana, tāhāṅ tomāra saṅgama,
nā pāile nā rahe jīvana

Śrī Caitanya-caritāmṛta (*Madhya-līlā* 13.138)

[Śrī Rādhā said:] Prāṇanātha, hear My true submission. My home is Vṛndāvana, and I wish to have Your association there. If not, it will be very difficult for Me to maintain My life.

Text 24

Pastimes during the first part of the night (*pradoṣa-līlā*) are described in *Govinda-līlāmṛta* (21.1):

rādhāṁ sālīgaṇāntām asita-sita-niśā-yogya-veśāṁ pradoṣe
dūtyā vṛndopadeśād abhisṛta-yamunā-tīra-kalpāga-kuñjām
kṛṣṇaṁ gopaiḥ sabhāyāṁ vihita-guṇi-kalālokanaṁ snigdha-mātrā
yatnād ānīya saṁśāyitam atha nibhṛtaṁ prāpta-kuñjaṁ smarāmi

In the evening, Śrī Vṛṣabhānu-nandinī cooks some preparations and sends them with Her *sakhīs* to Nanda-bhavana. Yaśodārāṇī is very affectionate and loving to Śrī Rādhā's maidservants. She feeds these preparations to the two brothers, Rāma and Kṛṣṇa, as well as to the other family members. Maiyā places the remaining *prasāda* in the hands of the maidservants to give to Śrī Rādhā. Kundalatā or Dhaniṣṭhā indicate the whereabouts of that night's meeting place to the maidservants, who give Śrī Rādhā the news from Nanda-bhavana as well as the remaining *prasāda*. They tell

Her, "Svāminī, Your *priyatama* lovingly ate the *manohara-laḍḍu* You made." Describing the mood with which Kṛṣṇa took each preparation, the *sakhīs* serve the rest of the *prasāda* and prepare Svāminī for Her rendezvous (*abhisāra*).

rādhā vṛndā upadeśe, yamunopakūladeśe,
sāṅketika kuñje abhisāre
sitāsita-niśā-yogya, dhari' veśa kṛṣṇa-bhogya,
sakhī-saṅge sānanda antare

gopa-sabhā-mājhe hari, nānā-guṇa-kalā heri',
mātṛ-yatne karila śayana
rādhā-saṅga soṅariyā, nibhṛte bāhira haiyā,
prāpta-kuñja kariye smaraṇa

Bhajana-rahasya-vṛtti

In accordance with Śrī Vṛndā-devī's indication, Śrīmatī Rādhikā goes to a *keli-kuñja* on the bank of the Yamunā for Her *abhisāra* with Kṛṣṇa, bringing a few faithful maidservants or some *priya-narma-sakhīs* with Her. These most beloved *sakhīs* dress Kiśorī in black cloth on dark nights and in white on moonlit nights, and then they very carefully and blissfully take Her for *abhisāra*.

At that time, Śrī Kṛṣṇa is watching a charming performance of music, singing, magical tricks, drama and other arts in the assembly of the cowherds. Later, He hears Yaśodā-maiyā sing Him a lullaby and He feigns sleep. Then, to attain the association of Kiśorī, He slips away from the royal palace and proceeds alone to the *kuñja* where They will meet.

The qualified *sādhaka*, while performing *harināma-kīrtana*, will lovingly remember these pastimes of the seventh *yāma*.

Thus ends the *Saptama-yāma-sādhana*,
Pradoṣa-kālīya-bhajana, of *Śrī Bhajana-rahasya*.

8

Aṣṭama-yāma-sādhana

Rātri-līlā – prema-bhajana sambhoga

(from midnight to three-and-a-half *praharas* of the night: approximately 00.00 A.M. – 3.30 A.M.)

Text 1

Steadiness in perfection – that is, one-pointed dependence on Kṛṣṇa – is described in *Śikṣāṣṭaka* (8):

āśliṣya vā pāda-ratāṁ pinaṣṭu mām
adarśanān marma-hatāṁ karotu vā
yathā tathā vā vidadhātu lampaṭo
mat-prāna-nāthas tu sa eva nāparaḥ

Let that debauchee (Kṛṣṇa) tightly embrace this maidservant, who is devoted to serving Him, and thus delight Me. Or, let Him trample Me under His feet, or break My heart by not giving Me His *darśana*. He may do whatever He desires. Even if He sports with His other beloveds directly in front of Me, He is still My *prāṇanātha*. In My heart there is none other than Him.

āmi – kṛṣṇa-pada-dāsī, teṅho – rasa-sukha-rāśi,
āliṅgiya kare ātmasātha
kibā nā deya daraśana, jārena mora tanu-mana,
tabu tiṅho mora prāṇanātha

Bhajana-rahasya-vṛtti

In relation to this Text, *Śrī Caitanya-caritāmṛta* (*Antya-līlā* 20.49–52) states:

sakhi he, śuna mora manera niścaya
kibā anurāga kare, kibā duḥkha diyā māre,
mora prāṇeśvara kṛṣṇa – anya naya

chāḍi' anya nārī-gaṇa, mora vaśa tanu-mana,
mora saubhāgya prakaṭa kariyā
tā-sabāre deya pīḍā, āmā-sane kare krīḍā,
sei nārī-gaṇe dekhāñā

kibā teṅho lampaṭa, śaṭha, dhṛṣṭa, sakapaṭa,
anya nārī-gaṇa kari' sātha
more dite manaḥ-pīḍā, mora āge kare krīḍā,
tabu teṅho – mora prāṇanātha

nā gaṇi āpana-duḥkha, sabe vāñchi tāṅra sukha,
tāṅra sukha – āmāra tātparya
more yadi diyā duḥkha, tāṅra haila mahā-sukha,
sei duḥkha – mora sukha-varya

[Śrīmatī Rādhikā said:] *Sakhī*, I am a maidservant of the lotus feet of *rasika-śekhara* Śrī Kṛṣṇa, who is an ocean of happiness. He may make Me joyful by tightly embracing Me, or He may trample Me beneath His feet. He may make Me happy by mercifully giving Me His *darśana*, or He may break My heart by not appearing before Me. He may not understand My inner desires; nonetheless, He is My *prāṇanātha*, the Lord of My life. *Sakhī*, I have decided that He may love Me and display My fortune by abandoning other beautiful ladies in order that He be controlled by Me; He may make them unhappy by sporting with Me in front of them, or, He may be deceitful, arrogant, duplicitous and debauched, and, just to provoke Me, He may torment Me by sporting before Me with other ladies. Still, He and only He is My *prāṇanātha*. I am not slightly concerned for My own suffering; I only desire His happiness, always. The goal of My life is to make Him happy in every way. If He feels happiness by giving Me distress, that distress is My greatest happiness.

Text 2

A devotee who remembers these pastimes is transcendental, being filled with eternality, knowledge and bliss (*sac-cid-ānanda*) just like Bhagavān. A Vaiṣṇava's body is non-different from Śrī Kṛṣṇa's body. In this regard, in *Śrīmad-Bhāgavatam* (11.29.34), Śrī Kṛṣṇa says to Uddhava:

martyo yadā tyakta-samasta-karmā
niveditātmā vicikīrṣito me
tadāmṛtatvaṁ pratipadyamāno
mayātma-bhūyāya ca kalpate vai

When a person abandons all fruitive activities and fully surrenders himself to Me, he becomes a recipient of special *prema*. This is a result of My merciful treatment towards him. I release him from old age and grant him entrance into My eternal pastimes, where he serves Me eternally.

sarva karma teyāgiyā, more ātma nivediyā,
yei kare āmāra sevana
amṛtatva-dharma pāñā, līlā-madhye praveśiyā,
āmā-saha karaye ramaṇa

Bhajana-rahasya-vṛtti

Having explained *sambandha-tattva* (the *jīva's* relationship with Bhagavān), *abhidheya-tattva* (the process to attain the supreme goal) and *prayojana-tattva* (the supreme goal) to His dear devotee Uddhava, here Bhagavān Śrī Kṛṣṇa describes the situation of a pure devotee who is exclusively surrendered to Him.

As the mortal *jīva* wanders throughout this material existence, he attains the association of Śrī Kṛṣṇa's eternal associates according to the extent of his *sukṛti.* Due to his association with pure devotees, the devotee relinquishes the desire for *nitya-karma* and *naimittika-karma* (daily and occasionally prescribed duties), sense enjoyment and liberation, and he cultivates pure *bhakti.* The darkness of his ignorance is removed by the light of *bhakti*, just as darkness is removed by the light of the sun. The devotee then serves Bhagavān with a full sense of possessiveness (*mamatā*) towards Him, and Bhagavān bestows upon that devotee a spiritual body appropriate for rendering eternal service to Him. That means He bestows a body, qualities, activities, service and so on according to the particular mood of the *sādhaka.*

As a result of associating with *svajātīya-snigdhāśaya-bhaktas*, affectionate devotees who are of the same mood as himself and more advanced, the *sādhaka* who is endowed with *mādhurya-rati* attains a desire in his heart to render service in the amorous mellow. And, by practising *bhakti* and by the mercy of devotees, he attains the state of perfection (*siddha-avasthā*). Such a devotee performs his *sādhana* internally under the guidance of Lalitā and other *sakhīs*, and by their mercy he receives bodily features equal to those of the *nitya-siddha-mañjarīs* and also obtains the pleasure of directly rendering *kuñja-sevā* in Śrī Vraja-dhāma. After this attainment of *svarūpa-siddhi*, the *jīva* achieves *vastu-siddhi* and for eternity serves Śrī Rādhā in the eternal land of Vṛndāvana. Such service is only attained by *sādhakas* in *mādhurya-rati*; it is not attained by others.

Text 3

Steadiness in *bhajana* is described in *Manaḥ-śikṣā* (2):

na dharmaṁ nādharmaṁ śruti-gaṇa-niruktaṁ kila kuru
vraje rādhā-kṛṣṇa-pracura-paricaryām iha tanu
śacī-sūnuṁ nandīśvara-pati-sutatve guru-varaṁ
mukunda-preṣṭhatve smara param ajasraṁ nanu manaḥ

O my dear mind, please do not perform either the *dharma*, which produces piety, or *adharma*, which gives rise to sin, that are mentioned in the Śrutis. Rather, render profuse loving service to Śrī Rādhā-Kṛṣṇa Yugala, who the Śrutis have ascertained to be supremely worshipful above all others and the topmost Truth. Always remember Śacīnandana Śrī Caitanya Mahāprabhu, who is endowed with the sentiments and bodily lustre of Śrī Rādhā, knowing Him to be non-different from Śrī Nanda-nandana; and always remember *śrī gurudeva*, knowing him to be most dear to Śrī Mukunda.

śruti-ukta-dharmādharma, vidhi-niṣedha-karmākarma,
chāḍi' bhaja rādhā-kṛṣṇa-pada
gaurāṅge śrī-kṛṣṇa jāna, guru kṛṣṇa-preṣtha māna,
ei bhāva tomāra sampada

Bhajana-rahasya-vṛtti

Dharma and *adharma* are defined in the Śrutis and literature pursuant to the Śrutis, such as the Smṛtis. Every activity a person performs falls into one of these two categories. If people were prohibited from performing *dharma* and *adharma*, it would be impossible for them to live a moment more. Therefore, Śrīla Raghunātha dāsa Gosvāmī has not prohibited all of the activities performed by the sense organs. Those who are ignorant are meant to perform *dharma* and auspicious activities, whereas learned *jīvas* who have attained knowledge of their spiritual identity are instructed to act on the platform of *ātma-rati*, or *kṛṣṇa-rati*. In other words they are instructed to perform loving service to Śrī Rādhā-Kṛṣṇa Yugala. The *sādhaka* should perform all his activities in a mood of service to Bhagavān. Householder devotees should worship deities at home and perform the activities of earning money, maintaining their family members and protecting their assets and home as services to their Lord. One should consider oneself a mere servant of the Lord.

Text 4

Śrīla Sanātana Gosvāmī's mood of humility is reflected in the following statement, which is imbued with the firm hope (*āśā-bandha*) characteristic of a *jāta-rati-bhakta* devoted to *bhajana*. This verse is quoted by Śrīla Rūpa Gosvāmī in *Bhakti-rasāmṛta-sindhu* (1.3.35):

na premā śravaṇādi-bhaktir api vā yogo 'tha vā vaiṣṇavo
jñānaṁ vā śubha-karma vā kiyad aho saj-jātir apy asti vā
hīnārthādhika-sādhake tvayi tathāpy acchedya-mūlā satī
he gopī-jana-vallabha vyathayate hā hā mad-āśaiva mām

My heart is devoid of *prema* for You, and I am not qualified to perform *bhakti* by hearing and chanting. I possess no knowledge, pious activities or qualifications of a Vaiṣṇava, nor have I taken birth in a high-class family. I am, therefore, unqualified in every respect. Nevertheless, O beloved of the *gopīs*, Your mercy also falls upon the lowest of the low. This firm hope of attaining You is making me very anxious.

śravaṇādi-bhakti, prema-bhakti, yoga hīna
jñāna-yoga-karma hīna, saj-janma-vihīna
kāṅgālera nātha tumi rādhā-prāṇa-dhana
tomā-pade dṛḍha-āśāya vyakulita mana

Bhajana-rahasya-vṛtti

Humility is the foundation of *bhakti*, and it is by humility that *bhakti* increases. Śrīla Sanātana Gosvāmī defines humility as follows: "When a person has all good qualities but feelings arise in his heart of being unqualified, wretched and inferior, this is called humility. In other words, humility is the utmost anxiety to attain Bhagavān. A person with humility is without false ego even though he possesses all good qualities." Only humility can attract Kṛṣṇa's mercy, and genuine humility only appears when *prema* is fully ripe. To attain such humility the *jāta-rati-sādhaka* prays, "O Prāṇa-vallabha, I have no attachment for You and am incapable of performing *śravaṇa* and the other practices in the ninefold path of devotion. My meditation is not unbroken like that of the *jñānīs*. I do not perform service according to *varṇāśrama*, I have not taken birth in a high-class family and I have not performed any pious activities. My hope is solely dependent on Your mercy, which all the *mahājanas* glorify. You are the master of the wretched, and You bestow Your mercy upon them."

Śrīla Sanātana Gosvāmī possesses all virtues, yet filled with humility, he spoke this verse. Although a *jāta-rati-sādhaka* performs abundant service, he thinks, "I perform no *sevā* at all." The *sādhaka's* only desire is to perform *prema-sevā*, pure *bhakti* that is devoid of *karma* and *jñāna*. This is *svarūpa-siddha-bhakti*, and it is attained only through *śravaṇa*, *kīrtana* and so forth. If a person is too attached to fruitive activities, whatever little devotion is in his heart disappears. And if someone desires material gain, adoration and fame, Bhakti-devī neglects that person. *Bhakti* only increases in the heart of one who is humble and sincere, and only humility that is thoroughly devoid of pride causes the flowing current of mercy to swell.

The method of performing *nāma-sādhana* is to chant the holy name while feeling more humble than a blade of grass. *Śrī Caitanya-caritāmṛta* (*Ādi-līlā* 17.31–3) says:

tṛṇād api sunīcena
taror api sahiṣṇunā
amāninā mānadena
kīrtanīyaḥ sadā hariḥ

ūrdhva-bāhu kari' kahoṅ, śuna sarva-loka
nāma-sūtre gāṅthi' para kaṇṭhe ei śloka

prabhu-ājñāya kara ei śloka ācaraṇa
avaśya pāibe tabe śrī-kṛṣṇa-caraṇa

"Considering oneself to be even lower and more worthless than insignificant grass that has been trampled beneath everyone's feet, being more tolerant than a tree, being prideless and offering respect to everyone according to their respective positions, one should continually chant the holy name of Śrī Hari. Raising My hands, I declare, 'Everyone please hear Me! For continuous remembrance, string this *śloka* on the thread of the holy name and wear it around your neck.'" One must strictly follow the principles given by Śrī Caitanya Mahāprabhu in this verse. If one simply follows in the footsteps of Śrīman Mahāprabhu and the Gosvāmīs, he will certainly achieve the ultimate goal of life, the lotus feet of Śrī Kṛṣṇa.

Text 5

The identity of a perfected soul (*siddha-paricaya*) is described in *Śrī Rādhā-rasa-sudhā-nidhi* (53):

dukūlaṁ vibhrāṇām atha kucataṭe kañcu-kapaṭaṁ
prasādaṁ svāminyāḥ svakara-tala-dattaṁ praṇayataḥ
sthitāṁ nityaṁ pārśve vividha-paricaryaika-caturāṁ
kiśorīm ātmānaṁ caṭula-parakīyāṁ nu kalaye

When will I remain near Svāminī eternally, intent on serving Her in various ways? When, wearing Her silken cloth and bodice that She affectionately gave me with Her own hands, will I be able to count myself as a clever and very beautiful *kiśorī*?

siddha-deha gopī āmi śrī-rādhikā kiṅkarī
rādhā-prasādita vastra-kañculikā pari

gṛhe pati parihari, kiśorī-vayase
rādhā-pada sevi kuñje rajanī-divase

Bhajana-rahasya-vṛtti

The *rasika-ācāryas* conclude that when the *sādhaka* enters the stage of perfection, he attains that *bhāva* upon which he meditated when he was in the stage of *sādhana*. The cherished desire of the Gauḍīya Vaiṣṇavas is to possess the self-identity (*abhimāna*) of being a maidservant of Śrī Rādhā. The appropriate *sādhana* to attain one's *svarūpa* and one's service to Śrī Rādhā is revealed by the spiritual master.

ātmānaṁ cintayet tatra
tāsāṁ madhye manoramām
rūpa-yauvana-sampannāṁ
kiśorīṁ pramadākṛtim

Sanat-kumāra-saṁhitā

sakhīnāṁ saṅginī-rūpām
ātmānaṁ vāsanā-mayīm
ājñā-sevā-parāṁ tat tat
kṛpālaṅkāra-bhūṣitām

Prema-bhakti-candrikā (5.11)

A *sādhaka* of *rāga-mārga* should internally perceive himself to be one of the young, beautiful *gopī* beloveds of Śrī Kṛṣṇa. He should meditate on his desired *svarūpa* as a female companion of Śrī Rādhā's maidservants, such as Śrī Rūpa Mañjarī and Śrī Rati Mañjarī, and adorned in the ornaments mercifully given by them, he should completely absorb himself in service to Śrī Rādhā-Mādhava according to their instructions.

The word *cintayet* in the above verse from the *Sanat-kumāra-saṁhitā* means that the *sādhaka* should nourish the following firm conception: "I am a *kiśorī* with the same moods and qualities as the *nitya-siddha-mañjarīs* of Śrī Rādhā." A Gauḍīya Vaiṣṇava *sādhaka* in deep meditation will maintain the conception that, "I am not this body, these senses and so forth; I am a maidservant of Śrī Rādhā and I am endowed with qualities such as the beauty and *rasa* of a *gopa-kiśorī*." This deep meditation on the soul (*ātma-cintana*) will quickly result in his giving up identification with the material body, and he will attain *svarūpa-siddhi*.

In this Text 5, Śrīla Prabodhānanda Sarasvatī describes the method of becoming a beautiful young *gopa-kiśorī*: "I will meditate on myself as a *kiśorī* adorned with the silken cloth and bodice that Svāminī gave me with Her own hands." The remnant objects Svāminī gives with Her own hands carry the mood of Her affectionate compassion, and the cloth and bodice remnants are connected with the sweet mood of the Divine Couple's amorous play (*vilāsa*). Absorption in one's internal *svarūpa* is accompanied by the rendering of *sevā* and a feeling of intimacy. For this reason, Śrīla Prabodhānanda Sarasvatī mentions the form of a clever *kiśorī* who is always close to Svāminī and intent on performing various services to Her. *Sevā-rasa*, which establishes one's *svarūpa*, takes place as a person serves Svāminī, who is the life and soul of Her maidservants. The main goal of the Gauḍīya Vaiṣṇavas is to become a *rādhā-dāsī*, a maidservant of Śrī Rādhā. The *sādhaka* remains ever fixed on this goal, just as the position of the pole star is fixed in the sky. By the mercy of *śrī guru*, the *sādhaka* is introduced to his eternal identity as a maidservant of Śrī Rādhā. Upon attaining that, he abandons his bodily identity as a servant of *māyā*, and he completely maintains the self-identity of being a *rādhā-dāsī*.

In his song *Śrī Rādhā-kṛṣṇa-pada-kamale*, Śrīla Bhaktivinoda Ṭhākura prays: "*lalitā sakhīra, ayogyā kiṅkarī vinoda dhariche pāya* – Vinoda, the unqualified maidservant of Lalitā Sakhī, clasps the lotus feet of the Divine Couple."

Text 6

The method of *bhajana* and place of residence of one who possesses the mood described in the previous Text is explained in *Upadeśāmṛta* (8):

tan-nāma-rūpa-caritādi-sukīrtanānu-
smṛtyoḥ krameṇa rasanā-manasī niyojya
tiṣṭhan vraje tad-anurāgi-janānugāmī
kālaṁ nayed akhilam ity upadeśa-sāram

While living in Vraja as a follower of those who are attached to Śrī Kṛṣṇa, one should utilise all his time by gradually transferring the absorption of his tongue and mind from matters other than Kṛṣṇa to the chanting and remembering of narrations of Śrī Kṛṣṇa's name, form, qualities and pastimes. This is the essence of all instruction.

kṛṣṇa-nāma-rūpa-guṇa-līlā-saṅkīrtana
anusmṛti-krame jihvā-manaḥ-saṁyojana
kuñje vāsa anurāgi-jana-dāsī haiyā
aṣṭa-kāla bhaji līlā majiyā majiyā

Bhajana-rahasya-vṛtti

The essential meaning of this Text is that, in accordance with his own *bhāva*, the *sādhaka* should remember his beloved Śrī Kṛṣṇa as well the devotees of Śrī Kṛṣṇa who possess the same mood as himself. One should reside in Vraja-maṇḍala while being immersed in chanting names of Śrī Kṛṣṇa, such as Rādhā-ramaṇa and Rādhā-rāsa-bihārī, that are favourable to his own *bhāva*, and in hearing narrations of pastimes connected to those names. If it is not possible to reside in Vraja physically, one should reside there mentally.

This Text explains both the process of *bhajana* and the best place to perform *bhajana*. No place is superior to Vraja-maṇḍala for performing *bhajana* of Śrī Rādhā-Kṛṣṇa. The most exalted devotees, such as Brahmā and Uddhava, therefore pray to take birth in Vraja as a blade of grass or a plant.

Text 7

The *rāgānuga-bhakta's* method of *bhajana* is to perform his desired perfectional service (*siddha-sevā*) under the constant guidance of the *guru*. *Bhakti-rasāmṛta-sindhu* (1.2.294) states:

kṛṣṇaṁ smaran janaṁ cāsya
preṣṭhaṁ nija-samīhitam
tat-tat-kathā-rataś cāsau
kuryād vāsaṁ vraje sadā

The devotee who desires *rāgānuga-bhakti* should constantly remember Vṛndāvana-Kṛṣṇa, along with Kṛṣna's beloved associates who have the same mood as himself. He should remain engrossed in hearing and speaking narrations of their pastimes and always reside in Vraja.

smari' kṛṣṇa, nija-kṛṣṇa-preṣṭha-vraja-jana
kṛṣṇa-kathā-rata, vraja-vāsa anukṣaṇa

Bhajana-rahasya-vṛtti

The process of *rāgānuga-bhakti* is that the *sādhaka* should remember his beloved and worshipful, ever-youthful Nanda-nandana Śrī Kṛṣṇa, as well as the dear *sakhīs*, such as Śrī Rūpa Mañjarī, who possess the mood that he cherishes. He should hear narrations about them while remaining a resident of Śrī Nandarāja's Vraja; that is, by physically residing in Vṛndāvana, Govardhana, Rādhā-kuṇḍa and other such places if he is able to do so. Or, if not, he should reside there mentally. These places are saturated with *śṛṅgāra-rasa*, and in *bhajana*, they are stimuli (*uddīpaka*) for *rasa* and *līlā*. Therefore, Śrī Bhaktivinoda

Ṭhākura prays: "*rādhā-kuṇḍa-taṭa-kuñja-kuṭīra, govardhana-parvata yāmuna-tīra* – a small cottage within a *kuñja* on the bank of Rādhā-kuṇḍa, Govardhana Hill, the banks of the Yamunā... ."

Such *sādhakas* should remember the narrations of Kṛṣṇa's dear associates, the *rasika* devotees of Vraja who are favourable for his *bhāva*, such as Śrī Rūpa Mañjarī and other *sakhīs*, and he should serve them. In this way, their moods will be transmitted into his heart. An example of this is Śrīla Raghunātha dāsa Gosvāmī who, under the guidance of Śrī Svarūpa Dāmodara and Śrīla Rūpa Gosvāmī, attained the summit of the *rasamayī-upāsanā* (devotional service in amorous love) of Vraja.

Text 8

The *premi-bhakta's* behaviour, characteristics and activities are expressed in *Śrīmad-Bhāgavatam* (11.2.40):

evaṁ-vrataḥ sva-priya-nāma-kīrtyā
jātānurāgo druta-citta uccaiḥ
hasaty atho roditi rauti gāyaty
unmāda-van nṛtyati loka-bāhyaḥ

In the heart of one who adopts such a transcendental vow, attachment for chanting the name of his most dear Lord arises and melts his heart. Now he rises above the condition of the general mass of people, and he is beyond caring for their opinions and views. In a natural way – not out of pretence – he acts as if mad. Sometimes he bursts out laughing and sometimes he sheds floods of tears. Sometimes, in a loud voice, he calls out to Bhagavān and sometimes, with a sweet voice, he sings Bhagavān's glories. At other times, when he perceives his beloved standing before his eyes, he even starts dancing in order to please Him.

ei vrate kṛṣṇa-nāma kīrtana kariyā
jāta-rāga drava-ccitta hāsiyā kāṅdiyā
cītkāra kariyā gāi loka-bāhya tyaji'
ei vyavahāre bhāi, preme kṛṣṇa bhaji

Bhajana-rahasya-vṛtti

The devotees of the Lord always chant the auspicious names of Bhagavān. As a result of this *kṛṣṇa-saṅkīrtana*, all kinds of *anarthas* are removed; the heart is purified; many lifetimes of sins and their result, transmigration, are destroyed; all kinds of good fortune arise; all the *sādhana* one needs to attain *prema-bhakti* is transmitted into the heart; *kṛṣṇa-prema* appears; one begins to relish the nectar of *prema*; one attains Śrī Kṛṣṇa; and finally one attains coolness and purity through completely immersing himself in the nectarean ocean of eternal service. At this stage, through the essential function of *hlādinī* (*hlādinī-sāra-vṛtti*), *śrī-kṛṣṇa-saṅkīrtana* boundlessly increases the living entity's natural bliss. Now the living entity is eternally fixed in one of the *rasas* (*dāsya*, *sakhya*, *vātsalya* or *mādhurya*), and moment by moment, he relishes complete nectar through an ever-fresh attachment for Śrī Kṛṣṇa. Śrī Kṛṣṇa's sweet pastimes appear in the devotee's heart and he repeatedly relishes the sweetness of all the Lord's qualities, such as His beauty. This ever-fresh sweetness astonishes the devotee and his heart melts.

While describing the glories of *śrī-kṛṣṇa-nāma-saṅkīrtana* to Prakāśānanda Sarasvatī, Śrīman Mahāprabhu said, "When I chant the name My *guru* gave Me, it automatically makes My heart melt. Sometimes this name makes Me dance, sometimes it makes Me laugh and at other times it makes Me cry." This is the nature of the *mahā-mantra*; it makes *kṛṣṇa-prema* arise within whomever chants it. *Kṛṣṇa-prema* is the topmost goal (*parama-puruṣārtha*); the other four *puruṣārthas* – *dharma*, *artha*, *kāma* and *mokṣa* – are insignificant in its presence. The nature of *prema* is that it gives rise to a restless heart, and the devotee who is controlled by this nature sometimes laughs, sometimes cries and sometimes, being maddened, starts dancing.

In his commentary on this verse, Viśvanātha Cakravartīpāda writes that by chanting the holy name, the *sādhaka* experiences a variety of pastimes as they naturally appear in his heart. He laughs when he hears Śrī Kṛṣṇa's joking words with the *vraja-devīs* during the *rāsa-līlā* or in the pastime of stealing butter, and he weeps when his vision of a pastime (*līlā-sphūrti*) ceases. He thinks, "I have relished the nectar of Your sweetness only once – when will I attain it again?" Lamenting like this, he rolls on the ground and, heaving long sighs, falls unconscious. Later, when he again sees Bhagavān everywhere, he is overwhelmed by happiness and becomes maddened. The devotee who performs such transcendental activities is devoid of bodily needs.

Text 9

Firm faith in *vraja-līlā* is found in this verse recited by Śrīman Mahāprabhu (*Padyāvalī* (386)):

yaḥ kaumāra-haraḥ sa eva hi varas tā eva caitra-kṣapās
te conmīlita-mālatī-surabhayaḥ prauḍhāḥ kadambānilāḥ
sā caivāsmi tathāpi tatra surata-vyāpāra-līlā-vidhau
revā-rodhasi vetasī-taru-tale cetaḥ samutkaṇṭhate

O friend, that beautiful one who stole my heart in my youth is now here. These are also the same pleasant nights of the month of Caitra, with the same fragrance of blossoming *mālatī* flowers and the same cool, gentle, fragrant breeze from the *kadamba* trees. I am also the same; my beloved, too. Nonetheless, my mind is eager for amorous play at the foot of the *vetasī* tree on the bank of the river Revā.

kaumāre bhajinu yāre sei ebe vara
sei ta' vasanta-niśi surabhi-pravara

sei nīpa, sei āmi, saṁyoga tāhāi
tathāpi se revā-taṭa sukha nāhi pāi

Bhajana-rahasya-vṛtti

Śrīman Mahāprabhu would recite this verse while dancing in front of Śrī Jagannātha's chariot. At that time, He was immersed in the *bhāva* of Śrī Rādhā, considering Himself to be Rādhā and Śrī Jagannātha to be Vrajendra-nandana Śyāmasundara. He was feeling that They were meeting each other at Kurukṣetra – this was His mood. At Kurukṣetra, Śrī Rādhā could not experience the same happiness She used to feel when meeting Śrī Kṛṣṇa in the solitary *nikuñjas* of Vṛndāvana. Absorbed in the mood of Rādhā, Mahāprabhu revealed the distress She felt as She spoke to Her *sakhī*. "O *sakhī*, I am that same Rādhā and He is that same Kṛṣṇa, and We are now meeting each other again; nonetheless, My mind is eager that We should meet and sport together in the secluded *nikuñjas* of Vṛndāvana."

Śrīman Mahāprabhu expressed His moods through this Text, taken from *Sāhitya-darpaṇa*. It is described there how a young unmarried *nāyikā* (heroine) became strongly attached to the qualities of a *nāyaka* (hero) and met with him on the bank of the river Revā. There, the *nāyaka* took her innocence. A *kumārī*, a very young, unmarried girl, naturally has no desire for union. When this desire arises, youth (*kaiśora*) begins. After some time, that *nāyikā* was married to the *nāyaka*. Upon the arrival of the month of Caitra, memories have come to the *nāyikā* of that charming, moonlit night in the *vetasī-kuñja* on the bank of the river Revā, and how the slow, gentle breeze carrying the fragrance of *mālatī* flowers stimulated their lust and increased their desire for union. Now, however, in the bonds of marriage, they do not have the same eagerness as then, even though there are no obstacles in their meeting. But her mind has gone to that bank of the river Revā, and happy memories have arisen in her heart of her first meeting with the beloved of her life and their amorous play under the *vetasī* tree.

In this verse, a mundane poet expresses the feelings of a mundane *nāyaka* and a mundane *nāyikā*, but through it, Mahāprabhu relished the sweetness of transcendental *śṛṅgāra-rasa*. In mundane poetry, such a union is considered impure and *rasābhāsa*, an overlapping of mellows, but Rādhā-Kṛṣṇa's pastimes are transcendental, with the supreme sweetness of *rasa* flowing through them. The meeting of an ordinary *nāyaka* and *nāyikā* is controlled by lust, *kāma*, that arises from illusion. When their lust is fulfilled, their feelings for each other become different. On the other hand, in transcendental amorous mellow (*śṛṅgāra-rasa*), the *nāyaka* and the *nāyikā* have *prema* for each other. This *prema* originates from the *svarūpa-śakti's* function of *hlādinī* and *saṁvit*, and its purpose is to give pleasure to Kṛṣṇa. In *kāma* one desires one's own enjoyment, but in *prema* one aims for Kṛṣṇa's happiness. This is confirmed in *Śrī Caitanya-caritāmṛta* (*Ādi-līlā* 4.165):

ātmendriya-prīti-vāñchā – tāre bali 'kāma'
kṛṣṇendriya-prīti-icchā dhare 'prema' nāma

Śrī Rādhā's desire to serve Kṛṣṇa is causeless and perpetual. The birth of a material desire, on the other hand, is caused and is therefore destroyed. The *nāyaka* and *nāyikā* who are tied by marriage have *svakīya-bhāva*, wedded love. Because they are with each other constantly, the variegatedness of *rasa* does not manifest in their meeting and the sweetness of *rasa* also remains concealed. However, the sweetness of a *nāyaka* and *nāyikā's prema* in *parakīya-bhāva*, paramour love, manifests in an extraordinary way because their *prema* is endowed with an exalted, radiant *rasa* (*samunnata-ujjvala-rasa*). The sweetness of the *vraja-devīs' parakīya-bhāva* is unprecedented. Because they do not always occur, their meetings with Kṛṣṇa are precious. Owing to the paramour relationship, their mood is characterised by contrariness, prohibition and secret amorous desires. This *bhāva* is the wealth of the *vraja-devīs* only. Its only *nāyaka* is the crown jewel of *rasikas*, Vrajendra-nandana Śrī Kṛṣṇa. The crown jewel of all the *gopīs* is Vṛṣabhānu-nandinī Śrī Rādhā. *Śrī Caitanya-caritāmṛta* (*Ādi-līlā* 4.80) states: "*bahu kāntā vinā nahe rasera ullāsa* – without many beloveds (*kāntās*), there is no rapture in *rasa*." Thus, to fulfil Śrī Kṛṣṇa's desire to taste paramour love, Śrī Rādhā manifests Herself as many beloveds. This *parakīya-bhāva* is manifest only in Vraja.

Text 10

Śrīla Rūpa Gosvāmī has explained the previous Text by composing this verse, which is found in *Padyāvalī* (387):

priyaḥ so 'yaṁ kṛṣṇaḥ sahacari kuru-kṣetra-militas
tathāhaṁ sā rādhā tad idam ubhayoḥ saṅgama-sukham
tathāpy antaḥ-khelan-madhura-muralī-pañcama-juṣe
mano me kālindī-pulina-vipināya spṛhayati

[After meeting Śrī Kṛṣṇa at Kurukṣetra, Śrī Rādhā said:] O *sakhī*, today at Kurukṣetra, I met My same *prāṇa-priya*, Kṛṣṇa. I am that same Rādhā and there is also happiness in Our meeting. But nonetheless, I deeply yearn for Vṛndāvana, for the *kuñja* on the bank of the Kālindī that is inundated by bliss as a result of Kṛṣṇa vibrating the fifth note on His playful *muralī*.

sei kṛṣṇa prāṇanātha, kurukṣetre pāinu
sei rādhā āmi, sei saṅgama labhinu

tathāpi āmāra mana vaṁśī-dhvanimaya
kālindī-puline spṛhā kare atiśaya

vṛndāvana-līlā-sama līlā nāhi āra
vaikuṇṭhādye ei līlāra nāhi paracāra

vraje yei līlā tāhe viccheda, sambhoga
dui ta' paramānanda, sadā kara bhoga

Bhajana-rahasya-vṛtti

Absorbed in the mood of Śrī Rādhā, Śrīman Mahāprabhu would recite the previous verse (Text 9) from *Sāhitya-darpaṇa* in front of Śrī Jagannātha at the time of Ratha-yātrā. Only Śrī Svarūpa Dāmodara knew the essence of the sweet mood of that verse. Śrī Rūpa Gosvāmī was also present at Ratha-yātrā. By Śrīman Mahāprabhu's mercy, he too was able to understand the mood of that verse, and he composed this Text 10 in the same mood. When Śrīman Mahāprabhu read it, He became overwhelmed with transcendental emotions.

Śrī Rādhā and Śrī Kṛṣṇa met each other at Kurukṣetra after a long separation from each other. Although this meeting was pleasurable like Their very first meeting in Vṛndāvana, the heart of Śrī Rādhā was not satisfied. She expressed this heartfelt mood to Her intimate *sakhī*: "O *sakhī*, My heart is very anxious to meet Śrī Kṛṣṇa in a *kuñja* on the bank of the Yamunā. When Kṛṣṇa performs sweet sports in the forests situated upon the banks of the Kālindī, He manifests an unprecedented sweetness by vibrating the fifth note on His flute. In the forest of Vṛndāvana, the heart is stimulated by the *ke-kā* sound of the peacocks and peahens, as well as by their captivating dance; by the cuckoos' *kuhū-kuhū* sound; by the humming of bumblebees around fragrant mango buds; by the life-giving air that is filled with the fragrance of *mādhavī* and *mālatī* flowers; by the male and female swans on the ponds; and by fragrant pollen from lotuses. In that

Vṛndāvana, the ever-youthful best of dancers, who has a peacock feather and flute and who is adorned with forest flowers, used to sport with Me. Here, at Kurukṣetra, there is not the slightest scent of any of this. Here I do not relish even a drop from the ocean of pleasure I received from My meetings with Him in Vṛndāvana. What's more, here I am surrounded by persons who are not like-minded. My innermost desire is to sport with Śrī Kṛṣṇa in the *nikuñjas* of that place which is well known to Me, Śrīdhāma Vṛndāvana."

Text 11

Śrī Rādhā-Kṛṣṇa's pastimes of meeting (*sambhoga-līlā*) are described in *Ujjvala-nılamaṇi* (15.222–4):

te tu sandarśanaṁ jalpaḥ
sparśanaṁ vartma-rodhanam
rāsa-vṛndāvana-krīḍā-
yamunādy-ambu-kelayaḥ

nau-khelā-līlayā cauryaṁ
ghaṭṭa-kuñjādi-līnatā
madhu-pānaṁ vadhū-veśa-
dhṛtiḥ kapaṭa-suptatā

dyūta-krīḍā-paṭākṛṣṭiś
cumbāśleṣau-nakhārpaṇam
bimbādhara-sudhāpānaṁ
samprayogādayo matāḥ

The *anubhāvas* of meeting (*sambhoga*) are: seeing each other (*sandarśana*); talking (*jalpa*); touching (*sparśana*); blocking each other's way in a contrary mood (*vartma-rodhana*); the *rāsa-līlā*; enjoying pleasure pastimes in Vṛndāvana (*vṛndāvana-krīḍā*); playing water-sports in the Yamunā and Mānasī-gaṅgā (*jala-keli*); enjoying boat pastimes (*nau-khelā*); stealing flowers, clothes and the flute (*līlā-caurya*); enjoying pastimes of demanding taxes (*ghaṭṭa*); playing hide-and-seek in the *kuñjas* (*kuñjādi-līnatā*); drinking honey (*madhu-pāna*); Kṛṣṇa dressing in female attire (*vadhū-veśa-dhṛti*); pretending to sleep (*kapaṭa-suptatā*); playing dice (*dyūta-krīḍā*); pulling off each other's garments (*paṭākṛṣti*); kissing (*cumba*); embracing (*āśleṣa*); making nail-marks on each other (*nakha-arpaṇa*); relishing the nectar of each other's lips, which are like *bimba* fruit (*bimba-adhara-sudhā-pāna*); and enjoying amorous union (*samprayoga*).

sandarśana, jalpa, sparśa, vartma-nirodhana
rāsa, vṛndāvana-krīḍā, yamunā-khelana

naukā-khelā, puṣpa-curi, ghaṭṭa, saṅgopana
madhupāna, vadhū-veśa, kapaṭa-svapana

dyūta-krīḍā, vastra-ṭānā, surata-vyāpāra
bimbādhara sudhāpāna, sambhoga prakāra

Text 12

Decorating Śrī Rādhā-Kṛṣṇa is described in *Stavāvalī* (*Sva-saṅkalpa-prakāśa-stotra* (9)):

sphuran-muktā guñjā maṇi sumanasāṁ hāra-racane
mudendor lekhā me racayatu tathā śikṣaṇa-vidhim
yatha taiḥ saṅkḷptair dayita-sarasī madhya-sadane
sphuṭaṁ rādhā-kṛṣṇāv ayam api jano bhūṣayati tau

May Indulekhā Sakhī, as *guru*, mercifully teach me the art of stringing very beautiful necklaces and garlands composed of pearls, jewels, *guñjā* berries and flowers. With these necklaces and garlands, I can decorate Śrī Rādhā-Kṛṣṇa for Their pleasure as They are seated on the jewelled throne in the middle of Rādhā-kuṇḍa.

muktā-guñjā-maṇi-puṣpa-hāra viracane
indulekhā-guru-kṛpā labhiba yatane

rādhā-kuṇḍa ratnamaya mandire duṅhāre
bhūṣita kariba āmi sulalita hāre

Bhajana-rahasya-vṛtti

In this Text, Śrī Raghunātha dāsa Gosvāmī, who is totally absorbed in his identity as a *mañjarī*, is drawing a delightful picture of his desire to serve Śrī Rādhā-Mādhava by decorating Them suitably in the *nikuñja* situated in the middle of Rādhā-kuṇḍa. Śrī Rādhā's *sakhīs* have a variety of natures with which they nourish many kinds of mellows (*rasas*). These *sakhīs* are proficient in knowledge of their own *rasa*, and sometimes they learn different arts from other *sakhīs*. By teaching all the *pālyadāsīs* Herself, Śrī Rādhā makes them expert in Her service.

Here Śrīla Dāsa Gosvāmī, in the mood of Rati Mañjarī, is praying to Śrīmatī Indulekhā, one of Śrī Rādhā's *aṣṭa-sakhīs*, to teach her the art of stringing necklaces of pearls, jewels and *guñjā* berries and making garlands of flowers, as well as other delightful arts. According to Śrīla Rūpa Gosvāmī's *Śrī Rādhā-kṛṣṇa-gaṇoddeśa-dīpikā*, Indulekhā is learned in scriptures dealing with snake-charming *mantras* and in the *sāmudrika-śāstra*. She is expert in stringing necklaces and garlands, drawing pictures, decorating the teeth, gemmology, weaving various kinds of cloth and writing auspicious *mantras*. She is also expert in generating the mutual attraction between Rādhā and Kṛṣṇa.

As Śrī Rādhā-Mādhava perform amorous sports (*rasa-vilāsa-krīḍā*) in the *vilāsa-kuñja* known as Madana-vāṭikā situated in the middle of Śrī Rādhā-kuṇḍa, Their necklaces of pearls, jewels and *guñjā* berries and Their garlands of flowers break and scatter. The *prāṇa-sakhīs* do not hesitate to enter the *kuñja* in order to rearrange Śrī Rādhā-Mādhava's clothes and ornaments. Śrīla Dāsa Gosvāmī is praying to Śrī Indulekhā, who is expert in all these arts, to impart knowledge about how to skilfully accomplish all these services. By their skill in stringing necklaces and garlands, the *pālyadāsī-mañjarīs* have their desires to please Śrī Rādhā-Mādhava fulfilled.

Text 13

For an understanding of *vipralambha-rasa* one should read *Gopī-gīta* (*Śrīmad-Bhāgavatam*, Tenth Canto, Chapter 31). Only those who distribute *bhagavat-kathā* are most munificent. *Śrīmad-Bhāgavatam* (10.31.9) states:

tava kathāmṛtaṁ tapta-jīvanaṁ
kavibhir īḍitaṁ kalmaṣāpaham
śravaṇa-maṅgalaṁ śrīmad ātataṁ
bhuvi gṛṇanti te bhūri-dā janāḥ

O Kṛṣṇa, nectar-filled narrations about You are the life and soul of persons suffering in separation from You, and they are sung by great, realised poets who are Your devotees. Just by hearing the all-auspicious narrations about You, all kinds of sins, such as *prārabdha* and *aprārabdha*, are removed, and all prosperity, in the form of *prema-bhakti*, arises in the heart. Therefore no one is equal to or more generous than he who chants and propagates narrations about You.

tava kathāmṛta kṛṣṇa! jīvanera sukha
kavi-gaṇa gāya yāte yāya pāpa-duḥkha
śravaṇa-maṅgala sadā saundarya-pūrita
sukṛta-janera mukhe nirantara gīta

Bhajana-rahasya-vṛtti

At the time of Ratha-yātrā, Gaurasundara, endowed with the mood of Śrī Rādhā, became tired and lay down to rest beneath a tree, extending His lotus feet. Within His mind, He relished the *vraja-devīs'* various moods. Mahārāja Pratāparudra came to Him dressed as an insignificant and lowly person and, in a humble mood, massaged Mahāprabhu's feet while gently singing this *śloka*.

In the previous verse of *Gopī-gīta*, which begins with the words *madhurayā girā*, the *gopīs* who were suffering in separation from Kṛṣṇa pray for the nectar of Śrī Kṛṣṇa's lips to cure their disease. In reply Śrī Kṛṣṇa says, "O *gopīs*, I cannot understand how you can remain alive in such a diseased condition."

The *gopīs* reply, "Śyāmasundara, we are alive only due to the nectar of narrations about You, which do not allow us to die. If You ask what this nectar is like, we will answer that it can even bring peace to someone who is afflicted with the intractable disease of suffering the threefold material miseries. The nectar of descriptions of You even calms a forest fire of miseries."

Kṛṣṇa may say, "O *gopīs*, I will bring you nectar from heaven. You can take that!"

The *gopīs* answer, "Dear Śyāmasundara, nectar from heaven will make the body healthy, but it will increase lust (*kāma*) and so forth, which cause much misfortune. Indra and the other demigods of Svarga have so much lust, anger, greed, illusion, pride and envy."

If Kṛṣṇa says, "O *gopīs*, take the nectar of liberation!" then the *gopīs* will reply, "Even if You offer liberation, Your devotees will not accept it because it is unfavourable for *prema-bhakti*. Where are the loving exchanges in liberation? Dhruva, Prahlāda, Brahmā, Nārada, Catuḥsana, Vyāsa, Śuka and other great devotees and poets glorify *hari-kathā*, descriptions of You. For those who aspire for liberation, this *kathā* is the immediately effective medicine to cure the disease of material existence. And for materialists, it gives pleasure to the ears and minds. Great personalities who are liberated within this world praise such narrations as nectar. Hearing them removes all the living entity's sins and offences and bestows auspiciousness. Just as with the arrival of the autumn season the water in rivers and ponds automatically becomes clean, similarly, by hearing descriptions of You, the dirt in the living entity's heart is removed. Such narrations give new life to the devotees who are burning in separation from You, and it bestows all kinds of beauty and wealth. One who distributes *kṛṣṇa-kathā* throughout the world is a truly benevolent person."

Text 14

When the *gopīs* think of Kṛṣṇa wandering in the forest, they experience great sorrow. A description of their deep love for Him at this time is given in *Śrīmad-Bhāgavatam* (10.31.11):

calasi yad vrajāc cārayan paśūn
nalina-sundaraṁ nātha te padam
śila-tṛṇāṅkuraiḥ sīdatīti naḥ
kalilatāṁ manaḥ kānta gacchati

O Prāṇa-vallabha! O Kānta! When You go to the forests of Vraja to herd the cows, the soles of Your soft lotus feet, which are like beautiful blue lotuses, must suffer as they are pricked by small stones and dry straw. Thought of this disturbs our hearts and minds.

dhenu la'ye vraja ha'te yabe yāo vane
nalina-sundara tava kamala-caraṇe
śilāṅkure kaṣṭa ha'be manete vicāri'
mahā-duḥkha pāi morā ohe cittahāri

Bhajana-rahasya-vṛtti

In the verse of *Gopī-gīta* that precedes this one and begins with the words *prahasitaṁ priya*, the *vraja-sundarīs* felt pain when they remembered *pūrva-rāga* – the loving glances of their *prāṇakānta* Śrī Kṛṣṇa, His gentle smile, His joking and talking with them in a secluded place, and so forth – and their hearts became disturbed. Now, they direct their words towards Śrī Kṛṣṇa, saying, "O deceiver of the heart, how we will ever attain peace, we do not know! Our hearts are anxious both when we meet with You and when we are separated from You; they are anxious in all conditions. O Kṛṣṇa, in the morning, You are surrounded by countless *sakhās* as You take innumerable cows to graze in the forest, and the Vrajavāsīs, deprived of Your *darśana*, are plunged into a deep ocean of separation from You. When we think of Your lotus feet, which are softer than a thousand-petalled lotus, being pierced by dry straw, thorns, sharp grass and so forth, we sink in unlimited anxiety. How can we tolerate pain to Your lotus feet, which we consider non-different from our hearts? First, we suffer in separation from You, and then, on top of that, we suffer the pain caused to Your crimson lotus feet. How can we tolerate this? Both types of pain break the barrier of our endurance. O Prāṇakānta, please do not abuse Your lotus feet. We remember that while roaming throughout the forest with You, You would ask us to remove the thorns that pricked Your feet. We would put Your feet on our body and remove the thorns gently and slowly. But when Your feet are pricked now, who will remove the thorns?"

Kānta kalilatāṁ mano gacchati – "We think, 'O Kānta, surely Your soft, tender, lotus feet will be pierced by thorns, sharp grass and stone chips.' By such thoughts, our minds begin to dispute with us.

"Our minds tell us, 'Doesn't Kṛṣṇa have eyes? He can see the thorns, sharp grass and stone chips as He walks, and He will avoid them.'

"To this we reply, 'O cruel mind, the foolish cows gallop off into rough places that are full of thorns, sharp grass and stones.

They do not feel them because they have hooves. But when Śyāmasundara runs after these galloping cows, will He see these things and tread carefully? His soft lotus feet will surely be pierced by thorns.'

"The mind argues, 'O ignorant milkmaids, don't you know that Vṛndāvana's thorns and stones are also very soft?'

"Then we say, 'O mind, we do not believe this. We used to remove thorns and sharp grass from Kṛṣṇa's lotus feet ourselves.'"

In this way, the *gopīs* quarrel with their minds. Finally, their minds say, "You can remain in such anxiety – I am going to Kṛṣṇa."

If Kṛṣṇa says, "O *gopīs,* why are you so worried about Me?" the *gopīs* will answer, "O Kānta, You make our minds restless and disturbed with transcendental lust, so our intelligence has become dull. O Prāṇanātha, please do not roam here and there in the forest. Quickly return and give us Your *darśana.*"

Text 15

Śrīmad-Bhāgavatam (10.31.15) describes that for the *gopīs,* even one moment seems like a hundred *yugas* when they do not have *darśana* of that beautiful face adorned with curling locks:

aṭati yad bhavān ahni kānanaṁ
truṭir yugāyate tvām apaśyatām
kuṭila-kuntalaṁ śrī-mukhaṁ ca te
jaḍa udīkṣatāṁ pakṣma-kṛd dṛśam

O Śyāmasundara, when You go to the forest to herd the cows during the day, the Vrajavāsīs are unable to see You and thus they feel one moment to be like a *yuga.* And in the evening, when You return and we see Your beautiful lotus face covered with curling locks, the blinking of our eyelids becomes painful because it obstructs our *darśana*. Is the Creator, who made these eyelids, ignorant, or is he foolish?

pūrvāhne kānane tumi yāo go-cāraṇe
truṭi yuga-sama haya tava adarśane

kuṭila-kuntala tava śrī-candra-vadana
darśane nimeṣa-dātā vidhira nindana

Bhajana-rahasya-vṛtti

Even a fraction of a second seems like a *yuga* for the *gopīs* when they are afflicted by separation from Śrī Kṛṣṇa, and when they meet Him, one *yuga* seems like a moment. This condition is called *mahābhāva*.

In this Text, the *gopīs* address Śrī Kṛṣṇa as *bhavān*. *Bhavān* is a term of honour, but here, the *gopīs* address Kṛṣṇa as such due to their jealous love.

Aṭati yad bhavān – The *gopīs* say, "O Kṛṣṇa! You are *arasajña*, ignorant of mellows. Even though we, who are *rasajña*, well-versed in mellows, are correct here, You continue to roam the forest. By roaming here and there with foolish cows, Your intelligence has become as dull as theirs. This is the effect of faulty association. By Your grazing animals all day, Your intelligence has become like that of an animal." The *gopīs*, who have been separated from Kṛṣṇa all day, eagerly await His return to Vraja so that they can have *darśana* of His beautiful lotus face. Upon hearing the *gopīs*, Śrī Kṛṣṇa may say, "O *vraja-devīs*, you are always seeing My face. What is so special about My face when I return from cowherding?"

The *vraja-devīs* reply, "*Kuṭila-kuntalaṁ śrī-mukhaṁ ca* – Your beautiful lotus face is decorated by curly locks, but because these locks of hair are scattered all over Your face, we cannot see it." With anger born of affection, the *vraja-devīs* are saying, "When this curly hair covers Your face, You are the only one to relish its sweetness. This further torments our minds, which are already burning in separation from You."

Udīkṣatām – The *gopīs* say, "Furthermore, we open our eyes wide and raise our faces in an endeavour to see You, but because the Creator, who fashioned our eyelids, is foolish (*dṛśāṁ pakṣma-kṛd jaḍaḥ*), we cannot take complete *darśana* of You. This Creator, being irrational and of meagre intelligence, has created eyelids for the eyes. For *darśana* of such a beautiful lotus face, he has only given two eyes, and on top of that, he has covered them with eyelids that constantly close and obstruct *darśana* of You."

Adhirūḍha-mahābhāva is characterised by the feeling that each moment is like a *kalpa* when one is separated from Kṛṣṇa, and the feeling that a *kalpa* is like a moment when one is meeting Him. In this Text, this *bhāva* is clearly visible in the *vraja-devīs*.

Text 16

The pre-eminent *gopī-bhāva* is intended solely for Kṛṣṇa's pleasure. *Śrīmad-Bhāgavatam* (10.31.19) states:

yat te sujāta-caraṇāmburuhaṁ staneṣu
bhītāḥ śanaiḥ priya dadhīmahi karkaśeṣu
tenāṭavīm aṭasi tad vyathate na kiṁ svit
kūrpādibhir bhramati dhīr bhavad-āyuṣāṁ naḥ

O beloved, Your beautiful feet are even softer than a lotus. When we massage those soft, tender, lotus feet we fearfully, slowly and gently place them on our breasts in such a way that our hard breasts may cause them no pain. With those same soft feet, You wander behind the cows in the deep forest. Will Your lotus feet not be pierced by sharp stones and the like? Such thoughts make us extremely anxious. O Prāṇanātha, You are our life, so please stop wandering in the forest. Please, appear before us.

tomāra caraṇāmbuja e karkaśa stane
sāvadhāne dhari sakhe! kleśa-bhīta mane

se pada-kamale vane kūrpādira duḥkha
haya pāche, śaṅkā kari' nāhi pāi sukha

Bhajana-rahasya-vṛtti

In this verse the *gopīs* express their extremely deep *prema*. In previous verses the *gopīs* described their condition in separation from Kṛṣṇa, but here their anxiety for His happiness is evident in their words. The *gopīs*, who are covered by *kāma* – that is, their love for Kṛṣṇa – tried very hard to conceal their *prema*, but because it flows so swiftly, it was revealed.

The *gopīs* suffer in their hearts at the thought of Kṛṣṇa coming to harm. This is the characteristic of *mahābhāva*. Only the *gopīs* are experienced in the sorrow of separation from their *prāṇa-priyatama*, and only the *gopīs* are experienced in the happiness of meeting with Him. In Text 14, the *gopīs* expressed how troubled they felt by the pain caused to Śrī Kṛṣṇa's lotus feet. That is why this Text, in which the suffering of Śrī Kṛṣṇa's lotus feet is again mentioned, came to be. Text 15 described separation from Him during the day, and this Text describes separation from Him at night. In the daytime, Kṛṣṇa roams here and there herding the cows, and He can easily protect Himself from the stone chips, thorns and sharp grass. But on the bank of the Yamunā, in the darkness of night, stones, thorns and sharp grass are not easily seen. Thinking of this, the *vraja-sundarīs'* hearts begin to melt and they express their moods with words of distress.

Śrī Vṛndā-devī puts great effort into making Śrī Kṛṣṇa's pastime-places, like the bank of the Yamunā, very pleasant and beautiful. There is no possibility of thorns or sharp grass being there, but nonetheless, the women of Vraja fear that Śrī Kṛṣṇa's lotus feet will suffer.

Afflicted by *prema*, the *gopīs* pray in this Text, "O life-giving Śyāmasundara, like beautifully blossoming lotus flowers, Your reddish lotus feet, which are endowed with fragrance and sweetness, mitigate any suffering. Now these reddish lotus feet must be suffering from the injuries caused by stones, sharp grass and so forth as You roam from forest to forest. We are saddened by such thoughts."

Upon hearing this, Śrī Kṛṣṇa might reply, "Oh, come now! What realisation do you have of My suffering?"

The *gopīs* answer, "*Priya karkaśeṣu staneṣu bhītāḥ śanair dadhīmahi* – O beloved, we consider You to be non-different from our bodies and to be the life of our lives. How can we place Your supremely beautiful, tender lotus feet on our hard breasts? Please listen for a moment. *Bhītāḥ śanaiḥ*, we place them there very slowly and gently so that You may feel no pain at all. Therefore, when You, Yourself, cause them pain, we drown in an ocean of sorrow."

Śrī Kṛṣṇa says, "O *gopīs* overwhelmed by *madana* (Cupid), why do you want to place My lotus feet on your hard breasts?"

"O Priya, You are our beloved, and the only duty of a lover is to increase the beloved's happiness. Placing Your lotus feet on our breasts gives You supreme pleasure, and if You are happy, we are, too. For this reason, we place Your lotus feet there, but as soon as we remember their softness, our hearts melt."

Kṛṣṇa says, "O mad *gopīs*, you all should perform some austerity to satisfy the Creator, and then pray to him for soft, tender breasts."

The *gopīs* reply, "We are ready to perform this austerity, but there is a consideration. If our breasts were soft, You still may not be pleased, and if they are hard, they will cause You pain. We are unable to determine what to do and what not to do. You, however, behave the same way You treat Your feet – mercilessly."

Hearing this Kṛṣṇa may reply, "O *gopīs*, what are you raving on about?"

The *gopīs* say, "O Śyāmasundara, we are unable to calm our hearts at all."

Kṛṣṇa replies, "Why do you suffer so much? Where is your affection for Me? What are the symptoms of affection? If the lover is unable to remain alive when the beloved is suffering severly, how is it that you are still alive?"

The *gopīs* say, "*Bhavad-āyuṣām.* You are our very life. Although we have endured much hardship, our lives do not end." With loving anger they continue, "O Śyāmasundara, not only are You cruel to us, but so is the Creator; he has given us such a long life – only to suffer."

This is the commentary of Śrī Viśvanātha Cakravartī Ṭhākura on this *śloka*, which expresses the deep suffering in separation from Kṛṣṇa of the *vraja-devīs*, who are filled with *mahābhāva.*

Text 17

The *gopīs' bhāvocchvāsa* (outburst of feeling that expresses the *bhāva* hidden in the heart) when meeting with Kṛṣṇa is described in *Kṛṣṇa-karṇāmṛta* (12):

nikhila-bhuvana-lakṣmī-nitya-līlāspadābhyāṁ
kamala-vipina-vīthī-garva-sarvāṅkaṣābhyāṁ
praṇamad-abhaya-dāna-prauḍhi-gāḍhādṛtābhyāṁ
kim api vahatu cetaḥ kṛṣṇa-pādāmbujābhyām

May my heart attain indescribable bliss at Śrī Kṛṣṇa's lotus feet, which are the eternal abode of pastimes for the original goddess of fortune, which thwart heaps of lotus flowers' pride in their beauty, and which are deeply respected everywhere for their great power in giving shelter to the surrendered souls.

nikhila-bhuvana-lakṣmī rādhikā-sundarī
tāṅra nitya-līlāspada parama-mādhurī

kamala-vipina-garva kṣaya yāhe haya
praṇata-abhaya-dāne prauḍha-śaktimaya

hena kṛṣṇa-pāda-padma, kṛṣṇa! mama mana
apūrva utsava-rati karuka vahana

Bhajana-rahasya-vṛtti

When Śrī Kṛṣṇa reappeared after disappearing from the *rāsa-līlā*, a *gopī* who was burning in the fire of separation from Him placed His lotus feet upon her breasts. Śrī Līlāśuka explains that this refers to Śrī Rādhā's keeping Kṛṣṇa's lotus feet on Her heart. Śrī Kṛṣṇa is sporting with Rādhā in a solitary *nikuñja*. As soon as He places His reddish lotus feet on Her breasts, they become even more reddish. May these lotus feet, smeared with *kuṅkuma*, fully manifest within our hearts.

In describing the speciality of Kṛṣṇa's lotus feet, he says that they defeat the pride of lotus flowers. How? The material lotus flower is cooling, fragrant, soft and beautiful for the five senses, and the bumblebee becomes mad by drinking its honey. But Śrī Kṛṣṇa's lotus feet are intoxicating in a different, exceptional way. These feet are the embodiment of beauty and wealth for all material and transcendental living beings, and they are the eternal abode of pastimes for the original goddess of fortune (*nikhila-bhuvana-lakṣmī*). The word *nikhila-bhuvana-lakṣmī* in this Text can also refer to all the *gopīs*, who offer their everything to these lotus feet. Śrī Kṛṣṇa removes the affliction of their *kāma* by touching them with His lotus feet. The young girls of Vraja affectionately keep these lotus feet on their hearts and serve them in every way.

Text 18

It is also said in *Kṛṣṇa-karṇāmṛta* (18):

taruṇāruṇa-karuṇāmaya-vipulāyata-nayanaṁ
kamalākuca-kalasībhara-vipulī-kṛta-pulakam
muralī-rava-taralī-kṛta-muni-mānasa-nalinaṁ
mama khelatu mada-cetasi madhurādharam amṛtam

His eyes are fresh and reddish like the early dawn, full of compassion and very long and wide; His bodily hair stands on end by the touch of the waterpot-like breasts of Śrī Rādhā; and the sound of His flute makes the *munis* restless like the *gopīs*. May the sweet nectar of His lips sport in my heart.

taruṇa aruṇa jini, karuṇā-svarūpa maṇi,
vipula nayana śobhe yāṅra
rādhā-kuca-dvaya bhara, preme deha gara gara,
vipula pulaka camatkāra

madhura-muralī svare, muni-mana padmavane,
taralita kare sarva-kṣaṇa
kṛṣṇera madhurādhara, parāmṛta śaśadhara,
citte mora karuka nartana

Bhajana-rahasya-vṛtti

Śrī Rādhā-Kṛṣṇa are in a solitary *nikuñja*, and no tinkle of ankle bells or any other sound comes from inside. Knowing that the Divine Couple's amorous pastimes (*surata-līlā*) have come to an end, the *sakhīs* look through the small eyelets in the *kuñja* at the intimacy of the pastime. Kṛṣṇa has risen from bed and is sitting up. To remove Śrī Rādhā's fatigue and to stimulate Her amorous desire, He massages Her limbs and cleverly fans Her with His scarf. Śrī Kṛṣṇa, who is the embodiment of nectar, maddens our *sakhī*, Śrī Rādhā, with the happiness of Her good fortune. Kṛṣṇa's naturally youthful, reddish eyes have become even more red by

His drinking the nectar of Rādhā's lips, and They are again becoming restless with intoxicating amorous desires. Full of tenderness, He fans Rādhā to remove Her perspiration. Seeing Śrī Rādhā's fatigue due to amorous sports, Kṛṣṇa's heart overflows with an ocean of compassion, and He endeavours in various ways to mitigate Her tiredness.

He places Śrī Rādhā on His lap, and the touch of each other's bodies drowns Them both in an ocean of *aṣṭa-sāttvika-bhāvas*. His endeavours to remove Her fatigue of amorous play increase Their desire to sport again.

Even the hard hearts of the *munis* become restless when Śrī Kṛṣṇa plays His flute. When Rādhā is in *māna*, Kṛṣṇa tries in various ways to pacify Her. This dense *māna* is not removed by His falling at Her feet and crying, but it is vanquished by His playing one note on the flute. The sound of Kṛṣṇa's flute enters Rādhā's ears and makes Her mad (*unmāda*). All glories to such a flute!

Text 19

The *mānasī-sevā*, service performed within the mind, of one who performs *bhajana* of pastimes in his eternal form (*siddha-deha*) is described in *Ujjvala-nīlamāṇī* (8.88–91):

mithaḥ prema-guṇotkīrtis
tayor āsakti-kāritā

abhisāra-dvayor eva
sakhyāḥ kṛṣṇe samarpaṇam
narmāśvāsana-nepathyaṁ
hṛdayodghāṭa-pāṭavam

chidra-saṁvṛtir etasyāḥ
paty-ādeḥ parivañcanā
śikṣā-saṅgamanaṁ kāle
sevanaṁ vyajanādibhiḥ

tayor dvayor upālambhaḥ
sandeśa-preṣaṇaṁ tathā
nāyikā-prāṇa-saṁrakṣā
prayatnādyāḥ sakhī-kriyāḥ

The sixteen activities of the *sakhīs* are: (1) to glorify the *prema* and qualities of the *nāyikā* to the *nāyaka* and vice versa; (2) to create attachment between the *nāyikā* and *nāyaka*; (3) to arrange for their *abhisāra*; (4) to offer their *sakhī* to Śrī Kṛṣṇa; (5) to joke; (6) to console; (7) to dress and decorate the *nāyikā* and *nāyaka*; (8) to skilfully hide the *nāyikā* and *nāyaka's* innermost feelings; (9) to conceal the *nāyikā's* faults; (10) to cheat their husbands and others; (11) to give favourable instructions; (12) to arrange for the *nāyikā* and *nāyaka* to meet at the appropriate time; (13) to fan and render other services; (14) to point out faults in the *nāyikā* and *nāyaka* and to instruct them; (15) to deliver the *nāyikā* and *nāyaka's* messages to each other; and (16) to endeavour to protect the *nāyikā's* life.

rādhā-kṛṣṇa guṇotkīrti, āsakti-vardhana
abhisāra-dvaya, kṛṣṇe rādhā-samarpaṇa

narmāśvāsa, veṣa-kārya, hṛdaya-sandhāna
chidra-gupti, gṛha-pati-gaṇera vañcana

śikṣādāna, jala āra vyajana-sevana
ubhaya-milana, sandeśādi-ānayana

nāyikāra prāṇa-rakṣāya prayatna pradhāna
sakhī-sevā jāni' yathā karaha vidhāna

Text 20

In *Stavāvalī* (*Vraja-vilāsa-stava* (38)) it is written:

tāmbūlārpaṇa-pāda-mardana-payodānābhisārādibhir
vṛndāraṇya-maheśvarīṁ priyatayā yās toṣayanti priyāḥ
prāṇa-preṣṭha-sakhī-kulād api kilāsaṅkocitā bhūmikāḥ
kelī-bhūmiṣu rūpa-mañjarī-mukhās tā dāsikāḥ saṁśraye

I take shelter of the maidservants of Śrīmatī Rādhikā, of whom Rūpa Mañjarī is prominent. Unlike the *priya-narma-sakhīs*, they can perform any service without hesitation. They perpetually and affectionately satisfy Śrīmatī Rādhikā with their various services, such as offering *tāmbūla*, massaging Her feet, bringing Her water and arranging for Her trysts with Kṛṣṇa.

tāmbūla-arpaṇa, duṅhāra caraṇa-mardana
payodāna, abhisāra, dāsī-sevā-dhana

Bhajana-rahasya-vṛtti

Śrī Rādhā's *sakhīs* are of five kinds. Among them, the service of the *nitya-sakhīs* and *prāṇa-sakhīs* (all of whom are *mañjarīs*) is topmost. When Śrī Rādhā-Kṛṣṇa become overwhelmed with ecstasy and become helpless while sporting in a solitary *nikuñja*, the *mañjarīs* enter without any hesitation to perform all varieties of services. Although the *mañjarīs* perform their service under the instruction of *priya-narma-sakhīs* such as Lalitā, Viśākhā and others, when Yugala-kiśora are in a solitary *nikuñja*, Lalitā and Viśākhā can only enter with the permission of Rūpa Mañjarī and Rati Mañjarī. In rank, the *priya-narma-sakhīs* are more eminent, but in the good fortune of service, the *mañjarīs* are more eminent. Even when the *priya-narma-sakhīs* cannot enter the *kuñja*, the *mañjarīs* freely serve the Divine Couple there. Often, when Śrī Kṛṣṇa desires to meet Śrī Rādhā, He must repeatedly entreat the *mañjarīs*; only then does He receive the opportunity to meet with Her.

Text 21

Pride in one's service is described in these words of Śrīla Raghunātha dāsa Gosvāmī from *Sva-saṅkalpa-prakāśa-stotra* (2):

navaṁ divyaṁ kāvyaṁ svakṛtam atulaṁ nāṭaka-kulaṁ
prahelī-gūḍhārthāḥ sakhi-rucira-vīṇā-dhvani-gatiḥ
kadā snehollāsair lalita-lalitā-preraṇa-balāt
salajjaṁ gāndharvā sa-rasam-asakṛc chikṣayati mām

Aho! When, in a secluded place, will I receive such fortune that Śrīmatī Rādhikā will, upon the request of Śrīmatī Lalitā-devī, affectionately and happily – yet shyly – teach me dramas composed by Herself, new poems, riddles with deep meanings, and melodies on the *vīṇā*?

svakṛta-nāṭaka āra navya kāvya-tati
gūḍhārtha-prahelī, divya vīṇā-rava-gati
lalitāra anurodhe snehollāse kabe
salajja gāndharvā more nibhṛte śikhābe

Bhajana-rahasya-vṛtti

Śrī Gaurasundara entrusted Śrīla Dāsa Gosvāmī to Śrīla Svarūpa Dāmodara. In *vraja-līlā* Śrī Svarūpa Dāmodara is Lalitā Sakhī. Under her guidance, Śrī Rādhā's *pālyadāsīs* learn how to serve the Divine Couple, and they attain the good fortune of directly serving Them. Śrīman Mahāprabhu is absorbed in the mood of Śrī Rādhā. Here Śrī Dāsa Gosvāmī, keeping the desire to serve Śrīman Mahāprabhu in his heart, is begging at the foot-dust of Śrī Rūpa Gosvāmī for his cherished desires to be fulfilled. He wants to attain expertise in all varieties of fine arts that are useful for *sevā*.

In order to engage Śrī Rati Mañjarī in *sevā* to Śrī Rādhā's lotus feet, Lalitā Sakhī took her by the hand to Śrī Rādhā and made the following request: "O Rādhā, this incomparably charming and beautiful girl is very qualified to serve Your lotus feet." Hearing this, Rādhā, feeling somewhat shy, spoke sweetly to Rati Mañjarī and embraced her to Her heart, moistening her with tears of compassion. Urged by the most charming Lalitā Sakhī, Gāndharvikā Śrī Rādhā, overwhelmed with great affection, instructed Rati Mañjarī on poetry, playing the *vīṇā*, drama, composing riddles and other arts. Śrī Rādhā is completely controlled by Lalitā Sakhī.

Vṛndāvana is the only subject matter of the new transcendental poetry that Śrī Rādhā teaches Rati Mañjarī. The *nāyaka* in this poetry is Vrajendra-nandana Śyāmasundara and the *nāyikās* are the *vraja-devīs*, the embodiments of *mahābhāva*. In this transcendental flow of *rasa* there ripples an unbroken stream of waves. The movement of these waves is unrestricted and has an ever-increasing freshness.

As well as teaching poetry, Śrī Rādhā also teaches the art of acting in dramas and the art of composing riddles with deep meanings. The *pālyadāsīs* employ this training to stimulate *śṛṅgāra-rasa* in Śrī Rādhā-Mukunda. The *sakhīs* ask Śrī Kṛṣṇa, "O best among clever persons, what is young (*bāla*) and old, both bound and liberated, and pure but also in darkness?" Perplexed, Śrī Kṛṣṇa begins to think. After some time, He laughs loudly and says, "Śrī Kiśorī's hair (*bāla*)!" at which point the *sakhīs* burst out laughing. The *sakhīs* please Śrī Kṛṣṇa with such riddles during *rāsa-vilāsa*, while roaming in the forest (*vana-vihāra*) and at other times. Śrī Rādhā, who is skilled in all arts, inspires Her *sakhīs* to please Kṛṣṇa in this way. Furthermore, when they play the captivating *vīṇā*, having learned the art from Śrī Rādhā, Śyāmasundara's heartstrings resound.

The *ācāryas* give the following conclusion for *sādhakas*: attachment (*āsakti*), eagerness (*utkaṇṭhā*) and service filled with the relish of *prema-rasa* are attained by associating with *rasika-bhaktas.* In *Prema-bhakti-candrikā* Śrī Narottama dāsa Ṭhākura says: "*rasika-bhakta-saṅge, rahiba pirīti raṅge, vraja-pure vasati kariyā* – one attains one's cherished desire by associating with and serving *rasika-bhaktas,* and by taking shelter of the land of Vraja."

Text 22

Sva-saṅkalpa-prakāśa-stotra (6) expresses the acceptance of Viśākhā Sakhī, whose beautiful voice defeats the sound of the cuckoo bird, as *śikṣā-guru*:

kuhū-kaṇṭhī-kaṇṭhād api kamala-kaṇṭhī mayi punar
viśākhā-gānasyāpi ca rucira-śikṣāṁ praṇayatu
yathāhaṁ tenaitad yuva-yugalam ullāsya sagaṇāl
labhe rāse tasmān maṇi-padaka-hārān iha muhuḥ

May Viśākhā, whose voice is sweeter than the cuckoo, teach me the captivating art of singing. With that singing, I will please the youthful couple Śrī Rādhā-Kṛṣṇa during the *rāsa* dance and will receive from Them gifts, such as jewelled lockets and necklaces, again and again.

kuhū-kaṇṭha-tiraskarī viśākhā-sundarī
gāna-vidyā śikhāibe more kṛpā kari'
sei gāne rādhā-kṛṣṇe rāse ullasiba
maṇi-padakādi pāritoṣika pāiba

Bhajana-rahasya-vṛtti

In this Text, Śrīla Raghunātha dāsa Gosvāmī prays to receive training in singing from Śrī Viśākhā-devī. With this training, Rati Mañjarī considers herself blessed to sing songs that are endowed with a variety of *rasa* and fragrant with cleverness in amorous *rasa.* She sings these songs to please the Divine Couple during the *rāsa-līlā*, the crown jewel of all pastimes, and thus receives many kinds of gifts from Them. Rati Mañjarī knows the desire of Śyāmasundara and, on the direction of Svāminī, she sings wonderfully melodious songs with her sweet, pleasing voice. She has learned to sing so beautifully from Viśākhā, whose soft, pleasant voice defeats the attractive *kuhū-kuhū* sound of the cuckoo bird. During the *rāsa* dance, which is filled with an abundance of tasteful mellows, Rati Mañjarī sings intoxicating, sweet notes in harmony with Viśākhā. Śrī Rādhā-Mādhava become overjoyed by this and give Their priceless necklaces and other ornaments to her as gifts. This remuneration makes the heart of Rati Mañjarī's *guru*, Viśākhā-devī, blossom with joy. Understanding that her efforts have been successful, Viśākhā-devī profusely praises Rati Mañjarī.

Viśākhā, who is both dear to and non-different from Śrī Rādhā, is zealous in Her service. She is extremely clever in the art of speaking, and she even defeats Śrī Kṛṣṇa in that art. Kṛṣṇa is also pleased by her smiling and laughing. Śrī Dāsa Gosvāmī, fixed in his *svarūpa* as Rati Mañjarī, is eager to learn speech that is full of joking, full of clever *rasa* and cooling like camphor. Therefore, to learn to speak in this supremely relishable, intoxicating way that is related to *mādhurya-rasa*, he accepts Viśākhā as *guru*.

Text 23

Śrī Gīta-govinda (1.12) describes the ecstasy of the *rāsa* dance, the eternal *rāsa-vilāsa* of Kṛṣṇa and the *vraja-sundarīs*:

viśveṣām anurañjanena janayann ānandam indīvara-
śreṇī śyāmala-komalair upanayann aṅgair anaṅgotsavam
svacchandaṁ vraja-sundarībhir abhitaḥ pratyaṅgam āliṅgitaḥ
śṛṅgāraḥ sakhi mūrtimān iva madhau mugdho hariḥ krīḍati

O *sakhī*, He who gives pleasure and bliss to all the *gopīs*; whose limbs are bluish-black, very soft and resemble blue lotuses; whose qualities awaken the festival of Kandarpa (Cupid) that lies dormant within the *gopīs'* hearts; and who is embraced by each and every limb of the *gopīs* – that Kṛṣṇa is sporting like amorous love personified in the spring season.

madhu-ṛtu madhukara-pāṅti
madhura kusuma madhu-māti

madhura vṛndāvana mājha
madhura-madhura rasa-rāja

madhura-naṭinīgaṇa-saṅga
madhura-madhura rasaraṅga

sumadhura yantra-rasāla
madhura-madhura karatāla

madhura-naṭana-gati-bhaṅga
madhura naṭanī-naṭa-raṅga

madhura-madhura rasa-gāna
madhura vidyāpati bhāṇa

Bhajana-rahasya-vṛtti

The crown jewel of connoisseurs of mellows, *dhīra-lalita-nāyaka* Vrajendra-nandana Śrī Kṛṣṇacandra, appears as Kāmadeva personified and relishes *śṛṅgāra-rasa* with the *vraja-devīs*. One *sakhī* informs her friend that in a nearby forest of *kuñjas*, Śrī Kṛṣṇa is absorbed in *rāsa-vilāsa* with the young *gopīs*. She says, "Look *sakhī*, look! Just see how Kṛṣṇa, possessed by an eager desire for captivating amorous sports, is bound by the embraces of the young women of Vraja." One *gopa-ramaṇī* is lovingly embracing Śrī Kṛṣṇa and sweetly singing. Another *gopī* is pressing against Śrī Kṛṣṇa with her uplifted, hard breasts. One *gopa-ramaṇī* with heavy hips is blooming with *prema*. On the pretext of whispering into His ear, she fulfils her heartfelt wish by kissing Him. Śrī Kṛṣṇa is also increasing the love of the beautiful women of Vraja by embracing and kissing them and pleasing them with His smiling sidelong glances. Śrī Hari, not considering right or wrong, displays His charming pastimes with the *gopa-ramaṇīs* in the spring season. He creates a great festival of Cupid by awarding the *rasa* longed for by the *vraja-sundarīs* with His soft, bluish-black limbs, which resemble a blue lotus. He is freely embracing and touching the *vraja-ramaṇīs*, thus manifesting Himself as the personification of *śṛṅgāra-rasa*.

The word *indīvara* in this Text indicates "coolness", the word *śreṇī* indicates "relishing ever-fresh mellows", *śyāmala* indicates "beauty" and *komala* indicates "extreme softness".

Text 24

Jagannātha-vallabha-nāṭaka (3.11) describes the happiness the *gopīs* feel upon attaining Śrī Kṛṣṇa's *darśana* after being separated from Him. In other words it describes the condition of the *gopīs* when they are meeting with Him:

yadā yāto daivān madhu-ripur asau locana-pathaṁ
tadāsmākaṁ ceto madana-hatakenāhṛtam abhūt
punar yasminn eṣa kṣaṇam api dṛśor eti padavīṁ
vidhāsyāmas tasminn akhila-ghaṭikā ratna-khacitāḥ

[Śrī Rādhā said:] From the moment Śrī Kṛṣṇa, the enemy of the Madhu demon, unexpectedly came before My eyes, wicked Cupid stole My heart. Nonetheless, if He will come within My vision again, I will decorate those moments with jewels.

ye kāle vā svapane, dekhinu vaṁśī-vadane,
sei kāle āilā dui vairī
'ānanda' āra 'madana', hari' nila mora mana,
dekhite nā pāiluṅ netra bhari'

punaḥ yadi kona kṣaṇa, karāya kṛṣṇa daraśana,
tabe sei ghaṭī kṣaṇa-pala
diyā mālya-candana, nānā ratna-ābharaṇa,
alaṅkṛta karimu sakala

Bhajana-rahasya-vṛtti

This Text, written by Śrī Rāya Rāmānanda, describes Śrī Rādhā's deep attachment for Śrī Kṛṣṇa, which She expresses to Her intimate friend Madanikā. Madanikā consoles Her, saying, "Why are You so sad? Just see! The captivating fragrance of the newly blossomed *ketakī* flowers attracts the bumblebee from afar. But if the bumblebee finds no honey in the flower over which it hovers, doesn't it abandon that flower? Similarly, You became attracted by seeing Śrī Kṛṣṇa's lotus face, but in Kṛṣṇa there was no *prema.* And even if Kṛṣṇa has *prema,* He has no understanding of how much *prema* You have, so it is only appropriate to give Him up."

Śrī Rādhā contained Herself and then said, "All right, I will now give Him up." She shuddered, Her heart full of fear, and then, with a trembling voice, said, "O *sakhī,* I have given Him up as you told Me, but I cannot give up My memories of His beauty and qualities. As much as I try to forget Him, to that degree memories arise in My mind of His gentle, soft, smiling lotus face and His reddish *bimba*-fruit-like lips on which the *vaṁśī* splendidly rests. When I receive this enchanting *darśana,* two enemies, *madana* (Cupid) and *ānanda* (joy), appear and obstruct My vision."

Saying this, Śrī Rādhā lost external consciousness and fainted. Such a condition resulted from Her increased longing to have Śrī Kṛṣṇa's *darśana.* This longing caused an inexpressible happiness to arise in Her heart, and She was overwhelmed by a deep yearning to serve Kṛṣṇa with Her body.

Later, Śrī Rādhā said to Madanikā, "O *sakhī,* if Kṛṣṇa gives Me His *darśana* now, I will not let these two enemies, *madana* and *ānanda,* enter My heart, and I will take *darśana* of Him to My full satisfaction. I will decorate the moments that give Me *darśana* of My beloved with garlands, sandalwood paste and various jewelled ornaments."

Text 25

The midnight pastimes (*rātri-līlā*) are described in *Govinda-līlāmṛta* (22.1):

tāv utkau labdha-saṅgau bahu-paricaraṇair vṛndayārādhyamānau
preṣṭhālībhir lasantau vipina-viharaṇair gāna-rāsādi-lāsyaiḥ
nānā-līlā-nitāntau praṇaya-sahacarī-vṛnda-saṁsevyamānau
rādhā-kṛṣṇau niśāyāṁ sukusuma-śayane prāpta-nidrau smarāmi

At night Rādhā and Kṛṣṇa, who are very anxious to see one another, finally meet. Their dear *gopīs* worship Them by performing many services. Rādhā and Kṛṣṇa become exhausted from roaming in the forest, singing, dancing in the *rāsa-līlā* and performing other pastimes with these most beloved *sakhīs*. Their group of loving maidservants then serve Them by fanning Them, offering Them camphor and *tāmbūla*, massaging Their feet and so forth. Then the Divine Couple go to sleep on a bed of flowers. I remember that Rādhā-Kṛṣṇa.

vṛndā-paricaryā pāñā, preṣṭhāli-gaṇere lañā,
rādhā-kṛṣṇa rāsādika-līlā
gīta-lāsya kaila kata, sevā kaila sakhī yata,
kusuma-śayyāya dūṅhe śuilā

niśā-bhāge nidrā gela, sabe ānandita haila,
sakhī-gaṇa parānande bhāse
e sukha śayana smari, bhaja mana rādhā hari,
sei līlā praveśera āśe

Bhajana-rahasya-vṛtti

The *sakhīs* return to Jāvaṭa-grāma from Nanda-bhavana with various kinds of food preparations, given by Dhaniṣṭhā or Kundalatā, that are mixed with Kṛṣṇa's *adharāmṛta*, the nectar of His lips. By the beauty and fragrance of these preparations, the eyes and nose of Svāminī and the other *sakhīs* are satisfied. The *sakhīs* also bring some indication of the place of rendezvous (*abhisāra*). At night, when everyone is sleeping, the *sakhīs* dress and decorate Śrī Svāminī with clothes and ornaments suitable to the phase of the moon, and take Her for *abhisāra*. Svāminī meets Her beloved at the designated place and They relish joking, playing dice, *rāsa-līlā* and other pastimes. The young couple then rest on a bed of flowers, which has been prepared by the *sakhīs*. At the end of the night, They awaken, much to the happiness of the *sakhīs*.

Śrīla Bhaktivinoda Ṭhākura's concluding words to Śrī Bhajana-rahasya

sādhanera saha aṣṭakāla-līlā-dhana
cintite cintite krame siddha bhāvāpana

svarūpa-siddhite vraje prakaṭāvasthāna
guṇamaya gopī-dehe līlāra vitāna

kṛṣṇa-kṛpā bale guṇamaya vapu tyaji'
aprakaṭa vraje gopī sālokyādi bhaji

nitya-kāla śuddha-dehe rādhā-kṛṣṇa-sevā
sthūla-liṅga-saṅga-bodha āra pāya kebā

'hare kṛṣṇa'-nāma gāne nitya-mukta-bhāve
pūrṇa-premānanda-lābha anāyāse pābe

dekha bhāi! sādhane siddhite eka-i bhāva
kabhu nāhi chāḍe nāma svakīya prabhāva

ataeva nāma gāo, nāma kara sāra
āra kona sādhanera nā kara vicāra

The *rāgānuga-bhakta*, and especially the *rūpānuga-bhakta*, remember Śrī Rādhā-Kṛṣṇa Yugala's night pastimes, and while chanting the holy name, they humbly pray, "When will I attain service in these pastimes?"

The *sādhaka* remembers these pastimes in the association of *rasika-bhaktas* and gradually attains perfection. Upon attaining *svarūpa-siddhi*, he takes birth in a *gopī's* house in *prakaṭa-līlā* by the arrangement of Yogamāyā. There, under the guidance of Kṛṣṇa's eternal associates, his *sevā* in the pastimes matures. He gives up his attachment to family etc. and attains the body of a *gopī* in the *aprakaṭa-līlā* of eternal Vṛndāvana. There, he is forever absorbed in serving Rādhā and Kṛṣṇa in his perfected body. At the time of *sādhana*, the gross and subtle bodies are obstacles in attaining one's eternal service. However, constant performance of Hare Kṛṣṇa *nāma-kīrtana* manifests the *sādhaka's* pure identity (*śuddha-svarūpa*). The *sādhaka-bhakta* who follows *rāga-mārga*, the path of spontaneous devotion, remembers pastimes by means of his internally contemplated body. The *bhāvas* upon which the *sādhaka* meditates at the time of *sādhana* will be attained by him at the time of perfection.

Thus ends the *Aṣṭama-yāma-sādhana*,
Rātri-līlā, of *Śrī Bhajana-rahasya*.
Thus ends *Śrī Bhajana-rahasya*.

Appendix

Śrī Gauḍīya Vaiṣṇavas'

Saṅkṣepa-arcana-paddhati

(abbreviated manual on deity worship)

Nāma-saṅkīrtana gives all perfection; nonetheless, in one's devotional life, some activities related to *arcana* give special benefit.

In the early morning, after taking bath, the *sādhaka* should sit on an *āsana* (seat) and face east. While touching the water in the *pañcapātra*, he should summon all the *tīrthas* by chanting the following *mantra*:

gaṅge ca yamune caiva
godāvari sarasvati
narmade sindho kāveri
jale 'smin sannidhiṁ kuru

O Gaṅgā, O Yamunā, O Godāvarī, O Sarasvatī, O Narmadā, O Sindhu, O Kāverī, please become present in this water.

He should sprinkle the water on his head, uttering *viṣṇuḥ* three times, and then perform *ācamana*. Thereafter he should apply *tilaka* in twelve places with *gopī-candana*. The *mantras* for applying *tilaka* are as follows:

lalāṭe keśavaṁ dhyāyen
nārāyaṇaṁ athodare
vakṣaḥ-sthale mādhavaṁ tu
govindaṁ kaṇṭha-kūpake

viṣṇuṁ ca dakṣiṇe kukṣau
bāhau ca madhusūdanam
trivikramaṁ kandhare tu
vāmanaṁ vāma-pārśvake

śrīdharaṁ vāma-bāhau tu
hṛṣīkeśaṁ ca kandhare
pṛṣṭhe tu padmanābhaṁ ca
kaṭyāṁ dāmodaraṁ nyaset

tat prakṣālana-toyaṁ tu
vāsudevāya mūrdhani

When one marks the forehead with *tilaka*, he must remember Keśava. When one marks the lower abdomen, he must remember Nārāyaṇa. For the chest, one should remember Mādhava, and when marking the hollow of the neck one should remember Govinda. Viṣṇu should be remembered while marking the right side of the belly, and Madhusūdana should be remembered when marking the right arm. Trivikrama should be remembered when marking the right shoulder, and Vāmana should be remembered when marking the left side of the belly. Śrīdhara should be remembered while marking the left arm, and Hṛṣīkeśa should be remembered when marking the left shoulder. Padmanābha and Dāmodara should be remembered when marking the back.

First, the *sādhaka* should worship his *guru* (*guru-pūjā*), and meditate on him as follows:

prātaḥ śrīman-navadvīpe
dvi-netraṁ dvi-bhujaṁ gurum
varābhaya-pradaṁ śāntaṁ
smaret tan-nāma-pūrvakam

> In the early morning, chant *śrī gurudeva's* name while remembering him as being situated in Śrī Navadvīpa or Śrī Vṛndāvana-dhāma, and possessing two eyes and two arms. He is the bestower of fearlessness and the embodiment of peacefulness.

At the Yogapīṭha in Śrī Māyāpura, in transcendental Navadvīpa, Śrī Caitanya Mahāprabhu is seated upon a jewelled platform. Śrī Nityānanda Prabhu is seated on His right, and Śrī Gadādhara Paṇḍita on His left. Śrī Advaita Ācārya stands at the front offering prayers with folded hands and Śrīvāsa Paṇḍita stands beside him holding an umbrella. The *guru* is seated on an altar below them. In this way one should meditate on sitting near *śrī gurudeva* and worship him by offering sixteen articles while chanting the appropriate *mantra* for each:

idam āsanam aiṁ gurudevāya namaḥ
etat pādyam aiṁ gurudevāya namaḥ
idam arghyam aiṁ gurudevāya namaḥ
idam ācamanīyam aiṁ gurudevāya namaḥ
eṣa madhuparkaḥ aiṁ gurudevāya namaḥ
idaṁ punar ācamanīyam aiṁ gurudevāya namaḥ
idaṁ snānīyam aiṁ gurudevāya namaḥ
idaṁ sottarīya-vastram aiṁ gurudevāya namaḥ
idam ābharaṇam aiṁ gurudevāya namaḥ
eṣa gandhaḥ aiṁ gurudevāya namaḥ
eṣa dhūpaḥ aiṁ gurudevāya namaḥ
eṣa dīpaḥ aiṁ gurudevāya namaḥ
idaṁ sacandana-puṣpam aiṁ gurudevāya namaḥ
idaṁ naivedyam aiṁ gurudevāya namaḥ
idaṁ pānīya-jalam aiṁ gurudevāya namaḥ
idaṁ punar ācamanīyam aiṁ gurudevāya namaḥ
idaṁ tāmbūlam aiṁ gurudevāya namaḥ
idaṁ sarvam aiṁ gurudevāya namaḥ

One should then chant the *guru-gāyatrī-mantra* according to one's capacity:

aiṁ gurudevāya vidmahe kṛṣṇānandāya
dhīmahi tan no guruḥ pracodayāt

Let us now meditate upon *śrī gurudeva*, who is always giving pleasure to Rādhā and Kṛṣṇa. Let us try to understand *śrī guru*. May he inspire and guide us from within.

After that one should offer obeisances to *guru*:

ajñāna-timirāndhasya
jñānāñjana-śalākayā
cakṣur unmīlitaṁ yena
tasmai śrī-gurave namaḥ

O Gurudeva, you are so merciful. I offer my humble obeisances unto you and am praying from the core of my heart that, with the torchlight of divine knowledge, you open my eyes, which have been blinded by the darkness of ignorance.

Then offer obeisances to the Vaiṣṇavas:

vāñchā-kalpa-tarubhyaś ca
kṛpā-sindhubhya eva ca
patitānāṁ pāvanebhyo
vaiṣṇavebhyo namo namaḥ

I offer obeisances unto the Vaiṣṇavas, who are just like wish-fulfilling desire trees, who are an ocean of mercy and who deliver the fallen, conditioned souls.

Thereafter one should perform *pūjā* of Śrī Gaurāṅga, who is comprised of five principles or truths, meditating on Him as follows:

śrīman-mauktikadāma-baddha-cikuraṁ susmera-candrānanaṁ
śrī-khaṇḍāguru-cāru-citra-vasanaṁ srag-divya-bhuṣāñcitam
nṛtyāveśa-rasānumoda-madhuraṁ kandarpa-veśojjvalaṁ
caitanyaṁ kanaka-dyutiṁ nija-janaiḥ saṁsevyamānaṁ bhaje

I worship Śrī Caitanyadeva, whose hair is intertwined with beautiful garlands of pearls, whose face is splendorous like a radiant moon, whose limbs are smeared with *candana* and *aguru* and who, adorned with wonderful clothes, garlands and transcendental, glittering ornaments, dances while absorbed in ecstasies of sweet mellows. His body of golden complexion, being adorned with the ornaments of *bhāva*, makes Him appear like an enchanting Cupid amidst the presence of His intimate associates.

Śrī gaura-pūjā:

idam āsanaṁ klīṁ kṛṣṇa-caitanyāya namaḥ
etat pādyaṁ klīṁ kṛṣṇa-caitanyāya namaḥ
idam arghyaṁ klīṁ kṛṣṇa-caitanyāya namaḥ
idam ācamanīyaṁ klīṁ kṛṣṇa-caitanyāya namaḥ
eṣa madhuparkaḥ klīṁ kṛṣṇa-caitanyāya namaḥ
idaṁ punar ācamanīyaṁ klīṁ kṛṣṇa-caitanyāya namaḥ
idam snānīyaṁ klīṁ kṛṣṇa-caitanyāya namaḥ
idaṁ sottarīya-vastraṁ klīṁ kṛṣṇa-caitanyāya namaḥ
idam ābharaṇaṁ klīṁ kṛṣṇa-caitanyāya namaḥ
eṣa gandhaḥ klīṁ kṛṣṇa-caitanyāya namaḥ
eṣa dhūpaḥ klīṁ kṛṣṇa-caitanyāya namaḥ
eṣa dīpaḥ klīṁ kṛṣṇa-caitanyāya namaḥ
idaṁ sacandana-puṣpaṁ klīṁ kṛṣṇa-caitanyāya namaḥ
idaṁ sacandana-tulasī-patraṁ klīṁ kṛṣṇa-caitanyāya namaḥ
idaṁ naivedyaṁ klīṁ kṛṣṇa-caitanyāya namaḥ
idaṁ pānīya-jalaṁ klīṁ kṛṣṇa-caitanyāya namaḥ
idaṁ punar ācamanīyaṁ klīṁ kṛṣṇa-caitanyāya namaḥ
idaṁ tāmbūlaṁ klīṁ kṛṣṇa-caitanyāya namaḥ
idaṁ mālyaṁ klīṁ kṛṣṇa-caitanyāya namaḥ
idaṁ sarvaṁ klīṁ kṛṣṇa-caitanyāya namaḥ

After completing worship of Śrī Gaura, one should chant the *gaura-gāyatrī* according to one's capacity:

klīṁ kṛṣṇa-caitanyāya vidmahe viśvambharāya
dhīmahi tan no gauraḥ pracodayāt

> Let us try to understand Śrī Kṛṣṇa Caitanya. Let us meditate upon Viśvambhara, who is maintaining the entire universe. May that golden-complexioned Gaura manifest within our hearts and inspire us.

Thereafter one should offer obeisances to Gaurasundara with the following *mantra*:

ānanda-līlā-maya-vigrahāya
hemābha-divyac-chavi-sundarāya
tasmai mahā-prema-rasa-pradāya
caitanya-candrāya namo namas te

> I offer obeisances unto Śrī Caitanya-candra, whose form is the embodiment of blissful, transcendental pastimes, whose golden complexion is divinely beautiful, and who bestows unlimited nectar in the mellows of *prema*.

One should then perform *arcana* of Śrī Rādhā-Kṛṣṇa with the consciousness that it is the mercy of *śrī guru* and Śrī Gaurāṅga. First, one should meditate on Śrī Vṛndāvana:

tato vṛndāvanaṁ dhyāyet
paramānanda-vardhanam
kālindī-jala-kallola-
saṅgi-māruta-sevitam

nānā-puṣpa-latābaddha-
vṛkṣa-ṣaṇḍaiś ca maṇḍitam
koṭi-sūrya-samā bhāsaṁ
vimuktaṁ ṣaṭ-taraṅgakaiḥ

tan-madhye ratna-khacitaṁ
svarṇa-siṁhāsanaṁ mahat

> Meditate on a great golden throne studded with jewels within the divine realm of Śrī Vṛndāvana-dhāma. A place of ever-increasing bliss, Vṛndāvana-dhāma is served by breezes that are cooled by

the touch of the Yamunā's waves and decorated with various types of flowers, creepers and trees. Its splendour is like that of millions of suns and it is ever free from the six waves of material nature (namely lust, anger, greed, envy, false ego and illusion).

Hereafter, one should meditate on Śrī Rādhā-Kṛṣṇa, who are sitting on a golden throne inlaid with jewels:

śrī-kṛṣṇaṁ śrī-ghanaśyāmaṁ
pūrṇānanda-kalevaram
dvibhujaṁ sarva-deveśaṁ
rādhāliṅgita-vigraham

I meditate on Śrī Kṛṣṇa, whose bluish-black colour resembles that of a fresh raincloud, whose body is full of transcendental bliss, who possesses two arms, who is the Lord of all the demigods and who is embraced by Śrīmatī Rādhikā.

Then, one should offer *pūjā* to Śrī Rādhā-Kṛṣṇa with sixteen articles:

idam āsanaṁ śrīṁ klīṁ rādhā-kṛṣṇābhyāṁ namaḥ
etat pādyaṁ śrīṁ klīṁ rādhā-kṛṣṇābhyāṁ namaḥ
idam arghyaṁ śrīṁ klīṁ rādhā-kṛṣṇābhyāṁ namaḥ
idam ācamanīyaṁ śrīṁ klīṁ rādhā-kṛṣṇābhyāṁ namaḥ
eṣa madhuparkaḥ śrīṁ klīṁ rādhā-kṛṣṇābhyāṁ namaḥ
idaṁ punar ācamanīyaṁ śrīṁ klīṁ rādhā-kṛṣṇābhyāṁ namaḥ
idaṁ snānīyaṁ śrīṁ klīṁ rādhā-kṛṣṇābhyāṁ namaḥ
idaṁ sottarīya-vastraṁ śrīṁ klīṁ rādhā-kṛṣṇābhyāṁ namaḥ
idam ābharaṇaṁ śrīṁ klīṁ rādhā-kṛṣṇābhyāṁ namaḥ
eṣa gandhaḥ śrīṁ klīṁ rādhā-kṛṣṇābhyāṁ namaḥ
eṣa dhūpaḥ śrīṁ klīṁ rādhā-kṛṣṇābhyāṁ namaḥ
eṣa dīpaḥ śrīṁ klīṁ rādhā-kṛṣṇābhyāṁ namaḥ
idaṁ sacandana-puṣpaṁ śrīṁ klīṁ rādhā-kṛṣṇābhyāṁ namaḥ
idaṁ sacandana-tulasī-patraṁ śrīṁ klīṁ rādhā-kṛṣṇābhyāṁ namaḥ
idaṁ naivedyaṁ śrīṁ klīṁ rādhā-kṛṣṇābhyāṁ namaḥ
idaṁ pānīya-jalam śrīṁ klīṁ rādhā-kṛṣṇābhyāṁ namaḥ

idaṁ punar ācamanīyaṁ śrīṁ klīṁ rādhā-kṛṣṇābhyāṁ namaḥ
idaṁ tāmbūlaṁ śrīṁ klīṁ rādhā-kṛṣṇābhyāṁ namaḥ
idaṁ mālyaṁ śrīṁ klīṁ rādhā-kṛṣṇābhyāṁ namaḥ
idaṁ sarvaṁ śrīṁ klīṁ rādhā-kṛṣṇābhyāṁ namaḥ

After the worship, one should chant this *yugala-gāyatrī-mantra* according to one's capacity:

klīṁ kṛṣṇāya vidmahe dāmodarāya
dhīmahi tan no kṛṣṇaḥ pracodayāt

Let us try to know the all-attractive Śrī Kṛṣṇa. Let us meditate upon Dāmodara, who is bound by the love of His devotees. May that Kṛṣṇa manifest in our hearts and inspire us.

śrīṁ rādhikāyai vidmahe prema-rūpāyai
dhīmahi tan no rādhā pracodayāt

Let us try to understand Śrīmatī Rādhikā. We meditate upon Her, who is the embodiment of *prema*. May that Rādhā manifest in our hearts and inspire us.

And then offer obeisances to Śrī Kṛṣṇa:

he kṛṣṇa karuṇā-sindho
dīna-bandho jagat-pate
gopeśa gopikā-kānta
rādhā-kānta namo 'stu te

I offer my unlimited obeisances unto You, O Kṛṣṇa! You are the ocean of mercy, friend of the fallen, Lord of creation and master of the cowherd community. You are Gopī-kānta, beloved of the *gopīs*, and above all You are Rādhā-kānta, the beloved of Śrīmatī Rādhikā.

And to Śrī Rādhā:

tapta-kāñcana-gaurāṅgi
rādhe vṛndāvaneśvari
vṛṣabhānu-sute devi
praṇamāmi hari-priye

O Gaurāṅgī, whose complexion is like molten gold! O Rādhā! Queen of Vṛndāvana! O daughter of Vṛṣabhānu Mahārāja! O Devī! O dearmost of Hari, obeisances unto You again and again!

After that, one should chant the *kāma-bīja, mūla-mantra* and *kāma-gāyatrī* according to one's capacity. And then, in the proper order, one should recite *padya-pañcaka* and *vijñapti-pañcaka* in a mood of distress.

Padya-pañcaka:

saṁsāra-sāgarān nātha
putra-mitra-gṛhāṅganāt
goptārau me yuvām eva
prapanna-bhaya-bhañjanau

O Śrī Rādha-Kṛṣṇa, You are my protectors from the ocean of material existence, which is characterised by sons, friends, household and land. Therefore You are known as the destroyers of fear for those who are surrendered unto You.

yo 'haṁ mamāsti yat kiñcid
iha loke paratra ca
tat sarvaṁ bhavato 'dyaiva
caraṇesu samarpitam

O Your Lordships, myself and whatever little I possess in this world and in the next – all this I now offer unto Your lotus feet.

aham apy aparādhānām
ālayas tyakta-sādhanaḥ
agatiś ca tato nāthau
bhavantau me parā gatiḥ

O Your Lordships, I am certainly the abode of many offences and I am completely devoid of any devotional practice. I don't have any other shelter; therefore, I regard You as my ultimate goal.

tavāsmi rādhikā-nātha
karmaṇā manasā girā
kṛṣṇa-kānte tavaivāsmi
yuvām eva gatir mama

O Master of Śrīmatī Rādhikā, I am Yours by actions, mind and words. O lover of Śrī Kṛṣṇa, Śrīmatī Rādhikā, I belong to You alone. You both are my only destination.

śaraṇaṁ vāṁ prapanno 'smi
karuṇā-nikarākarau
prasādaṁ kuru dāsyaṁ bho
mayi duṣṭe 'parādhini

O Śrī Rādhā-Kṛṣṇa, O oceans of mercy, I am taking shelter of You. Although I am fallen and an offender, kindly be pleased with me and make me Your servant.

Vijñapti-pañcaka:

mat-samo nāsti pāpātmā
nāparādhī ca kaścana
parihāre 'pi lajjā me
kiṁ bruve puruṣottama

O Puruṣottama, there is no one as sinful and offensive as I am. How can I describe myself? I even feel ashamed to give up my sins.

yuvatīnāṁ yathā yūni
yunāṁ ca yuvatau yathā
mano 'bhiramate tadvan
mano me ramatāṁ tvayi

Just as the minds of young ladies take pleasure in thinking of young men, and the minds of young men take pleasure in thinking of young women, kindly let my mind take pleasure in You alone.

bhūmau skhalita-pādānāṁ
bhūmir evāvalambanam
tvayi jātāparādhānāṁ
tvam eva śaraṇaṁ prabho

Just as the ground is the only support for those whose feet have slipped, so also You alone are the only shelter, even for those who have offended You.

govinda-vallabhe rādhe
prārthaye tvām ahaṁ sadā
tvadīyam iti jānātu
govindo māṁ tvayā saha

O Śrīmatī Rādhikā, dearest of Lord Govinda, this is always my request to You: may You and Govinda consider me to be Yours.

rādhe vṛndāvanādhīśe
karuṇāmṛta-vāhini
kṛpayā nija-pādābja-
dāsyaṁ mahyaṁ pradīyatām

O Śrīmatī Rādhikā, O queen of Vṛndāvana, You are a flowing river of nectarean compassion. Please be merciful unto me and grant me the service of Your lotus feet.

Thereafter, one should offer the remnants to *śrī guru* and Vaiṣṇavas:

etat mahā-prasāda nirmālyaṁ śrī-gurave namaḥ
etat pānīya-jalaṁ śrī-gurave namaḥ
etat prasāda-tāmbūlaṁ śrī-gurave namaḥ
etat sarvaṁ sarva-sakhībhyo namaḥ
śrī paurṇamāsyai namaḥ
sarva vraja-vāsibhyo namaḥ
sarva vaiṣṇavebhyo namaḥ

The *mantra* for picking *tulasī* before the *pūjā*:

tulasy-amṛta-janmāsi
sadā tvaṁ keśava-priye
keśavārthaṁ vicinomi
varadā bhava śobhane

O Tulasī of effulgent beauty, you have been produced from nectar during the churning of the milk ocean. You are always dear to Lord Keśava. I pick your leaves only for the worship of Śrī Kṛṣṇa. May you bestow upon me the benediction that my worship of Kṛṣṇa will obtain success.

Tulasī-pūjā:

nirmālya-gandha-puṣpādi-pānīya-jalaṁ
idam arghyaṁ śrī-tulasyai namaḥ

Tulasī-mantra:

nirmitā tvaṁ purā devair
arcitā tvaṁ surāsuraiḥ
tulasi hara me 'vidyāṁ
pūjāṁ gṛhna namo 'stu te

You came into being long ago, and are worshipped by gods and demons alike. O Tulasī, my obeisance unto you. Kindly dispel my ignorance and accept my worship.

Tulasī-praṇāma:

yā dṛṣṭā nikhilāgha-saṅgha-śamanī spṛṣṭā vapuḥ pāvanī
rogāṇām abhivanditā nirasanī siktā 'ntaka-trāsinī
pratyāsatti-vidhāyinī bhagavataḥ kṛṣṇasya saṁropitā
nyastā tac-caraṇe subhakti-phaladā tasyai tulasyai namaḥ

O Tulasī, I offer my respectful obeisances unto you. Simply by seeing you all sins are destroyed. Simply by touching you one's body is purified. By offering obeisances unto you all diseases are driven away. By offering water unto you the fear of death is dispelled. By planting you one obtains proximity to the Lord. By offering you unto the lotus feet of Śrī Kṛṣṇa, one obtains a special type of devotion, the rare fruit of *prema-bhakti.*

After offering obeisances to *tulasī*, one should chant the prescribed number of *kṛṣṇa-nāma* on *tulasī* beads with *sambandha-jñāna.* While chanting the holy name, which is supremely auspicious and the eternal truth, there is no consideration of time, place, purity or impurity. Thereafter, recite the following *mantra*, accept *śrī-kṛṣṇa-caraṇāmṛta* and then touch it to the head:

aśeṣa-kleśa-niḥśeṣa-
kāraṇaṁ śuddha-bhakti-dam
kṛṣṇa-pādodakaṁ pītvā
śirasā dhārayāmy aham

Having drunk the water from the lotus feet of Śrī Kṛṣṇa, which bestows pure *bhakti* and causes the destruction of unlimited miseries and pains, I take that water on my head.

After that one should chant the following *mantra* and accept some *mahā-prasāda*:

rudanti pātakāḥ sarve
niśvasanti muhur-muhuḥ
hā hā kṛtvā palāyanti
jagannāthānna-bhakṣaṇāt

When one simply takes the foodstuffs offered to Jagannātha, all types of sins gasp, and crying out "Alas! Alas!" flee for their lives.

Then, one should offer full prostrated obeisances with the following *mantra*:

dorbhyāṁ padbhyāṁ ca jānubhyām
urasā śirasā dṛśā
manasā vacasā ceti
praṇāmo 'ṣṭāṅga īritaḥ

I offer obeisances with eight parts: the arms, the feet, the knees, the chest, the forehead, the mind, vision and speech.

Thus ends the morning duties.

In the evening, one should chant the *kāma-bīja*, *mūla-mantra* and *kāma-gāyatrī* twelve times. One should never eat or drink anything that is not in the mode of goodness and not offered to Śrī Bhagavān.

pathyaṁ pūtam anāmayantam
āhāryaṁ sāttvikaṁ viduḥ
rājasam indriya-preṣṭhaṁ
tāmasam ārtido 'śuciḥ

Foods in the mode of goodness are wholesome, pure and do not cause pain. Foods in the mode of passion are dear to the senses. Foods in the mode of ignorance are unclean and cause suffering.

One should observe *vratas* on Śrī Ekādaśī, appearance days of *viṣṇu-tattva* and so forth, to one's capacity. One should never fall into bad association. Abandoning such association is the virtuous practice of a Vaiṣṇava.

Thus ends the *Saṅkṣepa-arcana-paddhati.*

Glossary

A

Abhisāra – rendezvous or tryst with Śrī Kṛṣṇa.

Ācamana – a ritual of purification in which one sips water from the palm of the right hand and then chants a particular name of Bhagavān.

Ācārya – spiritual preceptor, one who teaches by example.

Adhirūḍha-bhāva, adhirūḍha-mahābhāva – the highest state of *mahābhāva*, found only in the *gopīs* of Vraja. The mood in which all the *anubhāvas* that are manifested in resolute *mahābhāva* attain special characteristics that are even more astonishing than those *anubhāvas* in their normal forms. There are two types of *adhirūḍha-bhāva*: (1) *modana* and (2) *mādana*. (1) The *adhirūḍha* in which all the *sāttvika-bhāvas* of the *nāyaka* and *nāyikā* are aroused to a much greater extent than in the brightly burning (*uddīpta*) condition is called *modana*. *Modana* does not occur anywhere other than in Śrī Rādhā's group. In some special conditions of separation *modana* becomes *mohana*, and as an effect of this helpless condition of separation, all the *sāttvika-bhāvas* manifest in the blazing (*sūddīpta*) condition. (2) When *mahābhāva* increases even further it attains an extremely advanced condition. The paramount emotion in which it becomes jubilant due to the simultaneous manifestation of all types of transcendental emotions is called *mādana*. This *mādana-bhāva* is eternally and splendidly manifest only in Śrī Rādhā, and occurs only at the time of meeting. It is also referred to as *mādanākhya-mahābhāva.*

Ahaitukī-bhakti – unalloyed devotion.

Aiśvarya – opulence, splendour, majesty or supremacy; in regard to *bhakti*, this refers to devotion to Śrī Kṛṣṇa in a mood of awe and reverence rather than sweetness (*mādhurya*), thus restricting the intimacy of exchange between Śrī Bhagavān and His devotee.

Aiśvarya-jñāna – awareness of the aspect of divinity.

Ajāta-rati-sādhaka – a *sādhaka* who has not attained the stage of *bhāva*.

Akiñcana – without material possessions; one who considers he has nothing but Kṛṣṇa.

Ānanda – spiritual bliss, ecstasy, joy or happiness.

Anartha – (*an-artha* = non-value) unwanted desires, activities or habits that impede one's advancement in *bhakti*; in other words, everything that is against *bhakti*.

Anartha-nivṛtti – the clearing of all unwanted desires from the heart. This is the third stage in the development of the creeper of devotion, which occurs by the influence of *sādhu-saṅga* and *bhajana-kriyā*.

Aṇimā – the mystic perfection of being able to become small like a particle.

Anubhāvas – one of the five essential ingredients of *rasa*. The actions which display or reveal the spiritual emotions situated within the heart are called *anubhāvas*. They are thirteen in number: dancing (*nṛtya*), rolling on the ground (*viluṭhita*), singing (*gīta*), loud crying (*krośana*), writhing of the body (*tanu-moṭana*), roaring (*huṅkāra*), yawning (*jṛmbhaṇa*), breathing heavily (*śvāsa-bhūmā*), neglecting others (*lokānupekṣitā*), drooling (*lālāsrāva*), loud laughter (*aṭṭahāsa*), staggering about (*ghūrṇā*) and hiccups (*hikkā*).

Anurāga – (1) attachment, affection or love; (2) an intensified stage of *prema* which comes just prior to *mahābhāva*. In *Ujjvala-nīlamaṇi*

(14.146) *anurāga* has been defined as follows: "Although one regularly meets with the beloved and is well-acquainted with the beloved, the ever-fresh sentiment of intense attachment causes the beloved to be newly experienced at every moment as if one has never before had any experience of such a person. The attachment which inspires such a feeling is known as *anurāga*."

Aparādha – (*apa* = against, taking away; *rādha* = flow of affection) an offence committed against the holy name, Vaiṣṇavas, the spiritual master, the scriptures, holy places or the deity.

Aparāhna – late afternoon.

Aprārabdha – unfructified; the action has been performed and its result, although not yet manifested, is gradually coming to fruition.

Ārati – the ceremony of offering a deity articles of worship, such as incense, lamp, flowers and fan, accompanied by chanting and bell-ringing.

Arcana – deity worship; one of the nine primary processes of devotional service.

Artha – acquisition of wealth, economic development; one of the four goals of human life (*puruṣārthas*).

Ārya-patha – the path of honesty and chastity indicated in the scriptures.

Āsakti – attachment; this especially refers to attachment for the Lord and His eternal associates. *Āsakti* occurs when one's liking for *bhajana* leads to a direct and deep attachment for the personality who is the object of that *bhajana*. This is the sixth stage in the development of the creeper of devotion, and is awakened upon the maturing of one's taste for *bhajana*.

Āśrama – one of the four stages of life: *brahmācārī*, *gṛhastha*, *vānaprastha* and *sannyāsa*.

Aṣṭa-kālīya-līlā – the pastimes that Śrī Kṛṣṇa performs with His associates during the eight periods of the day. *Sādhakas* who are engaged in *smaraṇa* (remembrance) meditate on these pastimes: (1) *niśānta*-

līlā, pastimes at the end of night; (2) *prātaḥ-līlā*, pastimes at dawn; (3) *pūrvāhna-līlā*, morning pastimes; (4) *madhyāhna-līlā*, midday pastimes; (5) *aparāhna-līlā*, afternoon pastimes; (6) *sāyaṁ-līlā*, pastimes at dusk; (7) *pradoṣa-līlā*, evening pastimes; and (8) *rātri-līlā*, night pastimes.

Aṣṭāṅga-yoga – the *yoga* system consisting of eight parts: *yama* (control of the senses), *niyama* (control of the mind), *āsana* (bodily postures), *prāṇāyāma* (breath control), *pratyāhāra* (withdrawal of the mind from sensory perception), *dhāraṇā* (steadying the mind), *dhyāna* (meditation) and *samādhi* (deep and unbroken absorption on the Lord in the heart).

Aṣṭa-sakhīs – Śrīmatī Rādhikā's eight principal *gopīs*: Lalitā, Viśakhā, Citrā, Indulekha, Campakalatā, Raṅga-devī, Sudevī and Tuṅgavidyā.

Aṣṭa-sāttvika-bhāvas – see **Sāttvika-bhāvas**.

Aśvamedha-yajña – horse sacrifice.

Āvaraṇātmikā – one of the illusory energy's functions: to cover real knowledge, so the conditioned soul feels satisfied in any condition of life.

Avatāra – (literally means "one who descends") a partially or fully empowered incarnation of Śrī Bhagavān who is described in the scriptures. An *avatāra* descends from the spiritual world to the material universe with a particular mission.

B

Bahiraṅga-śakti – the Lord's external or material potency, also known as *māyā-śakti*. This potency is responsible for the creation of the material world, as well as all affairs pertaining to it. Because the Lord never directly contacts the material energy, this potency is known as *bahiraṅga*, external.

Bhagavān – the Supreme Lord; the Supreme Personality of Godhead. The *Viṣṇu Purāṇa* (6.5.72–4) defines Bhagavān as follows: "The word *bhagavat* is used to describe the Supreme Brahman who possesses all opulence, who is completely pure and who is the cause of all causes. In the word *bhagavat* the syllable *bha* has two meanings: (1) one who maintains all living entities and (2) one who causes all living entities to obtain the results of *karma* and *jñāna*. Complete opulence, religiosity, fame, beauty, knowledge and renunciation are known as *bhaga*, fortune." The suffix *vat* means possessing. Thus one who possesses these six fortunes is known as Bhagavān.

Bhagavat-kathā – see **Hari-kathā**.

Bhajana – (1) activities performed with the consciousness of being a servant of Śrī Kṛṣṇa. The *Garuḍa Purāṇa* (*Pūrva-khaṇḍa* 231.3) explains that the verbal root *bhaj* is used specifically in the sense of *sevā*, service; (2) in a general sense *bhajana* refers to the performance of spiritual practices, especially hearing, chanting and meditating upon Śrī Kṛṣṇa's name, form, qualities and pastimes.

Bhajana-kriyā – taking up the practices of *bhakti*, such as hearing and chanting. There are sixty-four primary limbs of *bhakti*, of which the first four are: to take shelter of the lotus feet of the spiritual master; to receive initiation (*dīkṣā*) and spiritual instruction (*śikṣā*); to serve one's *guru* with great affection; and to follow the path of *sādhus*. Without adopting these practices, there is no question of making any advancement in *bhajana*. This is the second stage in the development of the creeper of devotion, and it occurs by the influence of *sādhu-saṅga*.

Bhakta – a devotee.

Bhakti – loving devotional service to Śrī Kṛṣṇa. The word *bhakti* comes from the root *bhaj*, which means to serve; therefore the primary meaning of the word *bhakti* is to render service.

Bhāva – (1) spiritual emotions, love or sentiments; (2) the initial stage of perfection in devotion (*bhāva-bhakti*). A stage of *bhakti* in which *śuddha-sattva*, the essence of the Lord's internal potency consisting of spiritual knowledge and bliss, is transmitted into the heart of the practising devotee from the heart of the Lord's eternal associates and softens the heart by different kinds of taste. It is the sprout of *prema*, and it is also known as *rati*. This is the seventh stage of the creeper of devotion.

Brahmacārī – a member of the first *āśrama* (stage of life) in the *varṇāśrama* system; a celibate, unmarried student.

Brahman – the spiritual effulgence emanating from the transcendental body of the Lord; the all-pervading, indistinct feature of the Absolute. Depending on the context, this may sometimes refer to the Supreme Brahman, Śrī Kṛṣṇa, who is the source of Brahman.

Brāhma-muhūrta – the auspicious period of the day just before dawn, from one and a half hours to fifty minutes before sunrise.

Brāhmaṇa – the highest of the four *varṇas* (casts) in the *varṇāśrama* system; a priest or teacher.

Brāhmaṇī – a female *brāhmaṇa*; the wife of a *brāhmaṇa*.

C

Cakora bird – a bird that lives solely on moonlight.

Caraṇāmṛta – water that has been used to bathe the feet of Śrī Kṛṣṇa or His associates.

Cit-śakti – the poteny that relates to the cognisant aspect of the Supreme Lord. By this potency, He knows Himself and causes others to know Him. Knowledge of the Absolute Reality is only possible with the help of this potency.

D

Daṇḍa – a measurement of time; approximately 25–30 minutes; explained in *Śrīmad-Bhāgavatam*, Third Canto, Chapter 11 and in *Śrī Caitanya-caritāmṛta* (*Madhya-līlā* 387–90).

Daṇḍavat-praṇāma – *daṇḍa* = stick, *praṇāma* = obeisances; thus, *daṇḍavat-praṇāma* means obeisances by falling like a stick, prostrated obeisances.

Darśana – seeing, meeting, visiting or beholding (especially in regard to the deity, a sacred place or an exalted Vaiṣṇava).

Dāsī – a maidservant.

Dāsya – (1) the second of the five primary reationships with the Lord that is established in the stages of *bhāva* or *prema*; love or attraction to Kṛṣṇa which is expressed in the mood of a servant; (2) in this world the general relationship of practising devotees with Kṛṣṇa is known as *kṛṣṇa-dāsya* or *bhagavad-dāsya*. This means simply to recognise that one's true identity is that of being Kṛṣṇa's servant.

Devī-dhāma – the material world.

Dhāma – a holy place of pilgrimage; the abode of Śrī Bhagavān, where He appears and enacts His transcendental pastimes.

Dhāma-aparādha – offences committed towards the *dhāma*.

Dharma – (from the verbal root *dhṛ* = to sustain; thus, *dharma* means that which sustains). (1) religion in general; (2) the socio-religious duties prescribed in the scriptures for different classes of persons in the *varṇāśrama* system that are meant to liberate one to the platform of *bhakti*.

Dhīra-lalita-nāyaka – Śrī Kṛṣṇa as a hero who is expert in the sixty-four arts and in amorous sports, always situated in fresh youth, expert at joking, devoid of anxiety and controlled by the *prema* of His beloveds.

Dīkṣā – receiving initiation from a spiritual master.

Divyonmāda – a wonderful divine state that resembles a state of utter confusion. It occurs in the stage of *mohana-mahābhāva* and it has many different features such as *udghūrṇā* and *citra-jalpa*. It is found virtually only in Śrīmatī Rādhikā.

G

Gauḍīya Vaiṣṇava – (1) any Vaiṣṇava who follows the teachings of Śrī Caitanya Mahāprabhu; (2) a Vaiṣṇava born in Bengal.

Gopa – (1) a cowherd boy who serves Kṛṣṇa in a mood of intimate friendship; (2) an elderly associate of Nanda Mahārāja who serves Kṛṣṇa in a mood of parental affection.

Gopī, Gopikā – (1) one of the young cowherd maidens of Vraja headed by Śrīmatī Rādhikā who serve Kṛṣṇa in a mood of amorous love; (2) an elderly associate of Mother Yaśodā who serves Kṛṣṇa in a mood of parental affection.

Gṛhastha – a member of the second *āśrama* (stage of life) in the *varṇāśrama* system; a householder.

Guñjā – a small, bright red seed with a black patch on the top. This seed is said to represent Śrīmatī Rādhikā.

Guru-paramparā – the disciplic succession through which spiritual knowledge is transmitted by bona fide spiritual masters.

H

Hari-kathā – narrations of the holy names, form, qualities and pastimes of the Lord.

Harināma – the chanting of Śrī Kṛṣṇa's holy names. Unless accompanied by the word *saṅkīrtana*, it usually refers to the practice of chanting the Hare Kṛṣṇa *mahā-mantra* softly to oneself on a strand of *tulasī* beads.

Hlādinī-śakti – this refers to the *svarūpa-śakti* which is predominated by *hlādinī* (see **Svarūpa-śakti**). *Hlādinī* is the potency which relates to the bliss aspect (*ānanda*) of the Supreme Lord. Although the Supreme Lord is the embodiment of all pleasure, *hlādinī* is that potency by which He relishes transcendental bliss and causes others to taste bliss.

I

Īśvarī – queen, mistress or goddess.

Iṣṭadeva – one's worshipful deity; the particular form of Kṛṣṇa towards whom one is attracted, and who is the object of one's love and service.

J

Japa – loud chanting or soft utterance of the holy name of Kṛṣṇa to oneself; usually referring to the practice of chanting *harināma* on *tulasī* beads. The word *japa* comes from the verbal root *jap*, which means to utter repeatedly (especially prayers or incantations).

Jāta-rati-sādhaka – a *sādhaka* on the platform of *bhāva*.

Jīva – the eternal individual living entity who, in the conditioned state of material existence, assumes a material body in any of the innumerable species of life.

Jñāna – (1) knowledge in general; (2) knowledge leading to impersonal liberation.

Jñānī – one who pursues the path of *jñāna*, knowledge directed towards impersonal liberation.

K

Kali-yuga – the present age of quarrel and hypocrisy that began five thousand years ago. (Also see **Yuga**.)

Kalpa – the four *yugas* are calculated in terms of the heavenly calendars and accordingly are 12,000 years in terms of the heavenly planets. This is called a *divya-yuga*, and one thousand *divya-yugas* make one day of Brahmā. The creation during the day of Brahmā is called *kalpa*, and the creation of Brahmā is called *vikalpa*. When *vikalpas* are made possible by the breathing of Mahā-Viṣṇu, this is called a *mahā-kalpa*. There are regular and systematic cycles of these *mahā-kalpas*, *vikalpas* and *kalpas*.

Kāma – (1) lust to gratify the urges of the material senses; (2) the *gopīs'* transcendental desire to enjoy amorous pastimes with Śrī Kṛṣṇa.

Kaniṣṭha-adhikārī – a neophyte practitioner of *bhakti*.

Karma – (1) any activity performed in the course of material existence; (2) reward-seeking activities; pious activities leading to material gain in this world or in the heavenly planets after death;

(3) fate; previous actions which yield inevitable reactions.

Karma-kāṇḍa – a division of the Vedas that involves the performance of ceremonial acts and sacrificial rites directed towards material benefits or liberation.

Kiṅkarī – a maidservant.

Kila-kiñcita – bodily symptoms of ecstasy. They are explained in Śrīla Rūpa Gosvāmī's *Ujjvala-nīlamaṇi* (*Anubhāva-prakaraṇa* 39): "Pride, ambition, weeping, smiling, envy, fear and anger are the seven ecstatic loving symptoms manifested by a jubilant shrinking away, and these symptoms are called *kila-kiñcita-bhāvas.*"

Kīrtana – one of the nine most important limbs of *bhakti*; consisting of either: (1) congregational singing of Śrī Kṛṣṇa's holy names, sometimes accompanied by music; (2) loud individual chanting of the holy name; or (3) oral descriptions of the glories of Śrī Kṛṣṇa's names, forms, qualities, associates and pastimes.

Kiśora (Kiśorī) – an adolescent boy (girl).

Kṛṣṇa-kathā – see **Hari-kathā**.

Kṛṣṇa-anurāginī – a *gopī* filled with deep, loving attachment (*anurāga*) for Kṛṣṇa.

Kṣatriya – the second of the four *varṇas* (castes) in the *varṇāśrama* system; an administrator or warrior.

Kuṇḍalas – earrings.

Kuñja – a grove or bower; a natural shady retreat with a roof and walls formed by trees, vines, creepers and other climbing plants.

Kuṅkuma – a reddish powder or liquid used by married women to apply to the part in their hair.

L

Laghimā – the mystic perfection of making oneself lighter than a soft feather.

Lākha – one hundred thousand, written as 1,00,000.

Lālā – a Brajabhāṣā term of affectionate address for a young boy.

Līlā – the divine and astonishing pastimes of Śrī Bhagavān and His eternal associates, which grant all auspiciousness for the living entity, which have no connection with this mundane world and which lie beyond the grasp of the material senses and mind.

Līlā-avatāra – Kṛṣṇa's pastime (*līlā*) incarnation. There are innumerable such incarnations, such as Balarāma, Kūrma, Nṛsiṁhadeva and Matsya.

Līlā-mādhurya – see **Mādhurya**.

M

Mādana, Mādanākhya – see **Adhirūḍha-mahābhāva**.

Mādhurya-rasa – the mellow of amorous love, also known as *śṛṅgāra-rasa.*

Mādhurya – (1) sweetness or beauty; (2) Śrī Kṛṣṇa's four unique qualities: *līlā-mādhurya* – He is an undulating ocean of astonishing pastimes out of which the *rāsa-līlā* is supremely captivating; *prema-mādhurya* – He is surrounded by devotees who possess incomparable *mādhurya-prema,* which develops up to the stage of *mahābhāva*; *veṇu-mādhurya* – the sweet and mellow sound of His flute attracts the minds of everyone within the three worlds; and *rūpa-mādhurya* – His extraordinary beauty astonishes all moving and non-moving entities.

Madhyāhna – midday.

Madhyama-adhikārī – the practitioner of *bhakti* who has reached the intermediate stage of spiritual development.

Mahā-bhāgavata – a pure devotee of Bhagavān in the hightest stage of devotional life, who is expert in Vedic literature, has full faith in Śrī Kṛṣṇa and can deliver the whole world.

Mahābhāva – this highest stage of *prema* follows the stages of *sneha, māna, pranaya, rāga* and *anurāga,* and manifests when *anurāga* reaches a special state of intensity. Śrīla Rūpa Gosvāmī elaborately defines *mahābhāva* in *Ujjvala-nīlamaṇi* (14.154): "When *anurāga* reaches a special state of intensity, it is known as *mahābhāva*. This state of intensity has three characteristics: (1) *anurāga* reaches the state of *sva-saṁvedya*, which means that it becomes the object of its own experience; (2) it becomes *prakāśita*, radiantly manifest, which means that all eight *sāttvika-bhāvas* become prominently displayed; and (3) it attains the state of *yāvad-āśraya-vṛtti*, which means that the active ingredient of this intensified state of *anurāga* transmits the experience of Rādhā and Kṛṣṇa's *bhāvas* to whomever may be present and qualified to receive it. This includes both the *sādhaka-* and *siddha-bhaktas*."

Mahābhāva-vatī – endowed with *mahābhāva*, the highest loving sentiment.

Mahājana – a great personality who teaches the highest ideal and who by his conduct sets an example for others to follow.

Mahā-kalpa – see **Kalpa**.

Mahāmāyā, Māyā-śakti – the illusion-generating potency which is responsible for the manifestation of the material world, time and material activities. (Also see **Māyā**.)

Mahāpuruṣa – one who is expert in the imports of the scriptures, has realised the Supreme Brahman and is wholly detached from the material world.

Maharṣi – a great sage.

Māna – the sentiment that prevents the lover and beloved from meeting freely, although they are together and are attracted to each other. *Māna* gives rise to transient emotions like anger, despondency, doubt, restlessness, pride and jealousy.

Mānasī-sevā – service performed within the mind.

Mañjarī – a maidservant of Śrīmatī Rādhikā in the category of *nitya-sakhī* or *prāṇa-sakhī*.

Mantra – (*man* = mind; *tra* = deliverance) a spiritual sound vibration that delivers the mind from its material conditioning and illusion when repeated over and over; a Vedic hymn, prayer or chant.

Māyā – illusion; that which is not; Śrī Bhagavān's external potency which influences the living entities to accept the false egoism of being independent enjoyers of this material world. (Also see **Mahāmāyā**, **Māyā-śakti**.)

Māyāvādī – one who advocates the doctrine of impersonalism.

Mohana – see **Adhirūḍha-mahābhāva**.

Muni – a sage, ascetic, spiritual scholar or self-realised soul.

Muralī – one of Kṛṣṇa's flutes that is thirty-six inches long, has four holes on its body and a mouthpiece at the end, and produces a very enchanting sound.

N

Nāma – the holy name of Kṛṣṇa; chanted by devotees as the main limb of the practice of *sādhana-bhakti*.

Nāma-ābhāsa – a semblance of the holy name. The stage of chanting in which one is becoming cleared of sins and offences but has not yet attained pure chanting.

Nāma-aparādha – offensive chanting of the holy name. Chanting of the holy name that is not accompanied by the attempt to give up sinful and offensive behaviour in one's life.

Nāma-aparādhī – one who chants offensively.

Nāma-saṅkīrtana – the practice of chanting the holy name of Kṛṣṇa, especially congregational chanting.

Nāmī – Śrī Bhagavān; the person addressed by the name.

Nara-līlā – human-like pastimes.

Nāyaka – hero; especially refers to Śrī Kṛṣṇa.

Nāyikā – heroine; especially refers to Śrīmatī Rādhikā and the other *gopīs*.

Nikuñja – (also *kuñja*) bower, grove; a solitary place for the meeting and enjoyment of Rādhā and Kṛṣṇa.

Nirviśeṣa – devoid of variety; featureless impersonal aspect of the Absolute.

Niśānta – the end of the night just prior to dawn.

Niṣkiñcana – free from all material possessions, entirely destitute; a renunciant.

Niṣṭhā – firm faith; established devotional practice that does not waver at any time. The fourth stage in the development of the creeper of devotion.

Nitya-sakhī – see **Sakhī**.

Nitya-siddha-gopīs – eternally liberated *gopīs*.

Niyama – one of the practices of *aṣṭāṅga-yoga* (see **Aṣṭāṅga-yoga**).

P

Pālyadāsī – a maidservant of Śrīmatī Rādhikā. The word *pālya* means to be nourished, cared for and protected, and the word *dāsī* means a maidservant; thus, the *pālyadāsīs* are maidservants under the affectionate care of Śrīmatī Rādhikā.

Parabrahma – the Supreme Brahman, Śrī Bhagavān.

Parakīyā-bhāva – paramour love; an amorous relationship outside of marriage.

Paramahaṁsa – a topmost, God-realised, "swan-like" devotee of Śrī Bhagavān; the fourth and highest stage of *sannyāsa.*

Parama-tattva – the Supreme Absolute Truth, Śrī Bhagavān.

Paramātmā – the Supersoul situated in the hearts of all living entities as a witness and source of remembrance, knowledge and forgetfulness.

Parikramā – (1) circumambulation; (2) the path that encircles a sacred tract of land, such as Vṛndāvana or Vraja.

Paugaṇḍa – boyhood; from age six to ten.

Pītāmbara – the brilliant golden-yellow cloth that Śrī Kṛṣṇa wears.

Prabhu – title meaning "master", "lord" or "ruler".

Pradhāna – the original, dormant state of material nature, prior to the creation, when the material elements are unmanifest. In this state the three modes of nature are in balance and thus inactive.

Pradoṣa – evening.

Prahara – (same as *yāma*) a three-hour time period in the 24-hour day. The first *prahara* starts at *brahma-muhūrta.*

Prakaṭa-līlā – Kṛṣṇa's manifest pastimes.

Prāṇakānta – the beloved of one's life.

Praṇāma – an obeisance.

Prāṇanātha, Prāṇeśvara – literally means "the lord of one's life", but it carries the sense of one who is infinitely more dear to one than one's own life.

Prāṇa-preṣṭha-sakhī – same as *priya-narma-sakhī* (see **Sakhī**).

Prāṇa-priyatama – one who is more dear than one's own life.

Prāṇa-vallabha – the beloved of one's life.

Prāṇa-sakhī – see **Sakhī**.

Prārabdha-karma – the results of previous activities which have already begun to bear fruit.

Prasāda – (literally means "mercy") especially refers to the remnants of food offered to the deity; may also refer to the remnants of other articles offered to the deity, such as incense, flowers, garlands and clothing.

Prātaḥ – early morning, dawn.

Pravāsa – one of the four divisions of *vipralambha*, separation. *Pravāsa* is explained in *Ujjvala-nīlamaṇi* (*Vipralambha-prakaraṇa* 139) as follows: "*Pravāsa* is a word used to indicate the separation of lovers who were previously intimately associated. This separation is due to their being in different places." *Pravāsa* is the obstruction or hindrance between the *nāyaka* and *nāyikā* when they have been together and are now separated, either because they live in different countries or different villages, or because of a difference in mood, or because they are in different places. *Pravāsa* has two divisions: one is simply going out of sight (*pravāsa*) and the other is going to some distant place (*sudūra-pravāsa*).

Prema – (1) love for Kṛṣṇa which is extremely concentrated, which completely melts the heart and which gives rise to a deep sense of *mamatā*, possessiveness, in relation to Śrī Kṛṣṇa; (2) when *bhāva* becomes firmly rooted and unchecked by any obstacle it is known as *prema*. When some cause arises that could conceivably ruin the relationship between the lover and beloved and yet their bond remains completely unaffected, such an intimate loving relationship is known as *prema*. When *prema* is augmented it is gradually transformed into *sneha*, *māna*, *praṇaya*, *rāga*, *anurāga* and *mahābhāva*.

Prema-bhakti – a stage of *bhakti* which is characterised by the appearance of *prema* (see **Prema**); the perfectional stage of devotion; the eighth and fully blossomed state of the creeper of devotion.

Prema-mādhurya – see **Mādhurya**.

Premi-bhakta – a devotee on the stage of *prema*.

Priya-narma-sakhā – see **Sakhā**.

Priya-narma-sakhī – see **Sakhī**.

Priya-sakhī – see **Sakhī**.

Priyatama – dearmost beloved.

Pūjā – offering of worship.

Purāṇa – the eighteen historical supplements to the Vedas.

Puruṣārtha – the four goals of human life – *kāma*, *artha*, *dharma* and *mokṣa*.

Pūrvāhna – morning.

Pūrva-rāga – loving attraction for Kṛṣṇa prior to meeting. *Ujjvala-nīlamaṇi* describes *pūrva-rāga* as follows: "When attachment produced in the lover and beloved before their meeting by seeing, hearing and so on becomes very palatable by the mixture of four ingredients, such as *vibhāva* and *anubhāva*, it is called *pūrva-rāga*."

R

Rāga-mārga – the path of *rāga*, spontaneous attachment (see **Rāgānugā**).

Rāgānugā – *bhakti* that follows in the wake of Śrī Kṛṣṇa's eternal associates in Vraja, the *rāgātmikā-janas*, whose hearts are permeated with *rāga*, an unquenchable loving thirst for Kṛṣṇa which gives rise to spontaneous and intense absorption.

Rāgānuga-bhakta – a devotee on the path of spontaneous devotion.

Rāgātmikā – one in whose heart there naturally and eternally exists a deep spontaneous desire to love and serve Śrī Kṛṣṇa. This specifically refers to the eternal residents of Vraja.

Rājasūya-yajña – an elaborate fire sacrifice that establishes one as the emperor of the world.

Ramaṇī – a shy young girl who is expert in the various skills for awakening sweet emotions.

Rasa – (1) the spiritual transformation of the heart which takes place when the perfectional state of love for Śrī Kṛṣṇa, known as *rati*, is converted into "liquid" emotions by combining with various types of transcendental ecstasies; (2) taste, flavour.

Rāsa-līlā – Śrī Kṛṣṇa's dance with the *vraja-gopīs*, which is a pure exchange of spiritual love between Kṛṣṇa and the *gopīs*, His most confidential servitors.

Rāsa-maṇḍala – a circular arena in which Śrī Kṛṣṇa and the *gopīs* perform their *rāsa-līlā*.

Rasika – one who is expert at relishing *rasa*; a connoisseur of *rasa*.

Rasika-śekhara – a title of Kṛṣṇa meaning "the foremost enjoyer or master of the mellows of love".

Rati – (1) attachment, fondness for; (2) a stage in the development of *bhakti* which is synonymous with *bhāva* (see **Bhāva**).

Rātri – night.

Ṛṣi – a great sage learned in the Vedas.

Ruci – taste; *ruci* develops after one has acquired steadiness in *bhajana*. At this stage, with the awakening of actual taste, one's attraction to spiritual matters, such as hearing, chanting and other devotional practices, exceeds one's attraction to any type of material activity; this is the fifth stage in the development of the creeper of devotion.

Rūḍha-bhāva – the stage of *mahābhāva* in which all the *sāttvika-bhāvas* are manifest in the brightly burning (*uddīpta*) condition.

Rūpa-mādhurya – see **Mādhurya**.

Rūpānuga-bhakta – a devotee who follows Śrī Rūpa Gosvāmī on the path of spontaneous devotion.

S

Sādhaka – one who follows a spiritual discipline with the objective of achieving pure devotion for Śrī Kṛṣṇa, and more specifically, achieving *bhāva-bhakti*.

Sādhana – the method one adopts in order to obtain one's specific goal, *sādhya*.

Sādhu – (1) (in a general sense) a saintly person or devotee; (2) a highly realised soul who knows life's aim (*sādhya*), who is himself practising *sādhana*, and who can engage others in *sādhana*.

Sādhu-saṅga – association of highly advanced devotees; the first stage in the development of the creeper of devotion and the most important factor for advancement in *bhakti*.

Sakhā – a male friend, companion or attendant. There are four types of *sakhās* in Vraja: (1) *suhṛda* – those whose friendship is mixed with a scent of parental mood, who are slightly older than Kṛṣṇa, who bear a staff and other weapons and who always protect Kṛṣṇa from demons; e.g. Subhadra, Maṇḍalībhadra and Balabhadra; (2) *sakhā* – those whose friendship is mixed with a scent of servitorship, who are slightly younger than Kṛṣṇa and who are exclusively attached to the happiness of rendering service to Kṛṣṇa; e.g. Viśāla, Vṛṣabha and

Devaprastha; (3) *priya-sakhā* – those who are the same age as Kṛṣṇa and take the exclusive shelter of the attitude of friendship; e.g. Śrīdāma, Sudāma and Stoka-kṛṣṇa; and (4) *priya-narma-sakhā* – superior in every way to the three other types of *sakhās*, they are engaged in extremely confidential services and are possessed of a very special mood; e.g. Subala, Ujjvala and Madhumaṅgala.

Sakhī – a female friend, companion or attendant. Śrīmatī Rādhikā has five kinds of *sakhīs*: *sakhī*, *nitya-sakhī*, *prāṇa-sakhī*, *priya-sakhī* and *priya-narma-sakhī*. *Priya-narma-sakhī* is also known as *parama-preṣṭha-sakhī* or *prāṇa-preṣṭha-sakhī*. (1) *Sakhī* – Daniṣṭhā is an example. These *sakhīs* love and serve both Śrīmatī Rādhikā and Kṛṣṇa, but they are slightly more inclined towards Kṛṣṇa. (2) *Nitya-sakhīs* and (3) *prāṇa-sakhīs* – the only two kinds of *sakhīs* who are in the category of *tad-tat-bhāva-icchātmikā* (*mañjarī-sakhīs*). These *sakhīs* serve both Rādhā and Kṛṣṇa, with a tendency to favour Śrīmatī Rādhikā and render service to Her. They obey only Her. The *prāṇa-sakhīs*, like Rūpa Mañjarī and Rati Mañjarī, being even more intimately connected with Śrīmatī, are naturally the leaders of the *nitya-sakhīs*. (4) *Priya-sakhīs* and (5) *priya-narma-sakhīs* – Lalitā and Viśākhā are examples. Among the *sakhīs*, the *priya-sakhīs* and the *priya-narma-sakhīs* are most dear, and they both serve the youthful Divine Couple, but with a slight tendency towards Śrīmatī Rādhikā. Both these *sakhīs* have so much power that they can sometimes chastise Rādhikā and at other times chastise Kṛṣṇa.

Sakhya-rasa – love or attachment for Śrī Kṛṣṇa that is expressed in the mood of a friend; one of the five primary relationships with Kṛṣṇa.

Sālokya-mukti – liberation of residing on the same planet as Śrī Bhagavān.

Samādhi – meditation or deep trance.

Sambandha-jñāna – knowledge regarding *sambandha-tattva*, the mutual relationship between the Lord, the living entities and the material energy.

Sāmīpya-mukti – the liberation of becoming a personal associate of Śrī Bhagavān.

Sampradāya – a line of disciplic succession.

Saṁvit – the knowledge portion, cognisant aspect, of the Lord's spiritual potency. Although Bhagavān is the embodiment of knowledge, *saṁvit* is the potency by which He knows Himself and causes others to know Him.

Sañcāri-bhāvas – also known as *vyabhicāri-bhāvas*; thirty-three internal emotions which emerge from the nectarean ocean of *sthāyibhāva*, cause it to swell and then merge back into it. These include emotions such as despondency, jubilation, fear, anxiety and concealment of emotions.

Saṅkīrtana – congregational chanting of the names of Kṛṣṇa.

Sannyāsa – the fourth *āśrama* (stage of life) in the *varṇāśrama* system; renounced, ascetic life.

Sannyāsī – a member of the renounced order, a renunciant.

Sārī – a female parrot.

Sarovara – lake, pool or tank.

Sārṣṭi-mukti – in this liberation the opulence of the devotee is equal to the opulence of Bhagavān.

Sārūpya-mukti – in this liberation the bodily features of the devotee are exactly like those of Bhagavān apart from two or three symptoms found only on the body of the Lord.

Śaraṇāgati – surrender; approaching for refuge or protection. The six kinds of surrender are: (1) to accept that which is favourable to *kṛṣṇa-bhakti*; (2) to reject that which is unfavourable; (3) to have the strong faith "Bhagavān will protect me"; (4) to have dependence, thinking "Bhagavān will take care of me"; (5) to be fully self-surrendered (*ātma-samarpaṇa*); and (6) to be humble.

Śāstra – scripture, especially the Vedic scriptures.

Sāttvika-bhāvas – one of the five essential ingredients of *rasa* (see **Rasa**); eight symptoms of spiritual ecstasy arising exclusively from *viśuddha-sattva*, or in other words, when the heart is overwhelmed by emotions in connection with the five primary moods of affection for Kṛṣṇa or the seven secondary emotions. The eight (*aṣṭa*) *sāttvika-bhāvas* are: (1) becoming stunned, *stambha*; (2) perspiration, *sveda*; (3) standing of the hairs on end, *romāñca*; (4) faltering of the voice, *svarabheda*; (5) trembling, *kampa*; (6) loss of colour, *vaivarṇya*; (7) tears, *aśru*; and (8) loss of consciousness or fainting, *pralaya*.

Sāyam – dusk.

Sāyujya-mukti – the liberation of merging into the spiritual effulgence of the Lord.

Sevā – service, attendance on, reverence or devotion to.

Sevā-aparādha – offences in devotional service.

Siddha-deha – perfected spiritual body, which is beyond this gross and subtle material body, and fit to serve Rādhā and Kṛṣṇa.

Śikṣā-guru – the person from whom one receives instructions on how to progress on the path of *bhajana*; the instructing spiritual master.

Śloka – a Sanskrit verse.

Smaraṇam – rememberance of the names, forms, qualities and pastimes of Śrī Kṛṣṇa; one of the nine primary limbs of *bhakti*.

Smṛti – (literally "that which is remembered") the body of Vedic literature that is remembered, in contradistinction to Śruti, or that which is directly heard by or revealed to the *ṛṣis*. Smṛti includes the six Vedāṅgas, the *dharma-śāstras* such as *Manu-saṁhitā*, the Purāṇas and the *itihāsas*.

Śrāddha – a ceremony in honour of and for the benefit of deceased relatives, in which the forefathers are offered *piṇḍa*, an oblation of rice or flour, which endows them with a body suitable to attain *pitṛ-loka*, the planet of the forefathers.

Śraddhā – faith in the statements of the *śāstras* which is awakened after accumulating pious devotional activities over many births. Such faith is aroused in the association of *bhaktas* and it is the external manifestation of the seed of the creeper of devotion.

Śravaṇam – hearing the transcendental descriptions of Bhagavān's names, forms, qualities, pastimes and associates from the mouths of advanced *bhaktas*. One of the nine most important limbs of *bhakti*.

Śṛṅgāra-rasa – same as *mādhurya-rasa*, the amorous mellow.

Śruti – see **Smṛti**.

Sthāyibhāva – the permanent sentiment of love for Śrī Kṛṣṇa in one of five primary relationships of tranquility (*śānta*), servitude (*dāsya*), friendship (*sakhya*), parental affection (*vātsalya*) or amorous love (*mādhurya*). This also refers to the dominant sentiment in the seven secondary mellows of laughter, wonder, heroism, compassion, anger, fear and disgust.

Śuddha-sattva – the state of unalloyed goodness; the quality of existence which is beyond the influence of material nature.

Śūdra – the lowest of the four *varṇas* (castes) in the *varṇāśrama* system; artisans and labourers.

Śuka – a male parrot.

Sukṛti – piety, virtue; pious activity. *Sukṛti* is of two types: eternal (*nitya*) and temporary (*naimittika*). The *sukṛti* by which one obtains *sādhu-saṅga* and *bhakti* is *nitya-sukṛti* because it produces eternal fruit.

Svarūpa – constitutional nature, inherent identity; the eternal constitutional nature and identity of the self which is realised at the stage of *bhāva*.

Svarūpa-śakti – the Lord's divine potency. It is called *svarūpa-śakti* because it is situated in the Lord's form (*svarūpa*). This potency is *cinmaya*, fully conscious, and it is also known as *cit-śakti*, the potency endowed with consciousness. Because this potency is situated in the Lord's form, it is further known as *antaraṅga-śakti*, internal potency. Because it is superior to His marginal and external potencies, it is known as *parā-śakti*, superior potency. Thus, by its qualities, this potency is known by different names. The *svarūpa-śakti* has three divisions: *sandhinī*, *saṁvit* and *hlādinī*.

Svarūpa-siddhi – the stage in which a devotee's *svarūpa*, internal spiritual form and identity, becomes manifest.

Sva-saṁvedya – the word *saṁvedya* means capable of being known or realised; the word *sva* means oneself; so the term *sva-saṁvedya* literally means that which has the power to be fully tasted or experienced by itself. When *anurāga* reaches the state where it becomes the object of its own experience it is known as *sva-saṁvedya*. (Also see **Mahābhāva**.)

T

Tāmbūla – betel-nut.

Tapasya – voluntary acceptance of austerity for the purpose of detaching oneself from the sense objects.

Taṭasthā-śakti – the marginal potency (the living entities) of the Lord.

Tattva – truths, reality, philosophical principles; the essence or substance of anything (e.g. the truths relating to *bhakti* are known as *bhakti-tattva*).

Tilaka – clay markings worn on the forehead and other parts of the body by Vaiṣṇavas, signifying their devotion to Śrī Kṛṣṇa or Viṣṇu, and consecrating the body as the Lord's temple.

Tīrtha – holy place, place of pilgrimage.

Tulasī – a sacred plant whose leaves and blossoms are used by Vaiṣṇavas in the worship of Śrī Kṛṣṇa; the wood is also used for chanting beads and neck beads.

U

Udbhāsvaras – the symptoms which reveal the spiritual emotions situated within the heart are called *anubhāvas*. When they manifest mostly as external actions, they are known as *udbhāsvaras*. *Sāttvika-bhāvas* are also known as *anubhāvas* because they also reveal the emotions of the heart. The term *udbhāsvaras* is used, therefore, to distinguish between *anubhāvas* arising spontaneously from *sattva* (*sāttvika-bhāvas*) and those which manifest as external actions involving some conscious intention.

Udghūrṇā – a feature of *divyonmāda* (see **Divyonmāda**). A state in which many varieties of astounding and uncontrollable endeavours are manifest. Rādhikā experienced *udghūrṇā* when Kṛṣṇa departed for Mathurā. At that time, as if in complete forgetfulness due to feelings of separation from Kṛṣṇa, She thought, "Kṛṣṇa is coming; He will be here in just a moment." Thinking in this way She made the bed in Her *kuñja*.

Upaniṣads – 108 principal philosophical treatises that appear within the Vedas.

Uttama-adhikārī – the topmost devotee, who has attained perfection in his devotion unto Śrī Kṛṣṇa.

V

Vaidhī-bhakti – devotion prompted by the regulations of the scriptures. When *sādhana-bhakti* is not inspired by intense longing, but is instigated instead by the discipline of the scriptures, it is called *vaidhī-bhakti*.

Vaijayantī-mālā – a garland made of five varieties of flowers and which reaches the knees.

Vairāgya – detachment or indifference to this world; a spiritual discipline involving the acceptance of voluntary austerities to achieve detachment from the sense objects.

Vaiṣṇava – literally means one whose nature is "of Viṣṇu", in other words, one in whose heart and mind only Viṣṇu or Kṛṣṇa resides. A devotee of Śrī Kṛṣṇa or Viṣṇu.

Vaiśya – the third of the four *varṇas* (castes) in the *varṇāśrama* system; agriculturalists or businessmen.

Vaṁśī – one of Śrī Kṛṣṇa's flutes that is about thirteen inches long and has nine holes on its body. Kṛṣṇa also has a number of other, longer *vaṁśīs*: the *mahānandā*, or *sammohinī*, made of jewels; the *ākarṣiṇī* made of gold; and the *ānandinī*, technically named the *vaṁśulī*, made of bamboo.

Vānaprastha – a member of the third *āśrama* (stage of life) in the *varṇāśrama* system; retired life which entails freedom from family responsibilities and the acceptance of spiritual vows.

Varṇa – class, occupational division, caste; the four *varṇas* are: *brāhmaṇa*, *kṣatriya*, *vaiśya* and *śūdra*.

Varṇāśrama-dharma – the Vedic social system, which organises society into four occupational divisions and four stages of life (*varṇas* and *āśramas*).

Vastu-siddhi – the stage in which the *vastu*, or substantive entity known as the *jīva*, is fully liberated from matter. After giving up the material body, the living entity who has already attained *svarūpa-siddhi* enters into Śrī Kṛṣṇa's manifest pastimes, where he or she receives the association of Kṛṣṇa and His eternal associates for the first time. There one receives further training from His eternal associates. When one becomes established in the mood of their *prema* and one's eternal service to Kṛṣṇa, one gives up all connection with this world and enters His spiritual abode. At this point the *jīva* becomes situated in his pure identity as a *vastu*, and this is known as *vastu-siddhi*.

Vātsalya-bhāva – one of the five primary relationships with Śrī Kṛṣṇa, namely, love or attachment for Kṛṣṇa expressed in the mood of a parent.

Veda – the four primary books of knowledge compiled by Śrīla Vyāsadeva, namely, the *Ṛg Veda*, *Sāma Veda*, *Atharva Veda* and *Yajur Veda*.

Vedānta – "the conclusion of Vedic knowledge". The Upaniṣads are the latter portion of the Vedas and the *Vedānta-sūtra* summarises the philosophy of the Upaniṣads in concise statements. Therefore the word "Vedānta" especially refers to the *Vedānta-sūtra*.

Veṇu – (also called *pāvika*) one of Kṛṣṇa's flutes that is very small, not more than nine inches long, with six holes on its body.

Veṇu-mādhurya – see **Mādhurya**.

Vibhāva – is defined in *Bhakti-rasāmṛta-sindhu* (2.1.15) as follows: "That in which *rati* is tasted (*ālambana*) and that cause by which *rati* is tasted (*uddīpana*) is called *vibhāva*."

Vidhi-mārga – the path of *bhakti* which follows rules and regulations.

Vikṣepātmikā – one of the illusory energy's functions – the power to throw the living entity into the ocean of material existence; the spell of diversion that impels one to remain in conditioned life, fully satisfied by sense gratification.

Vilāsa – pastimes, especially the playful amorous pastimes of Śrī Rādhā-Kṛṣṇa.

Vīṇā – a stringed musical instrument of melodious sound, the favourite instrument of Nārada Muni and of various other celestial personalities.

Vipralambha-rasa – the mellow of separation.

Viraha – separation (same as *vipralambha*).

Viśuddha-sattva – see **Śuddha-sattva**.

Vraja-devīs, vraja-ramaṇīs, vraja-sundarīs – the *gopīs* of Vraja.

Vrajavāsī – a resident of Vraja.

Vrata – a vow undertaken for self-purification and spiritual benefit.

Vyabhicāri-bhāvas – same as *sañcāri-bhāvas* (see **Sañcāri-bhāvas**).

Y

Yajña – (1) a sacrifice in which a deity is propitiated by the chanting of prayers and *mantras* and the offering of ghee into the sacrificial fire; (2) any kind of intense endeavour which is directed at achieving a particular goal.

Yāma – (same as *prahara*) one of the eight periods of the day. Each *yāma* consists of approximately three hours.

Yāvad-āśraya-vṛtti – the highest state of *anurāga*. In the term *yāvad-āśraya-vṛtti*, *yāvad* means whomever and *āśraya* means the receptacle or abode of the experience of *anurāga*. This refers both to *sādhakas* and *siddha-bhaktas*. The word *vṛtti* means function or activity. *Yāvad-āśraya-vṛtti* is the function or transaction which extends its influence to whomever is in a position to receive it. (Also see **Mahābhāva**.)

Yoga – (1) union, meeting, connection or combination; (2) spiritual discipline to link one with the Supreme; to stabilise the mind so that it is not disturbed by sense objects. There are many different branches of *yoga* such as *karma-yoga*, *jñāna-yoga* and *bhakti-yoga*. Unless specified as such, the word *yoga* usually refers to the *aṣṭāṅga-yoga* system of Patañjali (see **Aṣṭāṅga-yoga**).

Yogamāyā – the internal potency of Bhagavān that engages in arranging and enhancing all His pastimes.

Yogī – one who practises the *yoga* system with the goal of realisation of the Supersoul or of merging into the Lord's personal body.

Yuga – one of the four ages described in the Vedas: Satya-yuga, Tretā-yuga, Dvāpara-yuga and Kali-yuga. The duration of each *yuga* is said to be respectively 1,728,000; 1,296,000; 864,000; and 432,000 years. The descending numbers represent a corresponding physical and moral deterioration of mankind in each age.

Verse Index

(main verses)

A

abhimānaṁ parityajya 205
abhisāra-dvayor eva 397
acirād eva sarvārthaḥ 49
ādau śraddhā tataḥ sādhu 22
aghacchit-smaraṇaṁ viṣṇor 13
aghadamana-yaśodā-nandanau 63
aham evāsam evāgre 102
ahaṁ hare tava pādaika-mūla 193
aho vidhātas tava na 322
āhuś ca te nalina-nābha 351
aihikeṣvaiṣaṇā pāra 75
alabdhe vā vinaṣṭe vā 158
āliṅganaṁ varaṁ manye 24
amaryādaḥ kṣudraś cala 142
amūny-adhanyāni dināntarāṇi 336
ānandaika-sukha-svāmī 54
anārādhya rādhā-padāmbhoja 201
anarthopaśamaṁ sākṣād 69
anāsaktasya viṣayān 116
aṅguṣṭha-parva-madhyasthaṁ 51
ānukūlyasya saṅkalpaḥ 127
āpannaḥ saṁsṛtiṁ ghorāṁ 78
aparādha-sahasra-bhājanaṁ 140
are cetaḥ prodyat-kapaṭa 93
āsaktis tad-guṇākhyāne 241
āsām aho caraṇa-reṇu 293
āśāsya dāsyaṁ vṛṣabhānu 210
āśliṣya vā pāda-ratāṁ 363
ataḥ śrī-kṛṣṇa-nāmādi 108
aṭati yad bhavān ahni 389

athāsaktis tato bhāvas 22
atyāhāraḥ prayāsaś ca 86
ayi dīna-dayārdra nātha he 319
ayi nanda-tanuja kiṅkaraṁ 185

B

barhāpīḍaṁ naṭa-vara-vapuḥ 272
bhagavāṁs tās tathā-bhūtā 353
bhakti-yogena manasi 69
bhaktiḥ pareśānubhavo viraktir 161
bhaktis tvayi sthiratarā 262
bhavantam evānucaran 139
bhāvena kenacit preṣṭha 120
bhayaṁ dvitīyābhiniveśataḥ 79

C

calasi yad vrajāc cārayan 387
ceto-darpaṇa-mārjanaṁ 28
chidra-saṁvṛtir etasyāḥ 397
cintātra jāgārodvegau 330
cirād āśā-mātraṁ tvayi 345
cittaṁ sukhena bhavatāpahṛtaṁ 175

D

dadāti pratigṛhṇāti 88
daivena te hata-dhiyo 68
dāna-vrata-tapas 65
devarṣi-bhūtāpta-nṛṇāṁ 99
devi duḥkha-kula-sāgarodare 220
dhanyāḥ sma mūḍha-gatayo 'pi 307
dharma-vrata-tyāga 95
dhātar yad asmin bhava 40
dhyāyantaṁ śikhi-piccha 212
dṛṣṭaiḥ svabhāva-janitair 90
dukūlaṁ vibhrāṇām atha 370
dūrād apāsya svajanān 207
dyūta-krīḍā-paṭākṛṣṭiś 382

E

ekāntino yasya na 42
etāḥ paraṁ tanu-bhṛto 296
etāvad eva jijñāsyaṁ 82
etāvān eva loke 'smin 58
evam ekāntināṁ prāyaḥ 120
evaṁ-vrataḥ sva-priya-nāma 375

G

gā gopakair anu-vanaṁ 316
go-puccha-sadṛśī kāryā 50
gopyaḥ kim ācarad ayaṁ 305
gopyaś ca kṛṣṇam upalabhya 348
gopyas tapaḥ kim acaran 299
guror avajñā 95

H

hā devi! kāku-bhara 226
hantāyam adrir abalā 313
harati śrī-kṛṣṇa-manaḥ 54
hare kṛṣṇa hare kṛṣṇa 49
harer apy aparādhān yaḥ 101
harer nāma harer nāma 56
harir eva sadārādhyaḥ 155
he deva! he dayita! 337

I

idaṁ śarīraṁ śata-sandhi 128
ihā haite sarva-siddhi 49
iti puṁsārpitā viṣṇau 191

ity acyutāṅghriṁ bhajato 190

J

jāta-śraddho mat-kathāsu 109
jaya nāmadheya! muni-vṛnda 46
jihvaikato 'cyuta vikarṣati 164

K

kadāhaṁ yamunā-tīre 259
kasyānubhāvo 'sya na deva 287
kim iha kṛṇumaḥ kasya 334
ko nv īśa te pāda 167
kṛṣṇaṁ smaran janaṁ cāsya 374
kṛṣṇa-nāma-svarūpeṣu 76
kṛṣṇa tvadīya-pada-paṅkaja 134
kṛṣṇa-varṇaṁ tviṣākṛṣṇaṁ 1
kṛṣṇeti yasya giri taṁ 114
kṛṣṇo rakṣati no jagat 132
kṣāntir avyartha-kālatvaṁ 240
kuhū-kaṇṭhī-kaṇṭhād api 402
kurvanti hi tvayi ratiṁ 199
kuryuḥ pratiṣṭhā-viṣṭhāyāḥ 121
kvacid rudanty acyuta 268

M

madhura-madhuram etan 39
madhyāhne 'nyonya-saṅgodita 182
manaḥ saṁharaṇaṁ śaucaṁ 51
māraḥ svayaṁ nu madhura 340
martyo yadā tyakta 365
māyā-mugdhasya jīvasya 72
mayi bhaktir hi bhūtānām 355
mayi prasādaṁ madhuraiḥ 147
mithaḥ prema-guṇotkīrtis 397

N

na deśa-kāla-niyamo 66
na dhanaṁ na janaṁ 151
na dharmaṁ nādharmaṁ 366
na dharma-niṣṭho 'smi 135
nadyas tadā tad upadhārya 310
nāhaṁ vipro na ca nara 248
naiṣkarmyam apy acyuta 36
naitan manas tava kathāsu 163
na kāmaye nātha tad 172
naktaṁ divā ca gatabhir 57
nāma cintāmaṇiḥ kṛṣṇaś 107
nāmāny anantasya hata 266
nāmāparādha-yuktānāṁ 101
nāmnām akāri bahudhā 61
nāmno 'sya yāvatī śaktiḥ 12
na mṛṣā paramārtham 141
na nāka-pṛṣṭhaṁ na ca 173
na ninditaṁ karma 136
na premā śravaṇādi-bhaktir 368
nārada-vīṇojjīvana 45
na śiṣyān anubadhnīta 156
naṣṭa-prāyeṣv abhadreṣu 186
nātaḥ paraṁ karma 38
nātiprasīdati tathopacitopacārair 129
nau-khelā-līlayā cauryaṁ 382
navaṁ divyaṁ kāvyaṁ 400
nāyaṁ śriyo 'ṅga u nitānta 289
nayanaṁ galad-aśru-dhārayā 237
nibaddha-mūrdhāñjalir eṣa 146
nijatve gauḍīyān jagati 8
nikhila-bhuvana-lakṣmī 394
nimajjato 'nanta 138
niṣkiñcanasya bhagavad 89

nṛtyaṁ viluṭhitaṁ gītaṁ 244

O

oṁ āsya jānanto 47
oṁ ity etad brahmaṇo 47

P

pādābjayos tava vinā 221
parasparānukathanaṁ 264
para-vyasaninī nārī 258
prabhu kahe kahilāma 49
prāṇa-vṛttyaiva santuṣyen 117
prāpañcikatayā buddhyā 98
pratiṣṭhāśā dhṛṣṭā 91
prema-ccheda-rujo 'vagacchati 330
premnas tu prathamāvasthā 238
priyaḥ so 'yaṁ kṛṣṇaḥ 380
pūrvāhne dhenu-mitrair 149

R

rādhāṁ sālīgaṇāntām 360
rādhāṁ snāta-vibhūṣitāṁ 122
rādhā-nāma sudhā-rasaṁ 217
rātryante trasta-vṛnderita 59
ṛte 'rthaṁ yat pratīyeta 103

S

sakṛd uccāritaṁ yena 38
sa mṛgyaḥ śreyasāṁ hetuḥ 118
saṅkīrtyamāno bhagavān 44
satāṁ nindā nāmnaḥ 95
satāṁ prasaṅgān mama 113
sā vidyā tan-matir yayā 41
sāyaṁ rādhāṁ sva-sakhyā 301
sevā sādhaka-rūpeṇa 251
śivasya śrī-viṣṇor 95
smarantaḥ smārayantaś ca 264
smartavyaḥ satataṁ viṣṇur 100
śokāmarṣādibhir bhāvair 159
sphuran-muktā guñjā maṇi 383
śravaṇaṁ kīrtanaṁ viṣṇoḥ 191
śreyaḥ-sṛtiṁ bhaktim 37
śrī-rādhāṁ prāpta-gehāṁ 233
śṛṇvan sato bhagavato 131
śṛṇvatāṁ sva-kathāḥ kṛṣṇaḥ 186
śrute 'pi nāma-māhātmye 95
śruti-smṛti-purāṇādi 119
sūditāśrita-janārtir-āśaye 33
sva-tattve para-tattve ca 74
svayaṁ tv asāmyātiśayas 284
sve sve 'dhikāre yā niṣṭhā 109
śyāmaṁ hiraṇya-paridhiṁ 271

T

tac chraddadhānā munayo 80
tadā rajas-tamo-bhāvāḥ 187
tad aśma-sāraṁ hṛdayaṁ 260
tad astu me nātha sa 166
tāmbūlārpaṇa-pāda-mardana 399
taṁ nirvyājaṁ bhaja 25
tan naḥ prasīda vṛjinārdana 194
tan-nāma-rūpa-caritādi 373
taruṇāruṇa-karuṇāmaya 396
tāsām āvirabhūc chauriḥ 342
tasmād ekena manasā 157
tasyā apāra-rasa-sāra 214
tasyaiva hetoḥ prayateta 168
tato bhajeta māṁ prītaḥ 109

tato 'bhūt trivṛd oṁkāro 48
tat te 'nukampāṁ 189
tāvad bhayaṁ draviṇa 153
tava dāsya-sukhaika 143
tava kathāmṛtaṁ 385
tāv utkau labdha-saṅgau 407
tayor dvayor upālambhaḥ 398
tebhyo namo 'stu 43
te stambha-sveda 245
te tu sandarśanaṁ jalpaḥ 382
tṛṇād api sunīcena 125
tucchāsaktiḥ kuṭīnāṭī 77
tulasī-kāṣṭha-ghaṭitair 50
tvaṁ pratyag ātmani tadā 178
tvayopabhukta-srag-gandha 230

U

utsāhān niścayād dhairyāt 111

V

vāco vegaṁ manasaḥ 84
vaidagdhī sāra-sarvasvaṁ 54
vapur-ādiṣu yo 'pi ko 'pi vā 144
varaṁ huta-vaha-jvālā 23
vāsudeve bhagavati 80
veṇuṁ karān nipatitaṁ 228
vihiteṣv eva nityeṣu 121
vijñāpya bhagavat-tattvaṁ 53
vīkṣyālakāvṛta-mukhaṁ 196
viśveṣāṁ anurañjanena 403
vṛttyā sva-bhāva-kṛtayā 117

Y

yad abhyarcya hariṁ bhaktyā 11
yadā yāto daivān madhu-ripur 405
yadā yāto gopī-hṛdaya 326
yad dharma-sūnor bata 281
yad icchasi paraṁ jñānaṁ 39
yaḥ kaumāra-haraḥ sa 377
yamādibhir yoga-pathaiḥ 34
yā nirvṛtis tanu-bhṛtāṁ 170
yan-martya-līlaupayikaṁ 276
yasyānanaṁ makara-kuṇḍala 278
yasyānurāga-lalita-smita 324
yasyānurāga-pluta-hāsa-rāsa 283
yasyāsti bhaktir bhagavaty 177
yasya yat-saṅgatiḥ puṁso 118
yā te līlā-rasa 346
yathā mahānti bhūtāni 105
yathā taror mūla-niṣecanena 154
yat-pāda-paṅkaja-palāśa 179
yat te sujāta-caraṇāmburuhaṁ 391
yāvatā syāt sva-nirvāhaḥ 160
yayā sammohito jīva 69
yena janma-śataiḥ pūrvaṁ 15
yugāyitaṁ nimeṣeṇa 303

Verse Index

(quoted verses)

A

aham apy aparādhānām 420
aiṁ gurudevāya vidmahe 414
ajāta-pakṣā iva mātaraṁ 242
ajñāna-timirāndhasya 414
āmiha nā jāni tāhā 333
ānanda-līlā-maya-vigrahāya 416
ananya-śrī-rādhā-pada 224
anayārādhito nūnaṁ 203
antaḥ kṛṣṇaṁ bahir-gauraṁ 6
antara bāhire, sama vyavahāra 227
antaś cintita tat 257
apagata-rādho yasmād 73
aprāpti-kāraṇaṁ ca 288
āśā bharair amṛta-sindhu 242
āśā hi paramaṁ duḥkham 335
āsan varṇās trayo hy asya 5
aśeṣa-kleśa-niḥśeṣa 423
āśliṣya vā pāda-ratām 22
ataeva 'triyuga' kari' 4
ātmānaṁ cintayet tatra 256, 371
ātma nivedana, tuyā pade kari 154
ātmendriya-prīti-vāñchā 379
āyāsya iti 211, 328
ayi nanda-tanuja 21

B

bahu kāntā vinā 380
bhakta āmā preme bāndhiyāche 106
bhakta-pada-dhūli āra 93, 232
bhāla nā khāibe āra 85

bhartuḥ śuśrūṣaṇaṁ 337
bhūmau skhalita-pādānāṁ 421

C

ceto-darpaṇa 20
chāḍi' anya nārī-gaṇa 364
channaḥ kalau yad 4
cittaṁ sukhena 337

D

daśāśvamedhī punar eti 134
dāsyāste kṛpaṇāyā me sakhe 146
'devī' kahi dyotamānā 221
dhāma-vāsī-jane praṇati 244
dharma-saṁsthāpanārthāya 6
dorbhyāṁ padbhyāṁ ca 424

E

ei tina-sevā haite 93
eka hari-nāme jata 13
ekala īśvara kṛṣṇa āra 249
emana nirghṛṇṇā 137

G

gaṅge ca yamune caiva 411
gaura āmāra ye saba 243
govinda-vallabhe rādhe 421
go vindayati iti 297
gṛhe vā vanete thāke 259

H

hare kṛṣṇety uccaiḥ 10
harer nāma harer nāma 12
hari-bhakti-mahādevyāḥ 168
he kṛṣṇa karuṇā-sindho 418

I

ihā vai āra nā bolibā bolāibā 243
ity ātmānaṁ vicintyaiva 256

J

jagāi mādhāi haite muñi 137
jagatera pitā kṛṣṇa 133
jīhvāra lālase yei 85
jñānī jīvan-mukta-daśā 35, 181

K

kali-yuge līlāvatāra 4
karma-kāṇḍa jñāna-kāṇḍa 178
karmāṇy ārabhamāṇā 76
kasyāḥ padāni caitāni 204
keha māne, kehā nā māne 133
khaṇḍa-khaṇḍa hai deha 50, 112
kibā teṅho lampaṭa 364
kīrtana prabhāve smaraṇa 267
klīṁ kṛṣṇa-caitanyāya 415
klīṁ kṛṣṇāya vidmahe 418
kṛṣṇa-bhakti-janma-mūla 144
kṛṣṇa-citta-sthitā rādhā 235
kṛṣṇake karāya śyāma-rasa 202
kṛṣṇa-līlāmṛta yadi 224
kṛṣṇa-varṇaṁ tviṣākṛṣṇaṁ 2
kṛṣṇera mādhurye kṛṣṇe 278
kṣāntir avyartha 19
kvacid api sa kathā 148

L

lalāṭe keśavaṁ dhyāyen 412

lalitā sakhīra, ayogyā 372

M

mad-īśā-nāthatve 212
mahā-bhāgavata dekhe 311
'mane' nija-siddha-deha 268
mat-samo nāsti pāpātmā 420
māyāpure bhaviṣyāmi 6
mo-viṣaye gopī-gaṇera 333

N

na dhanaṁ na janam 21
nā gaṇi āpana-duḥkha 364
nāhaṁ vipro na 145
nāma-saṅkīrtanaṁ proktaṁ 218
nāma-saṅkīrtanaṁ yasya 45
na me bhaktaḥ praṇaśyati 99
nāmnām akāri 20
nānā-puṣpa-latābaddha 416
nānā-śilpa-kalābhijñāṁ 256
nandaḥ kim akarod brahman 64
na pāraye 'haṁ 358
nayanaṁ galad-aśru 21
nehābhikrama-nāśo 'sti 14
nijābhīṣṭa kṛṣṇa-preṣṭha 268
nirantaraṁ vaśī-kṛta 215
nirmālya-gandha-puṣpādi 422
nirmitā tvaṁ purā devair 422

P

pahile dekhiluṅ tomāra 5
pakvāpakva mātra se vicāra 250, 266
patayaś ca vaḥ 337
pathyaṁ pūtam 424
prabhu-ājñāya kara 370
prabhu kahe – "kaun vidyā 42
prāṇa āche yāra 268
praṇata-dehināṁ 65
prāṇanātha, śuna mora 360
prātaḥ śrīman-navadvīpe 412
pratiyuge karena kṛṣṇa 4
prema-bhakti-sudhā-nidhi 208
prīty anudivasaṁ yatnāt 256
puṇya ye sukhera dhāma 208

R

rādhā-dāsyam apāsya 202
rādhā-kṛṣṇa kuñja-sevā 216
rādhā-kuṇḍa-taṭa 375
rādhā-padāṅkita-dhāma 203
rādhā-pada vinā 203
rādhāra svarūpa – kṛṣṇa-prema 224
rādhe vṛndāvanādhiśe 421
rādhikānucarīṁ nityaṁ 256
rādhikāra bhāva-kānti 6
rādhikā ujjvala-rasera ācārya 203
rāsaḥ parama-rasa 291
rasika-bhakta-saṅge 402
rātri-dina kuñje kriḍā 215, 263
rudanti pātakāḥ sarve 424

S

sādhakānāṁ hitārthāya 180
sādhana smaraṇa līlā 209
sādhane bhāviba yāhā 250, 265
sakhi he, nā bujhiye 332
sakhi he, śuna mora 364
sakhīnāṁ saṅginī-rūpām 371

sakhī vinā ei līlāya anyera 216
samo 'haṁ sarva-bhūteṣu 130
saṁsāra-sāgarān nātha 419
sannyāsa-kṛc chamaḥ 5
śaraṇaṁ vāṁ prapanno 'smi 420
sei ta parāṇa-nātha 9
smara-garala-khaṇḍanaṁ 213
smarati sa pitṛ-gehān 146
śokāmarṣādibhir-bhāvair 16
so 'yaṁ yuvā yuvati 331
śrīdharaṁ vāma-bāhau tu 412
śrī-kṛṣṇaṁ śrī-ghanaśyāmaṁ 417
śrīman-mauktikadāma 414
śrīṁ rādhikāyai vidmahe 418
śrī-rādhā-lalitā-saṅge 345
śruti-smṛti-purāṇādi 232, 254
sthāvara-jaṅgama dekhe 311
śyāma-varṇo 'yaṁ 202
śuddha-sattva-viśeṣātmā 238
sunileo bhāgya-hīnera 225
suvarṇa-varṇo hemāṅgo 5

T

tad eva manyate 218
tāmbūlārpaṇa-pāda-mardana 207
tan-madhye ratna-khacitaṁ 416
tan naḥ prasīda 337
tāṅra bhakta saṅge sadā 204
tapta-kāñcana-gaurāṅgi 419
tāra madhye mokṣa-vāñchā 174
tāsām āvirabhūc chauriḥ 341
tato vṛndāvanaṁ dhyāyet 416
tat prakṣālana-toyaṁ tu 412
tavāsmi rādhikā-nātha 420
teṣāṁ bhāvāptaye lubdho 228
teṣāṁ nityābhiyuktānāṁ 128
te taṁ bhuktvā svarga 171
tomāra sammukhe dekhi 5
tṛṇād api sunīcena 21, 369
tulasy-amṛta-janmāsi 422
tvaṁ rūpa mañjari sakhi 225

U

ūrdhva-bāhu kari' kahoṅ 369

V

vairāgya-yug bhakti-rasaṁ 162
vāñchā-kalpa-tarubhyaś ca 414
vāñchanti yad bhava 350
veṇuḥ karān nipatitaḥ 150
vidhi-mārga-rata-jane 253
viṣayīra anna khāile malina 89
viṣṇuṁ ca dakṣiṇe kukṣau 412
vraja-gopī-bhāva 251
vṛndāvana-purandara 345

Y

yadi cāha praṇaya rākhite 90
yā dṛṣṭā nikhilāgha-saṅgha 423
ya ekaṁ govindaṁ bhajati 202
yāḥ śrutvā tat-paro bhavet 72
yamunā-salila-āharaṇe giyā 260
yaśo dadāti 64
yasya yat-saṅgatiḥ 357
yathā dūra-care preṣṭhe 291
yat te sujāta-caraṇāmburuhaṁ 357
ye dharila rādhā-pada 203
ye yathā māṁ prapadyante 130

BOOK CATALOG 2003

Gauḍīya Vedānta Publications

Śrī Śrīmad Bhaktivedānta Nārāyaṇa Mahārāja

— and —

Śrī Śrīmad A.C. Bhaktivedānta Swami Prabhupāda

Jaiva-Dharma

The groundbreaking spiritual novel by Śrīla Bhaktivinoda Ṭhākura

Jaiva-dharma reveals the ultimate development of the path of pure devotion to the English-speaking world.

Hardbound, 5 x 7.5", 1077 pages, Bible paper, 8 color plates, glossaries of terms, indexes of quoted verses and general index. Code JDC $15.00

Śrīmad Bhagavad-Gītā

With extensive commentaries

This edition of *Bhagavad-gītā* contains two commentaries: the *Sārārtha-varṣiṇī Ṭīkā* by Śrīla Viśvanātha Cakravartī Ṭhākura and the *Sārārtha-varṣiṇī Prakāśikā-vṛtti* by Śrīla Bhaktivedānta Nārāyaṇa Mahārāja.

Hardbound, 5.5 x 8.5", 1120 pages, 12 color plates. Code SBG $15.00

Śrī Śrīmad Bhakti Prajñāna Keśava Gosvāmī

His Life and Teachings

A unique biography of a contemporary saint, the spiritual master of Śrīla Bhaktivedānta Nārāyaṇa Mahārāja and the *sannyāsa-guru* of Śrīla A.C. Bhaktivedānta Swami Prabhupāda.

Softbound, 5.5 x 8.5", 580 pages, 22 color illustrations. Code PKGB $15.00

Pinnacle of Devotion

An introduction to the most powerful yoga system

We all have a tendency to love, and no one can live without loving someone. The problem is, however, where to place our love.

Hardbound, 5.5 x 8.5", 200 pages. Code POD $10.00

Veṇu-Gīta

Tenth Canto, Chapter 21 of Śrīmad-Bhāgavatam

"By just hearing that flute-song that attracts the hearts of the whole universe, Sanaka and Sanandana and other *ātmārāma munis* became overwhelmed with joy and lost consciousness."

Softbound, 5.5 x 8.5", 188 pages, 8 color illustrations. Code VG $10.00

Bhakti-rasāmṛta-sindhu-bindu

A drop of the nectarean ocean of bhakti-rasa

This book is Viśvanātha Cakravartī Ṭhākura's summary of Śrīla Rūpa Gosvāmī's classic *Bhakti-rasāmṛta-sindhu* (*Nectar of Devotion*).

Softbound, 6 x 9", 305 pages, numerous diagrams. Code BRSB $8.00

Śrī Bhajana-rahasya

Deep analysis of the Hare Kṛṣṇa mahā-mantra

This revolutionary work by Śrīla Bhaktivinoda Ṭhākura presents an astounding analysis of the Hare Kṛṣṇa *mantra*, based on the eight verses of *Śrī Śikṣāṣṭakam*, covering all stages of *bhakti*.

Softbound, 5.5 x 8.5", 497 pages, 4 color plates. Code SBR $10.00

The Origin of Ratha-yātrā

The world's most ancient religious festival

Lectures by Śrīla Bhaktivedānta Nārāyaṇa Mahārāja on the Ratha-yātrā, or the Cart Festival of Lord Jagannātha.

Softbound, 5.5 x 8.5", 372 pages, 8 color plates. Code ORY $10.00

Śrī Brahma-saṁhitā

Lord Brahmā's prayers of devotion to Kṛṣṇa

These prayers offered at the dawn of creation by Brahmā, the secondary creator of the universe, contain all the essential truths of Vaiṣṇava philosophy.

Softbound, 5.5 x 8.5", 452 pages. Code SBS $10.00

Śrī Gauḍīya Gīti-guccha

An unprecedented collection of devotional songs

Sanskrit, Bengali and Hindi devotional poems, prayers, songs and *bhajanas* written by the Gauḍīya Vaiṣṇava *ācāryas* and compiled for the practicing devotee.

Spiral bound, 6 x 9", 224 pages.
Code GGG $10.00

Śrī Manaḥ-śikṣā

Instructions to the mind by
Śrīla Raghunātha dāsa Gosvāmī

Śrī Manaḥ-śikṣā consists of twelve verses composed by Raghunātha dāsa Gosvāmī that instruct the mind on how to make progress on the path of *bhajana*.

Softbound, 5.5 x 8.5", 153 pages. Code SMS $5.00

Jaiva-dharma, Part One

Part one of a spiritual novel by
Śrīla Bhaktivinoda Ṭhākura

"Out of all the books of Śrīla Ṭhākura Bhaktivinoda, *Jaiva-dharma* is considered to be the quintessence by religious thinkers of different countries."
– Śrīla Nārāyaṇa Mahārāja

Softbound, 5.5 x 8.5", 288 pages, 10 color illustrations.
Code JD1 $5.00

Secret Truths of the Bhāgavatam

Discourses on Śrīmad-Bhāgavatam

A series of lectures by Śrīla Nārāyaṇa Mahārāja at the New Vraja community in Badger, California, in June 1999.

Softbound, 5.5 x 8.5", 192 pages, 16 color illustrations. Code STB $5.00

Bhakti-tattva-viveka

The true nature of devotion

Śrīla Bhaktivinoda Ṭhākura has presented the grave and deep conclusions of devotional service, pure *bhakti*, in simple language that is accessible to any sincere reader.

Softbound, 5.5 x 8.5", 112 pages. Code BTV $4.00

Rays of Hope

A compilation of divine discourses, 1996–99

"The real connection with *guru* is through *bhāgavata-paramparā*. Even if one is not initiated by him in *guru-paramparā*, such a qualified disciple has understood his *guru's* mood."
– Śrīla Nārāyaṇa Mahārāja

Softbound, 5.5 x 8.5", 192 pages, 18 color photos and numerous illustrations. Code ROH $5.00

My Śikṣā-guru & Priya-bandhu

Remembrances by Śrīla Bhaktivedānta Nārāyaṇa Mahārāja

A deep and revealing account of the intimate relationship between Śrīla Bhaktivedānta Nārāyaṇa Mahārāja and his instructing spiritual master and dear friend, Śrīla A.C. Bhaktivedānta Swami Prabhupāda, from 1947 up until final instructions given in 1977.

Softbound, 5.5 x 8.5", 49 pages. Code SGPB $2.00

Their Lasting Relation

An Historical Account

A detailed and nectarean account of Śrīla A.C. Bhaktivedānta Swami Prabhupāda's long-standing relationship with both his *sannyāsa-guru*, Śrīla Bhakti Prajñāna Keśava Gosvāmī, and Śrīla Bhaktivedānta Nārāyaṇa Mahārāja.

Softbound, 5.5 x 8.5", 49 pages. Code TLR $2.00

Guru-Devatātmā

Accepting Śrī Guru as One's Life and Soul

Śrīla Bhaktivedānta Nārāyaṇa Mahārāja speaks on the importance of accepting a bona fide *guru*, who is more dear than life itself, the absolute necessity of second initiation, and other topics of *guru-tattva*.

Softbound, 5.5 x 8.5", 52 pages. Code GD $2.00

Our Gurus: One in Siddhānta, One in Heart

Clearing up the confusion

Nowadays some persons claim there are differences in the conclusions taught by Śrīla Bhaktivedānta Nārāyaṇa Mahārāja and Śrīla A.C. Bhaktivedānta Swami Prabhupāda. These authoritative responses to many of the objections will help the reader understand things as they are, without any politically motivated interpretation.

Softbound, 5.5 x 8.5", 61 pages. Code OIS $2.00

Śrī Hari-Nāma Mahā-Mantra

The transcendental holy name of the Lord

"When a qualified person chants *harināma*, this light diffuses, thus keeping the darkness of illusion away from the soul."

Softbound, 5.5 x 8.5", 64 pages. Code SHN $2.00

Happiness in a Fool's Paradise

The futility of material enjoyment

"Everyone wants to be happy, but generally we can find only a little happiness and affection in this world."

Softbound, 5.5 x 8.5", 32 pages, 6 color illustrations.
Code HFP $2.00

To Be Controlled By Love

The guru–disciple relationship

"Even Kṛṣṇa, the Supreme Personality of Godhead, wants to be controlled by love and affection."
– Śrīla Nārāyaṇa Mahārāja

Softbound, 5.5 x 8.5", 32 pages. Code CBL $2.00

The Butter Thief

The true nature of devotion

This book describes Kṛṣṇa's sweet childhood pastimes, in which He plays with Mother Yaśodā as an ordinary child.

Softbound, 5.5 x 8.5", 64 pages, 8 color illustrations.
Code TBT $2.00

The Essence of Bhagavad-gītā

Absorbing the mind in Śrī Kṛṣṇa

"Absorb your mind and heart in Me, become My devotee, worship Me, offer your obeisances to Me, and certainly you will come to Me."

Softbound, 5.5 x 8.5", 32 pages, 4 color illustrations.
Code EBG $2.00

Books by Śrīla A.C. Bhaktivedānta Swami Prabhupāda

These special editions are the authorized and approved versions, with the artwork and format specially designed by Śrīla Prabhupāda for introducing the Western world to Kṛṣṇa consciousness. Not one word or picture has been changed from Śrīla Prabhupāda's original version.

Kṛṣṇa: The Supreme Personality of Godhead

Who is Kṛṣṇa?

Śrīla Prabhupāda's summary of the entire Tenth Canto of *Śrīmad-Bhāgavatam*

Volume 1: hardbound, 7.5 x 10.5", 425 pages, 84 plates. Code KB1 $15.00
Volume 2: hardbound, 7.5 x 10.5", 400 pages, 24 plates. Code KB2 $15.00

Bhagavad-gītā As It Is

The most beloved of all Vedic literatures

Reprint of the historic original, authorized and approved 1972 Macmillan Complete Edition, with the original Sanskrit text, Roman transliteration, English synonyms, translation and elaborate purports.

Hardbound, 6.25 x 9.25", 1000 pages, 40 color illustrations. Code BG $15.00

Teachings of Lord Caitanya

The Golden Avatar

Lord Caitanya Mahāprabhu appeared in Bengal, India, in 1486, and began a revolution in spiritual consciousness that has profoundly affected the lives of millions.

Hardbound, 440 pages, many original color illustrations. Code TLC $15.00

Kṛṣṇa, the Reservoir of Pleasure

Eternal enjoyment through transcendental sound

"Kṛṣṇa – this sound is transcendental. Kṛṣṇa means the highest pleasure. All of us, every living being, seeks pleasure. But we do not know how to seek pleasure perfectly." – Śrīla Prabhupāda

Softbound, 5.5 x 8.5", 32 pages. Code ROP $1.00

The Perfection of Yoga

"There have been many *yoga* systems popularized in the Western world, especially in this century, but none of them have actually taught the perfection of *yoga*." The original, authorized and approved version.

Softbound, 4 x 7", 56 pages, 8 color plates. Code POY $2.00

U.S. Regional Book Distributors

Northwest (Seattle)

Mark Haines
11321 74th Ave. E
Puyallup, WA 98373
Attn: Maitreya Muni Prabhu
Phone: (866) HARIBOL (427-4265)
Email: maitreyamuni@yahoo.com

California Northern (Berkeley)

Westside & Company
5659 Telegraph Ave. #D
Berkeley, CA 94609
Attn: Kavidatta & Kṛtakarma Prabhus
Phone: (510) 655-5018, 883-0736
Email: kavidatta2000@yahoo.com

California Central (Badger)

Mt. Kailāsa Foundation
PO Box 99
Badger, CA 93603
Attn: Nanda-gopāla Prabhu
Phone: (559) 337-2448
Email: nandagopal@gaudiya.net

California Southern (Los Angeles)

IGVS
111 Dudley Ave
Venice, CA 90291
Attn: Jaga-mohana Prabhu
Phone: (310) 450-5371
Email: purebhakti@hotmail.com

California Southern (San Diego)

Padayatra America
PO Box 2179
La Jolla, CA 92038
Attn: Jayanta Prabhu
Phone: (858) 518-5209
Email: jayantadasa@yahoo.com

South (Houston)

IGVS - Houston
16119 Abergreen Trail
Houston, TX 77095
Attn: Kṛṣṇa dāsa Prabhu
Phone: (281) 550-2940
Email: kris4basics@hotmail.com

Eastern (Washington DC)

Rupa Raghunath Gaudiya Math
6925 Willow St. NW
Washington, DC 20012
Attn: Vamsivadana & Mukunda
Phone: (301) 864-3354
Email: ruparaghunatha@hotmail.com

Southeast (North Carolina)

Maria Christopher
4619 Timberwood Terr.
Efland, NC 27243
Attn: Rāma dāsa Prabhu
Phone: (919) 563-9464
Email: ramdas@mebtel.net

South (Florida)

Acolapissa Foundation
PO Box 1689
Alachua, FL 32616-1689
Attn: Bhāgavata Prabhu
(386) 418-2046 (800) 814-7316 Ext. 00
Email: Bhagavatdasa@msn.com

International Book Distributors

Canada - Western (Vancouver)

Stanley A. Gill
#25 - 15030 58th Ave.
Surrey, B.C. CANADA V3S 9G3
Attn: Prasasya Prabhu
Phone: (866) 575-9438
Email: stannshel@shaw.ca

Europe - UK (England)

Gour Govinda Gaudiya Math
32 Handsworth Wood Rd.
Birmingham B20 2DS, UK
Attn: Jīva-pāvana Prabhu
Phone: (44) 121 682 9159
Email: gourgovinda@hotmail.com

International Spanish Distributors

Vedic Cultural Association
1002 S. Austin St.
Santa Ana, CA 92704 USA
Attn: Haridāsa Prabhu
Phone: (714) 775-8760
Email: hsalas1@prodigy.net

For information on becoming a distributor in your area: e-mail vd@regalgift.com o isani@mail.com, or call Niścintya at 310-837-3518

Book Order Form

Book Code	Price each	Copies	Subtotal
	$		$
	$		$
	$		$
	$		$
	$		$
	$		$
	$		$
	$		$
	$		$
	$		$

Books Total $ ____________

Add 10% Shipping + $3 Handling $ ____________

ip to: Grand Total: $ ____________

me ____

dress ____

____

ephone____

ail ____

tructions: Fill in the book codes of the books you want to order, the price h, and the total number of copies you want. **Calculate the Grand Total and il this form and a check or money order to the Regional Distributor near- to you (listed on the previous page). Make your check or money order able to the name listed in bold type.** Please allow two weeks for delivery— re for international orders.

CENTERS AROUND THE WORLD

AUSTRALIA • **Murwillumbah** • Sri Giriraja Govardhan Gaudiya Matha • 56 Brisbane Street • Murwillumbah N.S.W 2482 ☎ +61 66-728499 🖃 lilasuka@bigpond.com •
GERMANY • **Berlin** • Gaudiya Vedanta Samiti Berlin • Emserstrasse 70 • 12051 Berlin ☎ +49 30 62 00 87 47 🖃 gvsberlin@yahoo.com •
INDIA • **Mathura** • Sri Keshavaji Gaudiya Matha • Opp. Dist. Hospital • Jawahar Hata • Mathura (U.P.) 281001 ☎ +91 565 250-2334 🖃 mathuramath@gaudiya.net ♦ **Navadwipa** • Sri Devananda Gaudiya Matha • Tegharipada, PO Navadwipa, D/O Nadiya, West Bengal ☎ +91 343 240-068 ♦ **New Delhi** • Sri Ramanvihari Gaudiya Math • OCF pocket, Block B-3, near musical fountain park • Janakpuri, New Delhi ☎ +91 11 2553-3568 ☎ +91 11 3230-2159 ♦ **Vrindavan** • Sri Rupa-Sanatana Gaudiya Matha • Danagali, Vrindavana U.P. ☎ +91 565 244-3270 •
INDONESIA • **Bali** • Ananta Gaudiya Math • Br. Juntal, Desa Kaba-Kaba • Kediri, Tabanan • Bali, Indonesia ☎ +62 361 830986 ☎ +62 361 830987 •
NETHERLANDS • **Rotterdam** • Preaching Center Rotterdam • 1e Pijnackerstraat 98 • 3035GV Rotterdam ☎ +31 010-2650405 🖃 sanga@worldmail.nl •
NEW ZEALAND • **Auckland** • Hare Krishna Vegetarian Restaurant • 214 Karangahape Road • Auckland ☎ +64 9 303-1560 ♦ **Wellington** • IGVS Wellington • 22 Wrights Hill Road • Karori, Wellington ☎ +64 4 476-6784 🖃 benhc@hotmail.com ♦ **Kati Kati & Whangamata** • IGVS Bay of Plenty • Kati Kati & Whangamata ☎ +64 7 552-0073 🖃 bhadradasi@hotmail.com •
PHILIPPINES • **Manila** • International Gaudiya Vedanta Society of the Philippines • Radha Krsna Gopala Mandir • 96 ROTC Hunters Clusters 23 Tatalon • Quezon City, Metro Manila 1113 ☎ +63 2783 0267 ☎ +63 91873-32659 🖃 jaipur_art@mailcity.com •
UNITED KINGDOM • **Birmingham** • Sri Gour Govinda Gaudiya Matha • 32 Handsworth Wood Road • Birmingham, B20 2DS ☎ +44 121 682 9159 🖃 gourgovinda@hotmail.com •
USA • **Los Angeles** • Sri Sri Radha-Govinda Gaudiya Math • 111 Dudley Ave. • Venice, CA 90291 ☎ +1 310-450-5371 🖃 purebhakti@hotmail.com ♦ **Miami** • Institute for Gaudiya Vaishnavism • 934 N. University Drive, #102 • Coral Springs, FL 33071 ☎ +1 754-245-2345 🖃 Mbuddhi@cs.com ♦ Sri Gaudiya Vedanta Samiti of South Florida • 701 N.W. 16th Ave. • Pompano Beach, FL 33069 ☎ +1 954-344-5404 🖃 alankar@adelphia.net ♦ **New York** • The Bhaktivedanta Gaudiya Matha • 134-06 95th Ave. • South Richmond Hill, NY 11419 ☎ +1 718-526-9835 🖃 unclepuru108@yahoo.com ♦ **Washington, DC** • Rupa Raghunath Gaudiya Math • 6925 Willow Ave. NW • Washington, DC 20012 ☎ +1 301-864-3354 🖃 ruparaghunatha@hotmail.com •
VENEZUELA • Sri Venezuela Kesavaji Gaudiya Math and Gaudiya Vedanta Publications (spanish) • Carrera 17, entre calles 50-51 • #50-47, Barquisimeto • Edo. Lara ☎ +58 51-452574 🖃 janardana@postmark.net

For more information please visit the following web sites: **www.gaudiya.net** and **www.purebhakti.com**